Early African American Print Culture

WITHDRAWN

MATERIAL TEXTS

Early African American Print Culture

Edited by

Lara Langer Cohen

and

Jordan Alexander Stein

PENN

PUBLISHED IN COOPERATION WITH
THE LIBRARY COMPANY OF PHILADELPHIA

UNIVERSITY OF PENNSYLVANIA PRESS
PHILADELPHIA

Published by
University of Pennsylvania Press
Philadelphia, Pennsylvania 19104-4112
www.upenn.edu/pennpress

Printed in the United States of America on acid-free paper
10 9 8 7 6 5 4 3 2 1

Library of Congress Cataloging-in-Publication Data
ISBN 978-0-8122-4425-0
Early African American print culture / edited by Lara
Langer Cohen and Jordan Alexander Stein. — 1st ed.
        p. cm. — (Material texts)
    Includes bibliographical references and index.
    ISBN 978-0-8122-4425-0 (hardcover : alk. paper)
        1. Literature publishing—United States—History—
18th century.   2. Literature publishing—United States—
History—19th century.   3. Authors and publishers—
United States—History—18th century.   4. Authors and
publishers—United States—History—19th century.
5. American literature—African American authors—
History and criticism.   I. Cohen, Lara Langer.   II. Stein,
Jordan Alexander.   III. Series: Material texts.
Z480.L58E17 2012
070.5097309'033—dc23

                                        2012002920

CONTENTS

PART IV. PUBLIC PERFORMANCES

Early African American Print Culture

LARA LANGER COHEN AND JORDAN ALEXANDER STEIN

The present volume takes its cue from a historical convergence. The late eighteenth and nineteenth centuries witnessed the consolidation of what historians have come to know as "print culture" in the United States. Spurred by technological improvements to the printing press, innovations in papermaking and binding, increasing divisions of labor and automation, and the expansion of distribution networks enabled by railroad and steamship, print shops turned out a huge variety of printed goods in unprecedented quantities. These goods included recognizably literary items such as books, newspapers, magazines, pamphlets, and broadsides, as well as nonliterary items such as stationery, lottery tickets, currency, and ledgers. Printed matter became a part of everyday life, mediating and reshaping the already fluctuating social relations of the early United States.

At the same time, these years also mark the inauguration of what scholars have identified as an African American literary tradition. Despite the fact that education was often explicitly prohibited for slaves, and effectively placed out of reach for many freepersons, publications by African American authors appeared in increasing numbers. The year 1760 saw both the first published poem by an African American, Jupiter Hammon's broadside "An Evening Thought: Salvation by Christ, with Penetential Cries," and the first published prose text, Briton Hammon's *A Narrative of the Uncommon Sufferings, and Surprizing Deliverance of Briton Hammon, a Negro Man.* (The first known poem by an African American, Lucy Terry's "Bar's Fight," probably composed in 1746, was transmitted orally before being committed to print in 1855.) The first black publishing house, the African Methodist Episcopal Book

Concern, was founded in 1817. The first black newspaper, *Freedom's Journal*, appeared in 1827, and over the next thirty years, black periodicals from Albany to Cleveland to New Orleans to San Francisco followed suit.[1] During the late eighteenth and early nineteenth centuries, African Americans also established numerous literary societies, circulating libraries, political conventions, and church organizations, all of which articulated themselves through print media.[2] African Americans worked alongside whites as compositors in print shops, as sailors transporting both raw and printed materials, and as educators instructing with books.

Yet despite this historical convergence, print culture and African American literature have rarely been considered in relation to one another. As Leon Jackson observes in a recent state-of-the-field essay on African American print culture, although the trope of the "talking book" remains one of the standbys of African American literary analysis, "we know very little about the production, dissemination, or consumption of the books that deployed that trope, and still less of the books that were begged, borrowed, stolen, owned, or encountered by the authors who wrote them"—to say nothing of African Americans' engagements with forms of print other than books.[3] To the extent that scholars of African American literature have addressed the matter of print, they have generally done so with a dependence on critical models that assume that print is a stabilizing technology that subtends the establishment of African American identity. Such models understand literature as a primary tool with which African Americans articulated their personhood, forged bonds of racial solidarity, and laid claims to history. These models have performed immensely valuable work for the study of African American literary history—not least, of course, by underwriting its formation *as* a field of study. But such models hit their limits in many of the earliest African American texts, whose meandering plots, numerous plagiarisms, and multiple rewritings defy nearly any notion of textual stability. These texts instead beckon to much recent scholarship in book history, which has shown how abstract concepts central to literary study—authorship, readership, intellectual property, textual integrity, literary professionalism, and, indeed, literature itself—were very much in flux during the eighteenth and nineteenth centuries.[4]

For their part, however, book historians have been slow to incorporate the evidence of African American literature into these theoretical interventions. As a result, if scholars of early African American texts have ignored much theoretical work in book history in favor of stable notions of identity and print, it is equally true that scholarship in book history has often ignored African American literature, however broadly conceived. Jackson, for one, combs the archives of book history and bibliography periodicals for essays on African American topics, with sparse results.[5] This neglect is all the more surprising given the abundance of potential material. In colonial and antebellum America, African Americans figured prominently in literary production both on the page (as writing subjects as well as subjects of writing) and off (as readers, editors, printers, engravers, compositors, papermakers, librarians, and so on). The sheer breadth and diversity of their experiences has a great deal to tell us about American print culture, while their omission from critical accounts renders even the freshest reconsiderations of the field inevitably partial.

Moreover, the rewards of studying African American print culture appear especially clear in light of growing efforts to consider how print culture studies and critical race studies might fit together. This conversation has produced excellent work on Hispanophone print archives (including studies by Anna Brickhouse, Kirsten Silva Gruesz, and Rodrigo Lazo) and Native American communications media (including the work of Matt Cohen, Jeff Glover, Andrew Newman, Birgit Brander Rasmussen, and Phillip Round), but as yet it has not produced an equivalent body of work on the eighteenth and nineteenth century's rich history of African American print culture.[6] To be sure, the field of African American literary studies boasts a long history of bibliographic scholarship and exceptional archival work, but these have, until very recently, tended to be more descriptive than critical.

Scholarship of the last decade or so suggests that book historians and critics of African American literature are beginning to turn this tide. Recent methodological essays by Frances Smith Foster, Xiomara Santamarina, and Leon Jackson have paired illuminating genealogies for African American print culture and its critical analysis with suggestions for new paths of inquiry.[7] Important books and articles by scholars including Sarah Blackwood, Michael Chaney, Jeannine Marie DeLombard, Marcy J. Dinius, John Ernest, Eric Gardner, Beth A. McCoy, Elizabeth McHenry, and Edlie Wong have taken a materialist approach to African American texts, with enlightening results.[8] Similar interdisciplinary work by historians such as Janet Duitsman Cornelius, David Waldstreicher, and Heather Andrea Williams has enhanced our understandings of African Americans' experiences with, uses of, and educations in print and literacy.[9] The second and third volumes of *A History of the Book in America* (covering the period 1790–1880) have each included a chapter devoted to African American print culture.[10] Vincent Carretta's controversial biography of Olaudah Equiano has urged scholars to see Equiano's *Narrative* as a book whose story is very different from that of its author, and it has in turn sparked new scholarship on the publication history of the narrative.[11] At the same time, critical investigations at the intersection of race and performance studies by scholars such as Daphne Brooks and Tavia Nyong'o have expanded our knowledge of African American representational practices and the methodologies we might use to understand them.[12] Such work brings together archival methods and African American literature in fresh ways that have helped sharpen this volume's focus on sustained textual and material analysis, as well as propel it toward an elaboration of the theoretical frameworks proper to such investigations.

Inspired and challenged by this scholarship, *Early African American Print Culture* focuses on bridging early African American literature and print culture studies. The essays that follow do not take a single approach to this project; nor do they attempt to map its contours comprehensively. Rather, they showcase the variety of discoveries scholars might make when they ask what early African American literature looks like when read with an attention to its material conditions, and what print culture looks like when it turns its attention to African American archives.

Definitions

If this volume thus proceeds from an understanding of how investigations into early African American print culture might be focused, it does not proceed from a single, agreed-upon understanding of what early African American print culture *is*. The following essays subject each of the terms in our titular phrase "Early African American Print Culture" to some reflexive scrutiny. Nevertheless, readers of these essays will notice the following definitional tendencies for each of the volume's key terms.

"Early," in the present usage, refers to African American print culture before the Harlem Renaissance. This aesthetic movement—along with an attendant constellation of developments in American culture, critical practices, and the literary marketplace—established an undeniable place for African American writing in the United States. But it did so in part by crystallizing a set of concepts, including "author," "literature," and even "African

American." These categories subsequently helped carve out claims for African American literature in the canon (including those made by post-1960s critics); but, conversely, their fixity seems to have hampered scholars' abilities to understand the terrain of African American print during a period before these definitions gained purchase. Viewed from the time following the Harlem Renaissance, the archives of earlier periods—with their often unknown authors, limited audiences, baffling narratives, and dubious claims on identity and plausibility—are consequently understood to be artless, immature, desultory, partial, unreadable, fraudulent, fragmentary, or, simply, unstable. As a result, the achievements of the Harlem Renaissance have ironically tended to obscure the more disparate racial, political, and cultural formations that existed before. While critical attention to print culture may tell us a great deal about the entire history of African American literature, then, such an interpretive task is especially pertinent with regard to the periods before the Harlem Renaissance's perceived high-water mark of African American writing.

This definition of "early" may strike some readers as quite late. However, its apparent dislocation reflects one of this volume's historiographic challenges: the periodization of early African American print culture does not necessarily coincide with more conventional (which is also to say, whiter) narratives of American literary history. Focusing on "early" African American print culture, our contributors have located surprising flash points in the convergence of African American print culture and racialization: the late eighteenth-century surge of gallows literature by the black condemned (DeLombard); John Marrant's immensely popular 1785 conversion narrative (Brooks, Dillon); the 1825 publication of *The Life of William Grimes*, the first book-length narrative of a fugitive slave written and copyrighted by the fugitive himself (Ashton); the black state conventions of the 1840s (Spires); the 1855 U.S. reprinting of Alfred, Lord Tennyson's poem "The Charge of the Light Brigade" (Hack). Other contributors take a radically nonlinear approach to temporality, emphasizing historical loops, gaps, and repetitions (Cohen, Jackson, Scruggs, Gillman). The diversity of these events (from publication to reprinting to citation) leads us to conclude that eighteenth- and nineteenth-century African Americans' experience of what Joanna Brooks calls "disrupted social fields" created temporalities whose significance has been underappreciated by the conventions of American literary history (Chapter 2).[13] However, rather than arguing for an alternative set of events that might anchor early African American print culture within the time of literary-historical convention,

these essays seek instead to open the issue to questions: what are the periodicities of African American print culture, when do they come into focus, and
how do they relate to other periodicities?

The definition of "African American" that emerges across this volume's
essays is similarly capacious, spanning hemispheric and transatlantic locations, and giving critical attention to editors, readers, printers, and distribu-
tors, as well as authors. In this respect, the volume resonates with Kenneth
Warren's recent contention that African American literature is defined not by
race but by racialization, such that "[a]bsent white suspicions of, or commitment to imposing, black inferiority, African American literature would not
have existed as a literature."[14] While Warren locates the mechanisms of racialization operative in the era of Jim Crow segregation as key for the production of African American literature as such, the following essays nevertheless
also find varieties of racialization at work in earlier periods, but find them
productive of a greater range of print and literary forms. In these accounts,
the "African American" texts examined achieve that designation by virtue of
their participation in a wide range of ideological and material ways that blackness becomes culturally "legible," from visual representations of the distinction
between blackness and whiteness (Senchyne, Capers, Scruggs) to the legally
"mixed character" of the slave as both person and property, which made criminality the clearest basis of early black personhood (DeLombard). The cultural
process of racialization both does and does not overlap with the more biographical details of race, and thus some of the following essays posit that it
might make heuristic sense to designate a text as African American even if its
author was not (Gillman, Clytus), or to argue that a text might usefully be
considered so despite its failure to conform to expected generic protocols of
African American literature (Ashton, Pratt). The very difficulty of pinning
down the category "African American" reflects one of the volume's key goals:
to recognize print's role in the process of racialization. Placing the emphasis
here, rather than on race and racial identity, means that the present volume
requires of its reader a willingness to engage the possibility that early African
American print culture might unmake identity as plausibly as make it, as this
volume posits that the richness of African American history can be told with
recourse to moments where identity diffuses as much as moments where
identity consolidates.

Many of the essays that follow treat the "American" in "African American" as a further site for investigation, for early African American print culture is not always confined by national boundaries. In part, this porousness

reflects a shifting historical understanding of the term: national boundaries were more coherent—and more frequently represented as coherent—in the United States after the 1870s. To be sure, African American print culture participated in nation formation, sometimes quite visibly and sometimes in ways that have gone unrecognized (Capers, Scruggs, Spires). At other times, however, African American print culture pushes against such national formations, positing alternative geographies, communities, and modes of belonging (Cohen, Hack, Ashton). And more often than not, the nation itself, too often seen by scholars as a uniform field, emerges here as quite an uneven one, furrowed by regional difference (Gardner, Pratt, Dillon). Thus, the following essays often take spatially comparative approaches (Rezek, McGill, Gillman), as well as temporally comparative ones.

Finally, the contributors to the volume try to think through "print culture" in a robust way that attends to different kinds of print media over different periods. Though we emphasize print, this volume is ultimately not a media-specific study, and its essays consider print in relation to the oral, visual, and manuscript mediations that nevertheless persist in a world where print has become commonplace. In saying so, we distinguish between "print," a technology that fixes impressions, and "print culture," a world in which print both integrates with other practices and assumes a life of its own.[15] This conceptual distinction emphasizes that print does not merely function as an instrument of human needs; it directs our attention instead to the ways that print affects (and sometimes effects) personhood, circulates to unintended readers, is subject to reiteration and reappropriation, solicits publics that may not yet recognize themselves as such, and allows equally for representation and misrepresentation. Such an expansive understanding of print yields a corresponding proliferation of "culture," and if "print culture" is therefore difficult to define adequately, this difficulty is part of the point. Throughout, the essays in this volume highlight the dynamic tension between "print" and "culture" rather than treating their pairing as a single reified entity.

Generically, the volume covers wide ground: book-length novels, journals, and narratives; broadsides and pamphlets; anthologies of poetry and biography; newspaper articles, serial fiction, poetry, and editorials; verbal and visual texts. Together, these demonstrate (but certainly do not exhaust) the broad array of early African American print production. But our contributors also aim to expand what we as readers take to be our texts—and what we read *for*—when we study print culture. Their objects of inquiry include not only the printed words of what we generally consider "the text" but also typography, format, and bindings (Rezek, McGill); frontispieces and mast-heads (Ashton, Clytus); engravings and photographs (Capers, Scruggs); and the very materials of paper and ink (Senchyne). Other chapters take up the ways that print indexes seeming antitheses such as music, performance, and bodily presence (McGill, Spires, Dillon).

Such a dynamic sense of print culture means that the essays suggest no congruence between the study of early African American print culture and the genres that have historically denoted it, such as the slave narrative. We suspect this is so because the abundance of work on this genre in particular has allowed our contributors to look outside of it, in part because the slave narrative has been so illuminatingly discussed by others, and in part because its very prominence calls for such a decentering. Speculations aside, the following essays clearly demonstrate that a host of other types of writing by and for African Americans flourished at the same historical time as the slave narrative—poetry, historiography, literary criticism, political speeches, conversion narratives, and more. The understandable tendency of literary critics studying slavery to focus on slave narratives can (unintentionally) create the impression that slavery only enters the picture when it is being recounted. And so our desire here to expatiate in other generic areas should be seen not only as bibliographical but also as political, as these essays show the much wider and more complex ways that slavery inflected early African American print culture, and indeed American culture more broadly. While slave narratives, then, may be noticeably absent in this volume, slavery makes its presence felt everywhere.

Organization

The volume's essays are grouped topically rather than chronologically, in order to bring diverse archives and historical periods into conversation. Focusing on circulation, representation, adaptation, and publics, respectively, the volume's four parts progress dialectically in their emphases between the questions of how African American literary production shapes print culture (Parts I and III) and how print culture shapes African American identity (Parts II and IV).

Part I, "Vectors of Movement," begins with circulation, one of the most widely theorized dimensions of print culture. Joseph Rezek's essay, "The Print

Atlantic: Phillis Wheatley, Ignatius Sancho, and the Cultural Significance of the Book," argues that "book publication, as distinguished from other kinds of printing, made these writers uniquely available to white readers as 'specimens,' as sites for the discussion of racial hierarchy, and, ultimately, as evidence either to support or to oppose the institution of slavery." Rezek demonstrates how cultural assumptions about the book—its significance, its materiality, its heft—shaped the ways that Wheatley's and Sancho's texts circulated. Stressing the importance of a media-specific approach to early black writings, Rezek encourages us to see that that a "black Atlantic" was born out of the movement of print, as well as people. Joanna Brooks's essay, "The Unfortunates: What the Life Spans of Early Black Books Tell Us About Book History," considers how race factors into the chances of survival for eighteenth- and nineteenth-century books. Using *The Journal of John Marrant* as a platform for articulating "a view of book history alternative to mainline histories of the book centering on the book trade," Brooks shows that the books most likely to endure had two "vectors of movement": they emerged out of social movements, and they appeared in mobile formats that traveled effectively across the fractured terrain of African Americans' lived experience. Likewise, in "Frances Ellen Watkins Harper and the Circuits of Abolitionist Poetry," Meredith McGill puts the movements of authors and texts into dialogue. She argues that in both their ephemeral print formats and their direct modes of address, Harper's poems supplement the temporal dislocation that characterized her own circulation on the lecture circuit. When we read Harper's work under the protocols of lyric poetry, individual authorship, or orientation toward a *book*, we overlook its aspirations to oratory and its solicitation of a collective response. Finally, Eric Gardner's "Early African American Print Culture and the American West" calls on scholars to extend the map of African American print culture beyond its usual northeastern perimeters. To demonstrate the contributions of western African American print culture, Gardner takes as his case study nineteenth-century San Francisco's burgeoning black press. He finds that African American writers and editors in San Francisco were particularly attuned to experiences of "black mobility"—both the geographic dislocations that characterized many African Americans' lives and the freedoms of movement particular individuals seized for themselves—while holding out California as "a destination where the versions of blackness that had been seeded in the East might finally flower." Treating in equal measure the movements of historical persons and material objects, this group of essays builds on existing theories of circulation by reading the movements of texts against both the forces that set them in motion and the consequences of those movements.

Following these studies of circulation, Part II, "Racialization and Identity Production," considers textual circulation's consequences for personhood. This cluster examines how African American identities in the early United States were constructed and reconstructed through multiple kinds of print production, from gallows narratives to genteel engravings, and from slave narratives to racist broadsides. Although the African American literary canon has historically privileged what Jeannine Marie DeLombard terms "exemplary blackness," in "Apprehending Early African American Literary History," she challenges this tradition to include the confessions of condemned criminals that enjoyed immense popularity in the late eighteenth century. DeLombard discerns that the legal system actually assigned African Americans dual identities: under civil law, they were treated as property, but under criminal law, they were punishable as persons. Thus gallows narratives have the ironic distinction of being the literature that first enabled black subjects to claim public personhood. In "Black Voices, White Print: Racial Practice, Print Publicity, and Order in the Early American Republic," Corey Capers interrogates how certain practices of publicity came to be marked as "black" in the first place. Examining the early nineteenth-century "Bobalition broadsides," which satirized African American celebrations of the abolition of the transatlantic slave trade, Capers shows that by translating abolitionist activism into ridiculous parades, malapropisms, and overeating, these accounts worked to make blackness synonymous with disorder. Susanna Ashton's "Slavery, Imprinted: The Life and Narrative of William Grimes" recovers one of the earliest and most successful self-conscious attempts by a slave to construct his own identity in print. Ashton argues that Grimes's narrative grapples with "his own fraught experiences with the print world," which confined and exploited him but also provided him with opportunities for self-definition—most crucially, by registering the first copyright by an African American author for a full-length book. The final essay in Part II, Jonathan Senchyne's "Bottles of Ink and Reams of Paper: *Clotel*, Racialization, and the Material Culture of Print," reexamines the language of blackness and whiteness that came to dominate printing in the nineteenth century, giving new meaning to Henri-Jean Martin's claim that the history of typography charts the "triumph of white . . . over black."[16] Senchyne points out that while stories of mixed-race women such as William Wells Brown's

Clotel hinge on their heroines' proximity to whiteness in order to critique ideologies of racial dualism, the accompanying engravings rely on techniques that graphically instantiate notions of white transparency and black markedness, producing illustrations that break down the texts' insistence on racial ambiguity. All the essays in this part illuminate the tensions and ironies by which print both enabled and compromised the agency that African Americans exerted in their acts of self-making and their claims to property. Together they complicate our understanding of African American literary producers' entry into U.S. print culture by showing that establishing identities in print meant contending with preestablished terms.

The widespread critical emphasis in African American literary studies on originality finds a powerful counterpoint in the collection's third part, "Adaptation, Citation, Deployment." The essays in this cluster emphasize the strategic and challenging ways that African American literary producers rewrote, repurposed, and imaginatively plagiarized from previously published materials. Lara Langer Cohen's essay, "Notes from the State of Saint Domingue: The Practice of Citation in *Clotel*," examines this aesthetic in William Wells Brown's 1853 novel, which stitches its narrative together with contemporary poetry, fiction, slave narratives, and newspaper reportage to make a kind of patchwork of a contemporary antislavery print culture. Focusing on Brown's use of passages from a biography of Haitian revolutionary Toussaint L'Ouverture to describe Nat Turner's failed rebellion, it hypothesizes a relation between citation as a form and these citations' counterfactual content, which "pits the print archive against history as we know it." In "The Canon in Front of Them: African American Deployments of 'The Charge of the Light Brigade,'" Daniel Hack investigates the surprising currency of Tennyson's poem in African American newspapers. Demonstrating that the poem became a key site to interrogate the intersections between nation, race, and culture, this essay asks what happens if we reconfigure an African American literary tradition to include engagements with non–African American texts. Holly Jackson's "Another Long Bridge: Reproduction and Reversion in *Hagar's Daughter*" begins with the observation that Pauline Hopkins's novel repeats almost verbatim the most famous scene in Brown's *Clotel*, in which the heroine, thwarted in her attempt to cross the Potomac to freedom, jumps to her death from the bridge instead. In a plot that does not so much unfold as fold back on itself, Hopkins likewise turns to history, invoking Brown to figure Reconstruction's failure to bring the nation into a new era of freedom. Turning from verbal to visual copies, Dalila Scruggs's "'Photographs to

Answer Our Purposes': Representations of the Liberian Landscape in Colonization Print Culture" explores the afterlives of two daguerreotypes of Monrovia taken by black photographer Augustus Washington. Scruggs follows the images as they are reproduced as wood engravings, cropped, and mobilized to new ends, using their history to trace "the American Colonization Society's efforts to manage the image of Liberia" amid the flurry of reprinting. Susan Gillman's essay, "Networking *Uncle Tom's Cabin*; or, Hyper Stowe in Early African American Print Culture," proposes that the "models of interactive digital scholarship" so popular today have their forebears in "African American traditions in print and performance." To demonstrate this claim, she turns to *Uncle Tom's Cabin*, which not only thematizes adaptation as an African American cultural practice but also generates an extensive web of text networks itself. If Harriet Beecher Stowe's novel seems like a surprising example of African American print culture, for Gillman, this is precisely the point, as her essay "works to question and potentially to redefine what counts as 'early African American print culture.'" By making a case for the interpretive significance of "unoriginality," the essays clustered in Part III argue that the instabilities they associate with early African American print culture challenge the most basic categories—author, text, identity—of both African American literature and print culture studies.

The book's final cluster, Part IV, "Public Performances," moves from the material conditions of texts to the phenomenological experiences of reading, identifying, and otherwise enacting a print "public." Lloyd Pratt's essay, "The Lyric Public of *Les Cenelles*," takes up the first anthology of African American literature, a collection of Francophone poetry published in New Orleans in 1845. Focusing on their use of apostrophe, Pratt argues that the poems in *Les Cenelles* offer "a mode of being in common with others" that cultivates multiple scales of affiliation—a mode of sociality that challenges both the individualism of lyric reading and the more rigid frameworks of the "spatial turn" in literary studies. In "Imagining a Nation of Fellow Citizens: Early African American Politics of Publicity in the Black State Conventions," Derrick Spires analyzes the printed proceedings of black state conventions in the 1840s, which he reads as "performative speech acts that seek to manufacture the very citizenship practices from which the delegates had been excluded." The convention proceedings' rhetorical strategies and modes of address, Spires argues, complicate models of a "counterpublic" often associated with African American discourse and suggest instead the possibility of a "mesopublic," which exists in the interstices between the state and the people. Radiclani

Clytus's study of the American Anti-Slavery Society's 1835 pamphlet campaign, "'Keep It Before the People': The Pictorialization of American Abolitionism," shifts the customary focus on the writings of the AASS to explore their "ocularcentric ethos." In the hundreds of thousands of illustrated materials that it distributed, as well as the visually inflected language it used, the AASS drew on Christian tropes of visual piety to propose that the best way to grasp slavery was to picture it. In the volume's final chapter, Elizabeth Maddock Dillon argues that early African American print culture is best understood not in terms of singular, reproducible texts but as a series performances or interactions with various publics—publisher, consumer, reader, critic. Her essay, "John Marrant Blows the French Horn: Print, Performance, and the Making of Publics in Early African American Literature," elaborates Marrant's signal position in the revisionary framework print culture offers. Marrant's narrative, which itself revolves around scenes of performance, helps dislodge the familiar notion that print fixes meaning and offers, a new, more dynamic way of reading print culture in its place. This final part, like the first, engages a critical term that has proved a central one for print culture studies. Rather than simply employing this term, however, the essays in Part IV problematize its use in relation to African American literary production, suggesting that we must understand print publics not as stable entities but as improvised and shifting scenes.

Insights

In the present usage, "early African American print culture" synthesizes and challenges the frameworks from which it emerges, yielding three sizable insights that resonate across the volume's essays. While those essays also yield far more local insights about early African American print culture than can be adequately described here, these larger points should be recognized as key elements of the overarching theoretical contribution this volume has to make and, moreover, as evidence of the ways that African American literature and print culture stand to transform one another.

First, these essays mount a collective challenge to the presumed universality of what we might call the print-capitalism thesis. Scholars of print culture customarily refer to "the literary marketplace" as shorthand for the circulation of print, a connection cemented by an influential tradition of scholarship on the economic underpinnings of print culture. The synonymy between print culture and economics was introduced at least as early as Lucien Febvre and Henri-Jean Martin's contention that the production of printed goods had to be "firmly based on a business footing" or "it was doomed to failure"; was reinforced by Jürgen Habermas's narrative of print commodities and the rise of the bourgeois "public sphere of letters"; and was condensed in Benedict Anderson's term "print-capitalism."[17] Anderson's argument insists that "nothing served to 'assemble'" disparate communities "more than capitalism," which "created mechanically reproduced print-languages capable of dissemination through the market."[18] The print-capitalism thesis possesses undeniable explanatory power. Yet the essays in this volume show that its model is not as generalizable as scholars tend to imagine, for the circulation of early African American print proves not to have been strictly (or even necessarily) an economic issue. Rather, the following essays demonstrate that print tracks with political movements (Brooks, Spires), racial ideologies (Rezek, DeLombard, Jackson), regional practices (Gardner, Pratt, Dillon), and generic conventions (McGill, Scruggs), all of which could be buttressed by economics, but, as these case studies show, all of which often are not. Economic circulation, these essays imply, is an aspect of social circulation in print culture, rather than the other way around.

Second, the essays in this volume provide an alternative paradigm to the study of "black authorship" that has for so long been the only significant paradigm by which to estimate African American print culture, and African American literature more generally. As literature written *by* (rather than *for* or *about*) African American persons is the almost universal criteria for defining African American literature, theoretical arguments for displacing the author have usually been read as hostile to the intellectual and political project that has carved out space for that literature. Twenty-five years ago Barbara Christian influentially articulated the terms of this supposed opposition, according to which recognition of "the literature of blacks, women of South America and Africa, etc., as overtly 'political' literature was being preempted by a new Western concept which proclaimed that reality does not exist, that everything is relative, and that every text is silent about something."[19] However, the following essays reject this opposition, by way of the collective insight that critical investigation into the idea of authorship complicates—and therefore does not and should not displace—attention to racialization or its historically lived experience. Taking for granted that African American literature may not exclusively count as literature by African American authors, the following essays consider African Americans variously as narrative protagonists

(DeLombard), performers (Dillon), booksellers (Brooks, Ashton), editors (Gardner, Cohen, Hack, Jackson), and signifiers (Capers, Senchyne, Scruggs, Clytus). These essays also find that print production is a collective endeavor, whose collaborations, for better *and* for worse, work across the color line (Rezek, DeLombard, Capers, Senchyne, Hack, Gillman, Scruggs, Clytus). Extending the force of these insights, we might further recognize that African Americans were printers, readers, laborers, teachers, subjects who desired literacy (and refused it), and, above all, participants in a rapidly emergent media culture whose impact on everyday life scholars are only beginning to understand. Authorship is one part of this story, to be sure; but it no longer seems necessary to insist that it is the only intellectually exciting or politically meaningful aspect of that story. Collectively, this volume demonstrates the uneven ways in which print culture enables the coexistence of historical subjects and rhetorical figures.

Following from critiques of both the print-capitalism thesis and the black authorship premise, the third major insight of this volume is an optimistic take on the importance of *not* being original. Copying—one of the most prominent and various aspects of any print culture—emerges as a central concept in this volume. Drawing on Meredith McGill's justly influential work on the antebellum "culture of reprinting," the essays in this volume track further variations on copying, including adaptation (Gillman), citation (Cohen), deployment (Hack), reproduction (Jackson), and cliché (Rezek). (We have chosen not to prioritize one of these terms over any other, in an effort to honor the varieties of creative unoriginality, with their distinct—in some cases idiosyncratic—political and historical valences.) Such copying usually embarrasses a marketplace that rewards novelty with economic success or a critical mode that privileges personal accomplishment with the sobriquet of genius. Yet as Peter Stallybrass has argued persuasively, "Learning requires imitation and inspiration, which today are marginalized by a concept of originality that produces as its inevitable double the specter of plagiarism, a specter rooted in the fear that we might have more to learn from others than from ourselves."[20] Putting varieties of copying at the conceptual center of this volume entails a rejection of the specious criteria that maintain that financially compensated original productions are the only meaningful mark of distinction in a print culture. Instead, financially uncompensated, generatively unoriginal productions are shown to be a cultural dominant of early African American print culture, pushing us to consider their prominence in early America print culture writ large.

These three insights underscore the present volume's aims to bring into focus the methodological interventions implicit in the conjunction of these fields, to ask how they intersect, and to suggest how each field may contribute to the other. Accordingly, a critique of the print-capitalism thesis should register as one of the ways in which attention to African American texts questions some of the assumptions of print culture studies, while the suspension of the singular value of black authorship should be read as one way in which print culture studies challenge the habits of African American literary studies. Moreover, the conceptual emphasis among this volume's essays on copying implies a disputation with any field—literary criticism and bibliography both included—that organizes itself around the author function.

As our interest in highlighting these mutually transformative encounters between African American literature and print culture suggests, part of the goal of this volume is to clear space for fresh *approaches* to underexamined material, as much as for that material itself. Thus while *Early African American Print Culture* participates in a critical tradition of expanding the archive through "recovery projects," it also asks how we might pursue our inquiries beyond the logic of "firsts" and "canons" that have often subtended such projects. For recovery requires more than the excavation of forgotten texts; it also requires the knowledge to read them. In addition to being an attempt to expand the fields of African American literature and print culture, then, this volume should be read as a series of methodological provocations or invitations. In this respect, we hope its claims will prove portable enough to generate a conversation about the theories that underwrite archival and recovery work, that pair critical race and material culture studies, and that shape the relationship between criticism and description that informs the most promising work in the field. After all, one key point of convergence for both African American literary studies and print culture studies is the insight that any book that is made by its authors can also be remade by its readers.

PART I

Vectors of Movement

The Print Atlantic: Phillis Wheatley, Ignatius Sancho, and the Cultural Significance of the Book

JOSEPH REZEK

TO BE SOLD. A Parcel of likely NEGROES, imported from *Africa*, cheap for Cash, or short Credit with Interest; enquire of *John Avery*, at his House next Door to the White-Horse, or at a Store adjoining to said *Avery's* Distill-House, at the South End, near the South Market: – Also if any Persons have any Negro Men, strong and hearty, tho' not of the best moral Character, which are proper Subjects for Transportation, may have an Exchange for small Negroes.

—*Boston Evening-Post*, August 3, 1761

PROPOSALS. For Printing in *London* by SUBSCRIPTION, A Volume of POEMS, DEDICATED by Permission to the Right Hon. the COUNTESS of HUNTINGDON. Written by *PHILLIS*, a NEGRO SERVANT to Mr. WHEATLEY of *Boston*, in *New-England*.

Terms of Subscription.

  I. The Book to be neatly printed in 12mo. on a new Type and a fine Paper, adorned with an elegant Frontispiece, representing the Author.

 II. That the Price to Subscribers shall be Two Shillings sewed, or Two Shillings and Six-pence neatly bound.

II[I]. That every Subscriber deposit One Shilling at the Time of
subscribing; and the Remainder to be paid on the Delivery
of the Book.

Subscriptions are received by Cox & BERRY, in *Boston*.
—*Massachusetts Gazette; and the Boston
Weekly News-Letter*, April 16, 1773

These advertisements are drawn from the print archives of two institutions
that shaped the culture of the Anglophone Atlantic: the trade in enslaved
Africans and the trade in books. The first advertisement, fairly typical of its
time, indicates a number of that culture's defining features. These include
tensions within commercial networks defined both by local knowledge ("enquire of *John Avery*, at his House") and a wide transatlantic reach; the use of
multiple devices for the exchange of goods (cash, credit, exchange); and the
radical contradictions of the slave economy, apparent in this advertisement's
description of Africans in both the stark language of commodification ("parcel," "imported," "cheap") and the language of subjectivity ("strong and hearty,"
"moral Character"). The advertisement also suggests one way that print, in this
case the newspaper, was used "to establish or reestablish confidence in slavery
and servitude," as David Waldstreicher writes of another group of advertisements, those for runaway slaves. It produces such confidence not only as it
constructs Africans as salable goods, but also as it projects its imagined audience as a slaveholding public with expertise about "Negroes," one that can
judge for itself whether or not certain individuals are "proper Subjects for
Transportation" and therefore unsuitable for the particular kind of household
slavery then prevalent in Boston.[1]

Household slavery in Boston enabled the production of another transatlantic commodity, announced in the second advertisement: the London-
printed book of poems "Written by *PHILLIS*, a Negro Servant to Mr.
Wheatley." In 1761, this poet was a young girl of seven or eight years of age,
one of the "small Negroes" brought from Africa to America that John Avery
advertised for sale in the *Boston Evening-Post*. The first advertisement sent
Susanna Wheatley, the poet's future mistress, educator, and promoter, to the
market for a slave. The second advertisement put that slave back in the marketplace, this time as an author who, exclusively through the mediation of her
identity in print, became a specimen for knowledge production and opinion

about Africans and their descendants. Phillis Wheatley's *Poems on Various Subjects, Religious and Moral* (1773), in contrast to the first advertisement, was an early example of how print lessened confidence in slavery and servitude, notably in Wheatley's own master, who freed her at the suggestion of the book's first readers.[2]

It was precisely the relationship between Wheatley's poems and their capacity to affect a reader's confidence in slavery that preoccupied her most notable early critic, the London shopkeeper and Afro-Briton writer Ignatius Sancho. Like Wheatley, Sancho was a victim of the slave trade—he was born on a slave ship crossing the Atlantic—whose only book, his posthumously published *Letters of the Late Ignatius Sancho* (1782), also made him a flash point in discussions about the intellectual capacity of Africans. Sancho encountered Wheatley's *Poems* along with a number of antislavery texts that Philadelphia Quaker Jabez Fisher sent him in 1778. In a letter to Fisher that appeared in the published *Letters*, Sancho criticizes the eminent Boston individuals who are listed in the famous "attestation" that was printed in Wheatley's volume and guaranteed the authenticity of her poems. He finds it appalling that none of them freed her from slavery: "[T]he list of splendid—titled—learned names, in confirmation of her being the real authoress.—alas! shews how very poor the acquisition of wealth and knowledge are—without generosity—feeling—and humanity. —These good great folks—all know—and perhaps admired—nay, praised Genius in bondage—and then, like the Priests and the Levites in sacred writ, passed by—not one good Samaritan amongst them." Elsewhere Sancho mentions less rarified conditions than "Genius" that make slavery unjust, including the "cruel carnage and depopulation" of the slave trade and the "diabolical usage of my brother Negroes," but in discussing Wheatley he is struck by what appears to be her ironic situation. Sancho thinks that "genius" is a trait that epitomizes freedom, while Wheatley, to the disgrace of her white patrons, remains "in bondage." Her case makes slavery seem particularly indefensible.[3]

The appearance of the first books by black writers forced readers in the Anglophone world to decide if they agreed with Sancho that there was a necessary irony in the enslavement of an author. This essay foregrounds the role that materiality could play in influencing such opinions. I argue that eighteenth-century print culture, and specifically the meanings readers assigned to the printed book as a class of material texts, helped determine the way writers like Wheatley and Sancho were received and how their work influenced debates about slavery. The dissemination of printed books by black authors presented readers with the unprecedented fact made clear by the two advertisements with which I began: black authors, unlike any others, were in their persons subject to commodification, just like the books they published. Book publication intensified the drama of this conjunction, as Sancho's comment about Wheatley suggests. Book publication also catalyzed aesthetic judgments that led readers to believe in a text's ability to represent the talents of an entire race. The cultural significance of the book helped make this leap of logic possible.

While scholars have consistently explored the political implications of early black writing, they have been less interested in how materiality carries a politics of its own. The politics of materiality can best be examined through considering Wheatley and Sancho together as writers of what Paul Gilroy has termed "the black Atlantic." A number of factors can explain the lack of serious scholarly comparison of these two authors, including the influence of nationally defined boundaries in literary study. Other differences separate the two writers: Wheatley was a female domestic slave who eventually died penniless in New England, while Sancho was a free black business owner in London who met gender and property qualifications to vote for Parliament as a resident in Westminster. However, the link between Wheatley's *Poems* and Sancho's *Letters* was obvious to eighteenth-century readers and should interest us now. Their books gathered meaning as objects in what I propose to call "the print Atlantic"—a term that emphasizes the role of print in connecting the English-speaking publics of the Atlantic into a single, though internally various, culture. I borrow the grammar of Gilroy's influential term to stress the importance of a media-specific approach to the writing of early black writers. In describing Wheatley and Sancho as writers of "the print Atlantic," then, I hope both to emphasize print's connective role in the Atlantic world and also to suggest a new way of talking about the black Atlantic that foregrounds print as a central concern.[4]

In what follows I will first explore readers' reactions to Wheatley and Sancho as the formats of their texts changed. Both authors were well known for their printed works before their books appeared—Wheatley for her elegy to George Whitefield and Sancho for his correspondence with Laurence Sterne. Yet only when their books appeared did readers begin to link their aesthetic judgments to claims about representativeness. Book publication, as distinguished from other kinds of printing, made these writers uniquely available to white readers as "specimens," as sites for the discussion of racial hierarchy, and, ultimately, as evidence either to support or to oppose the institution of slavery. Following this discussion, I proceed to a close reading of the textual history of Wheatley's famous poem to the Earl of Dartmouth to demonstrate that the cultural hierarchies that shaped the print Atlantic are apparent on the level of the word. I argue that Wheatley's poem encodes its material history as it links its reflections on the slave trade to the aesthetic experience books could produce.

The Politics of Format

In discussing early modern print culture, and the significance of Wheatley and Sancho in particular, it is imperative to speak carefully about format.[5] I therefore use the term "book" to mean a bound codex volume of a significant length, heft, and commodity status. Wheatley's *Poems* and Sancho's *Letters* have long been acknowledged as the first books published by black writers. Rather than assuming we know what we mean when we talk about books, however, we should historicize the cultural meanings that such objects would have had for the first readers who encountered them. Betsy Erkkila assesses the political implications of Wheatley this way: "the fact of a black woman reading, writing, and publishing poems was itself enough to splinter the categories of male and female, white and black, and undermine a social order grounded in notions of sexual and racial difference."[6] How much of Wheatley's potential as a disruptive political force depended on the existence of her poems in book form? The material and economic features of Wheatley's *Poems* intensified its potential as a politically disruptive object. The *Massachusetts Gazette* advertisement for Wheatley's *Poems*, for example, suggests the role that book publication played in accruing to her writing a claim to the status of art. The book has an aristocratic patron, the Countess of Huntingdon; it will be "neatly printed" with a "new Type" on "fine Paper"; it will include an "elegant Frontispiece" of the author; it will arrive as an object to be held in your hand and read, either "sewed" or "bound," and therefore also prepared for the shelf of a library; it will cost a significant amount of money, at least two shillings; and, finally, it will require submission to the "terms" of a contract—subscription publishing—which in this case requires the buyer to provide capital in advance and the seller to guarantee the printing and transatlantic importation of the book. Such details invoke all the agents involved in the production of this kind of commodity, from the manufacturing of type to its delivery to readers, and set this object apart from more ephemeral media that transmitted texts. In this regard, the advertisement for Wheatley's *Poems* invokes those aspects of a book that are designed to establish the cultural capital of a literary work. Its only unique feature, of course, remains the information it provides about the race of the author, "*PHILLIS*, a Negro Servant," which to most readers would have been incompatible with cultural capital of a familiar kind.

The disjunction between racial identity and cultural capital would have been apparent as well to readers of Sancho's *Letters*, which also was published by subscription and contained a frontispiece of its author. Sancho's book was even more impressive than Wheatley's volume in size and price: its first two-volume edition cost six shillings and totaled more than 500 pages, compared to Wheatley's 124 pages. Generally speaking, if we use distinguishing criteria like those highlighted in Wheatley's advertisement, we can count only three books of similar stature among the more than fifty discrete titles published by black authors in English before 1800, and they were all published first in London: Phillis Wheatley's *Poems* (1773), Ignatius Sancho's *Letters* (1782), and Olaudah Equiano's *Interesting Narrative* (1789).[7] These books contain more than 120 pages each; they were sold as single texts, either already bound or meant to be bound separately from other texts; they were printed with large type and with ample space between each line of text; they were advertised widely and published by subscription; and, significantly, they included frontispieces depicting the author. These books are thus distinguished from shorter, occasional, and more ephemeral texts by Jupiter Hammon, Briton Hammon, James Albert Ukawsaw Gronniosaw, Lemuel Heynes, Benjamin Banneker, Prince Hall, Absalom Jones, Richard Allen, and Venture Smith, as well as Wheatley's earlier pamphlets and broadsides, John Marrant's widely reprinted *Narrative* (1785), and Quobna Ottobah Cugoano's abridged *Thoughts and Sentiments on the Evil of Slavery* (1791). Two important texts shared some, but not all, the criteria that distinguishes those by Wheatley, Sancho, and Equiano: Cugoano's unabridged *Thoughts and Sentiments* (1787), which contained 154 pages but was printed with small and crowded type and without a frontispiece, and Marrant's *Journal* (1790), which was issued along with two sermons to make a book about as long as Wheatley's but which also used crowded type and contained no frontispiece.

The point here is that while any publication by an author of African descent threatened to disrupt the conventions of Anglophone print culture, not all printed texts were created equal. The material features of texts were freighted with cultural significance that could help determine the scandal a black-authored text produced. In distinguishing Wheatley, Sancho, and Equiano from other texts of the period, including more borderline cases like Cugoano and Marrant, I am using a narrow definition of the book to dramatize the importance of materiality to a culture accustomed to classifying texts according to format, a practice suggested by eighteenth-century library catalogs, which often listed books according to size—folio, quarto, octavo, duodecimo—as well as by title or author.[8] "Far from being secondary to content," Bradin Cormack and Carla Mazzio write, "the physical forms of the book generate content by making it available for particular kinds of use."[9] While no single material feature of a text in itself determined a reader's practice, the confluence of a number of distinguishing features, such as paper size or an authorial frontispiece, guided the use of a book by hailing a reader's attention and establishing cultural capital. In this period, for example, the use of a large typeface, of "leaded" type (which created space between lines of text), and of wide margins, indicated a claim to the importance of discourse. The difference is easily seen in comparing typical pages of Wheatley's and Sancho's first editions with the first printed edition of Marrant's *Narrative*, a pamphlet also published in London (see Figures 1.1–3).[10] Wheatley's *Poems* and Sancho's *Letters* were the first black-authored texts—of any kind—to leave so much empty space on the page.

The reception history of Wheatley and Sancho suggests that format was an important factor in shaping readers' aesthetic judgments. Before the appearance of their writing in book form, they were not used as evidence in serious arguments for or against the enslavement of Africans. This was true despite the wide dissemination of their work. Before her book was published, Wheatley's poems appeared in more than a dozen editions as pamphlets or broadsides in Boston, Newport, New York, Philadelphia, and London, and they were reprinted in periodicals such as the *London Magazine*, the *Newport Mercury*, the *New Hampshire Gazette*, the *Boston Evening-Post*, the *Massachusetts Gazette*, the *New-York Journal*, and the *Essex Gazette*. Sancho's letter to Laurence Sterne was printed first in Sterne's posthumous *Letters* and then reprinted in periodicals with transatlantic readerships, including the *Monthly Review*, *Dodsley's Annual Register*, and the *Gentleman's Magazine*. The first commentaries on Wheatley and Sancho treated their writings as the curious achievements of individuals, rather than as exemplary. In Wheatley's case this involved reactions both to her printed texts and to the scene of writing, as when Thomas Wooldridge reports his "astonish[ment]" at witnessing Wheatley at work. Knowledge of Wheatley's elegy to Whitefield brought Wooldridge

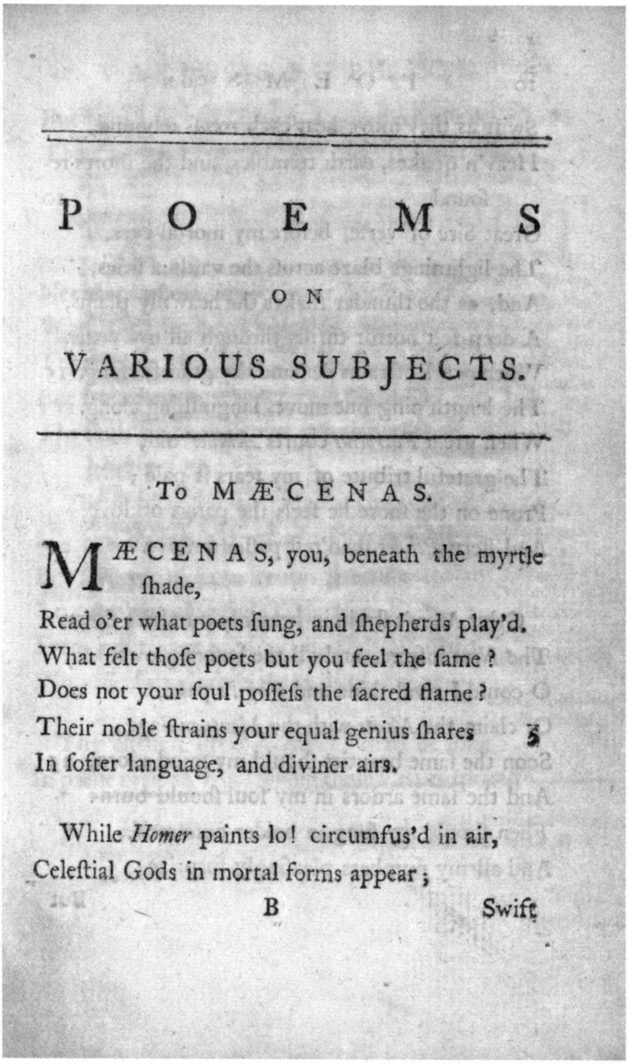

POEMS

ON

VARIOUS SUBJECTS.

To MÆCENAS.

MÆCENAS, you, beneath the myrtle
shade,
Read o'er what poets sung, and shepherds play'd.
What felt those poets but you feel the same?
Does not your soul possess the sacred flame?
Their noble strains your equal genius shares   5
In softer language, and diviner airs.

While *Homer* paints lo! circumfus'd in air,
Celestial Gods in mortal forms appear;

B   Swift

Figure 1.1. From Phillis Wheatley, *Poems on Various Subjects, Religious and Moral* (London, 1773). Courtesy of the Library Company of Philadelphia.

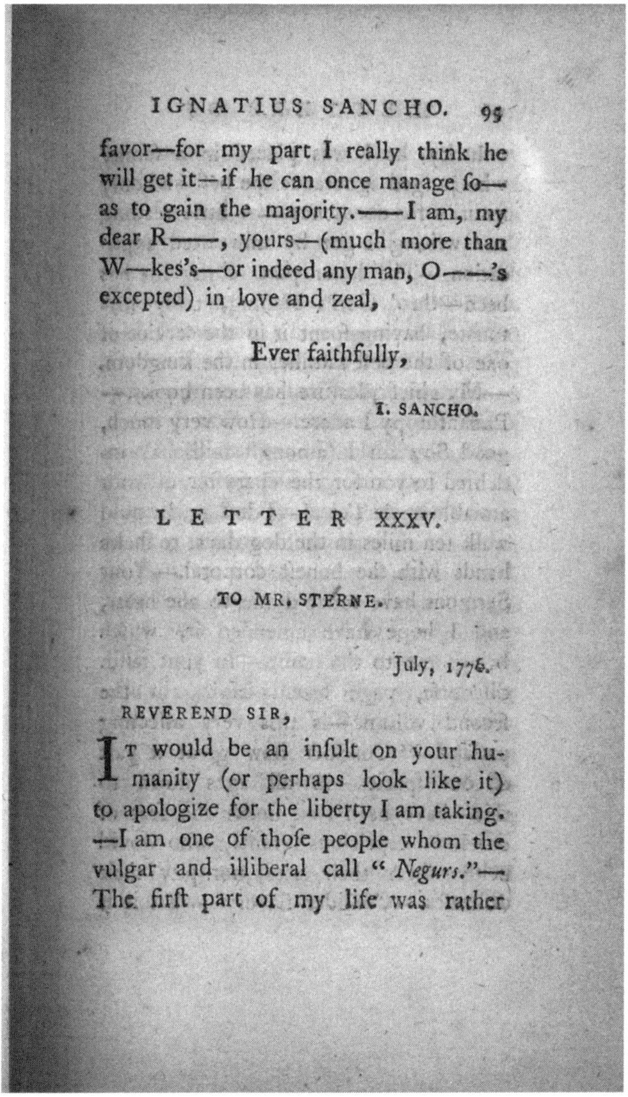

IGNATIUS SANCHO. 95

favor—for my part I really think he will get it—if he can once manage ſo—as to gain the majority.——I am, my dear R——, yours—(much more than W—kes's—or indeed any man, O——'s excepted) in love and zeal,

Ever faithfully,

I. SANCHO.

LETTER XXXV.

TO MR. STERNE.

July, 1776.

REVEREND SIR,

IT would be an inſult on your humanity (or perhaps look like it) to apologize for the liberty I am taking.—I am one of thoſe people whom the vulgar and illiberal call "*Negurs*."—The firſt part of my life was rather

Figure 1.2. From Ignatius Sancho, *Letters of the Late Ignatius Sancho, an African* (London, 1782). Courtesy of Singer-Mendenhall Collection. Courtesy of the Rare Book and Manuscript Library, University of Pennsylvania.

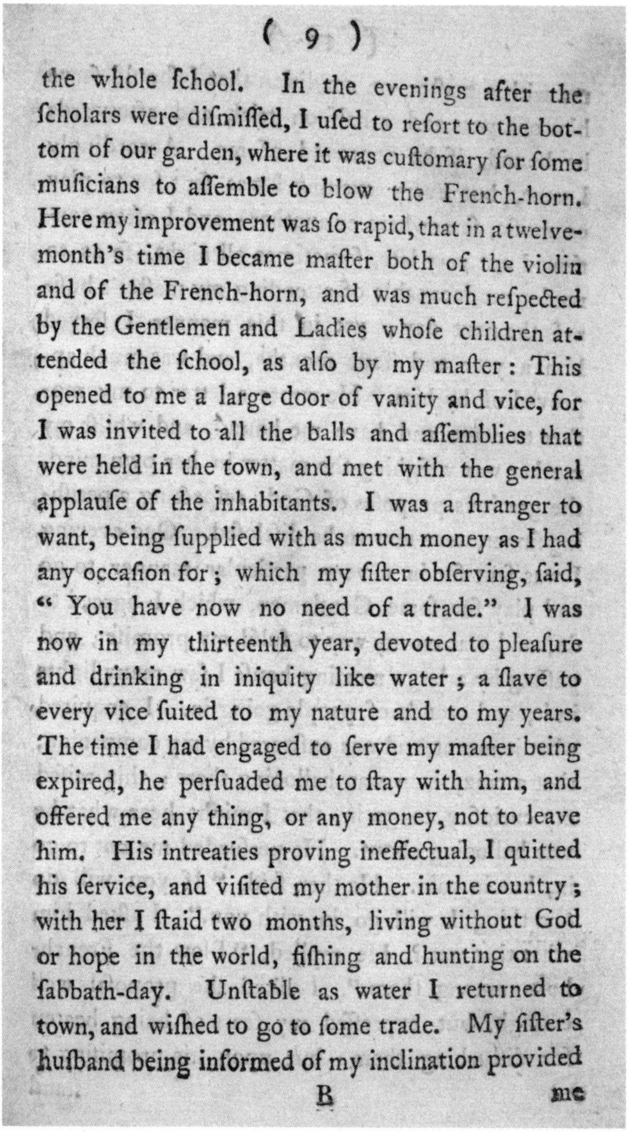

the whole fchool. In the evenings after the fcholars were difmiffed, I ufed to refort to the bottom of our garden, where it was cuftomary for fome muficians to affemble to blow the French-horn. Here my improvement was fo rapid, that in a twelvemonth's time I became mafter both of the violin and of the French-horn, and was much refpected by the Gentlemen and Ladies whofe children attended the fchool, as alfo by my mafter: This opened to me a large door of vanity and vice, for I was invited to all the balls and affemblies that were held in the town, and met with the general applaufe of the inhabitants. I was a ftranger to want, being fupplied with as much money as I had any occafion for; which my fifter obferving, faid, " You have now no need of a trade." I was now in my thirteenth year, devoted to pleafure and drinking in iniquity like water; a flave to every vice fuited to my nature and to my years. The time I had engaged to ferve my mafter being expired, he perfuaded me to ftay with him, and offered me any thing, or any money, not to leave him. His intreaties proving ineffectual, I quitted his fervice, and vifited my mother in the country; with her I ftaid two months, living without God or hope in the world, fifhing and hunting on the fabbath-day. Unftable as water I returned to town, and wifhed to go to fome trade. My fifter's hufband being informed of my inclination provided

B   me

Figure 1.3. From John Marrant, *A Narrative of the Lord's Wonderful Dealings* (London, 1785). Courtesy of the Newberry Library.

to call upon her in Boston, where in his presence she composed an epistle to his friend the Earl of Dartmouth. "I could hardly believe my eyes," Wooldridge writes to Dartmouth in a letter he sent with a copy of the poem, assuring him that this "very Extraordinary female Slave" is "no Imposter."[11] While Wheatley is interesting to Wooldridge because of her anomalousness, he refrains from drawing generalized conclusions from her achievements. Benjamin Rush may have been the first to employ Wheatley in the service of an argument against slavery, but his use of her was anonymous, tentative, and fleeting. Rush's footnote in an antislavery pamphlet printed before her *Poems* is meant to prove the abilities of Africans: "There is now in the town of Boston a Free Negro Girl, about 18 years of age, who has been but 9 years in the country, whose singular genius and accomplishments are such as not only do honor to her sex, but to human nature. Several of her poems have been printed, and read with pleasure by the public."[12] A response to this comment from proslavery writer Richard Nisbet led Rush to delete this footnote from the pamphlet's subsequent editions. Nisbet dismissed Wheatley as "a negro girl writing a few silly poems," a comment that reminds us that while Wheatley had by this time printed a number of poems, she had not yet published a book of poetry.[13]

Initial responses to Sancho's correspondence with Laurence Sterne are remarkable for their recourse to the language of interest rather than exemplarity. While Sancho's African identity was undoubtedly responsible for the wide reprinting of his letter to Sterne, and led commentators to trade in racist discourse, periodicals frame Sancho as an individual case. The *Monthly Review* calls his letter a "curiosity" written by "a very sensible Black" who "earn[s] a subsistence by keeping a little shop somewhere in Westminster."[14] The *Gentleman's Magazine* takes Sancho's letter as evidence of his unique nature, not the nature of his race: "the writer, though black as Othello, has a heart as humanized as any of the fairest about St. James's." There is no sense in the *Gentleman's Magazine* that this comment, notwithstanding its racialized generalization, implies that by writing Sancho proves anything—positive or negative—except his own character. As the magazine goes on to imagine the effects of the letter's publication, it points to Sancho's business as a shopkeeper, not to anyone's ideas about Africans in general; the letter "must certainly increase his custom."[15]

Later responses to Wheatley and Sancho suggest they became representative figures after book publication. When readers could hold an object in their hand, one that required a few hours to read and cost a few shillings, they generalized from the particular to the rule. These were objects that, given the frontispieces that depict authors of African descent, could by their material existence claim to *embody* the black body and reveal the black mind. Wheatley's first book reviewers highlighted her potential as a representative figure, and so did Sancho's editors and agents, who ushered his *Letters* to the press after his death. In introducing Wheatley's *Poems*, the *Monthly Review* considered its effect on the question of whether "ancient" mythology is correct in its claim that "genius is the offspring of the sun"; it offers Wheatley's poems as a single, though failed, "instance" of the creative efforts of "the sable race."[16] The editor of Sancho's *Letters* invites readers to generalize as she announces her motive for publishing his private correspondence: "the desire of shewing that an untutored African may possess abilities equal to an European."[17] In *Notes on the State of Virginia* (1784), Thomas Jefferson discusses Phillis Wheatley and Ignatius Sancho as examples of authors whose productions fail to convince him of racial equality; Wheatley's poems are "below the dignity of criticism" and Sancho's letters are "incoherent and eccentric."[18]

Jefferson's assessment is only the most well known of a number of discussions in the late eighteenth century that employed Wheatley and Sancho together in arguments about the capability of Africans. The association became somewhat of a cliché:

> Religion indeed has produced a Phyllis Whately [*sic*]; but it could not produce a poet. . . . Ignatius Sancho has approached nearer to merit in composition; yet his letters do more honour to the heart than to the head. (Thomas Jefferson, *Notes on the State of Virginia* [1784])

> [T]he letters of Ignatius Sancho, and the Poems of Phillis Wheatley, sufficiently prove that [Africans] are neither deficient in the feelings of humanity, nor the powers of the understanding. (Joseph Woods, *Thoughts on the Slavery of Negroes* [1784])

> The Poems of a *Negro* girl, and the Letters of *Ignatius Sancho*, are striking instances of genius contending against every disadvantage. (George Gregory, *Essays Historical and Moral* [1785])

> For a proof of [the talents of Africans] we appeal to the writings of an African girl. . . . Her poetical works . . . contain thirty-eight pieces on different subjects. . . . To this poetry we shall only add, as

a farther proof of their abilities, the Prose compositions of Ignatius
Sancho. (Thomas Clarkson, *Essay on the Slavery and Commerce of the
Human Species* [1786])

But the poems of Phillis Wheatley, and the letters of Ignatius Sancho,
are singular testimonies that the African mind is susceptible of very
superior improvement. (Thomas Burgess, *Considerations on the Abolition of Slavery and the Slave Trade* [1789])

[M]any instances are recorded of men of eminence amongst [Afri-
cans]: Witness, Ignatius Sancho, whose letters are admired by all men
of taste—Phillis Wheatley, who distinguished herself as a poetess.
(George Buchanan, *An Oration Upon the Moral and Political Evil of
Slavery* [1793])

Phillis Wheatley, who was a slave at *Boston* in New England . . .
wrote thirty-eight elegant pieces of poetry on different subjects,
which were published in 1773. . . . Ignatius Sancho . . . may also
be mentioned on this occasion. (John Stedman, *A Narrative of
Five Years' Expedition Against the Revolted Negroes of Surinam*
[1796])[19]

Jefferson's influence alone cannot explain the widespread occurrence of such
references to Wheatley and Sancho. Some of them are notable for invocations
of the materiality of the books they mention, as in Thomas Clarkson's reference to Wheatley's "thirty-eight pieces on different subjects," a figure tallied
from her table of contents, which John Stedman seems to have picked up
from him. Clarkson even adapts the language of the book's frontispiece in a
footnote identifying Wheatley by name: "Phillis Wheatley, a negro slave to
Mr. John Wheatley, of Boston, in New-England" (see Figure 1.4).[20] The publication of her book seems to have changed the opinion of Richard Nisbet.
Years after he dismissed her "few silly poems," Nisbet writes that "the more
natural and ingenious productions of Phillis Wheatley . . . [have] already
furnished a publick and ample testimony of, at least, as considerable a portion of mental ability, as falls to the lot of mankind in general."[21] The new
material setting for Wheatley's writing, within the pages of an "ample" book,
produced powerful claims about her relevance as a representative figure.
Clarkson highlights information about the book—such as the number of

Figure 1.4. Frontispiece to Phillis Wheatley, *Poems on Various Subjects, Religious and Moral* (London, 1773). Courtesy of the Library Company of Philadelphia.

poems—which a reader could easily glean from paratexts, reminding us that the use of a table of contents in Wheatley's *Poems* was another "first" for black authorship. Jefferson himself owned both books,[22] and while his discussion in *Notes* suggests he read the poems and letters they contain, other opinions about the two writers may derive more from widespread knowledge of their books than the writing within them.

The format of a printed text affected a reader's aesthetic judgments, a crucial fact for Wheatley and Sancho because it was on the basis of such judgments that readers tested their hierarchical thinking about race. Book publication raised the stakes because readers were also trained in hierarchical thinking about material texts. As Eric Gardner suggests in Chapter 4, such hierarchical thinking survives into our own time and is reflected in our strong preference for teaching and analyzing full-length books instead of shorter and more ephemeral texts. My analysis of the influence of format on the reception of Wheatley and Sancho contributes to a genealogy of this problem—of the privileging of the book—which, I have suggested, came into sharp relief as the first such objects were published by black authors. If the publication of books could make Wheatley and Sancho seem representative, it did so because the form of a book called for close readerly attention and, following this, promised unique entry into an authorial identity materiality helped to construct. Literary scholars are sometimes lured by the same promise, as we instinctively trust in the power of a book to represent whatever culture we assume it belongs to, the sort of assumption that would seem less convincing if the object of study were an anonymous text or a poem from a newspaper. The earliest commentaries on Wheatley's and Sancho's books display such assumptions in the extreme. In the sketch of Sancho's life that precedes his *Letters*, the biographer draws an implicit parallel between reading Sancho and understanding Africa: "He who could penetrate the interior of Africa might not improbably discover negro arts and polity. . . . And he who surveys the extent of intellect to which Ignatius Sancho had attained by self-education, will perhaps conclude, that the perfection of the reasoning faculties does not depend on a peculiar conformation of the scull."[23] The sketch asks us to survey the author as we would "penetrate" a continent, an imagined epistemological act formed by both the cultural work of racialized thinking and the aesthetic implications of book publication.

Book Publication and Textual Revision in Wheatley's Epistle to Dartmouth

So much for the perspective of readers. In Wheatley's poem addressed to the Earl of Dartmouth, we witness an author engaging with the hierarchies of the print Atlantic by embedding within a poem's textual history a record of its changing material existence. Three versions of the poem survive: in manuscript, in a newspaper, and within Wheatley's 1773 book.[24] Wheatley's changes to the poem emphasize the importance of format in determining a reader's level of engagement and therefore bear importantly on the question of representativeness and aesthetics. As I have mentioned, Wheatley wrote the poem at the prompting of Thomas Wooldridge, who called upon her in Boston in October 1772. The next month, Wooldridge forwarded the poem to the Earl of Dartmouth with a letter from himself describing her talents and a letter from Wheatley expressing her admiration. The poem was first printed in the *New-York Journal* seven months later, on June 3, 1773, while Wheatley was on her way to London to help oversee the publication of her book.[25] Variants to the poem in the newspaper version are minor and likely the work of an editor or compositor at the *New-York Journal*. For her book of poems, however, Wheatley deleted a number of lines from the manuscript version and made many significant changes. The most important changes occur in the passage where she invokes her reader and describes the injustice of the slave trade. The book version of this poem encodes the specific reading practices its medium makes possible.

In the poem's central moment, Wheatley steps back from a vehement defense of liberty to imagine the reactions of her reader. Compare the manuscript version of the passage, on the left, with the more well-known version from *Poems on Various Subjects*:

While you, my Lord, read
  o'er th' advent'rous Song
And wonder whence Such
  daring boldness Sprung:
Hence, flow my wishes for
  the common good
By feeling hearts alone, best
  understood.
From Native clime, when
  Seeming cruel fate
Me snatch'd from Afric's
  fancy'd happy Seat
Impetuous. —Ah! what
  bitter pangs molest
	Should you, my lord, while
	  you peruse my song,
	Wonder from whence my love
	  of *Freedom* sprung,
	Whence flow these wishes
	  from the common good,
	By feeling hearts alone best
	  understood,
	I, young in life, by seeming
	  cruel fate
	Was snatch'd from *Afric's*
	  fancy'd happy seat:
	What pangs excruciating
	  must molest,

What sorrows labour'd in the Parent breast!	What sorrows labour in my parent's breast?
That more than Stone, ne'er Soft compassion mov'd	Steel'd was that soul and by no misery mov'd
Who from its Father Seiz'd his much belov'd.	That from a father seiz'd his babe belov'd:
Such once my case. —Thus I deplore the day	Such, such my case. And can I then but pray
When Britons weep beneath Tyrannic sway.	Others may never feel tyrannic sway?

Both versions derive Wheatley's embrace of Britain's most cherished principle, liberty, from her experience of the empire's most offensive practice, the slave trade, thus exposing the foundational hypocrisy of her society. Both versions focus agony on the figure of her father; while here and elsewhere Wheatley expresses ambivalence about the consequences of her own "seeming cruel fate," she remains certain of her parent's misery. As a poet Wheatley specialized in the sorrows of parents, and in this poem she writes her own elegy, imagining the grieving father who lost his young daughter. This sets up a bitter and striking irony, because while in Wheatley's elegies the dead have been "snatch'd" to heaven, there is no consolation here for the worldly loss of a child to the slave trade.

These commonalities make the politics of the two versions of the passage seem identical, as one last similarity suggests: both versions invoke her reader—"my lord"—and put him on the same intellectual level with the speaker. This occurs through a remarkable mirroring effect, since the moment Wheatley poses a question about the earl's thought process she forces him to wonder about hers. The poem sets up the following transaction with the earl, which presents a radical argument for racial equality: as the earl reads over Wheatley's poem, he finds—when he gets to this passage—that she has decided to read his mind, which, perhaps only because of her inquiry, begins now to follow a path she traces for it straight into her own interiority, where a history of suffering led to her embrace of "Freedom." Wheatley shores up the depth of her own mind by granting depth to the earl's. This strategy asserts that her values have arisen not from assimilation into British culture, as the earl might suppose, but rather from reactions against its crimes. The passage is remarkable not only because of its biographical reference to

Africa, which has drawn notice from previous critics, but also because Wheatley uses the device of the interpolated reader. By raising the question of what the earl is thinking, Wheatley self-consciously guides her reader's thought process, responses, and conclusions.

As this poem goes from a manuscript written for a specific individual to a printed text within her book, though, the referent for the interpolated reader shifts: her addressee changes from the Earl of Dartmouth to a generalized reading public. On one level this occurs also in the *New-York Journal*, which gives the poem its first anonymous readership. However, the newspaper preserves the poem's initial specific address as well as its scene of composition through editorial remarks that direct readerly identification toward the person who demanded the poem (that is, Wooldridge) and away from the person who received it (the earl). The headnote in the *New-York Journal* explains that Wheatley wrote "in the presence" of a "Gentleman" who had visited her "in order to be satisfied" her earlier poems were "authentic."[26] The note asks readers to identify with the skeptical witness and invites them into the authenticating procedure as spectators. *Poems on Various Subjects* deflects such concern onto the general attestation that prefaces the entire volume, so it eliminates the authenticating scene of this particular poem. Within the book's pages we are free to identify entirely with the earl.

The central changes occur in revisions that manipulate the reader's interaction with the poem. They reflect its new significance as one of a large group of texts meant to produce an aesthetic judgment of a particular kind. In the new version Wheatley poses the whole question of a reader's curiosity as hypothetical. While in manuscript the poem presumes that the earl will definitely "wonder" about the origins of her politics, in the book Wheatley admits that such interest is merely possible. This change facilitates the identification of a more diverse range of readers than the manuscript poem, which, though the earl was unknown to Wheatley personally, still depended upon a higher degree of familiarity than a book marketed to strangers. Framing this readerly address as hypothetical eases an anonymous reader through the psychology of the passage. Furthermore, the opening comments are balanced by the new hypothetical question Wheatley poses at the end, which deletes her reference to "Britons" and generalizes her critique of tyranny: "And can I then but pray / Others may never feel tyrannic sway?" Kirstin Wilcox has rightly emphasized that as Wheatley turns to London away from Boston as the site for her book's publication, she modifies her plans and her poems to tone down local references and develop the image of a "practicing poet con-

cerned with the display of her belletristic mastery."[27] The infusion of hypothetical questions gives new authority to Wheatley's poetic voice, as do
changes that even out the prosody of the passage's middle couplets and deletions to other parts of the poem that tone down her rhetoric. Indeed, all these
changes make it more appropriate for its new status as book of poems printed
in London, the cultural capital of the Anglophone world.

The revised version of the passage modifies its description of an aesthetic
relation to poetry through a substitution that gestures, however subtly, toward
the material format of a book: in the first line, Wheatley substitutes "peruse"
for "read" in describing the earl's actions. This change is significant because of
connotations these terms carried in Wheatley's time. In their respective diction-
aries Samuel Johnson and Noah Webster define "to read" and "to peruse" as
synonyms that indicate the act of going over a text for comprehension. Both
lexicographers also signal an important difference: "to read" signifies discovery
and knowledge acquisition, while "to peruse" implies these things but carries a
secondary connotation of "to observe, to examine."[28] According to the *Oxford
English Dictionary*, the English word "peruse" has roots in the Anglo-Norman
word *peruser*, used to indicate an examination before a trial. Johnson's and
Webster's secondary definition of "peruse" has roots in this etymology and
implies a more deliberate activity than mere reading, one that requires careful
attention and a sense of purpose. This meaning differs from modern usage,
which casts perusal as the more superficial activity of browsing or skimming.
Eighteenth-century consumers *read* in order to learn something, but they *pe-
rused* in order to figure it out. When Wheatley writes "while you peruse my
song," she emphasizes the epistemological event for which readers during the
Enlightenment might prepare themselves, having picked up the first book they
had ever held written by an African. Such an event became an examination of
the African mind, as dozens of commentators imagined, and Wheatley's new
diction casts her book as a primary piece of evidence. Readers of Shakespeare,
from whom Johnson drew many illustrations, would have learned to associate the act of "perusal" with examining bodies as well as texts, training that
would prepare them to take Wheatley's book as an embodiment of her self and
of her race.[29] As Wheatley's poem describes a reader who "peruses my song," we
sense that he is called to consider not just the present poem but rather Wheatley's "song" writ large, her entire output as a poet. Readers are constructed as
part of an anonymous audience who carefully examine her book and her self.

This line is the only place we find the word "peruse" in *Poems on Various
Subjects*, with the striking exception of a sentence in the book's preface:

"With all their Imperfections, the Poems are now humbly submitted to the Perusal of the Public."[30] Among the other important material included in the book's front matter—the frontispiece, the dedication, the letter from John Wheatley, and the "attestation"—this preface is the one most interested in provoking an aesthetic response not dependent on Wheatley's biography. When Wheatley's poem to Dartmouth takes up the language of "perusal," it links this invocation of aesthetic judgment to the epistemology of examination. As such, the poem's embeddedness within *Poems* gestures toward a condition black authors faced as they printed books for a predominantly white readership: the conflation of readers' aesthetic responses and their opinions about racial difference. This passage from the poem to Dartmouth has long been recognized as a central moment in Wheatley's work because of her reflections about her father, Africa, and the slave trade. I believe it is the central moment in all of *Poems on Various Subjects* because it ties her consciousness of those things to a politics shaped by the medium that provides access to them. This is where Wheatley defines her readership, one she knows was used to handling, considering, examining, and perusing books.

Books helped give eighteenth-century readers confidence in their ability to interpret black texts as evidence of an author's identity and representativeness. Studies of the black Atlantic that take seriously the cultural significance of materiality can prevent us from making the same mistake. Despite continued attention to the instability of early black texts, especially those whose publications were controlled by white people and institutions, scholars of the early black Atlantic sometimes display a tendency to trace a direct line between literary expression and biographical experience that a media-specific study would disrupt.[31] The biographical focus of Gilroy's initial account of the black Atlantic can lead scholars to obscure the meanings black writers assigned to print as a medium, meanings that push back against a reading of their texts that would privilege personal experience above all else.[32] In this essay I have begun to trace the emergence of the logic that yokes the printed text uncritically to knowledge about experience. It is a logic that governs Ignatius Sancho's encounter with Wheatley, whose poems make him think about the paradox of her nature as a "genius in bondage." Vincent Carretta and Philip Gould have borrowed this phrase as the title of an important volume of scholarship, *Genius in Bondage: Literature of the Black Atlantic* (2001). In so doing they have emphasized the identity of the author and her experiences in a world defined by the structural inequalities of the slave system. To be sure, borrowing Sancho's language is entirely appropriate because the lives of the black Atlantic remain one important object of study. But the texts of the print Atlantic come to us mediated through institutions of dissemination, institutions to which authors like Wheatley often found themselves subject and in which, rarely, they wielded considerable power. A media-specific analysis of early black texts must not reconstruct an ontologically secure identity from the printed page; it must instead consider the levels of mediation that so often prevent such conclusions. Considering the effects of book publication on Wheatley's and Sancho's reception, and on their texts themselves, provides one account of the interpretive practices of eighteenth-century readers, a central goal in the study of the ideologies of slavery.

The Unfortunates: What the Life Spans of Early Black Books Tell Us About Book History

JOANNA BROOKS

Dead letters! does it not sound like dead men?

These lines from Herman Melville's classic short story "Bartleby, the Scrivener" capture for me the feeling of sorrow-tinged wonder I take away from studies of early African American writing. For just as the dead letter office comes to represent for Melville's narrator the power of randomness, loss, accident, anonymity, failure, and error in shaping human experience, every early black text I encounter raises questions of how many such books never made it to print or survived into contemporary memory. Even as new scholarship represented in this volume of essays discloses vital new information about how black print culture worked, much still remains lost and unknown. Few authors of color had individual access to the religious, educational, and governmental institutions that served as saving repositories for personal manuscripts. Similarly, nineteenth-century black newspapers and serials were for many years not cataloged and archived as well as white newspapers and serials. Even so apparently a lasting form as the printed book is vulnerable, especially individually authored printed and bound books of more than forty-eight pages. I estimate that apart from slave narratives published during the abolitionist movement, fewer than thirty such titles by authors of African descent were published in Great Britain and North America in the late eighteenth and early nineteenth centuries.

How do we think about race in connection with the life chances of these early black books?[1] Let's start from a basic definition of race. I think of race as a socially constructed, marked identity category designating a human being for greater vulnerability to political, social, and economic conditions threatening the quality, continuity, and longevity of life. We see this vulnerability to disruption and discontinuity at work in the generic shape of early African American literature, in the captivity, conversion, and slave narratives, if not the hybrid captivity-conversion-slave narratives by writers like Briton Hammon, John Marrant, Olaudah Equiano, and others, which are often nothing so much as a series of episodes of unfreedom and freedom, immobility and restored mobility, strung together, often without clear or final resolution. Cathy Davidson has identified this dynamic at work with Olaudah Equiano: "The most consistent trope structuring the plot of *The Interesting Narrative* might be termed 'the existential rug-pull.' Any time the author enjoys a transcendent seascape, the interesting customs of a new country, a handsome profit on a transaction, or the seeming kindness of a new (white) master, we can be sure that, in the very next scene, he will be cheated, extorted, beaten, 'mortified' (one of Equiano's most frequent and powerful emotions), accused of lying about his free state, and threatened with recapture, violence, or humiliation."[2]

Existential conditions of chronic discontinuity and disruption endemic to communities of color by reason of political and economic exploitation affect books and book cultures as well. Writing, purchasing, and reading a book require time, space, and resources. Purchasing several books (beyond a household Bible, a hymnal, an almanac) constitutes a material commitment of space and resources. It also implies a confidence on the part of the purchaser that his or her household is stable enough to support and maintain a collection of books. The bound octavo book was designed for portability, but a shelf or two or three shelves of octavo books oppose portability. And given the economic and social vulnerability of many early households of color, books are precisely the kind of item that would be left behind or sold away to make space in a wagon (presuming there were money enough to own or hire one) for tools, or seeds, or warm clothing, or a child. The Mohegan author Samson Occom once lost most of his household belongings including books crossing the Long Island Sound in a small boat. Such accidents happen to everyone, of course, but it is also the case that households of color in early America were categorically more vulnerable to misfortune, exploitation, and instability, to poverty, bankruptcy, tenancy, forced removal, destruction, imprisonment, migration, and death. Unstable contexts are environments challenging to book culture, and especially to the production, consumption, and collection of substantial books. In this respect, we might say that books and especially those substantial, more pricey books of more than forty-eight pages have life spans and life chances—lesser and greater chances of being written, published, sold, bought, read, reprinted, circulated, and then collected and preserved—that correlate positively with the race of the author.

There have been many outstanding recent studies of eighteenth-century book history, each one dealing to varying extents with the social facts shaping the life chances of books. William St. Clair's *The Reading Nation in the Romantic Period* (2004) and James Raven's *The Business of Books* (2008) tend to focus on intellectual property codes and the entrepreneurial savvy of booksellers as the structuring mechanisms of British book culture. A greater inclination to acknowledge the social contexts of book history is suggested in the closing pages of American book historian Matthew Brown's *The Pilgrim and the Bee* (2007), wherein Brown suggests a "book history that integrates the study of bibliographical transmission and cultural politics."[3] Meanwhile, Trish Loughran's *The Republic in Print* (2007) and Meredith McGill's *American Literature and the Culture of Reprinting* (2003) have dislodged the presumption enshrined in an earlier generation of American histories that print culture functioned evenly and uniformly across space and time and redirected our attention to the on-the-ground, local, unstable, and disrupted mechanisms of production, reproduction, and distribution. These scholars move us closer to something that might resemble book culture in early communities of color, something operating along the principles articulated by the original Subaltern Studies group, which argued that official "top down" histories of colonial societies are narrated in ways that homogenize historical fields and create false appearances of continuity and inevitability and do not capture the dynamics of subaltern societies or consciousnesses. The alternative is to attempt historiography that operates around discontinuity, contradiction, even failure: as Ranajit Guha describes it, a sequence of "loosely cobbled segments . . . necessarily charged with uncertainty."[4]

It is this tremendous sense of uncertainty that pervades early black book history, this awareness that the life chances of a given book are shaped by a social field of tremendous contradiction, that the chances of failure are always very real. In this essay, I will use the example of an early black book— one I would consider something of a failure, even though I am one of the people responsible for bringing it back into print more than two hundred years after its original publication—as a platform for articulating a view of book history alternative to mainline histories of the book centering on the book trade. This book is *The Journal of John Marrant*, a 127-page book published in London in 1790, a chronicle of the American-born Marrant's missionary travels among free blacks in Nova Scotia as an emissary of the London-based Huntingdon Connection. Written by Marrant to account for his missionary labors and to defend against suggestions that he had misused donations from his sponsors, the *Journal* is the most extensive account of a black man preaching in black communities before the mid-nineteenth century.

John Marrant described his life on the early black Atlantic as being "unstable as water." By the time he was twelve, his family had lived in New York, Florida, Georgia, and South Carolina. From this, Marrant wrote that he learned "we have no continuing city," a reference to Hebrews 13:14.[5] During his teenage years, he drifted between bound carpentry apprenticeships and a budding career as a violinist and French horn player, then experienced a dramatic conversion under the preaching of celebrity evangelist George Whitefield and a subsequent pilgrimage into the South Carolina backcountry where he was, by his own account, held captive by Cherokees, to whom he preached the gospel. Following his captivity, Marrant preached to blacks enslaved on South Carolina plantations, then was impressed into service as a musician (an occupation dominated by blacks) in the Royal Navy shortly after the outbreak of the American War of Independence, and was discharged in Plymouth, England. He worked in London (his last address is on Mile-End Road in the Stepney area) for three years as a servant to a merchant. During this time, Marrant began to preach on Monday nights at the Spa Fields Chapel in Islington, the central hub of Whitefield's Huntingdon Connexion. Marrant won the attention of the Connexion and was ordained to the ministry at the Huntingdon Connexion's chapel in Bath on May 15, 1785.

The account Marrant gave of his conversion and subsequent wanderings was transcribed as he delivered it by the Reverend William Aldridge of the dissenting Jewry-Street Chapel in Whitechapel and published in July 1785 in a thirty-eight-page edition. *A Narrative of the Lord's Wonderful Dealings with John Marrant, A Black (Now Going to Preach the Gospel in Nova-Scotia)* went through at least five editions in its first six months, and was soon carried "by all booksellers and newscarriers in town and country," as the title page of the fifth edition declared. One month after the publication of his *Narrative*, in August 1785, Marrant left London for Nova Scotia on orders to proselytize among free loyalist black refugees in Birchtown. Marrant stayed in Birchtown until January 1789, when communication and support from the Huntingdon Connexion broke down; the Connexion was in financial disarray, having overextended itself in the building of sixty-four new chapels in England, Ireland, and abroad, including one at Birchtown. After leaving Nova Scotia, Marrant traveled to Boston, where he lived for one year, associating himself with Prince Hall (1735–1807), the founder of the first African Lodge of Freemasons. Marrant joined the lodge, was appointed chaplain, and preached a public sermon to commemorate its celebration of St. John the Baptist Day on June 24, 1789. Marrant returned to London in March 1790. His Nova Scotia congregation, led by two Marrant trainees, emigrated to Sierra Leone in 1792.

During his missionary years, the often-penniless Marrant (who once pawned his coat to pay for a ferry crossing) apparently drew no benefit from five more editions of his *Narrative*, which appeared in London, Cork, and Dublin. Nor did his literary reputation secure him an easy reentry to London life. "Repeatedly sending home every opportunity to the connection for some support . . . [I] never had any of any kind, which forced me to come to England to know the reason," he explained. "With all the expence of coming, to pay myself, and when arrived, [I] was not permitted to speak for myself, and so remained, to the present, without any assistance, or even a Christian word out of them."[6] Abandoned and shunned by the Huntingdon Connection for reasons still unknown, Marrant found himself virtually stranded in London, thousands of miles from his family in South Carolina, his Nova Scotia followers, and his circle of friends in Boston. He made a home for himself on Black Horse Court in the Aldersgate neighborhood, near Islington. Why Aldersgate? London's black population (estimated at ten thousand) had no geographical center, and many black Londoners worked as nurses or servants and lived in white households.[7] Aldersgate seems to have been a neighborhood defined by religious monuments, such as St. Botolph Aldersgate Church, where John Wesley had been converted in 1738. Black Horse Court too seems to have had a particular history as a gathering place for musicians. Did Marrant settle in among old musician friends from the Royal Navy? Did he seek out the merchant he worked for before his mission? Or did he want to remain geographically proximate to the Islington headquarters of the Huntingdon Connexion, or to reestablish his reputation as a preacher in the dissenting chapels of Aldersgate?

Between March and June 1790, Marrant prepared his missionary journals for publication. He was motivated at least in part by a desire to defend his reputation and to say in print what he had not been permitted to say to the officers of the Huntingdon Connection. Maybe he also hoped to make a little money. Perhaps upon returning to London he discovered how popular the *Narrative* had been, although there is no indication he attempted to issue another authorized edition after 1790. Perhaps he was inspired by the example of Olaudah Equiano, whose two-volume, 530-page *Interesting Narrative* had been published in March 1789 and was by spring 1790 in its second edition. Like Equiano, Marrant published his book by subscription, a practice that as Vincent Carretta has observed had fallen out of favor in the late eighteenth-century book trade except among black authors.[8] A genius of literary and political self-fashioning, Equiano carefully designed and coordinated his subscription, promotion, and sales plans and recruited partial advance payments from more than 311 subscribers, among them some of the most eminent figures in British public life, including the Prince of Wales, the Duke of York, the Earl of Dartmouth, the Countess of Huntingdon, the bishop of London, Rev. John Wesley, Granville Sharp. Far more valuable than their financial investment was the social capital the names of these subscribers lent the *Interesting Narrative* and the political campaign against the slave trade. Equiano continued to build subscription lists as he toured England, Ireland, and Scotland in support of the book and against the slave trade, amassing in total over the course of nine editions 1,132 subscribers.[9]

By contrast, the list of subscribers for the *Journal of John Marrant* is very, very humble, in both size and stature. Perhaps the best-known subscriber (at least the only one with his own entry in the *Dictionary of National Biography*) was Thomas Mortimer (1730–1810), a trade and financial writer who had been deposed from his position as English vice-consul to the Netherlands after a minor political scandal and who later published a pamphlet entitled *The Remarkable Case of Thomas Mortimer, Esq.* (1770) in his own defense. Another subscriber was the Reverend Joseph Cartwright (1748–1800), a Calvinistic Methodist preacher who after failing to win ordination in the Church of England established his own chapel on Lant-Street in Southwark and allowed different ministers to take their turns at the pulpit, probably including Marrant.[10] A few of Marrant's subscribers lived in the Shoreditch or Spitalfields neighborhoods and worked in the textile industry. One of these, John Timmings, a silk broker, bought five copies. (Perhaps this is the merchant Marrant worked for in the mid-1780s when he lived on Mile-End Road?) The only public record we have of Timmings is that he went bankrupt in 1792.[11] The rest of the subscribers cannot be readily identified. Some names appear to have been misspelled, including that of one "Mr. Williams Ebeneza" and one "Mr. Victixker," suggesting that Marrant may have known some of his subscribers fairly casually or enlisted them on verbal promise.

What is even more telling are the names we do not see on his subscription list. There is no one associated with the Huntingdon Connection, not even his former amanuensis William Aldridge, who we can assume saw some benefit from the sales of Marrant's *Narrative* at his Jewry-Street Chapel. There is no one from Nova Scotia, or from his fairly well-connected circle of friends in Boston. No one can be identified from the small but mobilized community of Afro-Britons gathered around Olaudah Equiano, nor from the campaigns to abolish the slave trade or resettle blacks in Sierra Leone. As a lone black man with no immediate means of financial support, perhaps Marrant did not have time in the two-month interval between his arrival and the *Journal*'s publication to cultivate North American patronage or to work his way into high-powered black social networks. The community this once moderately famous black evangelist managed to cobble together for himself was one of failures and misfits: deposed trade officials, eccentric Baptist preachers, bankrupt silk brokers, and common Londoners whose lives have been lost to history.

After its publication in late June, Marrant sold the *Journal* from his home on Black Horse Court for two shillings, sixpence, which translates into fifteen or twenty dollars in today's currency. Of that, Marrant himself might have expected to take home about four to seven dollars per book.[12] The *Journal* was also sold by James Taylor, a bookseller operating under the south arch of the Royal Exchange, a London center of business for attorneys, insurance and stock brokers, merchant seamen, and city officials. The Royal Exchange was located a few miles from Marrant's Aldersgate home. It would not have been on his daily path after his return to London in 1790. How, then, did Marrant meet Taylor? Had Marrant conducted business at the Exchange for his merchant employer before his Nova Scotia mission? Had he visited the Exchange in the pursuit of financial recompense from the Huntingdon Connection? The picture is not clear. We do, however, have a sense of James Taylor's tastes and interests as a bookseller. In 1789 he had published an account of European lazarettos for plague sufferers, a collection of sermons preached for the benefit of the London Asylum, and an edition of *Robinson Crusoe*. In 1790, Taylor commissioned the printing of a new complete volume of the letters of Lady Mary Wortley Montague, as well as critique of mesmerism by London surgeon John Pearson (1758–1826), and an execution sermon and memoirs of accused forger Francis Fonton, a former clerk of the Bank of England.[13] Taylor appears to have had an appetite for the mildly exotic, as well as a taste for unfortunates and scoundrels. Perhaps this is what attracted him to Marrant, and his dramatic conversion narrative, and his tales of missionary suffering, and his need for vindication. Perhaps Taylor knew the success of Marrant's widely reprinted *Narrative* and hoped to build on it.

But the *Journal* was not the *Narrative*. The *Narrative* was a sensationally titled thirty-eight-page tale of dramatic conversion and Indian captivity, a performance piece steeped in theatrical orality. The *Journal*, on the other hand, was a sober chronicling of an exceedingly difficult but rather unglamorous foreign mission. To be sure, the *Journal* had its dramatic moments: preacherly battles, mob violence, near drownings in snowy swamps, bear encounters, literal and figurative deaths and resurrections. But these were interspersed between pages strictly recording miles traveled, scriptures preached, and money spent. Marrant wrote his *Journal* to vindicate his reputation. Its interest to modern scholars is in its theological subtexts, in the theology of black modern emancipation we see taking shape through his scripture references. Its interest to the readerly middling types who passed by James Taylor's bookstall after a day's work at the Royal Exchange? Unclear. So there sat the *Journal of John Marrant*, under the south arch of the Royal Exchange, alongside copies of *Robinson Crusoe* and the letters of Lady Montague, for about nine months, until Taylor's business dissolved in March 1791. One month later, in April 1791, John Marrant died from causes unknown and was buried in the Islington Chapel Ground. He was thirty-five years old.

The life of John Marrant is a sequence of discontinuous and contradictory episodes, or to return to the words of Ranajit Guha, a life made up of "loosely cobbled segments . . . necessarily charged with uncertainty." How does a substantial book come to being in the context of such a life? What happens to such a book when its author dies? Say that Marrant arranged for five hundred copies of the *Journal* to be printed. Book history experts estimate that the average eighteenth-century book may have sold through a first printing in seven to ten years. How many *Journals* did John Marrant sell in ten months? How many remained unsold by James Taylor, and what happened to them when his shop closed? How many remained at the home of John Marrant, and what happened to them when he died? Who came to clean out John Marrant's place at 2 Black Horse Court? Did Taylor or Marrant manage to arrange a shipment of his books to his circle of allies in increasingly literate black Boston? Did any make it to the black loyalists of

Birchtown? Who among them could have afforded such a book, let alone managed to carry it with them on the long and perilous 1792 sea journey to Sierra Leone? We know that a few copies did make it to North America, because today the only two known surviving copies of the *Journal* are at the Boston Public Library and the State Library of Pennsylvania.

What happened to the *Narrative* is a very different story. Cheaply reprintable in its thirty-eight-page paper-wrapped pamphlet form, it continued to live and travel, appearing after Marrant's death in twenty-six additional editions through 1850: in London, Leeds, York, Brighton, Newry, Yarmouth, Manchester, Newry, Ireland, Carmarthen, Wales, Halifax, Nova Scotia, Yarmouth, Nova Scotia, and even a Welsh-language edition at Caerdydd in 1818. Repackaged in its final decades as a narrative of the remarkable conversion of the "King of the Cherokees," the *Narrative* survived in the context of a thriving British evangelicalism emphasizing foreign missions.

What I take from the final years of John Marrant, and the short life span, even the failure of the *Journal* is that books need movement and movements. Books must move to live. They need constituencies, or dynamic social contexts. If books get stranded between places, between communities, they will have brief life spans. Highly motile, easily reprintable cheap print and pamphlets are better adapted to movement and thus have better chances at reaching more readers and staying in print longer. Longer, more substantial books are not adapted for mobility and thus truly depend on social movements to survive. We can test this observation by looking at other individually authored, substantial early black books published in Great Britain and North America in the late eighteenth and early nineteenth centuries. Books by black authors associated with the campaign to end the British slave trade thrived. Certainly, the success of Olaudah Equiano's *Interesting Narrative* arose in large part from Equiano's close coordination of its publication and promotion with the abolition campaign. So too did Ignatius Sancho's status as a human symbol of the injustice of the slave trade propel the posthumously published two-volume *Letters* (1782) to sell through three editions in its first two years, with two additional editions appearing in 1802 and 1803 for the financial benefit of Sancho's son William, and a final London reprinting in 1837. Ottobah Cugoano's 148-page *Thoughts and Sentiments on the Evil and Wicked Traffic and Commerce of the Human Species*, published in 1787 with Equiano's help, appeared in a French translation in Paris in 1788 and was reprinted in a condensed 46-page version in London in 1791. Phillis Wheatley was arguably as canny as Equiano in the construction of her public image, as assiduous in her use of newspaper and broadsheet publication, and as savvy in using social networks to promote of her book. But her 124-page *Poems on Various Subjects*, first published in four London editions totaling 1,800 copies in fall 1773,[14] did not see a second printing until 1786 when it was reissued posthumously in Philadelphia by the Quaker Joseph Crukshank, publisher of anti–slave trade writings by Thomas Clarkson, John Woolman, Granville Sharp, and Anthony Benezet. *Poems* was thereafter reprinted in Philadelphia and London in 1787, in Philadelphia in 1789, and in Albany in 1793. It appears that the resurgence of Wheatley's *Poems* in Philadelphia was connected to the growing Quaker movement against slavery and the slave trade.

The black church movement and the affiliated Afro-Protestant press, of course, produced many successful books, most of these in shorter pamphlet or serial forms. A more substantial book that thrived in the black church context was Richard Allen's forty-four-page *Collection of Hymns and Spiritual Songs*, which appeared in two editions in 1801, a book virtually designed for a movement and for motility. The African Methodist Episcopal Church founded the AME Book Concern in Philadelphia in 1817, with offices subsequently opened in Brooklyn in 1835 and Pittsburgh in 1848, before returning to Philadelphia in 1852. Its productions included the *AME Book of Discipline* (1817), the *AME Hymn Book* (1818), and the *Doctrine and Discipline of the AME Church* by Richard Allen and Jacob Tapisco (1819), before it shifted its focus to serials such as the *Church Magazine* (1841–49) and the *Christian Recorder* (1852–), the venue that premiered important nineteenth-century black authors such as Frances Watkins Harper and Julia C. Collins, author of the serialized novel the *Curse of Caste* (1865).[15] The Concern printed and distributed books and periodicals through church conferences and regional organizations.[16]

The transatlantic black Masonic movement was another influential force in print production and distribution. The Connecticut-born, Dartmouth-educated Prince Saunders (1775–1839) was a black Freemason who traveled the Atlantic world first as a proponent of colonization, but who was later recruited by William Wilberforce to serve as an adviser to Haitian emperor Henri Christophe and founded Masonic lodges in Haiti. His 228-page political commentary *Haytian Papers*, was published in London in 1816 and reprinted in Boston in 1818. Nancy Gardner Prince (1799–1856) published her eighty-seven page *Life* in Boston in 1850 and reissued in subsequent editions in 1853 and 1856. It probably helped that her husband Nero Prince was a former assistant to the Masonic order founder Prince Hall and onetime grand master of Boston's African Lodge of Freemasons.

Books conceived and executed as acts of individual entrepreneurial authorship rarely succeeded in early African America. We see this for a number of single-printing black books published with no connection to organized social movements such as the 204-page *Blind African Slave; or, Memoirs of Boyrereau Brinch, nick-named Jeffrey Brace*, published in Saint Alban's, Vermont (of all places), in 1810. Or the 68-page *Life of William Grimes, Runaway Slave*, published in New York in 1825, long before the beginnings of an organized mass abolitionist movement in that city. Even the 122-page *Essays* of Ann Plato, published for the author in Hartford, Connecticut, in 1841, did not see another reprinting, nor did Zilpha Elaw's 172-page religious autobiography, published in London in 1846, far from the North American Methodist circuits where Elaw had itinerated. A clear example of the vulnerability of isolated black books is *Our Nig* (1859), a novelistic autobiography by Harriet Wilson. Born and raised on the social and economic margins of New England, widowed at twenty-eight with one child, Wilson wrote *Our Nig* as an "experiment which shall aid me in maintaining myself and child," with an explicit appeal to her "colored brethren universally for patronage."[17] The appeal appears not to have worked. Although she went on to become a prominent medium and lecturer in the Spiritualist movement, *Our Nig* was not reprinted until recovered by literary historians in the late twentieth century.

A telling exception to this pattern is the spiritual autobiographer Jarena Lee (1783–?), the first woman authorized as an exhorter by African Methodist Episcopal Church founder Richard Allen, but whose long and highly mobile career as an itinerant preacher traversed political causes and religious denominations. One thousand copies of her *Religious Experiences* were printed in a highly motile twenty-four-page edition in Philadelphia in 1836; the book benefited not only from the support of the Mother Bethel AME Church community, but also from Lee's active distribution and promotion at political and religious camp meetings. Three years later, Lee had another one thousand copies printed in Cincinnati, Ohio, at the encouragement of local church officials. She developed two expanded editions (97 and 126 pages) of her *Experiences* in Philadelphia in 1849, publishing them without the support and in fact against the advice of the AME Book Committee. Lee, who was by then a leader of a movement of unlicensed black women preachers, apparently did not pay too much mind to institutional sanction. She was, as her long itinerant career shows, virtually a one-woman social movement.

If we can conclude from this overview of black book history that books by black authors without firm connections to social movements, especially books by authors who were (like John Marrant) geographically or socially isolated from robust black communities, had shorter life spans, then we can appreciate how the rise of a mass antislavery movement in the 1840s transformed black book publishing, one instance of this transformation being the phenomenal success of Frederick Douglass's much reprinted 125-page *Narrative* (1845) and his monumental 464-page *My Bondage and My Freedom* (1855). We might also extend a few observations about early black book history to serve as the platform for an alternative take on book history in general:

1. Discontinuity and disruption were structuring social facts that deeply shaped the life spans of books as well as people.
2. The life spans of many books depended on their ability to move across disrupted social fields.
3. The books that fared the best were adapted to mobility, either through their close association with social movements or their production in highly motile shorter forms.
4. Entrepreneurial authorship—a one-person social movement, if you will, focused on the survival of the author—rarely succeeded in early communities of color; the entrepreneurial book trade as a frame for understanding book history may bear reexamination.
5. As a corollary, we may find that we have underestimated the role of large institutions such as churches and governments in subsidizing the book trade and book publication. To what extent did the rise of modern bureaucracies and religious bodies that conducted many of their dealings in print mediums subsidize the ventures of publishers, printers, and booksellers into other more marginal forms? To what extent did the youth and vulnerability of bureaucratic institutional life in communities of color mediate the access to print of authors of color?
6. Factoring these institutional forces into the book history landscape, we may come to see that different subsets of books mobilize differently: as Ranajit Guha has observed of elite versus subaltern mobilization, the former being characterized by its "verticality," its access to hierarchies of cultural and political power, and the latter by its "horizontality," (which is again to say) its mobility across disrupted social fields.[18]

In summary, the life spans of early black books might nudge us to reconceive of books not as objects of exchange and consumption but as vectors of social movement. The magnitude of any individual book as vector is determined by social facts beyond the control of the author as well as the alignment of the book with social movements. To think of books in this way is to find ourselves gravitating slightly away from the richly informative but more economically mechanistic models of the book trade suggested, for example, by William St. Clair's characterization of books as "highly differentiated capital assets from which reading services were taken by purchasers and others" and toward something resembling Manuel Castell's concept of books as material forms supporting "time sharing social practices that work through flows," or Lisa Gitelman's definition of media as "socially realized structures of communication . . . includ[ing] both technological forms and their associated protocols."[19] We might, then, conceive of the work of the book as creating a form of experiential continuity across landscapes of profound discontinuity and disruption, and we might better appreciate how it is that authors like John Marrant and texts such as his *Journal* end up—in Herman Melville's words, dead letters, dead men—stranded in time.

CHAPTER 3

Frances Ellen Watkins Harper and the Circuits of Abolitionist Poetry

MEREDITH L. MCGILL

Can attention to the format of printed works change how we think about the history of literary genres, in particular, the history of poetic genres? Judging by the paucity of book history scholarship devoted to American poetry (despite its cultural prestige), and the lack of attention given to print culture by scholars of American poetry (outside of that which is lavished on our great printer-poet, Walt Whitman), one is tempted to conclude that the materiality of the printed poem is largely immaterial to how we understand its significance. Over the past thirty years or so, book history has done much to reshape the large-scale narratives of American literary history, providing nuanced accounts of literary authorship, publishing, and reading. Such accounts are, however, generally treated as external to histories of poetic form, which continue to be told as a set of relations between and among texts, and not books, institutions, practices, markets, systems of exchange, or media.[1] Is there something about poetry in general and lyric poetry in particular that produces transhistorical, dematerialized ways of reading? Will the uptake of book history into the discipline of media history—prompted in part by the remediation of large swaths of the printed record into easily searchable, digitally transmitted PDF images—pull the study of material texts even further away from the concerns of those of us who attend to histories of poetic form?

In her groundbreaking work *Dickinson's Misery*, Virginia Jackson surveys recent digital editions of Emily Dickinson, wondering if, for all of their promise of new approaches to Dickinson's work, these digital editions don't in the end offer us simply more of the same. Praising the new forms of access granted by the Dickinson Electronic Archive, Jackson nonetheless asks: "But will it change our reading of Dickinson's genre—or will readers still go to the Web as they have to the print editions in order to read more Dickinson poems? Won't readers still view—because they already expect to view—these poems as lyrics? Will the medium of the Internet have any effect on the imaginary lyric model that has guided the editing and interpretation of Dickinson for so long?"[2] To Jackson's disappointment, genre seems to trump medium, returning us again and again to lyric reading. But must genre always trump medium? Does medium matter for the study of poetry, and if so how?

Some of the difficulty in bringing these disciplines into closer relation stems from literary studies' and book and media history's often incommensurate periodizations and striking differences of scale in their address to their objects. From the perspective of media history, the concerns of literary criticism—modes of address, experiments in form, meter, or genre, differences between early and late style, the ebb and flow of literary movements—can seem small, even trifling. From the perspective of literary criticism, the concerns of media history—the life cycle of a medium, from novelty to viability and widespread adoption; the tension between innovation and standardization, dissemination and centralized control—can seem too broad and too remote from what matters about works of art that matter. The micromeasures of literary time—the impact of first printings, the efflorescence of styles or "isms," even the spans of authors' lives—can feel out of sync and out of scale with the slow time and transnational consequences of media shift.

Poetry compounds the difficulty of bringing media history and literary history into satisfying relation. Poetry has a long history of claiming multimedia status—threatening to overwhelm sense with sound, offering a different way of seeing, and toying with our consciousness of page (or screen). Poetry has promised to serve as tape recorder, jukebox, Auto-Tune, or synthesizer, while also competing for primacy with painting, illustration, photography, and other visual arts. Poetry's claim to be an aural and a visual *as well as* a verbal art makes it difficult to wrestle poetic history into the sequential narratives of media history, narratives that tend to proceed as if there were only one medium per epoch: handwriting, print, photography, film, radio, television, Internet. Can we imagine a book history or media history finely grained and supple enough to recognize the interventions in these histories made by poems and poetic genres? How can we plot the shifting relations of poetic forms to multiple media as media themselves are transformed by technological innovation, changing social and cultural values, and culturally galvanizing and rearranging works of art?

As a gesture in this direction, I propose stepping back from the larger units of book history and media history to consider the usefulness of the concept of "format," a word that has come into general use as a synonym for "medium" (video format), "structure" (formatting a computer disk), or "order" (the layout of a magazine), but that has a precise meaning within the discipline of bibliography, a precision I would like to draw on and extend. Analytic and descriptive bibliographers use the term "format" to describe the relationship between the size of the paper placed on the press and the way in which type pages were laid out and paper was folded in order to produce the signatures or gatherings that make up the text block of the book.[3] Technically speaking, "format" describes a relation between paper size and number of pages, which, at least for books produced in the handpress period, provides a reliable, shorthand description of the size and structure of the published book: "Crown quarto" or "Royal octavo."

Unlike the larger, vaguer "medium," this technical definition of "format" directs our attention to the set of choices printers and publishers make in publishing a work, with the potential field of a book's reception very much in mind. Format is where economic and technological limitations meet cultural expectations. There is a decorum to format, borne in part of the risk and uncertainty of publishing as a commercial venture. Particular formats get associated with particular kinds of texts, although these associations change over time. Across the history of its reprinting, a text might be published in number of different formats.

In using the concept of "format" to think about the relationship of poetic form to medium, I would like to loosen the term a bit from its strict bibliographic usage while retaining bibliographers' attention to the cultural hierarchies that become visible at the point of production. Thinking in terms of format can help disaggregate print into smaller units: rather than considering how poets position their work in relation to manuscript, print, recorded sound, or digital media, we can ask how different kinds of print mobilize poetic genres.

Format and Audience in Frances Ellen Watkins Harper's Poetry

Frances Ellen Watkins Harper offers a particularly good example of the difference an attention to format can make to our understanding of poetry, illuminating not only the field of circulation of particular works but also the poems themselves. Harper is best known to literary critics as the author of the 1892 novel *Iola Leroy*, but she first came into public prominence as an abolitionist lecturer and poet, traveling and publishing widely in the 1850s under her maiden name Frances Ellen Watkins. Watkins withdrew from the lecture circuit in 1860 when she married Fenton Harper, returning to the platform as "Mrs. Harper" after her husband's death in 1864. Her midcareer name change from "Watkins" to "Harper," therefore, signaled a significant transformation of her civil and social status. The end of the Civil War also brought her greater geographical mobility and a revitalized career lecturing to mixed audiences in churches and public buildings throughout the South. Harper became well known as a Reconstruction activist and as a leading black voice in the movements for temperance, women's education, and women's suffrage. Despite the demands of travel, lecturing, and contributing to numerous voluntary associations, she continued to publish poetry, including the ambitious blank-verse epic *Moses: A Story of the Nile* (1869), her second collection, *Poems* (1871), and a series of poems based on her Southern lecture tours, *Sketches of Southern Life* (1872); she also wrote serial novels for the African Methodist Episcopal Church weekly, the *Christian Recorder*.[4]

Critical attention to Harper's fiction and her postwar activism has largely eclipsed her antebellum career as a poet and abolitionist. Her mouthful of a name, which incorporates the recognizably abolitionist "Watkins" (her uncle William Watkins was a prominent Philadelphia abolitionist and educator, and her cousin William J. Watkins was also a traveling antislavery lecturer) into the lyrically appropriate "Harper," turns out to be part of the problem. Insofar as "Frances Ellen Watkins Harper" names a consolidated body of writing, it assimilates her early work to the norms of late nineteenth-century authorship and insists on a single identity across the radical personal and political changes of midcentury. Although the timing of her name change does not map cleanly onto the political and social transformations that would shape her postwar career—she gave a number of antislavery lectures as "Mrs. Harper" before embarking in 1867 on a series of extended lecture tours in the Reconstruction South—acknowledging a difference between Watkins and Harper is a critical first step toward breaking down the assumption that her writing is all of a piece, shaped by a continuity of poetic aims and means.[5]

The misleading coherence suggested by the inclusive authorial name works in tandem with a disregard for format, the assumption that all printed books are essentially the same. Literary critics' impulse to collect, sort, and make sense of Frances Ellen Watkins Harper's poetry under the sign of individual authorship has worked to minimize material differences between and among her published texts. For instance, critics frequently cite the number of books the poet published and sold across her career as an index of her popularity, but this general calculation glosses over the fact that the volumes of poetry published by Frances Ellen Watkins look nothing like the collections Frances Ellen Watkins Harper published toward the end of her career. Indeed, these early volumes aren't books at all, but rather small pamphlets or chapbooks, their print format suggesting conditions of circulation and assumptions about the cultural role of poetry quite different from those I had imagined for them. In hindsight, I could have teased out some of these differences from a careful reading of extant bibliographical information, but I failed, somehow, to take the measure of these details; I couldn't conjure the difference format made from brief descriptions of these volumes or from the two-dimensional PDFs on my computer screen.[6]

Compare, for instance, Watkins's *Poems on Miscellaneous Subjects* (printed and reprinted numerous times from 1854 to 1874) (Figure 3.1) to Harper's *Poems* (published in 1895 and 1900) (Figures 3.2 and 3.3). *Poems on Miscellaneous Subjects*, like nearly all of the poet's printed work through the 1880s,[7] is more of a pamphlet than a book. It is composed of three signatures (forty-eight pages) sewn in a stab binding with a pasted-on paper cover; some editions published after 1857 include seven new poems that take up an additional eight pages. Published in small print runs in successive batches to be given away or sold at her antislavery lectures, with no copyright notice overleaf, *Poems on Miscellaneous Subjects* bears in its format the traces of a strong relationship to oral performance—to the punctual meetings of reformers bent on miscellaneous reforms that were brought under the umbrella of antislavery, and to the songs that were sung and the songsters that provided a text held in common at these meetings.[8] The 1895 and 1900 editions of the *Poems*, however, with their floral-image, illustrated cloth covers, three-quarter-length author photo, facsimile signature, and copyright registration, mobilize a significantly different set of expectations as to what will be found in the book's pages, suggesting parlor display rather than activist uses, individual authorship and silent reading rather than the work of collectives that gathered to forge and sustain common aspirations.

Critical editions of Harper's work treat these books as items in a series composed of essentially the same thing—they are books of poetry. The

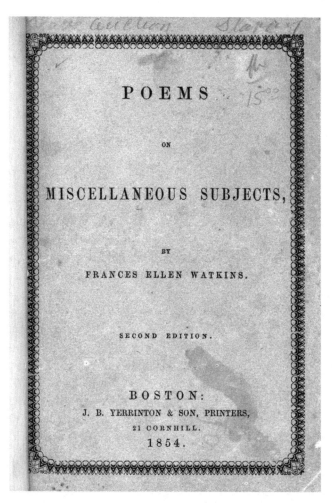

Figure 3.1. Paper covers, Frances Ellen Watkins, *Poems on Miscellaneous Subjects* (Boston: J. B. Yerrinton and Son, 1854), and *Poems on Miscellaneous Subjects* (Philadelphia: Merrihew and Thompson, 1857), Courtesy of Manuscripts, Archives, and Rare Books Division, Schomburg Center for Research in Black Culture, The New York Public Library, Astor, Lenox and Tilden Foundations.

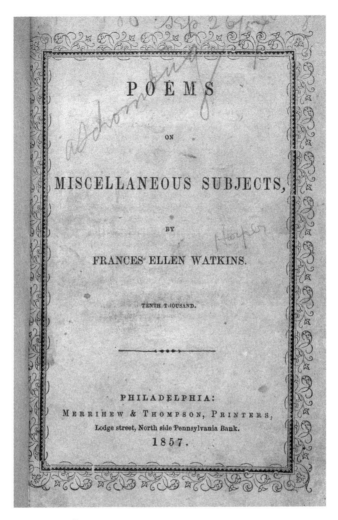

Figure 3.1. (Continued)

differences literary critics take care to account for and to remark on are predominantly verbal ones; the field of differences between and among printed texts gets rendered as linguistic, formal, and sequential variation.[9] While a book history approach to Harper's writing would surely take note of these radical differences in format, these differences would likely be normalized by being placed along the developmental arc of the poet's career rather than allowing differences in format to open up questions about the relationship

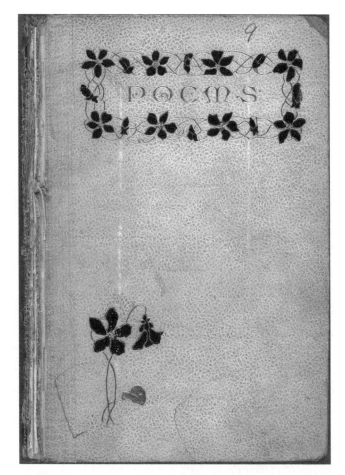

Figure 3.2. Cover, Frances E. W. Harper, *Poems* (Philadelphia: George S. Ferguson Co., 1900). Courtesy of Manuscripts, Archives, and Rare Books Division, Schomburg Center for Research in Black Culture, The New York Public Library, Astor, Lenox and Tilden Foundations.

of these collections of poems to other kinds of texts published in similar formats. Examining *Poems on Miscellaneous Subjects* through the lens of format instead of genre reveals its affinity with numerous texts that are similarly indexed to oral performance or that seek to contribute to the advancement of knowledge just outside of sanctioned institutions. Among the texts published by Frances Ellen Watkins's Boston and Philadelphia publishers in chapbook or pamphlet format are sermons, political and commemorative addresses,

CONTENTS.

Franced E. W. Harper

Figure 3.3. Frontispiece, Frances E. W. Harper, *Poems* (Philadelphia: George S. Ferguson Co., 1900). Courtesy of Manuscripts, Archives, and Rare Books Division, Schomburg Center for Research in Black Culture, The New York Public Library, Astor, Lenox and Tilden Foundations.

convention speeches, academic lectures, congressional speeches, government testimony, essays on reform, personal narratives, and amateur scientific essays.[10]

The vital first wave of recovery of Harper's life and writing, painstakingly pieced together and interpreted by Maryemma Graham, Frances Smith Foster, Melba Joyce Boyd, Joan R. Sherman, Carla Peterson, and others, bequeathed to us an extraordinary African American poet, novelist, essayist, and orator who had been well known in her day but who had been largely written out of the record that was made visible and sustained by twentieth-century literary criticism.[11] While in her later years, Harper worked to consolidate and preserve her literary legacy, the mid-nineteenth-century chapbook publication of her poems points at every turn *away* from the poet herself, *away* from a consistent poetic persona, and *away* from a stable poetic corpus toward frequently repeated oral performances and newspaper reports that helped strengthen opposition to slavery and knit together scattered communities of activists.

Frances Ellen Watkins Harper's identity as a black woman poet was crucial to the role she played in the antislavery movement, but her poems' publication in cheap pamphlets, their frequent appearance in abolitionist newspapers, and the structure of the poems themselves all suggest that they were not intended to be read as lyrics, but rather as instruments of exhortation, nodes for the condensation and transfer of oral authority, and vehicles for collective assent. Virginia Jackson has argued that our recognition of poems as lyrics depends on a carefully maintained distance from eloquence ("Eloquence is *heard*, poetry is *overheard*," in John Stuart Mill's influential 1833 coinage).[12] What then are we to make of poems that in their forms of address frequently abjure the lyric "I" for a collective "we" and, rather than staging their unconsciousness of a listener, go out of their way to conjure or to return the reader to scenes of collective listening? For instance, Harper's most widely anthologized poem "The Slave Mother" begins with the rhetorical question "Heard you that shriek?"[13] suggesting not the lyric's palpable disregard of an audience but rather a hyperconscious attempt to recast readers as listeners. In its forms of address and in its strategic generality, "The Slave Mother" seeks to produce not radical solitude but an architecture for easily iterable, collective witness.[14] Following format's lead, however, will take us beyond the anthology's approved, representative verses to the far messier world of serial antislavery lectures and the weekly newspapers that advertised and reported on them, keeping pace with small advances and setbacks in the abolitionist struggle.

Antislavery Poetry, Oratory, and Print

Frances Ellen Watkins circulated her poems in cheap pamphlets as she traveled from town to town on her antislavery lecture tours. She may have recited some of her poems as part of her oral performances,[15] but she certainly sold or gave away her chapbooks to those who came to hear her lecture, commissioning new issues and editions of *Poems on Miscellaneous Subjects* as her stock ran out.[16] Some of the formal features of this first collection of poems can be accounted for by recalling her need to address multiple audiences of would-be reformers in serial fashion. As many have noted, the very miscellaneousness of the volume seems designed for an audience drawn to the "sisterhood of reforms." Her poems depend heavily on stock figures ("The Slave Mother," "The Drunkard's Child," "The Dying Christian," "The Dying Fugitive"); they recirculate familiar stories from the Bible and from popular novels (*Uncle Tom's Cabin* [1852] and *Oliver Twist* [1838]); they strike generic postures and attitudes in predictable meter and simple rhymes (grave-slave, slave-save, strife-life, wrong-strong), and are jam-packed with rhetorical questions that seek to evoke a pragmatic, collective response from her readers.

These questions frequently urge assent to a counterfactual order of things. The pressure on the reader to add his or her voice to a gathering outcry is palpable in "The Slave Mother," in which a bystander to the separation of mother and child asks "Oh, Father, must they part?" (59), and in "The Contrast," which asks of a fallen woman "Would no one heed her anguish?" (73). Many poems presume or evoke the structure of call and response: "Ethiopia" begins "Yes!" (63), while the topically political "The Dismissal of Tyng" personifies an outraged Episcopal church's response to Stephen Tyng's antislavery sermon by echoing the last three words of the editorial statement quoted in the epigraph, "Served him right!" (83) (Whose voice is this? It is not Frances Ellen Watkins Harper's). Many of her poems are hortatory, oriented toward a future their readers are charged with bringing to pass: typically, the poem "Be Active"—an adaptation of her hymn "Freedom's Battle"—exhorts its readers to "See oppression," "Hurl the bloated tyrant," "See that sad, despairing mother," "Lay your hand upon her fetters," and "Crush these gory, reeking altars," all in the first six stanzas (76–77). These poems don't express states of feeling but rather ask readers to witness wrongs and to participate in their remedy.

The mutually reinforcing relationship between print and oratory within the antislavery movement, and the part played by poetry as a switch point between them, is readily apparent from the publishing history of Frances Ellen Watkins's 1860 poem "To Charles Sumner." These lines addressed to the Massachusetts senator were first published as a stand-alone poem in the black-owned *Weekly Anglo-African* and as part of correspondence with the editor of the *National Anti-Slavery Standard*; the poem was then reprinted in William Lloyd Garrison's *Liberator*.[17] "To Charles Sumner" commemorates "The Barbarism of Slavery," the first speech Sumner delivered on the floor of the Senate after his return to Congress more than three years after being brutally caned by the South Carolina congressman Preston Brooks. Bearing evidence in its headnote of the chain of like-minded papers that often reprinted each other's articles, Watkins's poem takes its place in the July 20, 1860, issue of the *Liberator* alongside a number of reprinted newspaper pieces that review or otherwise respond to Sumner's speech, expanding and materializing the field of circulation of a controversial and consequential oratorical performance. This issue of the *Liberator* also includes a front-page reprinted review of Sumner's speech in the London *Times*, which describes it as "offensively acrimonious" and a "foolish and vindictive harangue"; a letter to the editor of the *Dublin News* responding to this review; a report on the enthusiastic reception of Sumner when he delivered the speech for a second time in New York (along with the publication of a pseudonymous personal letter threatening murder if Sumner lingered in Washington, D.C., after the close of the Senate term); a letter from Sumner declining an invitation from the Boston mayor to speak at the city's Fourth of July festivities; and an announcement of Sumner's headlining a lecture series scheduled for the fall.

Why reprint a *poem* addressed to Sumner along with this outpouring of Sumner-related news and commentary? In general, the other Sumner material printed in this issue of the *Liberator* measures and seeks to control the effects of oratory. That the abolitionist newspaper served as a tool for extending the reach of prominent antislavery voices is reinforced by the fact that nearly half the paper is given over to an extensive "phonographic report," or transcript, of the speeches given at a recent antislavery celebration in Framingham, Massachusetts, a report that seeks to reproduce oral performance in print, complete with parenthetical acknowledgment of audience response, such as "(applause)," "(Loud laughter and applause)," and "(Renewed applause)."[18] By contrast, Watkins's poem is nearly context- and contentless. "To Charles Sumner" doesn't reproduce or report on speech, but rather arrogates the right to reply to Sumner directly, expressing relief at the very fact of his oration and describing how it sounded to his audience:

> Thank God! for thou hast spoken
> Words earnest, true, and brave:
> The lightning of thy lips has smote
> The fetters of the slave.
>
> I thought the shadows darkened,
> Round the pathway of the slave—
> That, one by one, his faithful friends
> Were dropping in the grave.
>
> When other hands grew feeble,
> And loosed their hold on life,
> Thy words rang like a clarion
> In Freedom's noble strife.
>
> Thy words were not soft echoes,
> Thy tones no syren song;
> They fell as battle-axes
> Upon our giant wrong.
>
> God grant thy words of power
> May fall as precious seeds,
> That yet shall leaf and blossom
> In high and holy deeds![19]

Despite the conceit that the poem refers to public speech—"Thank God! for thou hast spoken"—Watkins's audience is clearly one for whom Sumner's oration has been mediated by print. However, unlike the printed letter to the editor of the *Dublin News* or the transcript of speeches that had been delivered at Framingham, the poem's reply comes from nowhere in particular and thus could be claimed by any and all. Rather than responding to Sumner's assertions about the barbaric nature of slavery, the poem claims on behalf of those assertions a powerful if indeterminate set of effects (the speech has "smote /

The fetters of the slave" and has fallen "as battle-axes / Upon our giant wrong"). Although the second stanza introduces an "I" who fears that the antislavery cause has been derailed by the recent deaths of unnamed supporters, the poem works to dissolve individual doubt into collective confidence, exhorting readers to "high and holy deeds" that would translate into action the metaphorical effects claimed by the poet for Sumner's historic speech. The conceit that this poem is itself speech—a direct address to the heroic senator—creates a sense of intimacy without the individuation we are accustomed to find in lyric poems. Instead of a generalizable lyric inwardness we are left with a figurative rescattering—not of the speaker's feelings or of Sumner's words, exactly, but of the potential effects of these words.

As with "To Mrs. Harriet Beecher Stowe," which obliquely insists on the black poet's (and the black reader's) capacity to award "place" to the white antislavery activist,[20] "To Charles Sumner" claims a peculiar agency, conveying the stamp of black approval more in its provenance than in the poem itself, which maintains a strategic generality (Who are those "faithful friends" whose "hands grew feeble"? Does it matter who they were?). Reprinted by Garrison from a black abolitionist newspaper, but also published as part of the *National Anti-Slavery Standard*'s regular feature—the intermittently published report from the field of a traveling antislavery lecturer—the circulation of the poem in print bears witness to the diverse audiences that were loosely knit together by repeated courses of lectures and by the networks of communication drawn by reprinted items in the abolitionist press.

Like many of her antebellum poems, "To Charles Sumner" illustrates Frances Ellen Watkins's studious avoidance of the lyric "I," the carefully managed distance she maintains between the putative speaker and the figures she offers up for readerly identification, such as the "Slave Mother" ("Saw you those hands, so sadly clasped. . . . Saw you the sad, imploring eye" [59]) or "Eliza Harris" ("Like a fawn from the arrow, startled and wild / A woman swept by us, bearing a child" [60]). In both of these poems the speaker shares the reader's position as a bystander to the action. The poem becomes a vehicle for making available—circulating and recirculating—common reactions and stock postures for readers to inhabit.

Like the chapbook *Poems on Miscellaneous Subjects*, Frances Ellen Watkins's newspaper poetry is designed to circulate. Constituting a public in part by addressing it, her poems act as relays for abolitionist sentiment that neither originates with nor is captured or contained by the poems themselves. If much of the abolitionist press was keyed to oratory, announcing, transcribing, and reporting on speeches that were a vital part of local organizing, poems such as "To Charles Sumner," "The Dismissal of Tyng," "The Slave Mother," and "Eliza Harris" bear witness to how much this geographically dispersed movement depended on the abstraction of print and its many forms of repetition for coherence and visibility. Watkins's poems can seem trivial, ornamental, mere supplements to the more important, persuasive work of antislavery narrative and oratory. But they also offer something these modes cannot, or cannot do as easily or as well: a simulation of intimate address that is as general and iterable as print itself.

Temporality, Performance, and Poetic Address

Frances Ellen Watkins's poems circulated in close proximity to her circulating body, whether as keepsakes or extensions of her antislavery lectures, or as newspaper items that appeared along with occasional reports of her travels, advertisements of upcoming lecture tours, and letters from auditors who reported on her orations. It is impossible to say, finally, whether Frances Ellen Watkins's performances on the abolitionist lecture circuit served as a means for the circulation of her poetry, or whether her poetry and her status as a genteel black poetess sustained her career as a lecturer. Early on in her career, the black abolitionist William Still characterized *Poems on Miscellaneous Subjects* as a supplement to her lectures, one that might help audiences ratify the evidence of their senses. Announcing in a promotional letter to the black-owned and edited Canadian weekly the *Provincial Freeman* that a new edition—"making ten thousand copies"—has just been published, Still boasts that it "sells rapidly, and serves admirably no doubt to keep alive in the minds of many, the interest awakened by her lectures, proving her to be decidedly original."[21] In this account, Watkins's book of poems is not only a memento but also a means of verification. This supplementary logic is familiar from the paratexts that customarily buffered white reception of black-authored texts, but in this case, the corroborating evidence circulates under the auspices and control of the orator-author (and her patron and promoter).

It is clear from her published work that white abolitionists expected Frances Ellen Watkins to represent the possibility of uplift, to serve as a figure for an achievable future for the currently enslaved. William Lloyd Garrison's patronizing 1854 "Preface" to *Poems on Miscellaneous Subjects* argues that Watkins's poems offer white readers evidence of what freed slaves might be "capable of being and doing," which, without such exemplary figures, would be a mere matter "of supposition." Garrison's "Preface" shows how important the poet's "border-state heritage" is to her appeal: she is proximate to slavery but has never herself been enslaved; she is "identified in complexion and destiny" with "a depressed and outcast race" to which she also doesn't properly belong.[22] Often paired with, or scheduled so that her antislavery lectures directly followed those of a fugitive slave speaker such as William Wells Brown,[23] Watkins—a freeborn black Marylander—is able to give voice to the antislavery message, providing authenticity and a sense of urgency, without the stigma of ever having been enslaved.[24]

Frances Ellen Watkins's peculiar legal status was instrumental to her ability to carve a space for herself within antislavery discourse, enabling her to operate as an especially powerful vector for white women's identification. Initially, she had trouble breaking into the antislavery lecture circuit, landing her first speaking engagements only after the passage of an 1853 state law that decreed that free blacks reentering Maryland were vulnerable to imprisonment and enslavement. This law estranged her from the city of her birth and upbringing, transforming her into a kind of fugitive by proxy.[25] Throughout the antebellum period, Watkins's legal status enabled her to represent identification with the enslaved as a choice that was nonetheless compelled by law and by racial identity,[26] to strike a posture of genteel vulnerability that resonated thrillingly with many white abolitionists.

Take, for example, the elaborate description of her oratorical style published by the author and activist Grace Greenwood in response to one of the poet's performances in the aftermath of the Civil War. Reporting on a course of popular lectures held in Philadelphia in the spring of 1866, Greenwood borrowed a few lines from Elizabeth Barrett Browning's *Sonnets from the Portuguese* to describe the effects of "Mrs. Harper's" speech:

> She stands quietly beside her desk, and speaks without notes, with gestures few and fitting. Her manner is marked by dignity and composure. She is never assuming, never theatrical. In the first part of her lecture she was most impressive in her pleading for the race with whom her lot is cast. There was something touching in her attitude as their representative. The woe of two hundred years sighed through her tones. Every glance of her sad eyes was a mournful remonstrance against injustice and wrong. Feeling on her soul, as she must have felt it, the chilling weight of caste, she seemed to say:

"I lift my heavy heart up solemnly,
As once Electra her sepulchral urn."

* * * As I listened to her, there swept over me, in a chill wave of horror, the realization that this noble woman had she not been rescued from her mother's condition, might have been sold on the auction-block, to the highest bidder—her intellect, fancy, eloquence, the flashing wit, that might make the delight of a Parisian salon, and her pure Christian character all thrown in—the recollection that women like her could be dragged out of public conveyance in our own city, or frowned out of fashionable churches by Anglo-Saxon saints.[27]

For Greenwood, Harper's nonslave status paradoxically makes her a more effective "representative" of the condition of the slave. She is able to channel a long history of "woe" through the mere sound of her voice, her characteristic poetess's lament—that bottomless font of hypothetical feeling—connects the plight of the slave to an ancient history of effective if misdirected mourning (Electra mourns her brother's loss even as he stands beside her).[28] Frances Ellen Watkins Harper's genteel composure is rich with borrowed significance for her white auditors. For Garrison, her cultivation provides a glimpse into the slave's prospects; she is an apparition sent from the future to reassure wary abolitionists. For Greenwood, "Mrs. Harper" extends the repertoire of the poetess to the most pressing political issue of the day, becoming both a figure for and justification of vicarious identification. Harper provides a spectacle of thrilling vulnerability without actual compromise, one in which her agency and integrity is jeopardized, but somehow retained.

Of course, white abolitionists' complex investments in Watkins Harper's refinement must be imagined to differ from her own; as Tavia Nyong'o reminds us in *The Amalgamation Waltz*, African Americans' performance of respectability in the absence of civil rights is itself a kind of political action: "The respectability pursued by black male and female activists was virtual, a respectability to come. It was not based in a defense of extant social relations but enacted through a mimetic performative intervention into those relations, upon terms they well knew white supremacy might fund unacceptable. . . . In politicizing respectability, they moved the domestic into the political sphere."[29] What I want to suggest is a homology between the resonant future tense of Watkins Harper's performances—her enactment of a "respectability to come"—and her characteristic modes of address in her antebellum poems. Watkins Harper is not only or not simply an instrument of vicarious feeling, but rather a figure who is willing to embrace, even to cultivate, spatial and temporal dislocation in the interests of conjuring a radically different order of things.

Watkins Harper's willingness to take on the work of displacement—both her risky, exhausting travel along the abolitionist and Reconstruction lecture circuits and the oratorical performances themselves, in which she offered herself as an instrument for collective identification—can help clarify what the resources of poetry offered to abolitionists, why they would be so eager to reprint verses in their magazines and newspapers or to feature "Poetical Offerings from the Bards of Freedom" on important occasions, such as William Nell's 1858 Commemorative Festival of the Boston Massacre. This event was designed to protest the *Dred Scott* decision by celebrating black heroism during the American Revolution and the right to citizenship it ought to have conveyed. Yoking a painstakingly compiled, if patchwork historical counternarrative to a collective claim on rights withheld, the festival program juxtaposes evidence of African Americans' military service—in particular, Crispus Attucks's status as "the first martyr in the American Revolution"—with Chief Justice Taney's ruling, set out in large-type boldface, that colored men have "No rights that white men are bound to respect" (see Figure 3.4).[30] The festival's primary aim was to gather a community of dissent around the preservation of historical memory, assembling "Emblems—Relics—Engravings—Documents" that proved African American presence "at the dawn of the American Revolution." It is poetry, however, that serves to articulate the hinge between a past that is in danger of erasure and a future in which unrealized rights of citizenship might yet be conveyed.

"Freedom's Battle," the hymn that Frances Ellen Watkins composed "for the occasion" (see Figure 3.5), testifies to the limits of historical evidence—its inability to speak for itself—even as it seeks to capture the idiom of revolution to infuse a potentially stalled political struggle with a renewed sense of purpose:

Onward, O ye Sons of Freedom,
In the great and glorious strife;
You've a high and holy mission,
On the battle-fields of life.

CRISPUS ATTUCKS,

On the 5th of March, 1770, rallied a company of patriots in Dock square, marched up King Street, and in lifting his arm against Captain Preston, he received two musket balls, one in each breast, and fell. He being the first to attack, and himself the first Martyr in the American Revolution.

Peter Salem shot Major Pitcairn on Bunker Hill—and other Colored Americans shared the labors of Lexington, Dorchester Heights, Brandywine, Princeton, Monmouth, Stony Point, Fort Moultrie, Green Bank, Croton Heights, Catskill, Bennington, and Yorktown—besides signal services at New Orleans, and Naval exploits on the Lakes, in the War of 1812, which war was undertaken because of the impressment of three seamen, two of whom were colored, satisfactory proof, at least, that they were American citizens.

Extract from Treatise of Rev. Hosea Easton.

" In the first place, (we) the colored people, who are born in this country, are Americans in every sense of the word,—Americans by birth, genius, habits, language, &c. They are dependent on American climate, American aliment, American government, and American manners, to sustain their American bodies and minds, a withholding of the enjoyment of any American privilege from an American man, either governmental, ecclesiastical, civil, social, alimental, is in effect, taking away his means of subsistence; and consequently taking away his life. Every ecclesiastical body which denies an American the privilege of participating in its benefits, becomes his murderer.

" Every State which denies an American a citizenship with all its benefits, denies him his life. The claims the colored people set up, therefore, are the claims of Americans. Their claims are founded in an original agreement of the contracting parties, and there is nothing to show that Color was a consideration in the agreement.

" It is well known, that when the country belonged to Great Britain, the colored people were slaves. But when America revolted from Britain, they were held no longer by any legal power. There was no efficient law in the land except martial law, and that regarded no one as a slave. The inhabitants were governed by no other law, except by resolutions adopted from time to time by meetings convoked in the different colonies.

" Upon the face of the warrants by which these district and town meetings were called, there is not a word said about the color of the attendants.

" In convoking the Continental Congress of the 4th of September, 1774, there was not a word said about color. At a subsequent meeting, Congress met again, to get in readiness twelve thousand men to act in any emergency; at the same time, a request was forwarded to Connecticut, New Hampshire, and Rhode Island, to increase this army to twenty thousand men. Now, it is well known that hundreds of the men of which this army was composed, were Colored men, and recognized by Congress as Americans."

And yet Chief Justice Taney of the United States Supreme Court rules that colored men have

" No rights that white men are bound to respect."

To commemorate the names and services of Colored Americans in the wars of their country, and to Protest against the Dred Scott Decision which denies them Citizenship, is the motive prompting this appeal to Lovers of TRUTH, FREEDOM and JUSTICE.

Figure 3.4. From William Nell, *Boston Massacre, March 5th, 1770: The Day Which History Selects as the Dawn of the American Revolution; Commemorative Festival, at Faneuil Hall, Friday, March 5, 1858; Protest Against the Dred Scott Decision* (Boston: E. L. Balch, 1858), 2. Courtesy of the American Antiquarian Society.

PROGRAMME.

Among the Emblems,—Relics,—Engravings,—Documents,—together with a few Living Mementoes of Revolutionary and other Historic association, will be present the following: —

THE SCENE IN STATE ST., March 5th, 1770.

WASHINGTON CROSSING THE DELAWARE: in which Prince Whipple is seen pulling the stroke oar,—the same colored soldier that in other sketches is seen on horseback, quite prominent near the Commander-in-chief.

CERTIFICATE (in Gen. Washington's own handwriting,) of honorable discharge of Brister Baker, a colored soldier in the Connecticut Regiment, June, 1783.

Capt. WILLIAM TODD's RETURN OF HIS ARTILLERY COMPANY, including Negro Prince, October 31, 1778.

LETTER OF Capt. PERKINS to Brigadier Gen'l Green, on arresting Lieut. Whitmarsh for abusing a colored soldier, named Newport Rhode Island, in camp. Long Island, July 11, 1776.

Also, NEWPORT'S RECEIPT for Gun and Bayonet, January 9, 1776.

JOHN GRIDLEY'S RECEIPT for five Black Men, Boston, April 3d, 1770.

BILL OF LADING for Negro Girl Flora, consigned to John Powell, Boston, 1718.

SALE OF A NEGRO BOY and a Horse, Boston, Jan. 9, 1760.

INDENTURE OF SAMPSON NEGRO, Scituate, March, 1700.

APPOINTMENT OF POWER OF ATTORNEY for recovering prize-money earned by a colored seaman, Basil Garretson, on board the Private armed Schooner Mammoth, of Baltimore, said money claimed by his *reputed* master, J. C. Deshong, of Baltimore. Jan. 3d, 1815.

ARABIC SENTENCES written by a Black Man owned by Gen. Owen, of Wilmington, N. C.

PURCHASE OF SLAVE by Col. Titus, of Kansas notoriety. August, 1855.

GOBLET AND POWDER-HORN belonging to Crispus Attucks.

FLAG presented by Gov. Hancock (in front of his mansion in Beacon street) to the Bucks of America at close of Revolutionary War.

MRS. KAY, daughter of the Ensign who received the Flag, and (circumstances permitting.) Mrs. EUNICE AMES, aged 92, pensioned widow,—BARZILLAI LEW, and other descendants of colored Bunker Hill soldiers;—also GRANDMOTHER BOSTON, aged 105, and FATHER VASSALL, aged 88, will be present, to revive reminiscences of

GOOD OLD COLONY TIMES.

The following Poetic Offerings from the Bards of Freedom will impart inspiration to her chosen Orators.

Freedom's Battle.

Written for the occasion by Miss FRANCES ELLEN WATKINS.

Sung by Misses HESTER and PHEBE WHITEST, Miss ARIANNA COOLEY, Mr. JOHN GRIMES.

(AIR, GREENVILLE.)

Onward, O ye Sons of Freedom,
In the great and glorious strife;
You've a high and holy mission,
On the battle-fields of life.

See Oppression's heel of iron
Grinds a brother to the ground,
And from bleeding heart and bosom
Gapeth many a fearful wound.

On my blighted people's bosom
Mountain loads of sorrow lay;
Stop not, then, to ask the question,
Who shall roll the stone away?

O be faithful, O be valiant,
Trusting not in human might,
Know that in the darkest conflict
God is on the side of right.

Figure 3.5. From William Nell, *Boston Massacre, March 5th, 1770: The Day Which History Selects as the Dawn of the American Revolution; Commemorative Festival, at Faneuil Hall, Friday, March 5, 1858; Protest Against the Dred Scott Decision* (Boston: E. L. Balch, 1858), 3. Courtesy of the American Antiquarian Society.

See Oppression's heel of iron
Grinds a brother to the ground,
And from bleeding heart and bosom
Gapeth many a fearful wound.

On my blighted people's bosom
Mountain loads of sorrow lay;
Stop not, then, to ask the question,
Who shall roll the stone away?

O be faithful, O be valiant,
Trusting not in human might,
Know that in the darkest conflict
God is on the side of right.[31]

The poet's apostrophe arrogates the right to confer subjectivity on whomever or whatever the poet addresses, rather than, as so much antislavery discourse does, either describing a state of affairs or arguing for their amelioration. Despite legal disenfranchisement, you *are* Sons of Freedom, by virtue of being addressed as such and assenting to inclusion in this genealogy. The poet's fiat brings virtual worlds into being, if only for the duration of collective speaking or retrospective reading; you see Oppression's heel of iron, don't you? And what will you do about that fearful wound? The fragmentary and easily forgotten history Nell had assembled couldn't hope to countermand the bitter reality, in the wake of *Dred Scott*, of the legal withholding of the rights of citizenship without the strong imagination of a future in which such fragments would be gathered up and such sacrifice redeemed. "Poetic Offerings from the Bards of Freedom" provided an occasion for the collective summoning of an alternative history that exists only at the nexus of memory and desire. "Freedom's Battle" enjoins an orientation toward what might be, a world that readers and listeners might be empowered to bring to pass, not what is or has been (Onward!).

It is easy to lose hold of the importance of spatial and temporal dislocation to Frances Ellen Watkins Harper's career and writing when we read her poems as if they were written or somehow destined for the readers of a *book*. In carefully edited collections, such as Graham's and Foster's, her poems appear as only occasionally successful lyrics; it is hard to understand either why the poems were valued or how they work. Recovering these poems' circulation in pamphlets and newspapers lends significance to their forms of repetition, their elusive generality, and their use of direct address. Attending to print format helps to disclose the complex relation of these poems, and of antislavery poetry more generally, to oral performance, to recover the historical importance of the counterhistorical force of poetic address. It is not simply, as many critics would have it, that these poems bear the marks of oral tradition (or delivery) and therefore serve as forerunners of twentieth-century African American performance poetry.[32] Rather, they do all kinds of work at the intersection of print and performance: they serve as an adjunct or supplement to her lectures, a ratification of black genius, a cover for risky, boundary-crossing speech, a vehicle for collective witness, a reminder of black opinion, a personification of black response, a model of appropriate sentiment, a wormhole to other, possible worlds, reassurance of the persistence of alternative histories, an invocation of a better world to come. These poems don't simply circulate among lecture-goers or newspaper readers, they help to constitute these readers as part of a larger public, one of indeterminate extent. They help produce the sense of temporal dislocation necessary to sustain the abolitionist movement—the need for the activist, if only at intervals, to live outside of ordinary time.[33]

CHAPTER 4

Early African American Print Culture
and the American West

ERIC GARDNER

A handful of recovery efforts have begun to alert scholars to black textual presences outside of the urban Northeast, but the lively black print culture in the American West has often remained absent from consideration. This essay begins to treat crucial pieces of that print culture—specifically three nineteenth-century black San Francisco newspapers—to introduce scholars to the intrinsic richness of these texts (and their contexts) and to offer a case study that highlights key issues in the study of the black West as a location of early black print culture.

First, though, as absences and supposedly representative presences are deeply instructive, we should consider the factors that led to the black West's silencing and recognize some caveats necessary for "recovering" print in the black West. Certainly some of the silencing has to do with the forms of publication that dominated the nineteenth-century black West—especially the region's emphasis on newspapers rather than the bound books. Frances Smith Foster and a handful of other literary historians are struggling to remind the field of just how important the black press was within early black literary culture.[1] Partially rooted in literary studies' powerful, consistent privileging of what Joseph Rezek (Chapter 1) refers to as the "heft" of bound books, the separation of periodicals from the literary is directly responsible for part of what the editors of this volume note as a separation between two most vibrant areas for American Studies scholarship, the "inauguration of an African American literary tradition" and "the consolidation of American print culture"

(see Introduction). For figures as diverse as Daniel Payne, Frederick Douglass, Elisha Weaver, Philip Bell, Jennie Carter, and Harriet Jacobs, there was
no such separation: the black press—made possible in part by developments
in print technology and print culture generally—was crucial to *any* sense of
black textuality. Bound books of poetry and autobiography (especially in generic formations orbiting the slave narrative, like the few early black novels)
were only *part* of the story of early black literature. Critics favoring novelistic
narratives often severed that part from the larger whole by marking periodicals as nonliterary and ignoring short-form genres (for example, letters, editorials, travelogues, historical and biographical essays, religious explorations)
that dominated many black newspapers.

Similarly, as a discipline, African American literary studies still favors
and still expects primarily Southern (and occasionally northeastern) stories
that were published in northeastern urban venues; in this vein, it has largely
dismissed "western" stories as inherently not black. Through decades of in-
tensive recovery efforts, Houston Baker's assertion that "tales of pioneers enduring the hardships of the West for the promise of immense wealth are not
the tales of black America" has remained largely unquestioned.[2] Most of the
rare efforts to combat Baker's claim using pre-twentieth-century texts have
argued that black westerners *did* tell such stories—and so reached back to
Langston Hughes's famous call, "don't leave out the cowboys";[3] thus, recent
years have seen some attention to "cowboy" narratives like the autobiographies of James Beckwourth and Nat Love. The University of Nebraska's series
"Blacks in the American West" widens "cowboy" to include Henry Ossian
Flipper's military story as well as the narratives of James Williams, Mifflin
Gibbs, and Henry Bruce, but still focuses on extended novelistic forms; beyond these examples and Foster's edited reprinting of Thomas Detter's *Nellie
Brown,* few literary historians have challenged the unitary definition of western stories embodied in both Baker and Hughes's opposing rhetorics. We
need to recognize black presences beyond those tied to "cowboy genres," and
we need to move beyond the bound book, beyond our disciplinary preference
for novelistic narrative, and beyond geographic assumptions tied to specific
senses of blackness and of the West, as well as beyond the whiteness of much
print culture scholarship.[4]

Given this call for a wider and more varied sense of black letters, a caveat
is also necessary: we still do not have a full sense of just how large, complex,
and diverse my too-ambitious title phrase is. We should deconstruct the geographical boundaries suggested by "American West"—as the Indianapolis-

based AME *Repository of Religion and Literature*, for example, as well as the Saint Louis works of John Meachum and Cyprian Clamorgan, were arguably still fairly far "west" and self-identified as such. Among other examples, the print culture surrounding the Exodusters certainly demands consideration, as do the texts reflecting African American ties to British Columbia and even Japan. Thus, any "West" must recognize fluctuating boundaries tied to both temporal factors and cultural perceptions.[5] The title term "early" also demands examination—as the essay's subjects are certainly far later than, say, Phillis Wheatley; as both Indiana and California might be seen as different kinds of "frontiers" in the 1840s; and as San Francisco in the 1860s may have been just as cosmopolitan, urban, and important to black textual history as Rochester. Even the "and" in this essay's title is larger than it seems: I focus solely on print cultures *in* the West and do not discuss how black texts from other locations *represented* the West. Given this, the black press in San Francisco shouldn't be taken as representative of a unitary black West—because such might never have existed and because we do not have a full sense of the black West*s* such an example might need to represent.

In addition to studying black San Francisco's print culture as valuable in and of itself, this essay thus begins to approach its subject as one of many possible points of entry for considering the black West's print culture; in essence, in some ways, it is an introduction to an introduction. Specifically, through beginning to study the *Mirror of the Times*, the *Pacific Appeal*, and the *Elevator*—which together total some thirty years' worth of newspaper activity (though unfortunately extant runs of the papers are incomplete)—this essay considers how black Pacific Coast residents both literally and figuratively constructed black engagement with print. It emphasizes questions tied to the function of and authority behind black print ventures, the senses of public racial memory embodied in black texts, and the conceptions therein of geography, location, and mobility. In all, the essay thus considers the potential of black print to "fix"—to both place and to challenge, revise, and repair representations (and expectations) of and about—African Americans in the West, the larger nation, and American literary culture.

Print in the Black West

All available evidence suggests that many black westerners understood the importance of black print culture and that some came West as ready participants

in American print culture writ broadly.[6] For reasons tied to location, growing critical mass, and urban opportunities vis-à-vis print technology, San
Francisco became a hub of black culture in the West. The September 1, 1854,
Frederick Douglass' Paper reported that this group of perhaps 1,500 souls
boasted "two Methodist Churches, and one Baptist, 3 ordained ministers, 1
private school, 2 joint stock companies, with a capital of $16,000, 4 boot and
shoe stores, 4 clothing stores, 20 draymen, 8 express and job wagons, 2 furniture cars, 12 public houses, 2 restaurants, 2 billiard saloons, 16 barber shops, 2
bath houses," as well as community organizations including "1 brass band, 1
reading room and library, with 800 volumes, and 1 Masonic lodge" and property "to the amount of $1,000,000"—even though the California legal
system was "a shield to the white man" and made the African American
"an outcast." In the words of "Nubia"—black San Franciscan William H.
Newby—published three weeks later in the September 22, 1854, *Frederick
Douglass' Paper,* "You can form no idea of the progress made by the colored
people in this city."

This complex web of progress and oppression combined with the presence of a striking number of African Americans from the East's black elite,
California's youth as a state, and the state's difficulties in articulating coherent positions on slavery and race to quickly birth significant black cultural
entities—including churches, schools, and the above-mentioned reading
room, which was sponsored by the San Francisco Athenaeum literary society.
But these circumstances also led to calls for African Americans to organize
on a statewide level to fight for civil rights, and such calls resulted in the
statewide conventions in 1855, 1856, and 1857—events that function in fascinating dialogue to the rhetorics studied by Derrick Spires in Chapter 15 of
this volume and that proved crucial to black California's print culture.

The role of the convention movement in the murky history of the *Mirror
of the Times*—California's first black newspaper—demands much more
study, but even a brief examination demonstrates black California's sense of
the functions of and authority behind black print ventures. First, a word on
that murkiness: only two issues of the paper survive, and historians do not
definitively know the date of its first or last issue—although it clearly started
well before the December 1856 convention.[7] Extant records do, however,
show the paper's genesis in a brief resolution at the November 1855 state convention—a resolution that set up a committee to explore "the propriety of
establishing a paper for the use and benefit of the colored people of this State."[8]
Convention delegates clearly saw a newspaper presence as a tool for agitating

for equal rights—especially the right of blacks to testify in court against whites—and that solely political sense of print culture was likely what convinced many delegates to even entertain the issue, as the convention focused so heavily on California's testimony laws that a temperance motion brought by two important ministers was actually ruled out of order. The committee, it seems to have been expected, would report at the 1856 convention and recommend action.

However, by December 1856, William H. Newby and Jonas Holland Townsend—with the backing of San Francisco black businessmen and the support of some members the first convention's executive committee—had already founded the *Mirror of the Times* and were even already suffering the kinds of financial difficulties that plagued the black press across the nation.[9] Starting the paper before the 1856 convention was in many ways a politically savvy move: the 1855 convention was a large, slow-moving body, with delegates from across the state who wanted to be heard on an incredibly diverse range of individual and community concerns; as such, sessions often lapsed into debates over parliamentary procedure, personalities, credentials, and especially questions about the division of power and oversight. The 1856 delegates were thus *not* faced with whether to *begin* a paper (or whom to choose as editors, how to set up a press, where that press might be located, and so on). The press committee's resolutions foregrounded the much more focused question of supporting an existing paper run by a group of the convention's own. Newby and Townsend also undoubtedly knew that the question of finances went to the heart of several delegates' sense of racial elevation and pride: Jacob Francis asserted that "it would be a disgrace to let the *Mirror of the Times* go down"; David Lewis argued that the *Mirror*'s political potential made his "duty to support the paper" as clear as his need "to labor for my daily bread"; Townsend said simply "the colored people, resident in California, must represent themselves" and should "assume the *Mirror*."[10] If the function of a newspaper was to voice the people's concerns—to represent the people—it was incumbent upon the people to support that paper.

Still, Newby and Townsend could not forestall all discussion of who would have authority over the *Mirror*. Select delegates asserted ties between financial support and power and argued that the convention (or some convention subgroup) should control the paper. These questions came first from Peter Anderson, whose attempt to present relevant resolutions separate from the press committee's report was quashed on the convention's second day. Anderson rose again after the report and tried to amend the committee's first resolution, which read simply "That the *Mirror of the Times* be adopted as the State Organ of the colored people of California." Anderson specifically asked that the convention first "assume the ownership and responsibility of . . . the *Mirror*" and only then "take the entire control of its financial matters." Committee member Alexander Ferguson perceived this as a power grab and an attack on Newby and Townsend; he rushed to note that "their characters and their management have been beyond reproach" and that "we often fail in our efforts, from distrust of our leaders." Anderson backpedaled, asserted that he did not intend "to impugn" anyone, and said that he had "all confidence in those gentleman"; Townsend, probably recognizing that Anderson's "ownership and responsibility" did not *have* to mean day-to-day control, then offered tepid support of the amendment, which passed soon after.[11] The *Mirror* group's response was more aggressive when Thomas Detter offered a later resolution "that a committee of five be appointed to examine and decide upon the fitness and propriety of publishing articles" about the convention in the paper. Townsend tersely replied that "editors should decide upon the fitness of articles," sparking comments from E. A. Booth and John Jamison Moore that such power could amount to censorship; Townsend quickly shot back that committee control of an editor would mean that "no man, with ability and independence necessary to the efficient conducting of a paper, would willingly be confined." Detter's motion was tabled and never taken up again. Townsend, Newby, and supporters also fought off efforts to create a "Board of Trustees" for the paper, as well as a "State Central Committee of one from each county . . . who shall assume the direction of the *Mirror*."[12]

At issue, in short, was how a "state organ" should be controlled and whose voice(s) it should sound. For Anderson, the paper was without "father or mother; it is an orphan"; the convention, he argued, should "adopt and become its foster parents." This rhetoric was extended by Jacob Francis: "we have adopted this child, [so] let us assume the duties of a parent, take it by the hand and lead it to the Goddess of Liberty, and have it baptized." Townsend and Newby, however, asserted that the paper and its editors were grown, and the convention's final series of resolutions on the *Mirror* expanded this position—praising "the manly stand taken . . . in behalf of our injured and much abused people" and asserting that "we look upon the *Mirror of the Times* as a beacon light, shining brightly and clearly on the path . . . that as a free and intelligent people, we should occupy in common with our white fellow-citizens."[13] Such statements suggest a victory for individual editors as the authority over California's new black press—and evidence suggests that

Townsend exercised such power at some points: the account of the *Mirror* in Peter Cole's little-known pamphlet *War with Ignorance*, for example, contends that Cole's writing was consciously excluded from the paper.[14] The later legendary feud of Philip Bell and Peter Anderson similarly included competing claims that Bell's *Elevator* and Anderson's *Pacific Appeal* were excluding key voices (and truths) from their pages—often on editorial whim.

However, the editor's chair was actually much shakier. Townsend lost Newby relatively early in the *Mirror*'s history—when Newby moved to New York and then Haiti, hoping to work with the French consul there; Charles Buchannan, hired to replace Newby, left in August of 1857 to return to his home in New Bedford, Mass., ; Townsend himself returned east in 1858, and the *Mirror* seems to have stopped publication at about this time.[15] Bell was forced from the editor's chair of the *Appeal* after only a few months because his views conflicted *not* with any statewide group but with those of "proprietor" and then "editor and proprietor" Peter Anderson.[16] While Anderson's run with the *Appeal*—after Bell left—and Bell's with the *Elevator* were much, much longer, both figures consistently struggled to raise funds for their papers and had to carefully weigh (and actively limit) their editorial and (especially) censoring hands.[17] Beyond this, Anderson and Bell had been schooled in the eastern black press's tradition of multivocality—of publishing disagreements and viewing some forms of dissent as healthy. Bell, for example, continued to send work to the *Appeal* after he left the editorial chair, and Anderson continued to publish that work—and even defended Bell from letters that attacked him (which Anderson also published). Though the fight between the *Appeal* and the *Elevator* was bitter, Thomas Detter and James Monroe Whitfield wrote for and advertised in both, and several men— including Jennie Carter's husband Dennis D. Carter—worked as agents for both simultaneously.[18]

The unitary purpose of fighting for civil rights (first and foremost, for the right of testimony and then, after the Civil War, voting rights) grew to reflect the diversity of California's African Americans. What many convention delegates may have expected—a narrow focus tied to specific political actions—broadened to include a wide range of subjects and genres—from travelogues to book reviews, from national news to local news, and from strident speeches to poetry and even occasional fiction. In this regard, the *Elevator* became even more wide-ranging than the *Appeal*; Bell not only published all of the genres noted above but also encouraged writers to develop their own voices within and beyond established genres. He thus built a strong group of regular contributors—among them, Jennie Carter, who was best known for her multigeneric letters, but who also authored poetry that, though Bell didn't like, he published.

Carter not only serves as an example of the loosening of genre boundaries and editorial control; she acts as a reminder that conceptions of authorship broadened as San Francisco's black press grew. Public authority and print activism at the conventions were gendered male. However, by the 1860s, women were publishing under a variety of pseudonyms (from "Cassandra" and "Violet" to "Semper Fidelis") in the *Appeal* and the *Elevator*; later, more of their work appeared under either their own names or pseudonyms with thinner veils. Women's interactions with the San Francisco black press deserve more study—especially given the often-mistaken gendering of the American West—but, for our purposes, I simply want to recognize that the entry of women into the western black press was part and parcel of its growth from an attempt to be the "voice of the people" into being a collection of various voices *from* the people.

Black (Western) History

The diversification of voices, functions, and conceptions of authority helps explain the historical consciousness among San Francisco's early black press. That consciousness was, in turn, marked by the use of both geographic tropes and national connections to advocate for African Americans. The limited available evidence suggests that the *Mirror of the Times* followed its title emphasis on the present but did include brief historical items. However, the fact that the *Pacific Appeal* devoted close to a fourth of its second issue to the 1855 state convention shows an abiding sense that recording the state's black history—often within the activist rhetorics considered in John Ernest's *Liberation Historiography*—would quickly grow into a multigeneric and multivocal centerpiece of California's black press.[19] An early series in the *Appeal* offers perhaps the best introduction to how San Francisco's early black press fashioned historical memory as a tool for offering public racial presences and for making implicit and explicit arguments about blackness. Appearing roughly every other week in mid-1863, the "Colored Men of California" series consisted of an introduction and biographies of eight men, all authored by Bell and generally signed "C"—short for "Cosmopolite," Bell's pen name.[20]

Bell's introduction in the May 23, 1863, *Appeal* quickly set up several contexts: "Colored men are destined to perform an important part in the future history of California," he began, "as well as in the older States of this Republic. Here as there, they have been among the great pioneers of civilization. . . . The acquirements and abilities of colored men in California are not generally known, and where known are not fully appreciated, nor publicly acknowledged." First, then, the series offered such public knowledge, appreciation, and acknowledgment. But while all of the subjects Bell envisioned were "Americans in the fullest sense of the term," they were not necessarily the kinds of pioneers eastern readers—or twenty-first-century readers—might expect. Only three had any connection to mining, and all had left that field for other professions; none were cowboys. Instead, they were "orators who . . . can electrify an audience; divines eminent for their virtues . . . [;] writers, whose production would grace the library of the most . . . refined; mechanics, inventors, merchants, men of scientific attainments, men of wealth, professional men." Beyond the sense that California's black community and African America rested on the same kind of bedrock—participation in professions—Bell repeatedly pointed to his subjects' interventions in print culture, from Newby's work with the *Mirror* to Abner Francis's letters to *Frederick Douglass' Paper*. Even Isaac Sanks, who was considered in the November 28, 1863, *Appeal* and who "can barely read or write" in large part because "slaves are never sent to College," is noted as both an agent of the *Appeal* and the author of "short, pithy . . . communications" that "would do credit to a professional letter-writer."

Bell placed this textual work firmly within broader engagement with American culture, and so he noted Dennis Carter's importance to Frank Johnson's famous Philadelphia-based band, the convention work of William Hall and William Yates, Ezra Johnson's ties to James Forten, Thomas M. D. Ward's relationship with Daniel Payne, and Yates's oratorical "education" listening to statesmen like John Quincy Adams and Daniel Webster while working as a porter in various federal buildings. Bell was thus weaving the individual biographies of these "representative men" to form a narrative of California black history, African American national history, and American history; print presence and community activism were cornerstones of that narrative.[21] Each installment carried the series title, each balanced material on the subject's regional contributions with discussion of the subject's "representative" traits and actions, and each noted in some detail the subject's complexion and physicality—from Sanks and Newby's "pure black" skin to Abner Francis's "brown complexion" and "aldermanic proportions."[22] As important as the nation was to Bell's series, his descriptions of his subjects' western ventures also consciously created a timeline of events in the Pacific Coast's black history: Ward's founding of the African Methodist Episcopal Church's California conference; the statewide black conventions; the beginning of the *Mirror*; the founding of the San Francisco Athenaeum; early western Masonic work; and business ventures by several subjects. Bell also consistently intervened to remind readers that *he* was working in—and so that this history was being shared through—print: the series repeatedly speaks of Bell's "pen," discusses not only his subjects' newspaper work but also their efforts in other textual forms, and even quotes from texts written by and about his subjects. Bell was using the textual—and specifically the literary genre he referred to in his introduction as the "character sketch"—to not only firmly "fix" (place) black California in print but also to "fix" (repair) representations of black California in the world of print. Readers would have naturally put these (recent) historical events and arguments in dialogue with the news reports and commentary that surrounded them—for example, texts about efforts to gain the franchise, battles to desegregate San Francisco's Omnibus Railroad Company's cars, struggles to gain equal education, and the growing black interest in British Columbia. They thus would have been prepared for later items in the *Appeal* and the *Elevator*—from additional accounts of the early conventions and *Mirror* to Jennie Carter's *Elevator* reflections on the building of black Sacramento, and from reports of emancipation celebrations to memorials to community figures. In short, Bell's series encouraged readers to engage with their own history, to expand on the practices of individual and communal remembering, and to recognize the importance of print to those processes in ensuring that black memory had a lasting public place.

Black Mobility and a Black Nation

While Bell's adaptation of "representative" black Californian stories to tell a history of black progress in and beyond the West is essential to understanding the Pacific Coast's black print culture, his commentary on black mobility and location is even more fascinating. In part because of the demands of his genre, Bell discusses birthplaces, childhoods, and patterns of immigration to the West in some depth. His subjects suggest a stunning range of initial locations—from free African American sites in the Northeast like the birthplaces of Ward (Pennsylvania), Johnson (Massachusetts), and Francis (New Jersey) to more complicated multisite trajectories weaving together slavery and freedom. Bell talks, for example, of Newby's birth to a slave father and a free mother in Virginia and his subsequent exodus to Philadelphia with his mother; Carter's similar story, which would later be further detailed in Jennie Carter's columns; Yates and Hall's free births in Washington, D.C., and moves to New York City (forced by persecution tied to their race and work aiding fugitive slaves); and Sanks's wide travels in the South as a slave before his purchase by his wife (who Sanks had previously helped to buy her own freedom). But Bell's May 23, 1863, introduction emphasizes that while some of his *Appeal* subjects were initially located *in* slavery, all have been located *through and by* the nation's larger sense of slavery and race: "all have felt the baneful effects of that prejudice which American slavery engenders; all! all!! have suffered that martyrdom of the soul which the colored American has to bear." In short, from the beginning of the series, Bell recognized that "location"—including any location or act of locating in the black West—was more than just geographical; it represented a confluence of factors that said much about blackness in America.

Like accounts throughout the early black San Francisco press—as well as in various black periodicals in the East—Bell's sketches asserted that black Californians largely owed their presence in the West to their own exercise of mobility within and sometimes beyond the limits placed on African Americans throughout the nation. Thus, that challenged and challenging exercise became the base for both black California's history and the national narrative Bell and others fashioned—as well as a root of authority for conveying individual and communal voices through print. Even Bell's April 5, 1862, *Appeal* salutatory articulated such a trajectory—noting his youth New York City, his apprenticeship as "the humble assistant of that father of Colored Editors, the late Rev. Samuel E. Cornish," his studies with James McCune Smith, and his years with the New York–based *Colored American*. In this framework, California was a destination where the versions of blackness that had been seeded in the East might finally flower.

Both the *Appeal* and the *Elevator*, however, consistently also argued that African Americans in the West could and should be active contributors to the East and that they were not simply transplants: like the *Mirror*, they were also neither "orphans" nor in need of "baptism"; they were grown—and richly capable of helping their "parents," brothers, and sisters in the East and the nation. Bell's series thus regularly pointed out that many of his subjects were *still* sending texts to papers in the East (especially the *Weekly Anglo-African*). Perhaps the most notable early example of an East-West dialogue was published in the *Appeal* alongside the installments in Bell's "Colored Men of California" series. It started when one of those men, William Yates, reviewed William Wells Brown's *The Black Man* in the May 30, 1863, issue of the *Appeal* under the pen name "Amigo." Yates objected to Brown's limiting of major black figures to a comparatively small group—as well as to the fact that "Brown gives 17 pages to himself and but 7 to Banaker [Benjamin Banneker]" But Yates was most troubled not by Brown's "limited acquaintance with our people throughout the whole country" but with the fact that Brown's "knowledge is quite as imperfect in relation to California as to any other portion of the continent." Bell himself (under his pseudonym "Cosmopolite") followed with a more balanced review in the June 13, 1863, *Appeal* and, while recognizing *The Black Man* as "perhaps the best abused book of the day," praised *both* Brown and Yates as men of "genius and achievements."

But the storm had begun. Brown snapped back in the *Weekly Anglo-African*—in a piece republished in the September 12, 1863, *Appeal*—attacking his critics, calling Yates "the worst of these blunderers," using Yates's real name rather than his pseudonym, and challenging Yates with geographically inflected rhetoric: "Well, Mr. Yates, let us see with your 6,000 population and $3,000,000 wealth"—figures Yates cited in his review's description of black California—"what you can do. . . . With your profuse orators and distinguished poet, have you ever published a book advocating the rights and freedom of the race? True, you have the *Pacific Appeal*, a paper well conducted and showing talent; but with all your wealth and boast, I venture the assertion that it . . . has not 500 paying subscribers in California." Yates's biting two-and-a-half column response—published under his own name—appeared in the September 19, 1863, *Appeal* (only a week later), and an unsigned editorial (probably by Anderson) in the October 10, 1863, *Appeal* accused Brown of "flippantly" and falsely asserting that "we, as a people, do not properly appreciate each other's literary efforts." Certainly this debate demands more study, but key for this essay are the fact that the *Appeal* positioned itself as a voice on national questions of politics, print culture, and public memory, *and* actually *functioned* as such a voice—and did so with enough strength that Brown felt compelled to respond.

Bell was an especially ardent proponent of this sense of San Francisco's early black press as fully participant in larger African American and American cultures of letters. He knew, in essence, that print could be mobile. As San Francisco's agent for the *Weekly Anglo-African* and later the Pacific Coast's lead agent for William Still's *The Underground Rail Road*, he regularly included items clipped from black (and occasionally white) periodicals and books from across the country and offered commentary on them. But the basis for this kind of reprinting—a fascinating corollary to the areas considered in the landmark work of Meredith McGill—was the idea of exchange.[23] Many of the copies of newspapers Bell quoted from came to San Francisco because he sent out copies of the *Appeal* and especially the *Elevator* to newspaper offices across the nation. He urged all black papers to exchange regularly with each other—not simply to share sometimes geographically specific news and commentary, but also to build a richer black print culture. He pulled no punches when he saw black newspapers with typographical errors or weak design, and he was especially critical when issues were late in coming. But his criticism was sometimes recognized as useful, and, though his efforts to form a national black press organization were frustrated, he was recognized as one of the leaders of and in the black press.[24]

While black western voices' places in national dialogues in and about print culture jump beyond expected stories of the West, they also hint at a much more chaotic mobility embodied in many western African Americans' lives and textual presences. That mobility can even be seen in Bell's seemingly geographically fixed "Colored Men of California"—when, for example, in the June 6, 1863, account of the Reverend T. M. D. Ward, Bell recounted Ward's travels east on AME business but also, with a mixture of pride and loss, asserted that "Ward deserves a higher position than that which he now holds, and in which doubtless the heads of his Church in the Eastern States will ere long place him"; in other pieces he similarly discussed Newby's decision to move to Haiti, Francis's travels up and down the Pacific coast, and Johnson's near-decade return to New Bedford. And these sketches appeared next to texts from not just across California—Sacramento, Napa City, Los Angeles, Grass Valley, and so on—but also British Columbia and the territories that would become Nevada and Idaho, as well as New Orleans, Philadelphia, and New York City. California was thus not just a destination; it was also a springboard, a stopping point on all sorts of journeys, an important location—but not necessarily the only location—for black movement in the

West and the nation. This sense was echoed by the new series Bell began even before "Colored Men of California" was completed: a multipart travelogue titled "Notes of a Trip to Victoria" that reported on Bell's own transnational mobility, including subjects from his stop in Portland (to visit Jacob Francis, convention activist and Abner Francis's brother) to his observation of British Columbia's House of Assembly, and from his battles with Canadian senses of the Confederacy to his visit to Mifflin Gibbs's home outside of Vancouver. In short, Bell was "fixing" black mobility through and in print.

In many ways, such mobility through print was embodied even in the initial issues of the *Appeal*, which recognized that the paper's very title meant that its San Francisco location might, in the end, be less important than its status as a conduit for African American texts coming from and going to the entire region. A piece titled "Our Object" and published in the April 5, 1862, inaugural issue asserted that "We shall not confine ourselves particularly to California, nor to the States and Territories of the American government, but we include within the sphere of our duties the British Possessions" along the Pacific. The national and international scope intrinsic in being part of a "black Pacific" can also be seen in the paper's early listings of agents—including workers in Nevada, British Columbia, Texas, Oregon, and even Panama (a key stopping point on the sea journey west), as well as throughout California. Bell's *Elevator* was even more direct in depicting California as not just a destination but a springboard and a conduit—whether it was through reporting the fairly localized "immigration" of White Piners like James Monroe Whitfield (who moved to Nevada to try silver mining), the visits of Jennie Carter to Carson City, the much wider ranging travels of Thomas Detter throughout Idaho and Nevada, or the black possibilities in Japan shared in letters written by black expatriate Peter Cole. The *Elevator* boasted agents in all of these locations and more, from New York to China; the paper seems to have exchanged copies with other newspapers whenever possible and copied pieces from papers from the *Christian Recorder* to the *Japan Times*.

The broad, rich, and complex senses of (and responses to) black mobilities embodied in San Francisco's black press and introduced above—especially within the contexts of black California's senses of the authority, public presences, and historical memory of print culture—assert that we need new ways of thinking about black mobility and location vis-à-vis black print culture.[25] I thus want to end by submitting that we must extend our discussion of nineteenth-century black print culture in the American West if we want a fuller story *of* black stories.

That story has been radically circumscribed for far too long: even after the hard battles to end its long exclusion from the academy, it has often remained a narrow, reductive trajectory—limited readings of Phillis Wheatley and Olaudah Equiano leading to mid-nineteenth-century slave narratives (or, more often, solely the novelistic *Narrative* of Frederick Douglass and, more recently, Harriet Jacobs's *Incidents*) leading to the Harlem Renaissance leading to Toni Morrison. As this essay and this volume demonstrate, the stor*ies* of early African American print culture were actually much, much more diverse, diffuse, complex, and even contradictory than that seemingly linear progression suggests. As an "introduction to an introduction," this essay is thus as much a call as it is a response to my initial study of the black West and my longer engagement with black literature. It calls on libraries, database developers, publishers, and especially anthology editors to make available more of the content of black periodicals (especially those from the West)—content still too often uncollected, unindexed, and banished to microform drawers. It calls on scholars to move beyond expected texts and authors to do the much needed foundational work of a real understanding of the black press—contextual histories of major papers like the *Christian Recorder*, the *Weekly Anglo-African*, the *Pacific Appeal*, and the *Elevator*; studies of printing and distribution practices in the black press—and of networks of press workers and readers; and biocritical studies of early editors like Philip Bell (to say nothing of Elisha Weaver and the Hamilton family). It calls for the kinds of dialogues between historians of the book and print culture and students of African American literature embodied in many of the essays in this volume and in Leon Jackson's important "The Talking Book and the Talking Book Historian" to reconsider the production and circulation of black texts; in this, it calls on historians of black books to also become historians of periodicals and print broadly.[26] It calls on critics focused on narrow senses of "black Atlantics" to reconsider the *intra*national networks and print conduits even as they push for international, transnational, and cosmopolitan senses of black letters—thinking, for example, not just about Martin Delany or William Wells Brown's Atlantic sense but also the ways in which such might have circulated in a black West (and even, perhaps, the small black expatriate community in Japan). In short, this essay calls on all of us to rethink the supposedly representative presences—and to probe the purported absences—in nineteenth-century African American literature, in hopes of regaining a fuller sense of a print culture that was often ignored, forgotten, hidden, and suppressed.

PART II

Racialization and Identity Production

CHAPTER 5

Apprehending Early African American Literary History

JEANNINE MARIE DELOMBARD

The publication of Paul Gilroy's *Black Atlantic: Modernity and Double Consciousness* (1993) set the African American canon's clock back almost a full century. Previously, following the institutionalization of black studies in the 1960s and 1970s, the tradition was widely assumed to have commenced in political and aesthetic earnest—following fits and starts in the poetry of Lucy Terry, Phillis Wheatley, and Jupiter Hammon—with the antebellum slave narrative, specifically the *Narrative of the Life of Frederick Douglass* (1845). Featuring extended readings of Douglass, W. E. B. Du Bois, and Richard Wright, the *Black Atlantic* followed the canon's established timeline. But Gilroy's geographical reorientation of the field had the unexpected effect of prompting a corresponding (if less celebrated) chronological recalibration. Heeding the call to shift our gaze from national "roots" to crisscrossed diasporic "routes," scholars have come full circle, excavating the tradition's eighteenth-century littoral foundations.[1] Unmoored from the constraints of a (black) nationalist literary tradition, critics have developed a transatlantic Afro-diasporic canon that not only encompasses Du Bois's German years and Wright's French sojourn but also makes time for a refashioned John Marrant and a reborn Olaudah Equiano.[2]

As the latter examples suggest, rerouting the tradition has only rooted its origins more deeply in personal narrative. For, with the exception of Wheatley and Hammon, early Black Atlantic scholarship has tended to center on such cosmopolitan expositors of the Afro-diasporic self as Marrant, Equiano,

Briton Hammon, James Albert Ukawsaw Gronniosaw, Ottobah V. Cugoano, Ignatius Sancho, and Venture Smith. With this masculinist life writing serving as its prehistory, the antebellum slave narrative remains for many "the blood-stained gate" not only "to the hell of slavery," but to the canon proper.[3]

What would happen, though, if we were to think of the genre distinguished by the opening line "I was born" not as heralding the birth of a fully formed African American literature after a century-long gestation but as the second-generation scion of an important (if sometimes forgotten) and influential (if not always illustrious) literary family? For starters, we would have to acknowledge the skeleton dangling in the ancestral closet: black gallows literature.

Over the past two decades, critics have proven increasingly reluctant to avow the canon's penal origins. "The black writing that appeared during the eighteenth and early nineteenth centuries," Vincent Carretta and Philip Gould note in *Genius in Bondage: Literature of the Early Black Atlantic* (2001), "included the genres of spiritual autobiography, [Indian] captivity narrative, travel narrative, public epistle, sea adventure, and economic success story"— nearly all written in the first-person singular.[4] Oddly, this comprehensive list (like the volume itself) omits one of the most popular early print forms ascribed to black authors—the confessional crime narrative. Part of a broader scaffold tradition, this ephemera explicitly encompasses an Atlantic world that spans (in the words attributed to the black condemned) "Guinea" as well as "Old England" and "New."[5] Nevertheless, like others in the flotilla of anthologies and monographs bobbing in the wake of Gilroy's *Black Atlantic*, Carretta and Gould's excellent critical collection fails to welcome aboard these castaway texts.[6] That African American literary historiography (which persists, paeans to transatlantic border crossing notwithstanding) continues to look askance at gallows literature seems all the more remarkable given the shared interest in reception evinced by cultural studies, historicist criticism, and book history. After all, the confessing black malefactor would have been at least as familiar to early American readers as the African adventurer, the pious Negro, or the sable entrepreneur.[7]

With its disproportionate representation of condemned criminals of color, gallows literature provided some of early America's best-known print models of individual black experience, directly contributing to the eighteenth-century "emergence of the black narrator."[8] And if, as William Andrews notes, "the largest group of slave narratives published during this time" were "the confessions of condemned black felons," colonial and early national gallows literature is, conversely, disproportionately devoted to black malefactors.[9] Of the roughly two hundred works offering "sermons, moral discourses, narratives, last words, and dying sayings, and poems written for, by, and about persons executed for criminal activity" published from 1674 to the Civil War, at least sixty featured criminals of African heritage.[10]

Our first glimpse of the black condemned in colonial North America is the "Black Fellow-Sufferer" who, "for the very same Crime stands"—mutely—"in the same Condemnation" with "Elizabeth," the confessing, presumably white, infanticide who dominates Cotton Mather's *Warnings from the Dead* (1693).[11] Six years later, in *Pillars of Salt* (1699), the prolific Puritan divine would present "a Picture of *Hell* . . . in a *Negro* then *Burnt* to *Death* at the Stake, for *Burning* her Masters House, with some that were in it."[12] Despite these early examples, "the majority" of black gallows texts "concern slave-born men," who would become much more loquacious than their female predecessors.[13] From Mather's *Tremenda* (1721) to Thomas Gray's *Confessions of Nat Turner* (1831), crime ephemera was one of the primary print means by which the American public apprehended individual black experience from a putatively first-person perspective.

On both sides of the Atlantic, print extended the spatiotemporal effects of the Execution Day spectacle. English gallows literature was dominated by the *The Ordinary of Newgate's Account of the Behaviour, Confession and Dying Words of the Condemned Criminals* (1679–1772), with its more than four hundred editions containing biographies of some 2,500 executed criminals. In British North America, public executions ritualistically reminded the assembled spectators of the simultaneously punitive and redemptive power of God in the life of the individual and the community even as the day's carefully orchestrated exercises vividly displayed the terrifying power of local authorities.[14] People of both genders, all classes, and every hue traveled from great distances to attend, with crowds eventually reaching into the tens of thousands.[15] In Puritan New England, the scaffold ritual's theatrical and oratorical components were supplemented by the publication of execution sermons, which sometimes featured appendixes containing confessions by or interviews with the condemned. In 1717, notes historian Daniel A. Cohen, "[Cotton] Mather claimed that a local bookseller had sold off nearly one thousand copies of his newest execution sermon in just five days. Later that same year, at a time when published sermons typically appeared in editions of one to five hundred, a printer in Boston reportedly produced no fewer than twelve hundred copies of yet another of Mather's" more than a dozen "scaffold orations"—"one for approximately every ten inhabitants of the town, or about one for every two households."[16] Thus, whereas "many other published sermons were by necessity financed with public or private subsidies, execution discourses seem to have more than paid their own way, turning profits both spiritual and temporal."[17] The sermons' wide circulation resulted from their affordability (costing "only a small fraction of a single day's wages" for a typical unskilled worker), but also, like the executions on which they centered, from their comparatively wide geographic reach and broad demographic appeal.[18]

Over the course of the eighteenth century, gallows literature became more popular and secular. As printers replaced ministers and magistrates in transcribing, editing, and circulating these texts, the increasingly sensational confessions began to be published separately from the sermons to which they had been appended.[19] "Before the sun closes upon us this evening you will launch into an awful eternity, and go to appear at the tremendous bar of God, to give up an account of your conduct in the body," ministers conventionally admonished the condemned.[20] En route to the divine tribunal, many appeared to pause and account for themselves in print.

Given that a disproportionate number of the condemned were of African heritage, gallows texts might be seen as a grim realization of the "trope of the dying negro," which for Gould represents "the ultimate erasure of the African voice engaging in cultural critique."[21] Ministers often turned the black condemned to political account in the final section of their tripartite sermons, specifying the oration's "application" to others of their race or condition. Among the "Great Assembly" who had gathered in Boston's Old North Church to attend the execution sermon for Joseph Hanno, the "miserable African" sentenced to death for "Barbarously Murdering his Wife," Cotton Mather singled out bound people of color who evinced an inappropriate "*Fondness* for *Freedom*."[22] "The *Ethiopian*, and Other *Slaves* among us," instructed Mather, "may hear a *Dreadful Sound* in the Fate of their Unhappy Brother here before them; and they are to take warning from it."[23]

Treating other forms of personal narrative as stepping-stones on the long journey to an African American literature, critics have seen criminal confessions as more of a stumbling block. If, for Frances Smith Foster, these texts introduced a first-person perspective that asserted black humanity, the repressive conditions under which they were produced finally "limit their importance in the history of the slave narratives."[24] Noting that by the mid-nineteenth century "abolitionists and fugitive slaves would indict slavery itself as a cause of black transgressions against morality and law," Andrews finds that "the implication of almost all black criminal narratives is that the slave youth was at home in bondage."[25] Recognized as the "obvious literary ancestor" of the antebellum slave narrative, the criminal confession has served primarily to throw into relief its successor's "rhetorical achievements."[26]

These political and aesthetic concerns did not disappear in the swash of Gilroy's *Black Atlantic*. Quite the contrary: in the geographical and chronological dilation of the black canon's terraqueous borders, the early American gaol remains uniquely untouched. The problem is not obscurity or inaccessibility. Gallows texts attributed to the black condemned have long been available through *Evans Early American Imprints* (now digital); another online source is the University of North Carolina's virtual archive *Documenting the American South*, which, edited by Andrews, includes Northern slave narratives. Facsimile print editions for many works are also available in Paul Finkelman's monumental reprint series *Slavery, Race, and the American Legal System, 1700–1872* (1988). Two years before Richard Slotkin published his "Chronological Checklist of Narratives and Execution Sermons by or about Black Criminals, 1676–1800,"[27] Dorothy Porter included *The Life and Confession of Johnson Green* (1786) and *The Confession of John Joyce* (1808) in her *Early Negro Writing, 1760–1837* (1971). More recently, four of twenty works reprinted in Daniel E. Williams's *Pillars of Salt: An Anthology of Early American Criminal Narratives* (1993) portray the black condemned. One might expect the virtually simultaneous publication of Gilroy's *Black Atlantic*, Williams's gallows anthology, and Daniel A. Cohen's comprehensive *Pillars of Salt, Monuments of Grace: New England Crime Literature and the Origins of American Popular Culture, 1674–1860* (1993) to have pushed transatlantic black crime literature to the forefront of critical consciousness. Yet, now more than ever, scholars seem determined to ignore penality's formative role in African American literary history.

This studious disregard may well be a case of benign neglect. During the same thirty-year period in which the American canon grew to include a significant body of black-authored texts, the criminal justice system underwent a parallel expansion, incorporating unprecedented numbers of nonwhite offenders into carceral and supervised populations.[28] In 2008 the Pew Center on the States reported that "for the first time, more than one in every 100 adults is now confined in an American jail or prison," with African American men aged twenty to thirty-four experiencing the peak one-in-nine incarceration rate.[29] Due to felony disenfranchisement laws, "1.4 million African American men, or 13% of black men, are disenfranchised, a rate seven times the national average"; on the basis of these trends, "three in ten of the next generation of black men can expect to be disenfranchised at some point in their lifetime," with "as many as 40% of black men . . . permanently los[ing] their right to vote" in states that disenfranchise ex-offenders.[30]

In an era when, in the words of prison activist and philosopher Angela Y. Davis, "the racial imbalance in jails and prisons is treated . . . as proof of an assumed black monopoly on criminality," canon building has offered symbolic redress.[31] From the pious verses of Wheatley and Hammon and the conversion narratives of Gronniosaw and Marrant, to the success stories of Smith and Equiano and the monitory discourses of Absalom Jones and Richard Allen, the early black canon is replete with virtuous selves. Mounting a devastating insider critique of early American culture, these recovered accounts of exemplary blackness simultaneously ground a reassuring literary historical narrative of transcendent value, unassailable authority, and cultural authenticity—to say nothing of moral superiority. To found the canon in the colonial gallows tradition would be to undermine this narrative in unsettling ways. Such a critical endeavor risks topping centuries of hard-won cultural achievement only to shore up long-standing allegations of inherent black criminality.

Yet, even the best-known exemplars of black righteousness fashioned public selves in a late eighteenth-century Anglo-American culture where an "abundance of execution iconography" made "criminal law the lingua franca of popular politics."[32] A year before publishing her breakout elegy for the Reverend George Whitefield, nineteen-year-old Phillis Wheatley included "On The Death of Mr. Snider Murder'd by Richardson" (1770) in the prospectus for the volume of poetry she hoped to publish in Boston. Anglo-African activist Olaudah Equiano closed his *Interesting Narrative* (1789) by protesting his innocence of the "crimes he is accused" of having committed as "Commissary to the black Poor."[33] The following year, evangelist minister John Marrant offered his *Journal* (1790) as a rebuttal to similar charges of financial "impropriety."[34] Back in America, ministers Absalom Jones and Richard Allen published their *Narrative of the Proceedings of the Black People, During the Late Awful Calamity* (1794) to refute allegations that African American nurses cheated and robbed their white patients during Philadelphia's recent yellow fever epidemic. Allen, founder of African Methodist Episcopalism, went on to publish the *Confession of John Joyce* "for the benefit of Bethel Church."[35] Whether defending themselves or censuring others, the most virtuous black writers found incrimination closely correlated to print publicity. In such a climate, the published portrayals of culpable personhood attributed to their less savory counterparts helped to authorize more critical assertions of black political eligibility by a subsequent generation of activist writers.

Apprehending African American literary history in the manner proposed here provokes valid critical apprehensions. But such an endeavor might also offer its own form of redress by yielding a more politically and culturally relevant early black canon. Closer scrutiny of criminal confessions attributed to the black condemned could, for example, bring into sharper focus the works of peripheral figures like Chester Himes, Iceberg Slim, Donald Goines, George Jackson, Eldridge Cleaver, and Assata Shakur.[36] Widening the lens to include the writing of such imprisoned African authors as Ngugi wa Thiong'o, Nawal el Sadaawi, Wole Soyinka, and Ken Saro-Wiwa could, in turn, prompt an overview of the politics and poetics of Afro-diasporic penality, from the New World to the neo-colony. Finally, panning from early black crime ephemera to the global culture industry (and back again) could provide much-needed perspective on the popularity of today's "gangsta lit" and its Murder Inc. sound track.[37]

Publicizing Personhood

Law did not simply affect those involved in court cases or addressed by legislative enactments. It coursed through early American culture—animating, for example, the terms by which the enslaved appeared before the reading public: as items for sale or as security threats to be captured and punished. One of the more explicit efforts to publicize slaves' legally defined "character" appeared during the ratification debates over the U.S. Constitution, when "Publius" defended article 1, section 2's already notorious "three-fifths" clause.[38] The newspaper article that would become *Federalist* 54 refuted the notion "that slaves are considered merely as property, and in no respect whatever as persons," insisting that instead "they partake of both these qualities." In the former capacity, "in being compelled to labor, not for himself, but for a master; in being vendible by one master to another master; and in being subject at all times to be restrained in his liberty and chastised in his body, by the capricious will of another—the slave may appear to be degraded from the human rank, and classed with those irrational animals which fall under the legal denomination of property." But, Publius continued, "in being protected, on the other hand, in his life and in his limbs, against the violence of all others, even the master of his labor and his liberty; and in being punishable himself for all violence committed against others—the slave is no less evidently regarded by the law as a member of the society, not as a part of the irrational creation; as a moral person, not as a mere article of property."[39] The problem with the slave's "mixed character" was not that the laws authorizing and maintaining American slavery denied black humanity (state statutes only made the "slave . . . *appear* to be degraded from the human rank" in the eyes of the law). Rather, as the *Federalist*, countless judicial decisions, and modern scholars have made clear, the complications arose from what Colin Dayan has called the slave's "retractable personhood" under law, a condition that "accedes to the instrumental alternation between person and thing."[40]

Belied in practice, bedeviled by doctrinal complexities, the legal fiction of slaves' mixed character, with the corresponding distinction between civil and criminal agency, nevertheless held ideological sway as just that—a fiction. For when the black subject appeared in print as person rather than property in early America, it was more likely to be in sensationalized crime accounts or in the criminal code than in the belletristic works or exemplary accounts of piety, adventure, and enterprise on which we base our teaching and research. If, as Davis suggests, "crime is . . . one of the masquerades behind which 'race,' with all its menacing ideological complexity, mobilizes old public fears and creates new ones," criminality was nevertheless the guise under which the black persona routinely entered the public sphere of print in early America.[41]

To appreciate this point is radically to reconfigure the relations among African Americans, law, and publicity in the century leading up to Emancipation and the Reconstruction amendments. Influenced by Jürgen Habermas's controversial account of the eighteenth-century emergence of the public sphere, many of us share historian John L. Brooke's image of a liberal state where the deliberations of executive, legislative, and judicial officials at the governmental core are informed not only by the direct participation of enfranchised citizens (through jury duty, elections, and the like) but also by the indirect contributions of a much larger, more diverse cohort whose communications form the public sphere. In Brooke's schema, "civil outlaws" like slaves, insurgents, and criminals occupy a peripheral "arena of force," where their only "political voice is violence, and in turn they are met with state-sanctioned force," whereas other subordinates contribute not only to culture but to politics in its more limited, conventional sense through their persuasive interventions in the deliberative process.[42] Closed out of *both* the public sphere and the liberal state through their enslaved or outlaw status, how could the black majority ever achieve political membership in the form of citizenship?

Whether we picture eighteenth-century African American activists and writers creating a "black print counterpublic" through institution building and publishing efforts directed primarily toward constituencies of color, or we see these black publicists as "invad[ing] the public sphere and persuad[ing] Americans that they were equal citizens of the Republic in theory if not in reality," we tend to think of publicity as the avenue by which marginalized or excluded subordinates gained access to the polity.[43] Indeed, the enduring appeal of the antebellum fugitive slave narrative lies in the way it spatializes and materializes the slave's escape from the marginal "zone of force" into the public sphere: fleeing from the repressive South to the cultural centers of the North, the fugitive demonstrates African Americans' civic and political qualifications by publishing his personal narrative of bound servitude as a critique of the slaveholding legal regime. Yet movement was seldom so liberating for those facing "the predicament of territorialized freedom" in an Atlantic world structured by localized race slavery.[44] The lithographic and narrative "Resurrection of Henry Box Brown" notwithstanding, publicized geopolitical relocation alone could not bring the civilly dead to political life.[45]

Under the legal fiction of the slave's mixed character, however, criminality could do just that. Activating his personhood, the slave's offenses remove him from the extralegal zone of force, ushering him, through his arrest and prosecution, into the nucleus of state power. Having been transformed from human property into legal person, he is then transmuted from flesh-and-blood human being into print persona. Through published trial transcripts, press accounts, scaffold orations, gallows broadsides, or pamphlet confessions, the first-person black subject participates in the public sphere, thereby contributing to the popular opinion that cycles back into deliberative governmental processes.[46] Punitively affirming his political membership, passage through the criminal justice system made it possible to envision the black individual in alternative public, civic roles. Activist former slaves like Douglass could "talk 'lawyer like' about law" in their antebellum narratives because for well over a century the American reading public had become accustomed to seeing enslaved felons talk defendant-like about law in popular crime ephemera.[47]

The Death of the Condemned Black Author

Understanding the print performance of black authorship to be at least as important as its historical authenticity, the new African Americanist book history offers a way out of the critical impasse between the theoretical insistence upon the death of the author and the culturalist commitment to documenting black expression.[48] Directing hermeneutic attention toward the individualized black persona, and thus *away* from his flesh-and-blood historical referent, this essay does not attempt to discern "when we are hearing an authentic black voice instead of witnessing an act of literary ventriloquism."[49] Eschewing the imperative to discover a resistant black political consciousness in an authentic Afro-diasporic voice, this inquiry joins Dickson D. Bruce in seeking the "forms and conventions that seemed to provide, within a discursive world, a basis for a distinctively black intervention into the public sphere."[50] Regardless of whether such traces of "black authority"—of "an authoritative literary persona and a distinctive black perspective"—emanated from a black "hand" (or tongue), they nevertheless, to borrow the words of John Sekora, shaped "the terms of possibility for the slave narrative" as a more explicitly political form of African American print self-fashioning.[51]

Abandoning the pursuit of racial authenticity for a more generative account of black civic presence in print, we begin to see how gallows literature, rather than merely reinforcing the legal "designation of [enslaved] subjectivity [that] utterly negated the possibility of a nonpunitive, inviolate, or pleasurable embodiment," inadvertently thwarted the process by which "the black captive vanished in the chasm between object, criminal, pained body, and mortified flesh."[52] Publicizing official, punitive recognition of the legal personhood of individual Africans and African Americans, incrimination in print distinguished the black condemned from their more virtuous contemporaries, as well as from the mythic "Africanist presence" that pervaded America's white-authored literature.[53]

Tempting as it is to illustrate these claims with an exceptional work like the exuberant transatlantic rogue's narrative *Sketches of the Life of Joseph Mountain, a Negro* (1790), let us instead consider a typically brief, formulaic broadside, *The Life, and Dying Speech of Arthur, a Negro Man; Who Was Executed at Worcester, October 10, 1768; for a Rape Committed on the Body of One Deborah Metcalfe* (1768). Here is Arthur as he nears the end of his criminal career—and his life:

> [I] was discovered, and committed to *Worcester* Goal, where I continued 'till . . . I broke out with the late celebrated *FRASIER*, and a young Lad, who was confined for stealing. After which, at *Worcester*,

we broke into a Barber's Shop, from whence we stole a Quantity of Flour, a Comb, and a Razor: We then set off for *Boston*. At *Shrewsbury*, we stole a Goose from Mr. *Samuel Jennison*; and from the Widow *Kingsley*, in the same Place, we stole a Kettle, in which we boiled the Goose, in *Westborough* Woods. At *Marlborough*, we broke into a Distill-House, from whence we stole some Cyder Brandy: In the same Town we broke into a Shoe-maker's Shop, and took each of us a pair of Shoes. . . . At *Watertown* we stole a Brass Kettle from one Mrs. *White* of that Place. My Companions now left me; upon which I went to Mr. *Fisk's* in *Waltham*, who knew me: And having heard of my Escape from *Worcester* Goal, immediately secured me, and with the Assistance of another Man, brought me back again, where on the 17th of September following, I was tryed and found guilty. . . . And . . . I was, on the 24th of Sept. last, sentenced to be hanged, which I must confess is but too just a Reward for many notorious Crimes.[54]

We see here why gallows texts have been so unappealing to critics.[55] Notwithstanding the broadside's first-person voice and Arthur's claim to have learned to write as well as to read before running away, we can be excused for wondering whether the man hanged for raping Deborah Metcalfe actually wrote or even narrated this text. Arthur's closing endorsement of his hanging sounds less like the slippery, twenty-one-year-old jail-breaking recidivist portrayed here than the clerical and state authorities who often had a hand in producing gallows texts. This approbation, along with Arthur's stated reluctance to close his "Narrative, without gratefully acknowledging the unwearied Pains that was taken by the Rev. Mr. *McCarty*" to prompt Arthur's "own sincere Endeavours after true Repentance" suggests that we might better look to the minister, not the condemned man, as the text's source.

So what literary critical payoff can prosaic broadsides like *The Life, and Dying Speech of Arthur* possibly offer? "If all his enormous villainies, and wrongs to men, could be enumerated," the Reverend Aaron Hutchinson speculated in his own execution sermon for Arthur, "what a black catalogue would there be of his crimes . . . !"[56] To enumerate one's villainies was to generate cautionary or sensational black catalogs, not to compose great literature. These highly formulaic texts are narratives in only the strictest sense of the word, apparently more committed to inventorying stolen goods than telling the condemned malefactor's story. (A footnote in *Brief Account of the Life, and Abominable Thefts of the Notorious Isaac Frasier* [1768], the pamphlet attributed to Arthur's better-known white partner in crime, explains that such lists "are particularly mentioned at his desire, that the owners may know the articles taken by him, in order to exculpate others.") [57] Further complicating matters is the fact that, like *The Life and Confession of Johnson Green* and the *Life, Last Words and Dying Speech of Stephen Smith, a Black Man* (1797), *The Life, and Dying Speech of Arthur* differs little in content and style from the confessions attributed to white condemned malefactors like Frasier or the more famous Levi Ames. Why *black* gallows literature?

One answer lies in these very inventories of stolen goods. Typical of gallows texts, the *Life, and Dying Speech of Arthur* stresses not the condemned man's extraordinary capital crime but the everyday transgressions more commonly practiced in the larger community. Like other confessions, it centers on the property offenses that constitute the felon's prior criminal career. And it is in this identification of the narrator with such crimes that gallows texts register a subtle but signal difference between even the most formulaic print portrayals of the black condemned from those of their white counterparts, as well as from other contemporary forms of Afro-diasporic life writing.

Consider the broadside's opening lines:

> I was born at *Taunton*, January 15, 1747, in the house of *Richard Godfrey*, Esq., my Mother being his Slave, where I lived fourteen Years; was learned to read and write, and was treated very kindly by my Master; but was so unhappy as often to incur the Displeasure of my Mistress, which caused me then to run away: And this was the beginning of my many notorious Crimes, of which I have been guilty. I went first to *Sandwich*, where I lived two Months in a very dissolute Manner, frequently being guilty of Drunkenness and Fornication; for which crimes I have been since famous, and by which I am now brought to this untimely Death.
>
> At *Sandwich*, I stole a Shirt, was detected, and settled the Affair, by paying twenty Shillings. My Character being now known, I thought proper to leave the Place; and accordingly shipped myself on board a Whaling Sloop.

Telling the conventional story of Arthur's descent, through property crime, to death on the scaffold, the *Life, and Dying Speech* simultaneously depicts his ascent, also through property crime, from the civil death of the slave, via the culpable legal personhood of the felon, to the civil standing of the self-possessed, contracting individual.[58]

What sets the formulaic gallows texts of condemned criminals of color apart from those of their white colleagues is the way in which the recounted property crimes definitively distinguish their black perpetrators from the chattels they appropriate. Arthur's theft of chattels from the inaugural shirt in Sandwich to the culminating brass kettle in Watertown establishes in the text a fundamental, insistent difference between the legally liable person and the objects he appropriates. If, like "those irrational animals which fall under the legal denomination of property," slaves could resist, run away, or destroy things, by law they differed from livestock in the criminal responsibility that elevated them to the status of legal personhood. Brass kettles didn't steal brass kettles—and neither did livestock. "Would it not be an anomaly in judicial proceedings," proslavery lawyer George S. Sawyer would ask in his *Southern Institutes* (1859), "to organize a court for the trial and punishment of unruly horses and horned cattle?"[59] For Arthur, having a criminal "Character" was quite different from the loss of reputation it represented to a white man—even an indentured servant subject to whipping and sale, as Frasier had been. The slave's acquisition of such a public criminal "Character" marked the *attainment* rather than the diminution of recognized personhood. For the white man, such a reputation brought with it the loss of civil standing, but for the slave, criminal character marked the ascension from human chattel to legal person.

Just as the divergent effects of incrimination differentiate the narratives of the black and the white condemned, the recounting of such property crimes marks out the print subjects of confessions from other black Atlantic personal narratives. With his property offenses, the criminous slave sidesteps the liberal "trap" into which virtuous black autobiographers inevitably fall.[60] If, like Equiano, Smith, and Marrant, Arthur must pay to release himself from captivity, here the money is equivalent not to himself as property but to the shirt he, as a responsible legal person, has stolen. Rather than ensnaring him as fungible commodity in a seemingly inescapable mesh of property relations, Arthur's restitution for the stolen shirt has the opposite effect: affirming his responsibility for the crime, the payment likewise affirms rather than negates his personhood. Even prior to the criminal apprehension that will require his official acknowledgment as a legal person, Arthur's thefts change his position in the web of relations among persons and things, doubly consolidating his personhood as property holder and culpable criminal agent.

Puffed Up

Neither literary pretensions nor political intentions can explain the significance of black gallows texts, whose ideological transparency only illuminates their questionable provenance. The value of confessions attributed to the black condemned lies in the way that even fictive first-person participation in print culture filled out the partial, culpable personhood acknowledged by criminal proceedings. Print parlayed legal liability into civic presence.

We can glimpse that process at work in one of the earliest first-person portrayals of a black individual published in colonial America. The transcribed "Conference Between a Minister and the Prisoner, on the Day Before His Execution" appears as an appendix to Cotton Mather's *Tremenda: The Dreadful Sound with Which the Wicked Are to Be Thunderstruck*. When asked how he spent his "many Months in the Prison," Joseph Hanno answers, predictably, "In Reading and Praying, Sir." His rote catechistic reply is complicated, however, by the minister's outraged response: "In *Reading!* Of what, I pray? . . . you had no *Bible* with you."[61] Although Hanno's nonscriptural reading is lost to us, its civic implications resurface later in the interview. Exhorted to attain "Righteousness" through repentance and asked, "Do you understand what I say to you?" Hanno retorts, "Yes, Sir, I have a Great deal of Knowledge. No body of my Colour, in Old England or New, has so much"—prompting the curt ministerial rejoinder "I wish you were less *Puffed up* with it."[62] Presenting a black self "Puffed up" by its participation in the public sphere, Hanno belies Mather's portrayal of him in the sermon as a "*Black Thing . . .* in Irons."[63]

"As One within a Few Hours of an awful Eternity," Hanno was expected to turn to the Bible as a guide toward "*a Sincere and Serious Repentance*," in keeping with the Calvinist doctrine of *sola scriptura*.[64] Instead of leading to inward contemplation, Hanno's reading projects him beyond the confines of Boston's Queen Street jail, into the emergent republic of letters that, comprising "*Old England*" and "*New*," could also accommodate the "Knowledge" contained in a "body of [his] Colour." Through its publication Mather's *Tremenda* ensured the continued circulation of "Joseph Hanno" in Anglo-American print culture. Far from killing that nascent civic persona, the condemned man's execution, at once expiating his criminal act and occasioning the pamphlet, marked its birth.

CHAPTER 6

Black Voices, White Print: Racial Practice, Print Publicity, and Order in the Early American Republic

COREY CAPERS

On or about July 14, 1816, a broadside titled *Invitation, Addressed to the Marshals of the "Africum Shocietee," at the Commemoration of the "Abolition of the Slave Trade"* appeared in the Boston vicinity. *Invitation* simultaneously announced and satirized the commemoration of the end of the trade, which was organized and led by Bostonians of African descent but included white Bostonians who actively watched the processions, sometimes gave sermons, and even extended the celebration through complimentary newspaper announcements and reportage (Figure 6.1).[1] It was printed on rough paper measuring approximately eleven by eighteen inches, probably produced in a large run, sold for a few pennies, pasted on tavern walls, and read aloud for all within hearing range.[2] To the left of its centered title, it features an animal-like figure, in elegant dress and a cane, standing on a barrel apparently in the act of making an announcement. The body of the broadside is composed of two columns of text in a ridiculous fictive black dialect, featuring a letter of invitation and instructions to one of the commemoration's marshals and several toasts parodying Boston's African Society as the "Africum Shocietee" in a fictive black dialect.

As late colonial and early national newspapers and almanacs had frequently trafficked in jokes at the expense of African Americans, there is little noteworthy about *Invitation* itself.[3] It *is* interesting, however, as among the

INVITATION,

Addressed to the Marshals of the "Africum Shocietee," at the

Commemoration of the "Abolition of the Slave Trade,"

July 14th, 1816.

BOSTON, 11½ ²izteenth, ¹bôts.

BRODER OFFISAIR,

DE Afrikum Shocietee having done demself de high honour of pointing you one ob dare Marshal to inbiate in grand portunshum on Monday next, being de fourteen cay ob de weak, respectfully beg leave to present you de accompanying uniform an de badge which will be worn on dis splendied rocasion. It is expected by de Societee, dat you will make you repearance in de most superb style, wid you nose slit up and buttoned back, your shins rubbed down with brick bats, your eyebrows greased and black, balled in de neatest manner, and your face pulled up to heel, so as not to let de calf a leg interfere wid de shin bone; and dat if possibol, you will ware de white top boot polished wid Misser Fozzar's best Varnish, wid a butiful pair black buff cullered buckin breeches, and white silk tocking ob de same culler, which will compel de gemmen of the tarry heel to tand back in de rear, and make room for yourself an de rest of de Marshal to come up in de front. After dis brilliant ceremony has taken place dare will be (bien a toy tole what a fine dinner) giben, in commemoration of de bobolition of de slave trade; at which, when you are called upon for a shentiment, you will please take a chair, standin, keep your both eye well to de right about, grin wid all your trength, and dollar de following toast, accompanied by one gun and tree cheer.

"Misser Presidumpt Madimeson...in politie be no more jes de same like equal to de great Misser Prince Saradurs, dat two black bones ob anoder culler."

Earlyin de morning, fore sundown, you are desired to call on Misser J B, who supplies de Society with flour and candles to powder dare wool wid on dis gloris annisversary.

Per order ob de "Afrikum shocietee" for de
"Bobolition of de Slave Trade,"
MINGO MANTUN, Secretaree.

Notee Beane...In case of your neglect to repeat, on de pot terciely in mown street, at de roll call ½ o'cuock, de fine will be fifteen dollar, and on de contrary if you do repeat at dis time and plashe punctualim, it will not be more dan firty dollars.

The following are understood to be among the number of toasts pronounced by the "Afrikum Shocietee" on this occasion.

~~~~~

By a volunteer. De Afrikin fair. May dere butiful white charcoal eye cher flash fire onde enemy, dere troeg bref suffocate 'em and dere smilling oxy teak cher grin on the gemmen on de white top boot and buckin breeches wid de greatest approbation.
Tree cheer, one gun.

De memory of General Peter Gus. Only to tink dat he commanded de Afrikin army last year, and now he be gone to do debil to get new recruits.
Drad march in haul.

De Orator of de day. His eloquence demonish de Afrikin, and almost made my soul die a lafin.
Yankee Doodloum.

De fair creme coloured lady of de town of Boston. May day rull dere butiful white eye on de enemy whenever dey consuit 'em, and trow demself grinning for joy into the capricious white bosoms of the Afrikin marshal.
Rushum Dance.

De great Misser Prince Saradurs. Wid one foot he wash his calf de Atlantic, wid de odar he touch de calf a leg in de frog pond...de resplendum of his eloquence shine upon de nation like de full noon in eclipse, omy just he be as much abuperior to dem as two and two make six.
Tree gun, two cheer and a half.

De memory of Col. Middletun. Man dat is born of de woman be of few days and cheats full of wool.
Pleyel's Hymn.

Mr. Capt. Col. Kummins. May he shone brighter and brighter and brighter, like Misser Peter Gus going up to de grave.
Tree cheer, one grin.

De Afrikin Leetion. When de colored man shake poppaw on de common lection day, may no gemmen be allowed to cross de ring wid de feet carr'd, less he pick up two puzzleou.

De Orator of dis day ob our bolition. He bab truly told us dat we better be born a drug dan to ils feet wid a long trong chain tide about de neck.

Poor Pompey. Whenebor de enemy bab jes as much ag'n to say against him bi his father, may all true prius christchum exclaim wid one bref "Oh, don't, don't, do let de sod rest.

President Madimeson be no more like General Washerton den put de leg in de fire and take him out again.
Tree cheers, wid a grin.

American Eagle. May she nober clip her wing, nor lose her tail fedder.
Tree cheers, four gun.

"BOSTON de 14 day of Guly,
"To Mist. — 18,016   Hed Quarter,
'Bredder Ufficare,
"I ave de superb gratefecation to enform you dat de ranniversary of de bobolition of de strave trade tak place dis day at four quarter after six clock by de old sow...de cummittee ave done ranself de honor for mak you one marshall, to distend de progression thro' de treats. Massa—————was made de Marshall in de firs place, but he has informed de committee berg late dis morning, that he has got a bad faintezy, gone foul sock thro de solemly forscion...from dis reason de Committee of rangements hav pinted you to fulfill his place, you being de grandest and most celibrating milishy character among dem quantrake, and de hop you will disappear on de spot without display, and send your de incompiling badge of your high offis, to wear on de brilliant rocasion. It is expect dat were you march in de treets, you turn out your to, hold up your hed, but tak care de chappeo dont faul auff, and dat you try to meak as sublime a dispeatance as you can, as much like our mortal and latley diseased marshall and your friend Guss, as you can, it is expec dat wen you com to de fore end of State Street, you put your lef foot tire, and bring de hele up close; how your eyes right front and dress, &c. At distracting collashrom which will be divided for de rocashion, were you a called for on a toaste you must geb de preceading de brae fair sec, may he turn pale when he se enemy of the brae gemmens return from de parthe of stuctitude till dey turn to de left boute face. Or if you tink de rum spinchious rocashion preserve de forgetfulness of you at onner, you will give dis one. To dis aufole day of de activity of de brae hero of Afreco, may de rannoverarrie cume twice a year, an nebber be dri de, but may de licour flow from de great gug, like de swef from Hardy's forched, while he swepe down Marbro' Trees by moonlite. You high onner will do us de displeasure to xcuse us for de esli notis we make you, for we are so grate confitude of toblications to make out, dat it take all de time dat as bin giben to your most disounseld subject.

Secketaree to de Committy of Rangements for de cellebrashions of de bobblision of de Slave trade.
Tak notis...press carri your embriller wid you alweg to yess bos, for fear dat de rane fall and wet dis ranspicashus badge.

Printed Salem South Side de North Pump.

earliest iterations of a series of broadsides and newspaper accounts that figured African American celebrations of the abolition of the transatlantic slave
trade as "Bobalition," a corrupted form of "abolition." Circulating in print
through most of the United States and even in England until at least the
mid-1830s, Bobalition should be a matter of concern for students of early
African American print culture for several reasons. Bobalition provides us
with further evidence that some white writers and printers as well as their
audiences deemed African American processions and orations, as well as their
printed surrogates in newspapers and pamphlets, significant enough to comment upon, in celebration and execration. More important, Bobalition epitomizes the conditions of possibility of black writing in the early republic and
antebellum years, providing some sense of the logic, figures, and practices
against which black writers fought and necessarily engaged. Relatedly, as a
concept embodied in literary and graphic figures that were embodied in print
on paper that circulated widely in time and space over an increasingly dense
national and international communications infrastructure, Bobalition was a
technology for the production and maintenance of racial difference in a world
where the significance of class differences seemed to be melting away.

Building on earlier scholarship concerning Bobalition, which shows how
it excluded African Americans from legitimate participation in U.S. civil society, I am concerned here with how Bobalition was productive of new entities and new relations between the practice of racial distinction and the
emergent U.S. political order.[4] To that end, I examine Bobalition through
the lens of *racial practice,* a term I have coined to help grapple with the active
and contingent character of ordering the world along an axis of putative racial difference.[5] Among the most prominent means of Bobalition's racial
practice are translation and figuration.[6] As Eric Cheyfitz and scholars in science and technology studies have reminded us, one of the earliest meanings
of "to translate" is "to carry from one place to another."[7]

Discursively, translation is relevant to Bobalition in the substitution of
"Bobalition" for "abolition" that it entails. Likewise, in a perverse act of re-
figuration, the satiric broadsides and related news accounts that enact the
Bobalition discourse stand in the place of authentic news accounts of black
celebrations that, in turn, stand in lieu of the actual performances of African
Americans. In short, African American celebrations have been moved from
their initial locations and, in the process, transformed into farce.

Translation as a more explicitly material practice pertains to Bobalition
in terms of the repertoire of figuration drawn upon to create the broadsides.

C

The printer would have (self-consciously or not) chosen strategies of figuration and association from earlier contexts and assembled them together in a new material-semiotic figure in the form of Bobalition.[8] In view of the congealed material and semiotic labor embodied in and enacted through Bobalition, we should deal with it as a translating apparatus that filtered out the range of performance styles by actual black people and left us with *satiric public blackness* in its place.[9]

Through a careful examination of Bobalition, this essay explores the emergence of a satiric "public blackness" in the early national U.S. North from 1816 to 1834. By "public blackness," I mean the contested material-semiotic figure created in and through practices of publicity—by blacks and whites, racists and antiracists alike—that was partially concerned with the characteristics, condition, and place of people of African descent in the U.S. body, but also with the politics of everyday life more generally. I employ the term "public blackness" so as to interrupt the ease with which we tend to write of "race" and "racism" in general, that is, reductive, terms—construing the particularities of a general pattern of exclusion and distinction (as enacted in colonial Anglo-America and the U.S. racism) as adequate for specific instances of both such as Bobalition.[10] Attending to discrete enactments of public blackness (as in Bobalition) enables a more precise grasp of the situated and contingent relationships between black and white people in the early national United States as well as the emergent "whiteness" and "blackness" that they came to embody and signify. This essay argues that racial practice in the early American republic was neither merely the legacy of slavery, nor entirely the *result* of social changes. Instead, it was a form of practical politics and entertainment that drew on the history of racial slavery so as to intervene in the world of an increasingly nonslaveholding North, thus establishing something familiar but new that I call "satiric public blackness."

I am concerned with satiric public blackness in both its material production in popular print and its use as a strategy in political discourse. I examine both the rhetorical operations used to construct Bobalition's messages and the graphic as well as literary conventions employed to make them easily intelligible to their readers. In the first case, Bobalition satirizes both African American celebrations of abolition, literally (mis)translating "abolition" into the farce of "Bobalition." While actual black celebrations employed the discourse of republican virtue and the eschatology of Protestant millennialism to critique slavery and racism and build black civil institutions, Bobalition translated it into a comic satiric blackness composed of "black jokes," epistolary fictions, and satiric political commentary to discredit black independence and construct a generally unnamed white national body politic in racial terms. Bobalition's effect was both performative and pedagogical.[11] In its production and dissemination, Bobalition enacted black deviance as normative and, in so doing, trained Bobalition's audience to see *any* black performance as, in fact or fiction, deviant. This visual and literary mode of ordering joined blackness and disorder, making disorder a racial problem.[12] In the world of Bobalition, African Americans are developmentally challenged. They have neither mastered themselves nor the conventions of respectable celebration, so they are not ready for citizenship, but neither were those nonblack people who behaved as African Americans were alleged to have behaved.

The racial labor embodied in Bobalition was an intervention in early nineteenth-century northern U.S. politics that established the norms of citizenship in racial terms. Bobalition banished African American people to the margins of respectability, while their print surrogates, through contradistinction, served to fashion whiteness (without ever naming it as such) and join it with respectability, thereby making disorderly whites *racially* degenerate. This rhetorical fiat placed nonblack rowdy celebrants, along with the practices associated with them, below the boundary of blackness.[13]

By ridiculing black celebrants as disorderly because of who they were, but ultimately focusing on the *character* of the disorder figured in their caricatured surrogates, Bobalition turned "the form of democracy against its substance" combining "the rhetoric [and sentiments] of popular government with the hard reality of the iron law of oligarchy."[14] Using the media and conventions of popular print, Bobalition substituted the standardization of racially defined forms (of speech and public comportment generally) for the rule of putatively "disinterested" persons described in classical republican political theory and prescribed by Federalists.[15] This political strategy momentarily allowed for a rapprochement between the Federalist desire for proper order and the Jeffersonian Republican desire for a horizontal white national manhood, paving the way for herrenvolk democracy.[16]

Examining Bobalition as simultaneously a technology and a trope highlights both the principles and practices of classification (and association) that it relies on and also generates, showing how Bobalition differs from earlier forms of public blackness such as the "rhetoric of pretense" embodied in eighteenth-century runaway advertisements and the later corporeal satiric public blackness enacted in blackface minstrelsy.[17] My analysis explains the significance of the difference posited between people and practices labeled "white" and "black" in Bobalition, thus resolutely historicizing Bobalition itself. Moreover, it calls on interested scholars to examine more closely the material and semiotic *labor* that made whiteness the preeminent qualification for national belonging in the early national United States. In turn, it is this labor that accounts for the *wages of whiteness* described by W. E. B. Du Bois and made popular by David Roediger in his book of the same name.[18]

Translating Blackness and the Problem of Black Publicity

The earliest Abolition Day publicity occurred on May 10, 1807, in Philadelphia at a planning meeting chaired by the Reverend Richard Allen. According to the announcement in *Poulson's American Daily Advertiser*, the conveners of the meeting resolved to: "correspond with other religious societies in the Union"; commemorate the inaugural day of the abolition of the trade; give gratitude to the government and "friends of humanity" for produced abolition; form a committee to carry out the earlier resolutions; and hold "Divine service . . . on the 1st day of January at half past 10 o'clock in the forenoon."[19] This was followed by a meeting in New York City on October 3, 1807, held by "Coloured People . . . at the African School Room" where "it was agreed unanimously to commemorate the day" and to meet again with "the Colored People in General."[20] By mid-January of 1808 news of the meetings in Philadelphia and New York had appeared in print in Boston and Northampton, Massachusetts, alongside announcements of the "Political Jubilee, with Thanksgiving and Prayer."[21]

In spite of the decorous language and systematic planning evinced in the notices, a condescending response from a writer using the pseudonym "Humanitas" appeared in New York's *Public Advertiser* requesting that "the people of colour in this city" give due attention to decorum during their planned celebration. The choice of pseudonym is a clue to the writer's intent. "Humanitas," in the Ciceronian tradition, is the cultivation of sophisticated manners or the perfection of our natures.[22] Such a notion of humanitas is consistent with the writer's intent as laid out in his response to the notice of African American intent to celebrate. He writes:

> It will . . . become a matter of policy for yourselves . . . that your conduct should . . . be marked with that strict circumspection, which is one of the constituted virtues in an intelligent and rational mind . . .

it will behoove you to act with moderation and respectful decency—to be more than usually careful of every expression of language, and particularly attentive to that deportment of conduct which, according to its merit, will either be reprobated or approved. May you, therefore, particularly guard yourselves against every encroachment upon the peace of society, and evince to your fellow citizens and the *world*, that you are men, possessing those natural endowments which, if rightly cultivated, will enable you to become useful to yourselves, to one another, and ornaments to society.[23]

Humanitas frames the commemoration of the trade by Africans and their descendants as if the "people of colour" had not seen and likely participated in celebrations of national independence prior to their proposed undertaking. Moreover, Humanitas ignores that the announcement had already called attention to the "respectable" character of the previous meeting and probably did not need to be reminded to attend to correct language and "deportment of conduct." Regardless of its intent, such framing calls into question the decorum and propriety of the Africans and their descendants in the face of evidence that they were not likely to transgress the conventions of respectable celebration. It translates African American publicity into a scene of pedagogy, reminding the public (including his stated black audience) of the appropriate mode of celebration.[24]

Beginning in 1816 such pedagogical scenes had migrated to the discourse of Bobalition as manifested in three forms that I label "Bobalition," "replies," and "riot" texts. Each form explicitly parodies African American participation in U.S. civil society whether in celebration, self-defense, or the search for respectability. However, in the midst of ridiculing putative black pretension, the prints also target disorderly and licentious white Americans. The Bobalition versions poke fun at Jeffersonian politics, while the replies censure both the unknown authors of the initial broadsides and the rowdy white celebrants of the annual celebrations of artillery election and Squantum festivals. The riot broadsides are more complex in that they simultaneously define black gender relations as disorderly and dramatize the tyranny of white mobs that attack black households with excessive force. Though most scholars treat the broadsides satirizing Abolition Day celebrations and the replies to them as separate, I argue that they were part of a dialogic series; their producers intended them to be read in conversation with one another. Moreover, since they all share a medium (popular print), representational devices (caricature, mock epistles, Africanist dialogue), and a concern with establishing order through satire, we should read them in conversation with each other as well.

The politics of Bobalition are immediately apparent once we look past the black bodies and American Africanist dialect. For example, Cato Cudjoe, the speaker in *Grand Bobalition of Slavery* (ca. 1820; Figure 6.2), ironically comments on and critiques the leveling aspects of Jeffersonian Republicanism. Like the other personae in the world of Bobalition, Cato's speech presented in print is seemingly disordered, making *almost* no sense.

> Dear Sir—You Great Rascal!
> I habing been compointed de President of de day, it being no more dan juss and proper dat you mind what I say, else you stan chance to get a broke head, and dareby hab de nose-bleed on de shin. To day by virtue ob de autority of de Shocietee, I knock you down if I like, call you rogue, or juss such nam what suit me more betterer. To-morroo. I shake hand wid you, hell [help] you sweep de treet, or brack de boot and do noting at all almos besides.[25]

He recognizes that "Dear Sir" is the form of address appropriate for his letter's salutation, but renders it moot with the "You Great Rascal" that immediately follows. Likewise, he appreciates the authority vested in him as "President of de day," but lacks the virtue or discernment to utilize his authority with moderation. Thus, he threatens his audience with violence if they don't "mind what [he] says." Like catechisms, conduct books, or other forms of hortatory print, these jokes reiterate lessons in decorum in simple terms—the conventionally subordinate deserve to be in their positions because they lack the practical wit grounded in virtue and self-control to be anything else.

However, when extended to conventional politics, they make an additional point. After acknowledging that tomorrow he will return to his former status as a common man where he will help his peers to "sweep de treet, or brack de boot," or do nothing at all, Cato remarks, "and Massa Monro when he done being President, hab no more authority at all as? I do." This remark serves two purposes. First, it cites the classical republican principle of "rotation in office," which advocated frequent elections and limited individual terms so as to prevent political corruption in a not-so-subtle commentary on the duration of Jeffersonian Republican rule.[26] Relatedly, it serves as a warning to President James Monroe and all of those Republicans presently in office. As

Grand Bobalition of Slavery.

Grand and most helligunt Selebrashum of de Bobalition of Slabery in de Nited Tate ob Neu Englunt. and commonwet of Bosson in de country of Massa-chuse-it.

Order of de Presidum of de day, to de Shief Marshall, and all de rest of he understrayer.

marshall, company wid de music of de band, and discharge of a popgun.

How sweet be de rum, and de sugar and water,
When enuf you can get in de belly to fill,
But sweeter he Cato nose toootiful daughter,

Figure 6.2. *Grand Bobalition of Slavery: Grand and most helligunt Selebrashum of de Bobalition of Slabery . . .*, detail (Boston, ca. 1820). Courtesy of the John Hay Library, Brown University.

their future positions parallel that of the Abolition Day president, they should *now* be prudent in their exercise of authority. This is a clear comment on the potential self-interest inherent in the republicanism of the Jeffersonians in contrast to the disinterested virtue of the Whig republicanism out of which it emerged. The putatively comic black figure makes the serious point that politics requires both the individual virtue of moderation and, implicitly, the collective political virtue of a return to first principles.

Dreadful Riot on Negro Hill! (1816; Figure 6.3) describes the "late riot on Negro Hill," via the device of "a copy of an intercepted Letter from Phillis to her Sister in the Country," thus drawing on a long tradition of Anglo-American epistolary fiction, satirical and otherwise.[27] Its source is an actual 1815 riot against a "disorderly house" in Boston's West End neighborhood known at the time as "Negro Hill."[28] *Dreadful Riot* features a black woman named Phillis protecting her family from an attacking white mob, while, Pompey, her wounded husband (on crutches), walks away while holding the hand of their infant child Kate.

By depicting Phillis as the family's defender, the print suggests that gender relations in the black household did not fit the norms of classical or emergent democratic republicanism.[29] In the terms of the broadside, their domestic disorder allows the sanctity of their home—along with its genteel furnishings described by Phillis to her sister—to be defiled and corrupted. Indeed, the intercepted letter's pretense mimics the corruption, putting its readers in a voyeuristic position, making the conventionally private public, thus corrupting the integrity of the black family it portrays. While the inversion of patriarchal authority and transgression of republican standards of virtue clearly mark Phillis and Pompey's relationship as *conventionally* disorderly, they also—in terms of the same republican standards—simultaneously render the mob tyrannical in its use of excessive force against a feminized opponent.[30]

Dreadful Riot is an allegory of the corruption of the body politic under the tyranny of "the democracy" rendered in racial terms. It focuses on the boundary between public and private space as well as vice and virtue. In the upside down world of *Dreadful Riot*, African American families and communities are too weak to protect themselves from the tyrannical excess of the mob. The black father cannot defend his family from the multitude, leaving Phillis to take on what would conventionally be *his* masculine position.[31] In turn, however, the white mob oversteps its bounds and stands in for "the hand of power" always haunting the pamphlets of the American Revolution.

Figure 6.3. *Dreadful Riot on Negro Hill* (Boston, 1816). Courtesy of the Library Company of Philadelphia.

Together they stand in for a corrupt society—the black family for an ill-defended liberty and the mob for a tyrannical power. Their attempts at respectability, like the attempts of the Bobalition celebrants, fail due to a lack of self-mastery.

Reply to Bobalition of Slavery: Dialogue between Scipio and Cato, and Sambo and Phillis, occasioned by reading the account of Bobalition proceedings, as detailed in a letter from Cesar Gobbo, to his friend Marco Mushy, residing in the country (see Figure 6.4) joins the Bobalition version's concern with civil society and the riot version's concern with domestic life and virtue.[32] In doing so, it offers an almost panoramic view of the Bobalition genre's concerns and clarifies the scope of its critique. Its speakers, Cato and Scipio, discredit the false accounts of the abolition celebration's proceedings and recall rowdy white celebrations where the "greater part ob um get drunk, and mose break he neck, and den pay to doctor for to mend him agin." Cato claims to not care about the carrying on of white celebrants "if dey didn't set bad sample to some of our Sochietee." By way of example, he refers to the bad influence that Tommy and Tabaty Tightlace (two white dandies) have had on the once respectable Sambo (the servant of Tommy Tightlace's father) and Phillis who, coincidentally, just happen to enter the scene. Unseen, Scipio and Cato stand to the side to listen to the "dandy antics" of Sambo and Phillis. Sambo complains of his plight as a fashion-conscious man. He had bought his suit of clothes on credit and when he could not pay was dragged off to jail. Likewise, Phillis complains that her tight-laced corset is making her faint. When Phillis complains that Sambo doesn't "stend out" his hand to support her, he begs her forgiveness as he was "so rap in meditation deep, dat for a little time I did forget de mose pol[i]tess rule, which Massa Chesafield [Chesterfield] lay down."[33] Here both parties suffer unnecessarily because of their licentious overindulgence in fashion and luxury—two more sins according to the civil religion of republicanism.[34]

Scipio responds to this comedy of manners with choice words and suggestions as to how to put a stop to the nonsensical behavior of Phillis and Sambo, which they learned through the "mimetic corruption" from their white betters.[35]

> Why I tink Sambo deblish fool, and dat he make you cousin Phillis what de shopkeeper call ditto. I tell you what, Cato—de nex time de Shociete hab a meeting, I mean to expose [read "propose"] dat all dem member who make himself like be white dandy be turn out,

Figure 6.4. *Reply to Bobalition of Slavery* (Boston, 1819). Courtesy of the Library of Congress.

and no suffer to sellybrate annuder Bobalition forty-ten year to
come—so by dis time, I gess dey know what long to good manner,
and de speck du to de Shocietee. So let you and I now get our grog,
and leab dem to himself till he find out dat me spise um for he deb-
lish nonsense.

This passage reveals the primary aim of the broadside—to critique and
correct pretentious behavior generally whether embodied in white or black
skin. Scipio's proposal to expel, or "turn out," dandified black members of
the African Society for fifty years until they learn better behavior mirrors the
emergent reform politics of the age. In fashioning fictive representations of
black celebrants and substituting them for actual black celebrants, the broadside satires remove the actual black celebrants from the social world in which
they live, placing them outside the norms of "respectable" society. The fictive
Africanist characters stand in their place and, through ventriloquized speech,
repeat the operation of alienation onto unruly white celebrants, placing them
outside of social norms defined in terms of an unmarked "whiteness."

Scurrility and Satire: Disciplining Civil Society

The attention directed at the range of figures, pedagogic intent, and anti-
Jeffersonian sentiment in Bobalition points to its partial connection to another body of understudied popular print—the Federalist satiric newspapers
that shared many of Bobalition's devices and concerns: Philadelphia's *Tickler*
(1807–13) and Boston's *Scourge* and *Satirist* (1811–12). It is in part from these
sources that Bobalition emerged. *Invitation*'s topic and graphic figure were
quite literally taken from two accounts in the *Satirist*, showing that the partial connections between these texts and Bobalition is more than coincidental. With names such as the *Tickler*, *Satirist*, and *Scourge*, it is easy to see why
scholars might have discounted these prints. Clarence S. Brigham claimed
that "Scurrility and vilification became commonplace and, now [1800] that
the Republicans were in power, the Federalist newspapers descended to the
most improper forms of abuse, attacking Jefferson without mercy or regard
for truth."[36] Twenty years later Frank Luther Mott would characterize the
period between 1801 and 1833 as "a kind of 'Dark Ages' of American journalism" largely because, "So far as scurrility and vulgar attack . . . were concerned, the period . . . exceeded all that had been known before. . . . Humor,

indeed, had always played a considerable part in political lampooning, but
vile innuendo and open accusation of personal turpitude are scarcely funny."[37]
Perhaps. Nonetheless, these prints provide insight regarding the turn in Federalist political strategy that can only be induced from Bobalition. They show
how Federalists sometimes abandoned the high-toned Augustan mode of
their earlier publications and employed popular forms to maintain their concern with proper order.

Philadelphia's *Tickler* was one of the first U.S. newspapers to employ
graphic caricature. In a period of less than two months in the fall of 1807, it
featured two woodcuts attacking William Duane, the arch-Republican editor of the *Aurora*. One figures Duane in Ireland (his birthplace) fighting with
his mother, who has accused him of stealing her whiskey (see Figure 6.5). Its
composition mirrors *Dreadful Riot* and like the Bobalition broadsides more
generally, it is embellished with doggerel poetry and a fictive dialogue between the two caricatured figures. The major difference is that the dialogue is
what purports to be Irish speech. Perhaps more important, it also implicitly
comments on the Duane household. There is no father or any other head to
guide its subordinate members and keep them in check. The other woodcut
presents Duane in India "riding the stang" in an Indian version of the Anglo-
American popular punishment (see Figure 6.6).[38]

The mock-procession notices joining politics and putatively degraded
and/or alien speech that characterize the Bobalition form were also ubiqui-
tous in the earlier Federalist satiric press. They were mastered by the *Tickler*
years earlier, appearing as "marching follies" in the guise of "battalion mus-
ter" reports described in letters from Georgia, the ironic "Grand Army of
Pennsylvania," sham European celebrations of the Fourth of July, and Fourth
of July celebrations in Georgia. [39] Boston's press featured similar reports in
the *Scourge's* "Grand Democratic General Caucus" [40] and the *Satirist's* March
12, 1812, report on the "Grand Republican Caucus," followed by an ode entitled "Mobocratical Celebration; or, Festival of the Disclosure" that roundly
satirizes the Republican administration for employing a British spy on the
eve of the War of 1812.[41] In the center of this mock news item is the cartoon
figure heading *Invitation* some four years later. The figure reappears in conversation with a female dandy (see Figure 6.7) a month later with text prefig-
uring the critique of white dandies in the 1819 *Reply to Bobalition of Slavery*.[42]

Finally, the *Tickler* and the *Scourge* both featured several different forms
of mock epistle in fictive vernacular dialect including the Africanist version.
"African Tammany Society Celebration" (1809) featured a mock report of

THE TENDER CONFLICT; OR FLIGHT FROM IRELAND.

At nineteen years old they could get little good of me,
I then ran away which you've all understood of me,
I next got drunk, and myself for the blood of me
    Couldn't tell what I did ail,

Dear! dear! what can the matter be?
Och! dear! faatt can de matter be?
Arrah blood-o'nouns what can the matter be?
Billy's as drunk as a pig.

Mother. Ubhubboo! you whiskey staling thief, would stale your own dear mudder's life's blood? Och to de divil I pitch you!
Son. I'll not go to de divil, dis bout, mammy; I'm bound to de Senate!

Figure 6.5. "The Tender Conflict; or, Flight from Ireland," Philadelphia *Tickler*,
October 12, 1807. Courtesy of Readex/Newsbank.

said society's Fourth of July celebration in Africanist dialect along with mock
toasts to the society, their red brothers, and, of course, to Phillis. [43] One
month later, the *Tickler* featured a reply that critiques the "Frenchified" (read
"Jeffersonian Republican") white Tammany Society. "If Massa Genet or any
oder Frenchmens wants to turn Indians, we tink dat he better go to de toder
Tammany Society. And we whish, besides, dat de peoples would mind der
won business," a sentiment implied in the replies to Bobalition.[44] In the next
several years, the *Tickler* added to its stock of fictive voices those of characters
in German, French, and several with white dialect speech.[45] The *Satirist*

The Asiatic mode of exalting Merit.

" In fair India, still they tell us,
How the knight of dauntless soul,
After he had 'scap'd the gallows,
Gallantly bestrode the *Pole*."

[Vide Tickler, No. 6.]

1st HINDOO. Ha Billy, you make dam ugly face, he ! he ! he !
2d HINDOO   Hi Yah ! him no like me bamboo he.
3d HINDOO. He chum printer no like de pole-horse.
O'DUNN.   By de Hill o' Hoath . dis same pole is sharper den my mammy's husband's drum-sticks.

Figure 6.6. "The Asiatic Mode of Exalting Merit," Philadelphia *Tickler*, November 25, 1807. Courtesy of Readex/Newsbank.

continued the tradition with a series entitled "Intercepted Letters," and the *Scourge* published fictive letters from Tom Webb and Eben B——L.[46]

In spite of their shared topics and tactics, the earlier prints differ from Bobalition in that their objective is much clearer and more obviously violent, making a stronger connection between print ridicule and punishment—popular and otherwise. They have much in common with rituals of popular punishment such as skimmington and rough music as discussed by social historians.[47] The important difference is that the bodies they punished and shamed were embodied in print instead of flesh. While the printed lash

' *Mistakes of a Night.*' We have been favored with a copy of a new *farce*, under the above title. The plot is founded on the story of a young man having made so unfortunate a mistake one night as obliged him to marry the mother of the young lady to whom he was paying his addresses. The subsequent plate is prefixed to the work. Whether this curious production has a local application we know not. At any rate the frontispiece, of which the following is a correct copy, is an admirable satire on the prevalent fashions.

Figure 6.7. "Mistakes of a Night," Boston *Satirist*, April 20, 1812. Courtesy of Readex/Newsbank.

avoided the physical punishment and allegations of tyranny associated with crowd actions, it allowed the judgment of popular punishment to be disseminated as far as the print network would go, doing national harm to the reputations of its victims. Despite the difference in reach, the distinction between physical attacks and their print counterparts was neither clear nor definite.

The punishment in the pages of the *Tickler* was not coincidental. It was part of these papers' mission. All three share mastheads featuring cat-o'-nine-tales being applied to punish dogs (in the case of the *Satirist* and *Tickler*) or a penitent tied to a whipping pole (in the case of the *Scourge*). Moreover, each paper's motto advocates the targeted application of the lash. The *Scourge's* reads, "Weak men demand our Pity—Bad men deserve our stripes." Lodowick Lash'em, the editorial persona of the *Satirist*, asserts his paper's main object to be "to lash vice and folly, in whatever shape it may be found."[48] Even the more moderate sounding persona of the *Tickler*, Toby Scratch'em, grants the violence of his intent, writing in October of 1809 that "Satirists use the public as pedants do a naughty boy ready horsed for discipline; expostulate, then plead the necessity of the rod and conclude every period with a lash."[49] Each editor seems to see himself as a necessary part of government, an adjunct to its state institutions. As an anonymous writer in the *Satirist* claimed: "He [the satirist] may be considered as a sort of supplement to the legislative authority and penal afflictions of his country, as assisting the unavoidable defects of all legal institutions for the regulations of manners. . . . The strongest defense, perhaps against the inroads of vice, amongst the more cultivated part of our species, is well[-]directed ridicule. They, who fear nothing else, dread to be exposed to the contempt and indignation of the world."[50] Perhaps the sentiment was expressed best across the Atlantic and nearly a century before, when Richard Steele wrote in the *Tatler*, "In a Nation of Liberty, there is hardly a Person in the whole Mass of the People more absolutely necessary than a Censor."[51]

The Federalist satiric newspaper prefigured the genre of Bobalition and most likely served as its model. Given the continuity between their explicit and implicit methods and ends, it seems that Bobalition embodies a change in strategy. Where the earlier prints dramatized their violence and targeted the lower orders directly, Bobalition hides its violence behind comedy and, launches its critique of the lower orders through the predicament of African Americans whose ventures into civil society were more easily contested. If, as Jeffrey Pasley has written, the early Federalist satirists were indeed out of touch with their Augustan satire, as the Republican ascendancy began to seem more permanent, they learned to improvise and innovate.[52] Instead of retreating from politics into an aesthetic world of artistic letters as William Dowling has maintained, some Federalist writers merely changed strategies.[53] They maintained their appreciation of Augustan satire and used it to fashion more vernacular satiric forms to address the people generally. As the promise of a "speaking aristocracy and a silent democracy" waned, some Federalist-leaning printers became innovators in shaping public sentiment.[54] Through the ideology and practice of racial difference, they disseminated the norms of democratic comportment and speech. While the Federalists may have been somewhat sympathetic to the real black people whom they used as models for their caricatures, the populace seems to have learned their lesson well and more fervently maintained racial boundaries, refusing to mix the form of American citizenship with the out-of-place matter of African descended bodies.

Like the earlier Federalist satiric papers, Bobalition served to instruct the public. The graphic carnivalesque component of these prints directed the white public to see black people as inherently different, unable to speak, and subject to public ridicule. Likewise, they suggested to Americans of African descent that, regardless of their actual behavior, white Americans would likely see them as unruly and out of order. Coupled with the graphic, the literary component attempted to train the public (black people included) in the standards of orderly and appropriate performance through constructing a fictive and caricatured "blackness" and associating that blackness with disorder and impropriety, rendering the two virtually synonymous. These anti-black prints forcefully and repeatedly asserted racial difference as a means of simultaneously constructing and maintaining the boundaries of a new popular democracy while instructing potential citizens and subjects in the appropriate manner of performing their positions, in opposition to the caricatures of "blackness," as *white*.

CHAPTER 7

Slavery, Imprinted: The Life and Narrative of William Grimes

SUSANNA ASHTON

In 1824, in a fury over the injustices of slavery, racism in the North, and exploitation of the workingman, William Grimes wrote the story of his life. *The Life of William Grimes, the Runaway Slave* (1825) ends with a visceral and violent image of literary sacrifice: Grimes offers to skin himself in order to authorize the national story of the United States:

> If it were not for the stripes on my back which were made while I was a slave, I would in my will leave my skin as a legacy to the gover[n]ment, desiring that it might be taken off and made into parchment, and then bind the constitution of glorious, happy, and free America. Let the skin of an American slave bind the charter of American liberty![1]

Grimes's memoir, the first detailed autobiography written by a fugitive slave in the United States, rendered visible the contradictions of a national ideology that could marry freedom and slavery; his status as "bound" also "bound" the legal freedoms enshrined in the United States' founding documents. And that he made this claim by invoking the imaginative language of print was no coincidence. Not only had Grimes worked as a hired slave to a prominent printer in Savannah, and was thus conversant in both the practice and language of print culture, but he was challenging the sacred status of print in Western culture. I see this passage as not only an opportunity for him to display slavery's literal and figurative inscription on his skin, as William Andrews has aptly noted, but also as a cry that could seize upon an image that had a personal resonance.[2] This image arose from his own fraught experiences with the print world, by which he was occasionally exploited but from which he also occasionally benefited. His challenge, "Let the skin . . . bind the charter of American liberty," played out, too, in his very copyright registration of his own bound life story, the first U.S. copyright claimed for a full-length black-authored book. By boldly asserting his rights of intellectual property he was, in effect, cauterizing the injuries slavery had imprinted upon him. His experiences with how print culture could both entrench and unseat a system that enslaved him lent Grimes language both figurative and literal to shape not only his expressions but also his actions. His intellectual property claim was essentially synecdochic—his copyright claim could thus stand in as a broader claim to his own self, a man who had been "bound" in slavery. That is to say, while both literal and figurative texts betrayed him (as he suggested the Constitution did, for example) they also could be harnessed for his own benefit (as the letters he wrote negotiating his own "value" demonstrated). The upshot was that Grimes understood himself as a full-fledged participant in textual world—a participant shaped by text but also a participant who could assert the material and immaterial power of text to his own benefit as well.

William Grimes's narrative is a notable text not merely because of its rich and troubling contents but also because of its status as the first published, book-length runaway slave narrative in the United States that was almost certainly, in its first edition, written by the runaway himself.[3] Moreover, the fact that he went to the expense and effort to have his copyright asserted under the jurisdiction of the 1790 Copyright Act, the first federal copyright act in the United States, also illustrates how his work marked a transitional moment of national conceptions about citizenry, civic rights, the public sphere, and property itself.[4] The 1790 law required, in no uncertain terms, U.S. citizenship on the part of the claimant.[5] By claiming his own copyright—and all evidence suggests that he was the first African American to claim copyright for a book-length work under the 1790 act—Grimes marked 1825 as a moment in which conflicting notions of citizenship and civic rights might be exploited to his advantage.[6] It is, of course, possible that a publisher filed the copyright on his behalf, but since the phrasing of the title-claim reads that Grimes "hath deposited in this Office the title of a Book" it seems probable that Grimes himself made an appearance and the clerk knowingly recognized him as a man with citizenship rights sufficient to file the claim (see Figure 7.1).[7]

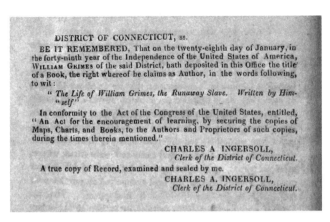

DISTRICT OF CONNECTICUT, ss.

BE IT REMEMBERED, That on the twenty-eighth day of January, in the forty-ninth year of the Independence of the United States of America, WILLIAM GRIMES of the said District, hath deposited in this Office the title of a Book, the right whereof he claims as Author, in the words following, to wit:

"*The Life of William Grimes, the Runaway Slave. Written by Himself.*"

In conformity to the Act of the Congress of the United States, entitled, "An Act for the encouragement of learning, by securing the copies of Maps, Charts, and Books, to the Authors and Proprietors of such copies, during the times therein mentioned."

CHARLES A INGERSOLL,
Clerk of the District of Connecticut.

A true copy of Record, examined and sealed by me.

CHARLES A. INGERSOLL,
Clerk of the District of Connecticut.

Figure 7.1. Copyright notes from the 1825 edition of *The Life of William Grimes.* Courtesy of Z. Smith Reynolds Library Special Collections and Archives, Wake Forest University, Winston-Salem, North Carolina.

Since the Connecticut State Constitution specifically denied free black males the right to vote in 1818 and yet receiving copyright was predicated upon one's citizenship, Grimes's success demonstrates the variable levels and definitions of citizenship as effectively practiced in the antebellum era. Indeed, one might also argue that his claim had even more import because it was one of his very first rights exercised as a freeman. For it was only after he had, under duress, purchased his freedom and relinquished his identity as a fugitive slave, that he could he invoke any kind of citizenship rights at all.

The fact that it took at least thirteen more years after Grimes for another black person to claim a U.S. copyright on anything other than a protest pamphlet suggests, too, that we might view Grimes and his copyright as a singular aberration.[8] Other black writers (David Walker, for instance) wrote books and political pamphlets under their own names that were not copyrighted until well after Grimes's 1825 narrative had been published. And yet Grimes's 1825 copyright claim raises questions that reveal much about the historical period as well as about his individual situation. What made it possible to register that claim, for example, and what made it of interest to Grimes in the first place? How did the unfettered nature of his literary production, a book neither introduced nor framed with the imprimatur of white patrons, inform his decision? And how had his previous experience with the print trade informed his decision to compose and register his work? In the work that follows, I argue that just as his offer to skin himself was constructed to reveal the contradictions of American polity in the figurative terms most likely to reverberate with violent irony, so too his successful assertion of copyright was a calculated act that not only powerfully asserted his own claims but also made visible the hypocrisy of a nation through the legal language of textual property rights.

The Life of Grimes

Grimes's expectations for an audience and some attendant profits may have been highly ambitious in 1824, before slave narratives were a widespread print phenomenon, but they weren't unreasonable. No known book-length slave narrative, unambiguously authored by a slave, had ever been published in the United States. His experiences with the educated, socially influential, and politically active populations of New Haven and Litchfield, Connecticut, surely shaped his hopes that a story, his story, which testified to a new perspective on American freedom and citizenship, might find an audience.

For his story did demand notice: born in 1784 in Virginia, he led a peripatetic life, continually torn away from what was familiar. He was owned by at least nine masters (and was lent to, employed by, and hired out to many more than that), he was moved from place to place, and he was assigned a variety of both menial and artisan tasks, from plowing to assisting with medical procedures and from working as a coachman for a printer to, possibly, working in a print shop. At various times he was a house slave, a farmhand, a field slave, and what we might understand as an urban hustler—enslaved but nonetheless operating with some considerable autonomy in the city of Savannah, Georgia. Grimes details extensive physical and psychological suffering under cruel masters; at one point he even tries to use an ax to break his own leg to avoid working for a particularly vicious man. He is repeatedly betrayed by enslavers who keep him hostage to their hollow promises of freeing him.

His accounts of suffering do not end when, in 1815, aided by black sailors, he escaped by boat from Savannah. Fully half of his narrative thereafter consists of his experiences as a fugitive in the North—experiences that were anything but easy. He made it to New York City and from there to New Haven, Connecticut, and elsewhere, but even in the northern states (slavery wasn't fully abolished in Connecticut until 1848) he was still not free from the power of the slave system and the social problems attendant upon poverty.

Even as a fugitive, Grimes became a familiar figure around the Litchfield law school in Litchfield, Connecticut, and also at Yale University in New Haven, where he cut hair, ran errands for students, founded a "victualing shop," traded furniture, and became deeply embroiled in the often raucous world of university and city life. His barbering work, in particular, allowed him access and networking with lawyers, statesmen, academics, students, and even the governor of Connecticut. By 1823, Grimes realized that his Savannah master knew of his Connecticut whereabouts and that inquiries were being made. Grimes also knew that, if he were taken up or accosted by agents working for his master while on the streets of New Haven, he might not have the opportunity to negotiate for his freedom. Calculating that he could fare better in the smaller and more regulated community of Litchfield, Connecticut, where he had already founded some good relationships, he fled potential capture in New Haven and settled his family in Litchfield.

His strategy paid off. Although he was shortly thereafter tracked to Litchfield and forced to purchase his freedom through intermediaries, losing all his money and incurring considerable debts, the fact that he was even able to conduct such a complex transaction—which involved mortgaging his property and using various levels of sympathetic legal representation—was thanks to the remarkable political and social culture of that town. His connections with the professional community in Litchfield—home not only to the famous Beecher family from 1810 to 1826 but also home of the first law school in the United States and indubitably one of the most prominent gatherings of legal and intellectual minds in the nation—were ultimately what saved him. In Litchfield, he found prominent men who were willing to negotiate his price and arrange for the humiliating but necessary transaction.

Still shaken from nearly being returned to slavery, Grimes immediately went to work on his memoir to recoup his losses and managed to publish it early in 1825, only a few months after becoming a free man. Incredibly, considering all his disadvantages of caste and class, William Grimes's story continued for another twenty-six years. He had more children and continued to deepen his relationships and ties to the community, especially with the students of Yale. A "William Grimes" was listed as living in New Haven in the 1830 census, and again in the 1840 census, this time with several children and a woman, presumably his wife. The 1846 New Haven city directory lists no profession for him, but notes "William Grimes" is "col'd" (colored) and lives at 21 Rose Street. His early years may have been nomadic (even after his 1825 edition he reports living in various Connecticut towns such as Bridgeport, Stratford, Norwalk, Fairfield, and Stratford Point), but he evidently settled down into a poor yet somewhat more stable life in New Haven when, by 1855, he could claim eighteen children, of whom twelve were still living.

As slave narratives began to sweep the country in the wake of the growing abolitionist movement from the 1830s and beyond, Grimes tracked down an old copy of his 1825 memoir and had it reset. In 1855 he had it reprinted with some addenda concerning his later years and his family, perhaps hoping to cash in on the growing market for slave memoirs—a market that his extraordinary narrative had been just too early for the first time around. This 1855 version (see Figure 7.3), which didn't receive a copyright, seems also to have been ignored by the abolitionist press (with no references to it in any copies of major abolitionist newspapers), but its reappearance some thirty years after the original bookends, both literally and figuratively, a life that refused encasement.

A handful of obituaries marked Grimes's death in August of 1865, and they marked a triumph for him in a number of ways. On August 25, 1865, William Lloyd Garrison's Boston-based newspaper the *Liberator* noted his passing, although it didn't mention his literary career and ran the same announcement that appeared elsewhere, merely stating that

"Old Grimes is Dead"
New Haven Aug. 21
Wm. Grimes, better known as "Old Grimes" a quaint old darkey, once a slave, known to all our citizens, and to thousands of Yale College graduates, died in this city yesterday at an advanced age—probably ninety years.[9]

Grimes's beloved public persona as a "quaint old darkey" popularly known by a nursery rhyme title and repeated in such terms by the *Liberator* indicates perhaps a sad or ironic disappearance of his rebellious early reputation. Or, alternatively, perhaps it marks a triumph, signifying his successful infiltration of a self-created, unthreatening identity into print. Either way, it didn't do him the justice of his final appearance in print. That honor belonged to his most important eulogy; the one that ran in the *New Haven Daily Palladium* a day after its official boilerplate Grimes obituary had appeared. This far more intriguing follow-up notice declares:

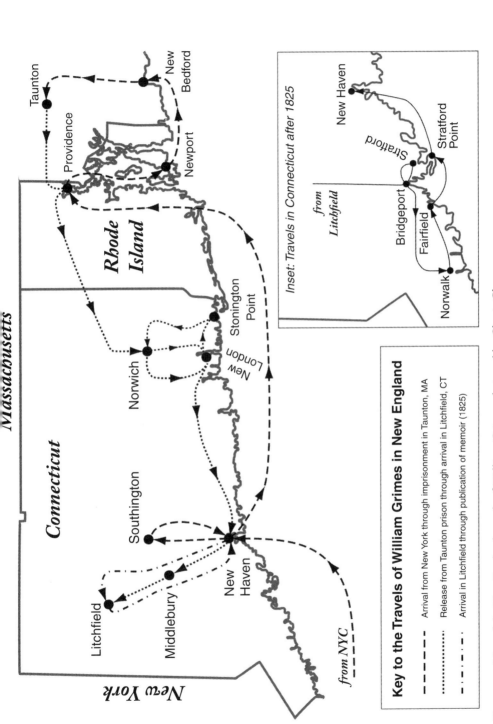

Figure 7.2. Map of the New England travels of William Grimes, designed by Charis Chapman.

Key to the Travels of William Grimes in New England

- – – – – Arrival from New York through imprisonment in Taunton, MA
- ·········· Release from Taunton prison through arrival in Litchfield, CT
- – · – · – Arrival in Litchfield through publication of memoir (1825)

Inset: Travels in Connecticut after 1825

LIFE

OF

WILLIAM GRIMES,

THE

RUNAWAY SLAVE,

BROUGHT DOWN

TO THE PRESENT TIME.

WRITTEN BY HIMSELF.

NEW HAVEN:
PUBLISHED BY THE AUTHOR.
1855.

Figure 7.3. The 1855 edition of *Life of William Grimes*. Cover page image courtesy of the research library at the Connecticut Historical Society Museum, Hartford.

Old Grimes—We have received a copy of the "Life of William Grimes," a work which thousands of New Haveners have read, and which was printed by S. H. Harris, at T. J. Stafford's establishment. It may not be uninteresting to our readers to know that the concluding portion of this narrative was written by Mr. Harris one day in the composing room. Old Grimes was sitting by, "basket in hand," furnishing the writer with the heads.

While the basket doubtless refers to the basket he was known for carrying throughout New Haven and with which he is pictured on the cover of his 1855 edition (see Figure 7.3), the word "heads" here presumably refers to what we might call headlines or perhaps organizing ideas. Thus in this notice we are directed to imagine Grimes sitting in a print shop narrating or at least shaping, his conclusion, engaged in the very bosom of the print world. We learn that "thousands" of New Haveners would have read his book and that Samuel H. Harris, who was soon to become the president of the New Haven Typographical Union, had worked closely with Grimes, a fellow veteran or denizen of print shops, to produce his final edition. Truly, this notice placed Grimes's life achievements firmly where they belonged, in the world of print production—indeed, in the composing room itself.

Bound and Printed

The distinct lack of conciliatory rhetoric marks Grimes's text as different from many of the slave narratives that later became understood as representative of the nineteenth-century experience. Indeed, his recognition in the *Liberator* and elsewhere as a "quaint old darkey" makes less sense as an accurate character description than as an indication of the extent to which the condescending culture of the radical press—to say nothing of the mainstream one—could not acknowledge his rebellious legacy. Beholden to no organization for sponsoring his life story, Grimes had no incentive to mitigate any critiques of slavery or express his loyalty to the United States. When, by the 1830s and 1840s, the abolitionist movement realized the hortatory power of first-person narratives to raise money, they became published and distributed aggressively, albeit with introductory letters or authenticating documents from prominent white abolitionists, ministers, statesmen, and, occasionally, even printers, vouching for the truthfulness of the encased narrative.[10]

This was not, however, the case with Grimes's 1825 edition or even his later edition in 1855. The sole framing device Grimes employs is not a character reference but is simply an initial statement of title deposit and the claiming of authorship, witnessed by the clerk of the District of Connecticut in 1825 (see Figure 7.1).[11] Nonetheless, when Grimes publicly establishes his right to claim the book as his own, he effectively invokes a paratextual space (in this case in the form of a copyright or depository announcement) that here may be understood as symbolic resistance to dominant conceptions of authority, authenticity, and external valuation.

Grimes's gamble that the official witnessing enacted by the imprimatur of the copyright clerk would serve him in any logistical way beyond that of adhering to legal publication formalities proved incorrect.[12] Decades later, when he wanted to reissue a copy of his narrative but had lost any complete copies of his own, the District of Connecticut clerk's office evidently did not or could not provide him with his book. Grimes was thus forced to advertise in the papers for his own memoir, so that he might be able to update it and attempt a second edition.[13] While he was eventually able to obtain a surviving copy of the 1825 edition in this manner and was thus able to update it for a second edition in 1855, the incident provided yet another bitter example of how even his own book proved elusive to him—a fact consistent with many other incidents he recounts about his dealings with paper.[14] It is difficult to say precisely how this initial self-publication was arranged, but his hands-on involvement is certainly a possibility. He discusses paying the printer in New Haven, but he also had knowledge of the print world beyond cursory reading and writing, and it seems likely he was able to employ a printer with at least an informed sense of the trade at hand, if not a more direct involvement in the production or printing of the text. And even if he wasn't involved in the production of his own material text, his self-publication and assertion of authorship in the District of Connecticut clerk's office suggests a considerable familiarity with how the world of print needed to be publicly negotiated.

This knowledge may have come in part from his early experiences in Savannah, Georgia. As a teenager, young Grimes was hired out for a few months by his master to work for Philip D. Woolhopter.[15] Whether or not Grimes was literate at that point or involved in some aspect of typesetting at this stage, we can still legitimately speculate that a strong young man capable of pulling down a press iron might well have lent a hand from time to time in the pressroom. When we consider that Woolhopter, like many early printers, ran a variety of jobs and doubtless had periods of heavy orders, it seems certain that Grimes had many opportunities to become familiar with the language and mechanics of printing regardless of how involved he may or may not have been with the pressroom.[16]

There is only slight evidence about the literary matter Grimes could have come in contact with while working for Woolhopter. We do know that Woolhopter was the official printer for the seat of Georgia's government and the *Columbian Museum and Savannah Advertiser* newspaper (which regularly ran advertisements for slave auctions and for runaways) and also printed sermons and other sorts of religious pamphlets in Savannah.[17] Moreover during the time Grimes was with Woolhopter, the *Columbian Museum* specifically advertised a stationery store also set up by Woolhopter that marketed pens, paper, and a variety of reference books and novels, so certainly Grimes was surrounded by the commerce and discourse of the print trade. In the years preceding Grimes's presence in the print shop, numerous titles of interest were published by Woolhopter, including the *Doctrine of Perpetual Bondage Reconciled with Infinite Justice of God*, written by John Beck and published in 1800, and the complete collection of Georgia state laws and supplementary federal documents, including the Declaration of Independence and the Constitution, that were printed in one volume in 1802. While Grimes wasn't with the print shop during those precise years, he could not have been oblivious to the irony of slave labor being used to produce titles, texts, newspapers, and legal documents promoting slaves' own bondage. Thus the manner in which he framed his life story as one shaped by the literal and figurative presence of texts adds a dimension of self-conscious argument about his own presence as an objectified subject in uneasy relationship to a subjectified object.

To be clear: we cannot know if he read or participated specifically in printing and binding books promoting his own bondage. But we do know that he worked for a printer who made his living upon the labor of people who were forced collaborators in their own oppression. The comforting reconciliation that author John Beck offered in his doctrine justifying slavery might have provided very strange comfort indeed to the slaves who worked for that printer. The culpable language of "book" and "slave" in a book like Beck's *Doctrine*, which promoted the Good Book as irrefutable textual evidence justifying slavery, would be hard for any man in bondage to ignore. Similarly, the irony of slaves printing government documents that included the Declaration of Independence and collections of Georgia state laws regulating slavery would have been obvious to anyone forced to work on their production. When scholars seek to define what early black print culture might have been, they would be wise to expand their definitions to consider the culture discourse of print in which even illiterate slaves would have participated.

Grimes's ability to secure copyright in 1825 is the result of inconsistent enforcement of federal regulations, to be sure. Legal cases in Connecticut and elsewhere abounded in the 1820s and 1830s that ruled variously about whether free black people could be "citizens."[18] And perhaps we could view his copyright registration as a fortunate confluence of his light coloring with the happenstance of a good day with a sympathetic clerk. As Joanna Brooks argues elsewhere in this collection, books "depend on social movements to survive" (see Chapter 2).[19] The fact that copies of his 1825 edition were lost even to Grimes underscores Brooks's point about a necessary support system. The historical circumstance that demands note here, though, is that while Grimes didn't produce his memoir during the decades of abolitionist publishing and thus it nearly disappeared from view, his ability to produce it at all, much less his confidence in copyrighting it, were nonetheless the product of a social world that was increasingly open to the democratization of practices hitherto restricted to elites. Grimes was familiar with the cultural and intellectual worlds of New Haven and Litchfield and was aware how individuals he had access to were well placed to subscribe to or distribute his work. The growth of print and book culture in the republican culture of Savannah, much less the printed dissemination of laws done by the very printer who had held him, must have allowed Grimes to imagine that he himself could someday harness print to his own ends.

At various points in the 1825 edition and even more so in his 1855 edition, Grimes identifies himself as a citizen in a reference that may seem obscure now but that would have been commonly recognized. Each time he referred to himself as "Old Grimes" or each time he cited the song "Old Grimes," he was claiming a legitimized presence in the nation's history, for the song was, as he informs us, to be sung to the popular tune of "John Gilpin Was a Citizen."[20] For a black man and ex-slave to assert citizenship was an audacious act even if done with some facetiousness via musical referencing. But for Grimes, who asserted citizenship rights by registering his copyright claim, it was in keeping with the multivalenced textual and literal poses he assumed; he might be an ex-slave and a trickster, for sure, but he was like John Gilpin, defiantly a citizen.

William Grimes's narrative is a synecdoche of the entire slave-narrative tradition that was to follow. As he saw it, his text made flesh and his flesh made text. While we might see his memoir primarily as an early launching point for the narrative tradition of slave memoirs that came into full form by the mid-nineteenth century, that wouldn't give Grimes the full credit that he deserves. He set out the story of his life as an individual with all of his most human flaws and virtues on display and he did so via the medium of the book, an object Joseph Rezek describes as singularly placed to demonstrate "the disjunction between racial identity and cultural capital." (see Chapter 1). As if that weren't enough, Grimes registered the title of his story as "The Life of William Grimes, the Runaway Slave," but perhaps we should understand the titular emphasis as being placed not upon "slave" but instead upon his own name, claimed and copyrighted at great cost: "William Grimes." He might not be able to fully claim the American identity promised by the Constitution, but by constructing a narrative and asserting his a copyright, he effectively claimed a citizenship that would enable him to dissolve constitutional bindings.

CHAPTER 8

Bottles of Ink and Reams of Paper: *Clotel,* Racialization, and the Material Culture of Print

JONATHAN SENCHYNE

Stereotypical

William Wells Brown carried stereotypes with him. So we learn in an 1849 letter from William Lloyd Garrison to a British abolitionist who had inquired about the American Anti-Slavery Society's role in Brown's English lecture circuit. Brown carried letters of introduction and other credentials from influential Americans, but he went to England a free agent, relying on the generosity of friends and book sales to pay his way. "Mr. Brown does not go out officially from any anti-slavery society, simply because he prefers to stand alone responsible for what he may say and do," Garrison replied. "Nor does he go out to be a pecuniary burden or to make himself an unwelcome guest to any one; but he hopes that, by the sale of his Narrative, (the stereotype plates of which he takes with him,) he shall be able to meet such expenses as may arise beyond what the hospitality of friends may cover."[1] Existing interpretive frameworks for early African American literature tend to privilege literacy and writing in the attainment of agency and subjectivity, exploring how, William L. Andrews writes, "the *writing* of autobiography [is] in some way self-liberating."[2] As Garrison explains, however, Brown's freedom in Europe from the reaches of kidnappers and from the management of white abolitionists alike depended on his relation to the material conditions of print production as much as it did his own literacy. The stereotype plates in Brown's traveling case remind us that producing oneself as a free subject in print and in life is embedded within a set of material textual practices— practices that are (as the double meaning of stereotype suggests) also constitutive in processes of racialization.

Contrast Brown's carrying stereotype plates of his narrative as a sign and source of his independence with an event Brown recounts in the narrative itself. He describes an incident that occurred while enslaved in Saint Louis, during the period when he was hired out to Elijah Lovejoy, the publisher of the *Saint Louis Times* who would, years later, become an abolitionist printer and famous First Amendment martyr. Brown recounts how he was often sent to the office of another newspaper to retrieve forms of standing type and on one occasion was stopped and harassed by local youth. "Once while returning to the office with type, I was attacked by several large boys, sons of slaveholders, who pelted me with snow-balls. Having the heavy form of type in my hands, I could not make my escape by running; so I laid down the type and gave them battle. They gathered around me, pelting me with stones and sticks, until they overpowered me, and would have captured me, if I had not resorted to my heels. Upon my retreat, they took possession of the type; and what to do to regain it I could not devise."[3] Just before this passage, Brown notes that his first acquaintance with literacy was made while working at Lovejoy's press, probably while sorting or setting type. "I am chiefly indebted to [Lovejoy], and to my employment in the printing office, for what little learning I obtained in slavery."[4] To perform basic tasks in the shop Brown would have needed, at minimum, the ability to recognize basic letter shapes in order to sort pieces of type in the cases.

The beginning of literacy, commonly associated with the beginning of freedom in nineteenth-century African American narrative, does seem to stem from Brown's access to letters, but it is an alphabet in the type cases before it is an alphabet in the mind. And while Brown's literacy grows out of the material practice of print production, it is the awkward heft of these materials that encumbers him physically. As an enslaved person, Brown's movement is already restricted to the circuit between two newspaper offices, but the wooden form, furniture, quoins, and leaden type only frustrates his "escape" and exposes him to threat of "capture." Compared to frames of type, the stereotype is freeing. Of course, I am intentionally stressing the similarities and differences between stereotype printing plates and stereotypical representations in order to highlight the links between technologies of print and technologies of racialization. A stereotype plate is created from a mold of moveable type, producing a lightweight replica in a single piece of metal; while the thousands of pieces of movable type are redistributed for new uses, the stereotype can be reprinted over and again, unchanged.[5] Thus Brown can carry his stereotypes across the Atlantic and around England without remaining tethered to a publisher or a particular print shop's type. This mobility is documented in an edition of Brown's narrative from 1849 that lists Charles Gilpin as publisher and London as place of publication on the title page, yet on the very next page we find: "Printed, chiefly from the American Stereotype Plates, by Webb and Chapman, Great Brunswick-street, Dublin."[6]

This essay argues that greater attention to the significance of the material culture of print, especially in early African American print culture, shows how technologies of racialization emerge in conjunction with technologies of printed words and images. The stereotype is perhaps the most familiar case. In one sense it offers quick reproduction of legible text, and in another it offers quick reproduction of a legible social type. In the rest of this essay, I examine how another technology of legibility, black/white dualism, structures both print legibility and racial legibility. This essay proposes that the material culture of whiteness in antebellum print culture participates in nineteenth-century racial formation by modeling how whiteness is to be seen while unseen, providing the structural backdrop against which marks or types become legible.[7] I will focus on the materiality of paper (and to a lesser extent, ink) because, as Brown himself suggests in the opening sentences of the 1867 edition of *Clotel*, these materials transmit the author's writing about racial categorizations of blackness and whiteness while they also shape the *sensus communis* about whiteness, blackness, and structures of legibility and visibility.[8] Reading print relies on making meaning out of the difference between black and white, and in the antebellum period where black ink and white paper were racially coded, the black/white dualism underwriting print legibility further naturalized black/white racial dualism by implying the possibility of "reading" bodies in relation to one another. Finally, I turn to "The Death of Clotel," a wood engraving providing the only illustration of Brown's novel's namesake, as a moment when the materiality of the text, and the racialized meaning of whiteness in paper, forces a foreclosure of the novel's exploration of racial ambiguity by "filling in" Clotel's face with ink, signifying racial content instead of the absence implied in white paper (see Figure 8.1).

Figure 8.1. "The Death of Clotel," the only illustration of the novel's eponymous character, was printed in each bound edition of *Clotel*. Courtesy of the American Antiquarian Society.

On display in such a moment is print's role in the construction and maintenance of dualism as a technology for making sense out of difference both in
print culture and antebellum racial discourse.[9]

Black and White and Read All Over

The minstrel riddle "What's black and white and re(a)d all over? (Answer: the
newspaper)" turns on the multiple meanings of white and black and is complicated by the homophonic "red"/"read." It is a racially inflected joke, not
only in its formal use of minstrelsy's comic indirection but also in the way it
trades in the racialized meanings of color. The demand to think these colors
together is frustrated by the assumption that a body is ultimately identified
only by one color, or racial identification, "all over."[10] The resolution arrives
in the replacement of racial significations with a printed thing that can, without contradiction, be black and white simultaneously. Titles of scholarship in
African American literature that announce a focus on American literature
"in black and white" also play on the heart of this riddle. Such play retraces
the historical process in which, through the printed page, black and white
became sensible as binary opposites. Print provided a binary black/white
structure that would later be used as a key form for the articulation of racial
difference.

The emergence of the printed letter and image between the fifteenth and
sixteenth centuries precipitated the partitioning of black and white from the
domain of the full color spectrum, setting them in their now-familiar opposition. The visual experience of the codex shifted from the medieval manuscript culture's rich illuminations to modern print culture's black/white
contrast. John Calvin, for example, saw in the stark contrast of black print
against white paper the model for an aesthetic in which "the most beautiful
ornament in the church must be the word of God." For the "people of the
Book," the word of God appeared in black and white. Michel Pastoureau
places ink, paper, and the engraved image at the center of a modern revolution in perception:

> It was the circulation of the printed book and engraved images
> that . . . led to black and white becoming colors 'apart.' And even
> more than the book itself, it was undoubtedly the engraved and

printed image—in black ink on white paper—that played the primary role. All or almost all medieval images were polychromatic. The great majority of images in the modern period, circulated in and outside of books, were black and white. This signified a cultural revolution of considerable scope not only in the domain of knowledge but also in the domain of sensibility.[11]

The printed book, then, quite literally redefined "black" and "white." According to the *Oxford English Dictionary*, in 1594 "white" began to mean "blank space between certain letters or types . . . space left blank between words and lines," and four years later, "black" began to signify both "writing fluid" and "characters upon . . . paper; writing."[12] Black/white dualism is assumed in these definitions: white is sensible between black marks, and black against paper, which is white by definition.

If the black/white binary of print is an analogue of the black/white binary of race, then it seems important to ask how much cultural work this analogue performed. In other words, does the material contrast between black ink and the white page really have significant meaning with respect to the ideological contrast between black and white racially identified bodies in the period during which Brown was writing? The archives of paper mills, stationers, and publishers reveal the degree to which professionals of the material text were occupied with the production and preservation of whiteness. Professional roles in the print shop such as the "printer's devil" were part of the daily practice of maintaining the purity of paper from staining ink, and even a surprising amount of children's literature was produced to discipline children's experience of the page. The paper industry's preoccupation with and protection of whiteness as a valuable commodity cannot be seen in isolation from the production of what George Lipsitz calls the "possessive investment in whiteness."[13] Print legibility does indeed require contrast, but the adoption of whiteness as a central metaphor makes paper inextricable from the processes by which blackness becomes difference and whiteness the unmarked center. In what follows, I offer a range of contexts for the use of whiteness in the paper industry, suggest its convergences with racial discourse, and read how these convergences are at work in parts of *Clotel*.

In his 1814 *American Artist's Manual*, James Cutbush states a fact about papermaking so well known that it seems axiomatic in its presentation: "I will suppose that the object of the manufacturer is to obtain paper of a beautiful white."[14] Despite actual differences in the color of finished product, the paper industry adopted white and brown as signifiers of quality loosely related to appearance. The idea of white as pure, unmarked, and beautiful lent itself well to the purposes of an industry in search of an unobtrusive background that contrasted with black ink. "White" was adopted to signify paper with a suitably light and refined surface for printing, and "brown" to signify darker and coarser paper for wrapping and other uses.[15] Until 1867, paper in the United States was still primarily produced from cloth rags, a perpetually scarce resource. Because of the further scarcity of rags considered clean enough to make white paper for printing, both white paper and the "white rags" used to make it commanded high prices.

Writing to Boston papermakers Tileston and Hollingsworth, one salesman explicitly linked whiteness to quality and the promise of great profit: "If you continue to send in as *good* an article as the first 50 reams, I have a prospect of selling a considerable amount of it. . . . I hope you will keep up the quality, make it as *white* as possible."[16] But white paper wasn't necessarily visually white; "white" served as a metaphor for refinement and lightness in tone. The way whiteness functions in white paper begins to look like the function of whiteness under racial dualism: it is representative of supposed refinement and desirability and only loosely associated with the visual experience of a certain color.[17]

The first order of business in the papermaking process was to distinguish between rags that could be used to make "white" paper from those that would make "brown." This was known not only to millworkers or printers, but also to the general public. The separation and appraisal of rags was taught even to children and linked to literacy itself. For example, in an 1837 version of "Jack and the Beanstalk," an illiterate Jack does not find a giant in the clouds, but rather a paper mill, a type foundry, printing press, bindery, and a schoolhouse. While at the paper mill, Jack joins a group of children working in the rag pile: "[Jack] found himself in a room where there were a great many boys and girls sitting round, and picking among huge piles of cloth of every size, shape, and color, and as they picked they sang,—Pick, pick the black from the white, Assort the whole bundle before it is night. . . . The mill and the water and man with care have turned dirty rags into paper fair." Jack selects white from black through equation with dirtiness and fairness. The story's rhyming refrain, "pick, pick the black from the white," shows that metaphors of dualism structured the perception of rags and the paper they

would become, despite whatever actual color the linens were. Upon returning to his mother, Jack says, "I should like to know what they are going to do
with all this white paper," and later learns about writing that distinguishing
black from white is also the most basic skill required in the acquisition of
literacy: "I see some strange-looking things of black on a white board . . . but
I do not know what they mean."[18]

The professional practices of the print shop were shaped by the need to
maintain white paper's virginal state, keeping ink away except for intentional
marks. Shops were set up such that workers who touched ink never touched
paper. The apprentice who applied ink to the type and who touched the
leaden forms was called the "printer's devil," a "term [that] originated in reference to the fact that the young apprentice would inevitably become stained
black from the printing ink."[19] Paper mills and print shops were structured
by metaphors of purity/deviance and cleanliness/filth constructed and circulated in the service of preserving white from black.

One papermaker, however, suggested that the orientation toward whiteness distracted from making the best quality paper, showing the preference
for whiteness to be ideological, not functional. The focus on cleanliness and
whiteness of rags and paper is misplaced, he claimed, and the rage for whiteness predominated other important qualities: "The degrees of fineness and
whiteness, distinguished with little care, are thought to be the only objects of
importance; whereas the hardness and softness, the being more or less worn,
are very essential in this selection."[20] Instead of obsessing over color as a de-
terminant of quality, papermakers are here urged to make stronger paper by
selecting rags for their texture, not color. Some readers even took a contrary
position on what made for the most legible paper color, arguing that the contrast of white and black was painful to the eye and that brown paper was superior. "Brown paper preserves the eye better than white," argued one reader,
"and when authors and readers agree to be wise, we shall avoid printing on a
glaring white paper."[21]

These indicate that white color in paper was less a utilitarian need than a
reflection of the importance of whiteness in the antebellum imagination.[22]
Toni Morrison suggests that Herman Melville, when writing *Moby-Dick*,
"was overwhelmed by the philosophical and metaphysical inconsistencies of
an extraordinary and unprecedented idea that had its fullest manifestation in
his own time in his own country, and that . . . idea was the successful assertion of whiteness as ideology."[23] In a similar deployment, the desire to have

paper "as *white* as possible" made papermakers, printers, and readers into actors in the production of this pervasive ideology of whiteness in the nineteenth century.

Bottles of Ink and Reams of Paper

The widespread and repeated experience of ink and paper established black and white in the binary opposition that gave substance and support to the logic of racial dualism that dominated social and legal understandings of race in the nineteenth-century United States inhabited by African American writers such as William Wells Brown. The reliance of racial discourse on the binary black/white color metaphor—and the critique of this racial binary—is a key subject in much of Brown's work.

Clotel was first published in London in 1853 while Brown was on the aforementioned European lecture circuit. Tracing the lives of women (Clotel, Althesa, and their daughters) who are descended from Thomas Jefferson and an enslaved woman named Currer (a thinly veiled Sally Hemings), Brown devotes much of the novel to parsing the different forms of whiteness that these figures simultaneously do and do not inhabit. Clotel and Althesa are described in the novel as white women when whiteness refers to a tone of skin, but as the novel unfolds, their legal and social status as blacks under enslavement reveals itself, like the logic of hypodescent, as prevailing over all else. Though Clotel's light skin color and refined manners allow her temporary inhabitance of white domesticity, she and her daughter are abandoned by the white man who, though he has promised to be a husband and father, cannot finally overcome the legal and social structures that make him their owner. After Althesa's death from fever, her daughters learn of their "true" racial status and are sold into sexual slavery to pay debts. In this way, the novel both bends binaries by indicating how unstable the chromatic metaphors for race are and explores how antebellum U.S. practices forcibly insisted that racial legibility be maintained by settling racial identification into the binary relation of black and white.[24]

As critics in the field of race studies have shown, racial binaries are unstable and socially constructed, yet nonetheless are embedded in legal and social discourse. Addressing the rigidity of racial and symbolic dualisms compared to the slipperiness of the visual, Richard Dyer writes that "white as a symbol, especially when paired with black, seems more stable than white as a hue or skin tone." "White as a skin colour," he explains, "is [an] unstable, unbounded . . . category," a "category that is internally variable and unclear at the edges."[25] As a symbol adopted by law, however, white is, as Cheryl Harris describes, more rigidly defined: a legal construct that "defined and affirmed critical aspects of identity (who is white); of privilege (what benefits accrue to its status); and of property (what *legal* entitlements arise from that status)."[26] Brown never misses an opportunity to complicate supposed congruities between the visual and legal syntaxes of race implied in the terms "black" and "white." Characters dwell in the spaces between apparent skin color and the legal/social privilege metaphorized through racial color. Clotel has a "complexion as white as" white men and features "as finely defined as any" white women. Clotel appears to be "Anglo-Saxon," even "Real Albino," which stresses the congruence between racial whiteness and extreme visual whiteness, while also confusing that congruence by locating it in Clotel's "black" body.[27] Althesa is "as white as most white women in a southern clime," but "was born a slave."[28] Brown turns a phrase that puts white next to *white*, elegantly demonstrating the difference between visual and legal registers of race.

Despite Brown's interest in deconstructing a black/white racial binary, as a writer and printer, he traded in a material world structured by a black/white binary. And indeed, success in that world—printing—depended, one might say, on his ability to present ideas in black and white. Brown seems attuned to the contradiction that his work as a racial theorist constantly interrogated the decipherability of whiteness and blackness in opposition to one another, but that as a writer/printer his work would always depend upon this very structure. Yet, in the final revision of his novel in 1867, Brown seems to capitalize on this irony. In order to theorize the difference between print legibility and racial legibility, Brown figures printing, the putting of black ink onto white paper, as racial intermixture, describing "Quadroon women" as products of ink and paper.

These lines open the 1867 edition:

For many years the South has been noted for its beautiful Quadroon women. Bottles of ink, and reams of paper, have been used to portray the "finely-cut and well-moulded features," the "silken-curls," the "dark and brilliant eyes," the "splendid forms," the "fascinating smiles," and "accomplished manners" of these impassioned and voluptuous daughters of the two races.[29]

As Brown suggests, "mulatta" narratives were quite popular, and one in particular rewrote the limits of the possible in the book industry.[30] "One Hundred thousand volumes issued in eight weeks!" exclaimed the *New York Independent* on the publication of Harriet Beecher Stowe's *Uncle Tom's Cabin*, "The demand continues without abatement. . . . It has taken 3000 reams of medium paper, weighing 30 lbs. to the ream—90,000 lbs. of paper."[31] But, *Clotel*'s final opening passage does more than highlight the expanding scale of print production. Brown opens with print production in order to theorize the concept of legibility. Where earlier editions of *Clotel* begin with a discussion of racial intermixture under slavery, this one discusses the production of representations of racial intermixture. The first edition begins with a description of an actual population of people, described as a "fearful increase of half whites, most of whose fathers are slaveowners, and their mothers slaves."[32] In 1867, however, white fathers and black mothers are replaced with black ink and white paper, and the defining characteristics of "Quadroon women" are put under quotation: "silken-curls," "dark and brilliant eyes," and so on. Brown shifts from discussing the birth of actual mixed-race people to the production of the literary trope of the mulatta that over "many years" of "portray[al]" has become synonymous with these features. As Ann duCille has written, this passage seems concerned with the problem of representation, or the hypervisibility of the mulatta trope in antebellum popular culture, and that Brown is unlikely, for example, to have uncritically figured mixed-race women as "voluptuous." Even the replacement of "half whites" with "Quadroon women" recalls "The Quadroons," the 1842 short story by Lydia Maria Child out of which Brown built *Clotel*. Brown suggests that racial mixture is most legible, then, as a set of literary tropes as the appearance of "silken-curls," "dark . . . eyes," and "voluptuous" bodies immediately orients readers to a set of standard characteristics and plots.[33] These figures are mixtures of black and white both because they have "fathers [who are] slaveowners, and . . . mothers [who are] slaves," and because they are formed from "bottles of ink, and reams of paper." It is only in print, however, in assembling lists of features like "silken-curls," that these figures are legible within a structure of black/white dualism, for, as Brown emphasizes in *Clotel*, the mixture of "black" and "white" in mixed-race people does not produce the legibly "black" body demanded by the laws and logics of hypodescent.

If the portrayal of mixed-race figures like Clotel involves the mixture of black ink and white paper, then Brown's 1867 introduction also begs a practical question: how does an illustrator visually represent racial ambiguity when the tools at hand are contrasting fields of white paper and black ink? The question is particularly pertinent in the case of *Clotel* because the only illustration of Brown's eponymous heroine, "The Death of Clotel" (see Figure 8.1), contradicts the author's repeated descriptions of the character's light skin and the importance of her whiteness in the narrative. Clotel looks, Brown writes, "as white as . . . those who . . . wish to become her purchasers," yet, in the engraving she is visibly darker than the men surrounding her. This disconnect between the verbal and visual text has not escaped scholars. Russ Castronovo, for example, notes that "even though Brown repeatedly states that Clotel . . . is so close to appearing white that she can pass as an Italian or Spanish gentleman, the illustration darkly shades her face."[34] It is not uncommon for the visual and verbal texts within a work to create tension; "The Death of Clotel" presents what W. J. T. Mitchell calls "image/text," or "relations of the visual and verbal" that create a "problematic gap, cleavage, or rupture in representation."[35] In this instance, the rupture arises out of the link between black/white dualism in print legibility and racial legibility. Brown's deconstruction of dualism threatens to eradicate the system of black/presence and white/absence through which engravers make meaning.

Mixed-race figures break down the false logic of black/white dualism, presenting a problem for artists whose renderings are dependent upon engraving as a practice of presence and absence that cannot easily mix black and white. What engravings, or "finely-cut" portrayals, like "The Death of Clotel" reveal in their attempts to depict mixed-race women is the problem of racial presence and absence, the idea of blackness as raced and whiteness as normalized, neutral, or transparent, which racial theorists ultimately expose as false. For the illustrator, though, these structures of race and legibility constitute the very form of engraving. In wood engraving, the whiteness of the page literally *is* the racial whiteness of legally white figures who go unmarked in two senses: their faces are not inked, and they are not generally understood to be "raced." The whiteness of the page makes type legible at the same time as it naturalizes the social structure of whiteness as absence, making race appear "present" on the body of its others. Working out this binary on the surface of the body was even part of an engraver's training (see Figure 8.2).

Michael Gaudio argues that instead of "explain[ing] away the physical substance of the engraving as the neutral agent of symbolic meaning," literary scholarship must grant attention "to the peculiar materiality of the engraver's art." Engravings have "a syntax," according to Gaudio, a system of meaning making constructed through "the visible sign of a wood-engraver's

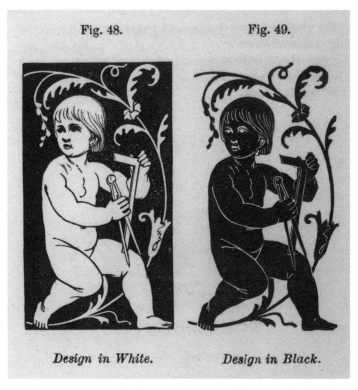

Figure 8.2. "Design in White" and "Design in Black," from the *Hand-book of Wood Engraving*, by William A. Emerson (East Douglas, Mass.: C. J. Batcheller, 1876). Courtesy of the American Antiquarian Society.

concentrated efforts with his tools," the "insistently present, insistently interfering, insistently *material* lines of the engraver."[36] The material lines marking Clotel's face actualize the racial coding of the whiteness of paper and the blackness of ink, rendering Clotel's racial status legible by making it readable on the surface her skin (see Figure 8.3).

"The Death of Clotel" was originally engraved for the first edition of the novel published by Partridge and Oakey, the same Protestant press that a year before had issued one of the first illustrated London editions of *Uncle Tom's Cabin*. In sharing a publisher, Brown's and Stowe's novels also had a common illustrator, Henry Anelay, and an engraver, James Johnston, a team recognizable enough to attract top billing alongside Stowe on the edition's

Figure 8.3. The face of Clotel. From "The Death of Clotel," detail. Courtesy of the American Antiquarian Society.

title page.[37] Their images may even have surpassed Stowe's prose in the eyes of literary tastemakers:

> All criticism on the subject of the story of Uncle Tom is superfluous; the public have settled the matter effectually by accepting the book as a sort of anti-slavery Bible not to be spoken against. The question among publishers now is, who can sell the best edition for the money? So far as real art is concerned in the illustrations, the volume before us, to our thinking, answers that question most satisfactorily. The designs of Anelay, engraved by Johnston, which adorn this edition, are alone worth the money it sells for.[38]

The pair of well-known illustrators applied the same representational strategies in their depictions of both Eliza Harris and Clotel (see Figure 8.4).

Anelay and Johnston's Clotel and Eliza each have faces similarly marked by striations designed to index a racial difference located in "blood" but not skin color. Not all engravers approached Eliza similarly. George Cruikshank, for example, does not use such lines to mark Eliza's complexion. Anelay and Johnston's lines try to register a "tint" between white and black, both visually and racially. "At one time, cross-hatching was much employed in representing flesh, which is now generally cut in tints, with white lines crossing," instructed one manual for engravers. "The lines that are [not cut away] receive ink in printing, and the lines that are cut out appear white. The quality of the plain tint depends on the evenness of the lines, which make it both black and

Figure 8.4. The faces of Eliza Harris and Harry Harris. From "Eliza, with Her Child, Escaping from Haley," detail. The year before illustrating the first edition of *Clotel*, Johnston and Anelay illustrated Harriet Beecher Stowe's *Uncle Tom's Cabin; or, The History of a Christian Slave* (London: Partridge and Oakey, 1852). Courtesy of the American Antiquarian Society.

white."[39] Anelay and Johnston's attempt to present Clotel and Eliza in "both black and white" goes beyond Brown's and Stowe's texts in order to present racial nonwhiteness as always legible on the surface of their white bodies and the surface of the white paper they inhabit. This poetics of racial representation in which "color" must be registered on the surface of the skin reflects popular thinking about the visibility of race.[40]

It is useful here to recall how strongly white paper was associated with meanings of whiteness that overlap with racial significance. A poem attributed to Benjamin Franklin demonstrates the extent to which white paper was associated with white femininity, the status ultimately denied Clotel. Franklin's "Paper: A Poem" explicitly connects white paper and white femininity. Reprinted in the popular oratorical schoolbook *The Columbian Orator*, the poem was widely circulated during the first half of the nineteenth century. Expanding on John Locke's comparison of the human subject to paper ("white Paper receives any characters"),[41] the poem organizes social types as types of paper in varying degrees of quality and purpose: "Men are as various; and, if right I scan, / Each sort of *paper* represents some *man*."

SOME wit of old,—such wits of old there were,—
Whole hints show'd meaning, whose allusions, care,
By one brave stroke, to mark all human kind,
Called clear blank paper every infant mind;
Where still, as opening sense her dictates wrote,
Fair virtue put a seal, or vice a blot.

After several stanzas classifying different social types according to different kinds of paper (fools/foolscap and so on), the reader comes to a stanza that aligns fine white paper with white femininity:

Observe the maiden, innocently sweet,
She's fair *white paper*, an unsullied sheet;
On which the happy man, whom fate ordains,
May write his *name*, and take her for his pains.[42]

The clean white sheet signals virtuous white femininity: the virginity, inno-cence, and purity of spirit that awaits the writing of a man's name in marriage and sexual consummation. Locke's tabula rasa takes on a sense of feminine passivity as the clean white sheet awaits the receipt of a man's "character."[43]

Despite her appearance as a white woman in the texts, Clotel is denied even the visual status of nineteenth-century white womanhood. That intersec-tion of race and gender depends on ideas of racial unmarkedness and spiritual/genetic purity largely denied to mixed-race women, and incompatible with the metaphorical construction of paper most clearly articulated when Franklin equates the "unsullied sheet" of "fair white paper" to "the maiden, innocently sweet." The material lines of the engraver externalize the racial blackness forbidding Clotel from entering into legal marriage with Horatio Green and indexing the sexual history of her parentage that disallows her ever having been a properly "unsullied sheet."

Given the senses of purity, beauty, refinement, and even overt white femininity sedimented on the surface page, it then seems like no surprise that Anelay and Johnston cannot, within these racial logics, let the whiteness of the page equal the whiteness of Clotel's face described in the text. What hap-pens on the surface of Clotel's skin here becomes inextricable from the pro-cesses of wood engraving. The wood engraver works by cutting away wood where the "white" should show, preserving the whiteness of the page from the impression of ink. Wood left raised accepts the ink and impresses it into the paper. The wood engraver, then, works by producing absences, cutting away voids that create the "invisible" whites that structure the visible blacks. Following Dyer and Lipsitz, from a visual standpoint, race, especially when articulated in color metaphors, is commonly held to be a "content" or "presence" that nonwhites carry on the surface of their bodies, a content that becomes legible as racial difference against the "background" of whiteness that claims for itself the privilege of invisibility or absence.[44] This describes the same structure through which wood engravings negotiate the figure/ground relationship: a passive, yet structuring whiteness makes visible the black marks that contrast it. But the work of the engraver actively produces these absences, just like the papermaker engages in great effort to produce a whiteness that purposefully fades out of sight. On the surface of the engraved woodblock, areas carved away (absence) "print" white, maintaining the whiteness of the page, whereas areas left raised (presence) "print" black because, they accept ink from the press marking the surface of the page. Illustrating Clotel "as white as most of those . . . waiting to become her purchasers" would have required Anelay and Johnston to cut away the wood within the borders of the figure's face, creating a void, or making actual the ideology of whiteness as the absence of marking. Indeed, this is how the faces of the white men surrounding her are crafted. Leaving the wood in place to transfer ink to Clotel materially creates racial marking as presence, a "face" filled with wood on the engraving block and color on the page. Anelay and Johnston's illustrations of Clotel and Eliza demonstrate the extent to which the ideology of a racially marked blackness and a racially unmarked whiteness, reinforced in the legal institutions of "blood," guided the work of engravers for whom whiteness was literal absence and blackness literal presence.

In *Pictorial Victorians*, Julia Thomas suggests that black figures were perfect subjects for Victorian engravers seeking to demonstrate their talent:

> At a time when wood engraving was the most popular form of illustration, the reproduction of the Negro provided an opportunity for the artist and engraver to demonstrate their skills. The technique of cutting away the white parts of the image on the block and leaving the part to be inked in relief seemed designed specifically for the representation of whites. The skin could be cut away more or less in its entirety, while the inked lines served to demarcate the features. . . . Manipulating the wood engraving process and leaving

all the skin in relief and therefore black, however, not only blurred the distinction between outline and content, but could obliterate the features, making the appearance of the figure too dark. The solution was to produce tonal effects by cross-hatching, cutting the wood between sets of crossed lines. . . . Such techniques . . . tested the skill and patience of the engraver, but they also showed wood engraving at its best, giving the Negro more visual impact than his white counterpart.[45]

Thomas's reading fails in its assumption that there is a discernable visual difference between "the Negro" and "whites." The image most resonant with this reading is that of Eva sitting in Uncle Tom's lap, one white and one black in visual contrast. As Brown and several other nineteenth-century writers (including Stowe) point out, however, visually identifying the legal construct of "the Negro" by complexion is not viable. Illustrating mixed-race figures that complicate the notion of racial dualism pressures both the technological limits of engraving and the tendency to equate racial status with the presence of "color." Perhaps, when he wrote the opening to the final revision of *Clotel*, Brown meant to emphasize that his title character challenged the duochromatic media through which she had been represented since the novel's first edition. Victorian engravers may have felt that "the Negro" figure was a showcase for the richness and possibility of the art, but once the dualisms that premise the form come under question, the figure of the mulatta collapses the binaries upon which wood engravings are encoded.

In "The Quadroon's Home," a chapter in *Clotel* that strategically edits Child's "The Quadroons," Brown repeats Child's characterization of Clotel's daughter, Mary, as an "octoroon." "Their first-born was named Mary, and her complexion was still lighter than her mother. Indeed she was not darker than other white children. As the child grew older, it more and more resembled its mother. The iris of her large dark eye had the melting mezzotinto, which remains the last vestige of African ancestry."[46] Though Mary has the "dark and brilliant eyes" of her mother, she is imagined outside of the black/white ink/paper dualisms. Mezzotint is a different process of engraving that produces more refined shades of gray than wood or copper engraving. Rather than black lines and white lines, mezzotint creates its effects in "tones" and "halftones." In place of wood engraving's rigid separations, the mezzotint "melts" between shades. In the illustration this use of the term "mezzotint" imagines, then, that Mary's whiteness can be represented outside the black/

white binary of the printed page. In place of white and black are shades of darkness and lightness. Capable of producing more mimetic representations of skin tone than the black/white dualism of wood engraving's presences and absences, the "melting mezzotinto" seems better suited to work outside the boundaries of a racial dualism never adequate to represent the people it nonetheless inscribed. William Wells Brown worked in this material world of print, a world saturated with ideological meanings related to racial difference. *Clotel* works in, through, and against these materialities and ideologies when it thematically, verbally, and visually trades in forms of legibility and illegibility—in their construction and deconstruction—and the forms of freedom and unfreedom they afford.

PART III

Adaptation, Citation, Deployment

CHAPTER 9

Notes from the State of Saint Domingue: The Practice of Citation in *Clotel*

LARA LANGER COHEN

The primary claim to fame of William Wells Brown's 1853 novel *Clotel; or, The President's Daughter* lies in its priority: it is routinely hailed as the first African American novel. Yet as numerous readers have discovered, this claim, which honors originality and authenticity, has little in common with the literary mode of *Clotel* itself, which traffics in citation and iteration. Beginning with William Farrison's 1969 biography of Brown, scholars have shown that he raided countless sources, including John Relly Beard's biography of Toussaint L'Ouverture, Lydia Maria Child's short story "The Quadroons," Grace Greenwood's poem "The Leap from the Long Bridge," his own previous works, and a host of anonymous newspaper articles, to construct a collage of contemporary antislavery print culture.[1] Moreover, in the fourteen years following *Clotel*'s publication, Brown would reproduce the novel itself in three different revisions—*Miralda; or, The Beautiful Quadroon* (1860–61); *Clotelle: A Tale of the Southern States* (1864); and *Clotelle; or, The Colored Heroine* (1867). *Clotel*'s extraordinary awkwardness—its textual clutter and general excess—continues to challenge literary critics, leading many to conclude that "the *first* Black American novelist must be . . . the *worst* Black American novelist," as Robert Reid-Pharr has put it.[2] And if Brown's citational practices dismay readers in search of originality, they equally fail to comport with more gratifying models of citation like signifying, mimicry, or performativity, for while sometimes Brown transfigures his sources ironically, more often he copies them faithfully.[3]

Yet *Clotel* demands our attention precisely because we cannot readily account for it. In particular, it challenges familiar accounts of literature by former slaves, which tend to depend upon the importance of authorship. Robert B. Stepto's influential taxonomy of slave narratives, for instance, charts a progression from the "eclectic narrative," characterized by a flurry of documentation and a lack of authorial control, to authors' increasing ability to shake off an authenticating apparatus and step forth unaccompanied, and even authenticate others' texts.[4] This longing for unhindered authorship likewise propels William L. Andrews's foundational study *To Tell a Free Story*, whose title's catachresis evocatively conflates the freedom of story and storyteller. These books (which I continue to find brilliant and compelling, despite my disagreements), as well as the critical consensus I take them to represent, value the literature of former slaves to the extent that it produces both words and selfhood. Such an approach makes two assumptions: that selves produce words, and that words produce selves.

In other words, the study of literature by former slaves, more than most fields, has been tightly organized around the author function. Elsewhere, we have eagerly followed Michel Foucault's command that "the subject . . . must be stripped of its creative role," but it feels painful to apply this logic to writers so systematically denied any agency—indeed, any subjectivity—to begin with.[5] It is more appealing to see authorship as the counterweight to slavery, an approach that requires authors to wield power in proportion to that which slavery seizes. Certainly, many former slaves adopted liberal models of authorial self-making; Frederick Douglass is the most obvious example. Brown himself elsewhere embraces the role of author, especially in his 1847 slave narrative (and arguably also in later versions of *Clotel*). But a reliance on this model has left critics at a loss for what to do with other works, like the 1853 *Clotel*, that do not fit its mold. I would argue that, as productive as the author function proved for some former slaves, its appeal was not universal. Indeed, it has led us to overlook the possibility that a former slave, especially, might not necessarily have favored a model of writing that conceives the book for sale as continuous with the person who wrote it. Measuring literary achievement by the production of selfhood reproduces the logic of slavery by making persons and objects *fungible*, by equating a story's "freedom" with its author's. Moreover, this approach makes personhood *alienable*, by asserting that it can be transferred to a book. And finally, it does so by making that personhood *salable*, such that a former slave derives power from transforming his or her life into a commodity. Thus it seems hardly surprising that when Augustine St. Clare buys Tom in *Uncle Tom's Cabin*, he wryly imagines that the slave already embodies a book, "all the moral and Christian virtues bound in black morocco," an image that represents Tom's interiority as his contents while punning on the condition of both books and slaves as "bound." But St. Clare's follow-up question, "What's the damage?" begins to sound very different, linking the price of this remarkable literary commodity with the human cost it exacts.[6] Our attachment to an interpretive model that equates the books and persons of former slaves might likewise speak more to the enduring power of slavery's market logic than to the evidence of the texts themselves. And certainly, if "the name of an author poses all the problems related to the category of the proper name," as Foucault insists, then these problems become all the more intractable when the author's name is not fully his own but that of a former master, or, in the case of Brown, a white benefactor.[7]

Perhaps, then, it is not so surprising that in *Clotel*, whose haphazard plot defies recapitulation, Brown seems uninterested in presenting a *story*—and, his partiality for other authors' words suggests, still less interested in the act of *telling* one. Indeed, nearly all of Brown's writings recycle other texts, including his own, making his authorship less a matter of origination, as Andrews and Stepto see it, than something akin to the work of an editor. In one especially jarring instance, Brown turns his own stint as an assistant to a slave trader, recounted in the *Narrative of William W. Brown, a Fugitive Slave* (1847), into a queasily comic episode in *Clotel* in which a caricatured slave named Pompey plays Brown's part, recasting memoir as minstrelsy. (This repetition surely elicited a double take from readers, since Brown prefaced *Clotel* with a new edition of the *Narrative*.) An anecdote in *Clotel*, in turn, resurfaces in Brown's historical study *The Negro in the American Rebellion* (1867), as does a story about the naming of a fugitive slave that Brown first recorded as autobiography in the *Narrative*, later repurposed as biography in his composite history *The Black Man: His Antecedents, His Genius, and His Achievements* (1863), and finally transformed into a tale of the Revolutionary War in *The Negro in the American Rebellion*. It is "[a]s if he forgot for a while that he was writing history," as Brown's exasperated biographer Farrison puts it. "Since this sketch is as much imaginary as factual, it obviously does not belong in this book any more than it belongs in *The Black Man*."[8] Farrison's propriety about "belonging," however, clearly holds little interest for Brown (who, after all, properly "belonged" to a St. Louis merchant named Enoch Price), just as the opposition between "imaginary" and "factual" presumably fails to mean much to a man who named his own daughter Clotelle.

Moreover, Brown's patchwork aesthetic extended far more widely than author-centric literary histories would indicate, suggesting that these models' efforts to locate an elusive author in a text have obscured those texts' efforts to locate themselves proximate to other texts.[9] Citations perforate (or perhaps stitch together) well-known books like David Walker's *Appeal . . . to the Coloured Citizens of the World* (1829), as well as less remembered ones like Robert Benjamin Lewis's Afrocentric history *Light and Truth: Collected from the Bible and Ancient and Modern History* (1836, revised 1844).[10] Citation constitutes in its entirety one of the most widely read books of the antislavery movement, Theodore Dwight Weld's massive compendium *American Slavery as It Is: Testimony of a Thousand Witnesses* (1839). *Uncle Tom's Cabin* proliferated such numerous reiterations as fiction, stage plays, songs, advertisements, board games, and so on that Lauren Berlant describes it as a "supertext" for an enduring national culture of sentimentality.[11] Berlant singles out the scene of Eliza crossing the ice as the most frequently cited in the novel, reproduced faithfully in one version after another, regardless of medium or message. But Stowe seems to have cited the scene itself from Brown's *Original Panoramic Views of the Scenes in the Life of an American Slave*, which pictures a runaway slave holding her child and trembling on the banks of the Ohio River as her pursuers grow closer, then stepping onto the ice, which "cracked under her feet" as she "went from mass to mass."[12]

I propose that we read this scene as not just exemplifying the practice of citation but also emblematizing it. The prehistory and afterlives of Eliza's river crossing demonstrate that the practice of citation has gone underrecognized, but the action of the scene also intimates something of how that practice might work: a textual strategy of leaping from fragment to fragment, cutting across the current's flow. In this context, *Clotel* starts to look less anomalous and more representative. Accordingly, it demands fresh forms of analysis that would recognize citation as an important technique of African American print culture, theorizing modes of textual production that exceed origination to encompass reading, maneuvering, and rearrangement. Instead of relegating *Clotel*'s citations to footnotes, we need to restore their disorienting presence within the text. The remainder of this essay attempts to read *Clotel* through its citations. It focuses on those from the novel's most frequent and, in many ways, least predictable source, Beard's *The Life of Toussaint*

L'Ouverture, the Negro Patriot of Hayti, a largely sympathetic biography published in London the same year as *Clotel*. Following a reading of Brown's
incongruous use of Beard, I conclude by hypothesizing a relation between
citation as a form and these citations' counterfactual content, one that pits
the print archive against history as we know it.

"All These Combined Have Made Up My Story"

Any attempt to understand *Clotel*'s radical intertextuality must begin by acknowledging that citation and reprinting were common practice in antebellum print culture.[13] Working in the printing office of Elijah P. Lovejoy's *Saint
Louis Times* while still a slave, Brown would have had firsthand experience of
editors' everyday recycling of copy, illustrations, and actual printing plates.
Such practices tended to mine proven moments of rhetorical efficacy or simply save the effort of rewriting. Yet as often as not, *Clotel*'s patchwork approach fulfills neither of these objectives. The inclusion of Grace Greenwood's
tragic poem "The Leap from the Long Bridge" caps the novel's own emotional
high point, but Brown does not use any particularly affecting or memorable
moments from *The Life of Toussaint L'Ouverture*. And incorporating the
novel's many sources must have been arduous, not labor-saving, since the
original materials rarely correspond to the story Brown constructs from
them. The citations, that is, appear to serve no practical purpose. Furthermore, although citation may have been the norm in early nineteenth-century
print culture, attitudes to literary property had a tendency to splinter along the
color line. As John Ernest reminds us, "[a]t a time when it was important for
black writers to secure the authority of authorship ('written by himself'),
Brown's practice carried risks."[14]

Moreover, few of the antebellum period's patchwork productions showed
their seams—indeed, showed off their seams—so boldly as *Clotel* does. To
the eternal frustration of readers, the story makes little pretense of coherence,
jumping from one plotline to another with no apparent motive. The citations
themselves are more juxtaposed than incorporated in the text, creating awkward disruptions, and the pages themselves are visually pitted with offset
quotations from other sources. In the conclusion, Brown announces that
even unmarked components of the novel have been imported. "Some of the
narratives I have derived from other sources," he writes, including personal
communications with fugitive slaves. "Of their relations I have made free use.

To Mrs. Child, of New York, I am indebted for part of a short story. American Abolitionist journals are another source from whence some of the characters appearing in my narrative are taken. All these combined have made up my story." In fact, Brown borrows from many more texts than he lists here, but the important point is his willingness to "acknowledge . . . my resources," as he puts it.[15]

In response to generations of critical embarrassment at Brown's "free use" of these resources, several recent critics have tried to recuperate the value of *Clotel*'s citational practices. Certainly, this textual assemblage seems to complement the novel's plot. The excisions and recombinations of text pattern the wrenching divisions and regroupings of families, who are constantly "to be separated, and form new relations and companions," as Brown writes in the 1864 *Clotelle*.[16] At a formal level, then, the novel's uncompromising heterogeneity witnesses its story's assertion that a whole is impossible. In this respect, it rhymes with the novel's peculiar organizing principle, its orientation around genealogy rather than narrative progression—an orientation it doggedly preserves despite the fact that its genealogies are constantly disrupted, or perhaps for this precise reason. The novel's structure proves bitterly ironic: although the family tree would seem to guarantee a coherent narrative structure, in which elements will be figuratively because literally related, in fact *Clotel* is incredibly difficult to read because the women's connections are continually, brutally severed.

Some have countered the critical dismay over *Clotel*'s citations by arguing that, far from revealing a tenuous grasp of authorship, they function as a tactic for constructing personal and political authority. Noting that "plagiarism" has its roots in the Latin word for kidnapping children or slaves, Robert Levine contends that Brown's "stunning example of literary pastiche" gives slaveholders a taste of their own medicine: "[H]e steals the texts of a culture that steals black bodies. Writing *Clotel* in the wake of the Fugitive Slave Law's edict to return escaped blacks to their 'proper' places on the southern plantation, Brown attempts to liberate a variety of texts by placing them in 'improper' relation within his revisionary narrative."[17] According to Levine, Brown's technique achieves two victories: one, it mirrors back to slaveholders their own theft; and two, it "liberate[s]" the plagiarized texts by releasing them from the circumstances in which Brown found them. In this same vein it is also tempting to see the fugitive slave Brown highlighting what his contemporaries referred to as "fugitive," or occasional and uncollected, literary works, assembling them into a speaking whole. These readings allow us to envision

Brown striking a blow against slavery in not only the content of *Clotel* but also its form, or "engag[ing] . . . in verbal acts of violating the violator," in Ezra Greenspan's words. Yet as Greenspan adds, as compelling as this interpretation is, it "oversimplifies" Brown's textual practice, since he also appropriated the words of black writers.[18] It also seems limited by the extent that, for all its investment in pastiche rather than origination, it pivots on the figure of the commanding author, who constructs the text in order to construct his own authority. The repudiation of authorship, according to this logic, becomes the definitive sign of authorial power.

Another approach critics have used to apprehend *Clotel*'s citations focuses on what John Ernest calls "untelling." These readings are less concerned with how the novel constructs its author's identity than with how it deconstructs the master narratives of national founding that it takes as its subject. Ernest includes Brown's writing, but *Clotel* especially, in a body of antebellum African American historical "interventions" whose fragmented forms bespeak an effort "less . . . to tell the story of history than to undermine, to untell, the story that has been told."[19] Here, too, however, Brown's sources complicate the argument. If *Clotel* aims to make a hash of white supremacist history, Brown's choice of materials seems inapt; he draws far more heavily from the archives of antislavery print culture than from those of white nationalist ideology, although inevitably the two overlapped at times. Still, we are left with the perplexing notion of Brown trying to deconstruct the slave narrative of William and Ellen Craft, an exercise whose payoff is difficult to fathom.

The two interpretive camps I've outlined find different meanings in Brown's use of citation: either the novel's apparent lack of authorial control is a ruse that actually confirms authorial control, or its heterogeneity questions the grounds of textual authority. But I want to propose that the most interesting thing about *Clotel*'s citations is that they unite these two seemingly dichotomous positions. As appropriations, they are evidently talking back, but they seem determined not to *say* anything. To make sense of such expansive inaccessibility, we need to take a closer look not only at the existence of *Clotel*'s citations but also at their substance.

The Reenactment of St. Domingo

If *Clotel*'s patchwork draws attention to the seams and spaces of history, it also pieces together an aggregate otherwise, for Brown made not just fragmentation but juxtaposition and reassembly mainstays of his work. These practices appear not only in *Clotel* but also in the *Anti-Slavery Harp*, the abolitionist songbook he compiled in 1849; in the panorama of slavery he exhibited around Great Britain in 1850, in which a scene of a coffle led to a scene of the U.S. Capitol, for instance; and in his two race histories, *The Black Man* and *The Rising Son; or, The Antecedents and Advancement of the Colored Race* (1874). These last two make for particularly interesting limit cases, because both initially appear to collect biographies of the heroes of the black diaspora: the Revolutionary War martyr Crispus Attucks, the French novelist Alexandre Dumas, the generals of the Haitian Revolution. Yet Brown rejects the genre. *The Black Man*'s entry on Nat Turner begins: "Biography is individual history, as distinguished from that of communities, of nations, and of worlds. Eulogy is that deserved applause which springs from the virtues and attaches itself to the characters of men. This is not intended either as a biography or a eulogy, but simply a sketch of one whose history has hitherto been neglected, and to the memory of whom the American people are not prepared to do justice."[20] As long as "the American people are not prepared to do justice" to the memory of black men and women, recovering any "individual history" proves an impossible task. Yet if white supremacy renders black biography unwritable, the vacuum it creates around black personhood also opens up a space where Brown may imagine a collective history embodied in individuals, such that the singular entities of these two books' titles— "The Black Man" and "The Rising Son"—prove to contain "communities . . . nations . . . worlds." While antebellum U.S. culture persistently conflated African American persons and texts, Brown imagines any given person of African descent as something closer to an archive.

Unmoored from his own individual history, it is perhaps not surprising that Nat Turner makes an anachronistic guest appearance in *Clotel*. (While the references to Jefferson place the novel's initial action around 1815, only a few years pass before the scene turns to Nat Turner's 1831 rebellion.) When Clotel travels to Richmond in disguise to try to find her daughter Mary, she finds herself caught in the panic sown by the recent uprising. All strangers are subject to scrutiny, and Clotel is searched and her identity as a fugitive slave discovered. These scenes' blend of fact and fiction, like many others in the novel, does not so much authenticate the story as make it more fantastic; they "skew rather than anchor," as Trish Loughran observes.[21]

More striking than Nat Turner's presence in the novel, perhaps, is the even unlikelier presence of one of the other subjects of *The Black Man* and

The Rising Son: Toussaint L'Ouverture, who died in 1803 without, of course, ever having set foot in Virginia. The leader of the Haitian Revolution does not appear in person, exactly. Rather, Brown summons his presence through citations from Beard's *The Life of Toussaint L'Ouverture*. In a novel thick with quotations, *The Life of Toussaint L'Ouverture* is *Clotel*'s most frequently cited text. In certain ways, this is not surprising: over the course of Brown's career as an antislavery activist, he wrote extensively on the Haitian Revolution. Yet where many of the texts Brown borrows overlap with *Clotel*'s plot—likewise depicting abandoned mixed-race mistresses or pursued fugitive slaves, for instance—*The Life of Toussaint L'Ouverture* recounts events far removed from it. The passages Brown selects from Beard likewise seem unrelated to the action of the novel; they consist of descriptions of a yellow fever epidemic, simmering rebelliousness among the slaves, and the Haitian revolutionary Lamour de Rance. I will discuss the substance of these disorienting transpositions in greater detail below. For now, however, I simply want to note their apparent ill fit with *Clotel*'s domestic (in both the national and familial senses of the word) melodrama, which makes them especially illuminating cases of citation.

Brown introduces Nat Turner's rebellion with the following observation:

> The evils consequent on slavery are not lessened by the incoming of one or two rays of light. If the slave only becomes aware of his condition, and conscious of the injustice under which he suffers, if he obtains but a faint idea of these things, he will seize the first opportunity to possess himself of what he conceives to belong to him. The infusion of Anglo-Saxon with African blood has created an insurrectionary feeling among the slaves of America hitherto unknown. Aware of their blood connection with their owners, these mulattoes labour under the sense of their personal and social injuries; and tolerate, if they do not encourage in themselves, low and vindictive passions.[22]

Brown here seems to echo Augustine St. Clare's warning in *Uncle Tom's Cabin* that the "infusion of Anglo-Saxon blood" with "African" will ineluctably ring in the "San Domingo hour." But where St. Clare's argument is quasi-biological, based on the growth of "our calculating firmness and foresight" in the slaves' veins, Brown's argument is social: the knowledge of blood ties destabilizes the black/white binary on which slavery depends, opening up a rift in its explanatory logic.[23] If these sentiments, however interesting, seem oddly irrelevant to the story of Nat Turner ("a full-blooded negro," Brown tells us), this may be because the lines themselves were inherited from the very different racial dynamics of Saint Domingue. The paragraph fuses two passages from *The Life of Toussaint L'Ouverture*:

> *The evils consequent on slavery are not lessened by the incoming of one or two stray rays of light. If the slave becomes conscious of his condition, and aware of the injustice under which he suffers, if he obtains but a faint idea of these things* . . . then a new element of evil is added to those which before were only too powerful. . . . In the agitation of the public mind of the world, which preceded the French Revolution, such feelings could not be excluded from any community on earth: they entered the plantations of Hayti, and they aided in preparing the terrific struggle, which, through alarm, agitation, and slaughter, issued in the independence of the island.

> *On their side, the men of color labouring under the sense of their personal and social injuries, tolerated, if they did not encourage in themselves, low and vindictive passions.* . . . The mulattoes, therefore, were a hot-bed of dissatisfaction, and a furnace for turbulence. Aware by their education of the new ideas which were fermenting in Europe and in the United States, they were also ever on the watch to seize opportunities to avenge their wrongs.[24]

Beard's model of revolutionary thought is positively kinetic: the "faint idea[s]" of particular people are magnetized by the "agitation of the public mind of the world," and once they have joined this formation, they can "not be excluded from any community on earth." Quickened by the revolutionary "ferment" of Europe and the United States, then, "they enter . . . the plantations of Hayti." These passages picture revolution as an almost physical but distinctly free-spirited entity, heedless of borders or persons. Brown seems to have imbibed Beard's historical vision; a year later, when he offered his own sketch of Toussaint L'Ouverture in the lecture "St. Domingo: Its Revolutions and Its Patriots," he pictured the hero as a kind of accident. "[A]ll appeared to look with hope to the rising up of a black chief, who should prove himself adequate to the emergency," until "[i]n the midst of disorders that threatened on all sides, the negro chief made his appearance in the form of an old slave named Toussaint."[25] Toussaint becomes the fortuitous embodiment of revolution, a "form" possessed by the spectral "negro chief." Brown's uncanny dialectic anticipates C. L. R. James's formulation nearly a century later: "Toussaint did not make the revolution. It was the revolution that made Toussaint. And even that is not the whole truth."[26]

In *Clotel*, Brown enacts this idea of revolutionary possession as a textual practice. When Brown defies space and time to requisition Beard's account of the Haitian Revolution for his account of Nat Turner's rebellion, the combination is particularly jolting because it fuses the most famously successful slave rebellion with the most famously failed one. In other words, it pictures quite literally the possibility so many Southerners feared—that Turner might be another L'Ouverture. In fact, Brown was certain that the events of Saint Domingue would be repeated stateside. As he concluded in "St. Domingo": "Who knows but that a Toussaint, a Christophe, a Rigaud, a Clervaux, and a Dessalines, may some day appear in the Southern States of this Union? That they are there, no one will doubt. That their souls are thirsting for liberty, all will admit. The spirit that caused the blacks to take up arms, and to shed their blood in the American revolutionary war, is still amongst the slaves of the south; and, if we are not mistaken, the day is not far distant when the revolution of St. Domingo will be reenacted in South Carolina and Louisiana."[27] Here again, revolution stalks the United States, a "spirit . . . still amongst the slaves of the south," so that while the passage begins by positing the future appearance of the Haitian revolutionaries' U.S. counterparts, Brown quickly concludes that they are already here. *Clotel*, however, goes further by cutting and mixing historical record. Its seemingly misplaced citation of *The Life of Toussaint L'Ouverture* asks us to imagine not that Saint Domingue *might* recur, or even that it *will* recur, but that it already *has*, compelling the reader to envision Turner's defeated rebellion as commensurate with L'Ouverture's victorious one. Several years later, in *The Black Man*, Brown would bring his inexorable historical vision full circle. The entry on Nat Turner ends portentously (which is also to say recursively): "Every eye is now turned towards the south, looking for another Nat Turner."[28]

Brown skews historical record still further by equipping Turner with an ally: an Afro-Cuban slave named Picquilo, who in fact eclipses Turner in Brown's account of the Southampton insurrection. Picquilo is "from one of the barbarous tribes in Africa, and claimed that country as his native land," but he was sold to Cuba as a boy and later smuggled into Virginia in defiance of the ban on the international slave trade. When we meet him, he has been living in the Dismal Swamp for two years, wearing just "a girdle around his loins, made of skins of wild beasts which he had killed; his only token of authority among those that he led, was a pair of epaulettes made from the tail of a fox, and tied to his shoulder by a cord."[29] Picquilo has no precedent in the histories of Nat Turner's rebellion. However, he has a near relative in Beard's history of the Haitian Revolution, the guerrilla Lamour de Rance. The leader of a tribe of "untamed Africans" who escaped slavery and made their home in the mountains, de Rance is "an adroit, stern, savage man, half-naked, with epaulettes tied by a cord for his only token of authority."[30] But where Beard notes of Lamour de Rance, "His dress, his manners, his character, his mode of fighting . . . were objects of curiosity and amusement with the French army," Brown turns de Rance's African roots from the object of the French army's derision into the source of Picquilo's strength: "His dress, his character, his manners, his mode of fighting, were all in keeping with the early training he had received in the land of his birth," such that "neither the thickness of the trees, nor the depth of the water could stop him."[31] More-over, while Picquilo's textual history links him to the Haitian Revolution, his personal history as a recent immigrant from Cuba links him to the aborted slave revolt known as La Escalera, which had sent tremors through Cuba's planter class (as well as anxious U.S. observers) in 1844. In other words, he conjures a double vision of Caribbean insurrection. (Indeed, Picquilo's name may echo that of Cuba's famous enslaved poet, Plácido, who was executed for his role in the alleged conspiracy, and to whom Brown devoted a chapter of *The Black Man*.) A kind of diasporic palimpsest, Picquilo's hybrid Virginian-Haitian-Cuban insurgency triangulates the revolutionary past of the Americas into a fantastic convergence.

If appropriating Beard's history of the Haitian Revolution to portray Nat Turner's rebellion allows Brown to envision "the horrors of Saint Domingue" infecting the United States, his final citation from Beard stages this contagion at a more literal level. Clotel's sister Althesa is sold in New Orleans, where she attracts the notice of a white doctor who purchases her freedom and marries her. The couple lives together peacefully for several years and, in keeping with the novel's bleakly repetitive rule of reproduction, they in turn have two daughters. But their happiness crumbles when the yellow fever—one of those "epidemics of a most destructive nature" to which "all tropical climates are subject"—ravages New Orleans in the summer of 1831 and carries off both parents. Brown's account of the disease is exception-ally gruesome:

The disorder began in the brain, by an oppressive pain accompanied or followed by fever. The patient was devoured with burning thirst. The stomach, distracted by pains, in vain sought relief in efforts to disburden itself. Fiery veins streaked the eye; the face was inflamed, and dyed of a dark red color; the ears from time to time rang painfully. Now mucous secretions surcharged the tongue, and took away the power of speech; now the sick one spoke, but in speaking had a foresight of death. When the violence of the disease approached the heart, the gums were blackened. The sleep, broken, troubled by convulsions, or by frightful visions, was worse than the waking hours; and when the reason sank under a delirium which had its seat in the brain, repose utterly forsook the patient's couch. The progress of the heat within was marked by yellowish spots, which spread over the surface of the body. If, then, a happy crisis came not, all hope was gone. Soon the breath infected the air with a fetid odour, the lips were glazed, despair painted itself in the eyes, and sobs, with long intervals of silence, formed the only language. From each side of the mouth spread foam, tinged with black and burnt blood. Blue streaks mingled with the yellow all over the frame. All remedies were useless.[32]

In fact, cholera, another "tropical epidemic," struck New Orleans in 1832. But Brown bases his account not on the reports of that outbreak, but on the yellow fever that spread through Saint Domingue in 1802, devastating the French army. The passage above nearly word for word copies Beard's description of the event, which he portrays as both the turning point of the war and retribution for it, a "terrible punishment which fell on the predatory expedition sent by the Corsican adventurer against the hero and patriot of St. Domingo."[33] In visiting Saint Domingue's yellow fever upon New Orleans, Brown follows the belief that the disease was endemic to a "tropical climate" that included both places. Beyond this environmental connection, however, and against the odds of time and space, Brown's citation also brings 1802 Saint Domingue's *revolutionary* climate to 1831 New Orleans. As Beard emphasizes the disease's crucial role in defeating the French army and even invests its fury with purpose, yellow fever becomes itself a metaphor for slave revolt. Given this correlation of yellow fever with revolution, it makes sense that Brown preserved what otherwise is surely the most peculiar feature of Beard's account, the disease's capacity to turn victims a rainbow of colors, which produces bodies with "dark red" faces, "blackened" gums, "yellowish spots" on the skin, "black and burnt blood" on the mouth, and "[b]lue streaks mingled with . . . yellow all over the frame." Yellow fever's name refers to jaundice, a common symptom, but Beard's (and Brown's) accounts dramatically expand the disease's color spectrum. Little surprise, then, that it militates against racial slavery so effectively in the text, for its symptoms themselves undermine the taxonomy of skin color on which that system depends. In the context of a medical discourse that understood the disease as native to the tropics, yellow fever makes an especially unsettling metaphor for insurrection, because it imagines the latter, as much as the former, as endemic to the plantation zone.

In *Clotel*'s imaginary New Orleans yellow fever outbreak, as in the Southampton scenes, the forces of the Haitian Revolution—this time pathological rather than military—once again slip into the United States through the historical rift that Brown's citations open. And here Brown may be borrowing a page from Beard's book for his method as well as its materials, for throughout *The Life of Toussaint L'Ouverture* Beard obsesses over the significance of his hero's surname, which translates as "the opening." Beard offers various explanations for how he acquired the name, but he favors the theory that "Toussaint assumed the epithet, in order to announce to his people that he was about to open the door to them of a better future. . . . Whenever they saw Toussaint, they were reminded of the opening; whenever they pronounced his name, they were encouraged to advance toward the opening."[34] Evidently fascinated by the association, in which Toussaint himself comes to embody what Lenin would call a "revolutionary situation," Beard makes these words a refrain that runs throughout the book. Thus when France proposes an alliance with the slaves, "Toussaint L'Ouverture accepted *the opening*," and as his influence over the French authorities grows, he "now see[s] 'the opening' in clear outline before him."[35] At last, when he is named commander in chief of the army of Saint Domingue, "[t]he opening was made."[36] While readers frustrated by *Clotel*'s temporal and textual patchwork often complain that the novel is of full of holes, we might consider these the result of Brown's efforts to turn Beard's "openings" into a literary device.

From History to Archive

Clotel frequently gets classified as a counterhistory, an intervention that unearths the events suppressed by official record. This designation underscores the challenge the novel poses to triumphant nationalist historiography, especially to the legacy of Thomas Jefferson, by restoring to the founding fathers their forgotten foundlings. But even as it searches out the past's hidden truths, *Clotel*'s incongruous citations reject any truth claims at all. What Ann duCille calls the novel's "unreal estate"—its "blending of the 'real,' the 'incredible,' and, most particularly, the 'borrowed'"—has hampered its canonization, despite its precedence.[37] "The trouble with *Clotel* as an originary novel," duCille explains, "is not that it speaks a suppressed historical truth that has now been scientifically authenticated, but that it does not."[38] Yet we might also find our way to value these "openings," which refuse to acknowledge historical outcomes as being any more meaningful than the possibilities they foreclose. Even as the novel narrates one scene, its citations harbor another, so that the story it tells resides neither in the words on the page nor in the sources they quote, but somewhere in the space opened up between them.

In this respect, the content of *Clotel*'s citations mirrors their form, for the former refuses the integrity of the historical event just as surely as the latter refuses the integrity of authorship. Indeed, Jacques Rancière contends that "the impropriety of . . . words and the anachronism of . . . events" go hand in hand, and that the two together constitute the idiom of revolution, whose "violence is identified with the theoretical scandal of the event in general."

> This scandal of the event is that of the conflagration of discourses and the confusion of time periods. Every event, among speakers, is tied to an excess of speech in the specific form of a displacement of the *statement*: an appropriation 'outside the truth' of the speech of the other (of the formulas of sovereignty, of the ancient text, of the sacred word) that makes it signify differently—that makes the voice of Antiquity resonate in the present, the language of prophecy or of *belles lettres* in the common life. The event draws its paradoxical novelty from that which is tied to something restated, to something stated out of context, inappropriately. The impropriety of expression is also an undue superimposition of time periods. The event has the novelty of the anachronistic.[39]

One would be hard-pressed for a better gloss on *Clotel* than we find in Rancière's description of the event's voracious appetite for familiar yet inappropriate words: "an appropriation 'outside the truth' of the speech of the other."

Whereas Marx sees anachronism as the sign of revolutionary failure, a flight from the new and unknown, Rancière counters that anachronism is the only possible means of imagining revolution, and derivativeness its signature style. Brown differs from Rancière's historians, however, insofar as these become not strategies for articulating the newness of the present, but for reanimating the past. As a result, *Clotel* crafts a print archive that works to keep alive, interstitially, what might have been—and what might yet be.

Given *Clotel*'s combination of the counterhistorical and the messianic, its intimations of unwon revolutions, it is tempting to recognize in Brown an anticipatory version of Walter Benjamin's archetypal historical materialist. But I would go further and say that Brown lends new meaning to the term, by fortifying "materialism" in the Marxist sense of the word with its more colloquial sense. Benjamin's historical materialist works by viewing his available materials "with cautious detachment." Since "[t]here is no document of civilization which is not at the same time a document of barbarism," "[a] historical materialist therefore dissociates himself from it as far as possible."[40] But *Clotel*, as I have argued, eschews authorial agency and consistently lets its documents speak instead. In making citation, not narration, the mode of its historical intervention, the novel envisions a materialist history in the most literal sense: one that would not be the work of a historian but could lurk in the materials themselves.

Thus even when *Clotel*'s citations do not explicitly counter historical record, as in the excerpts from Beard, they nonetheless turn history inside out, by suggesting that this story has been part of the historical record all along. When Brown follows a harrowing episode about the execution of a runaway slave with a report from the *Mississippi Free Trader*, for example, the newspaper does not bear out the events of the novel; instead, Brown assures us that his character was a "witness" to the events the *newspaper* recounts.[41] Similarly, as Holly Jackson points out in Chapter 11 of this volume, Clotel's suicidal leap into the Potomac copies Congressman Seth M. Gates's widely reprinted account of a real event, which likewise became the basis for Grace Greenwood's "The Leap from the Long Bridge." Brown ends this chapter by quoting Greenwood's poem in full, but he rather dizzyingly contends that the poem derives from his heroine, rather than the other way around: "A few days after the death of Clotel," he explains, it "appeared in one of the newspapers."[42] The nineteenth century's deep controversies over race and slavery papered the United States with an enormous body of literature about African

Americans, as this volume's own tremendous archive attests. At once documentary and counterfactual, *Clotel* shows intense fidelity to this print archive, while prying it apart from what we know as history. Instead, the novel insists that its story is immanent in the archive, even if the archive has not told it until now. Against the apparent finality of print, it compels the archive to speak otherwise.

The Canon in Front of Them: African American Deployments of "The Charge of the Light Brigade"

DANIEL HACK

In a 1990 episode of the television sitcom *The Fresh Prince of Bel Air* wittily titled "Def Poets' Society," Will Smith joins the school poetry club. Commending this newfound interest in poetry (which of course is really an interest in girls), Geoffrey, the family's excruciatingly proper Afro-British butler, informs Will that he too loves poetry and in fact received first prize at the All-Devonshire Poetry Recital of 1963. Reliving his triumph, he begins to recite:

> Cannon to the right of them,
> Cannon to the left of them,
> Cannon in front of them
> Volleyed and thundered.

The choice of "The Charge of the Light Brigade" by the makers of *The Fresh Prince* accurately reflects its status as an enduring favorite for the study of elocution.[1] What I want to call attention to is the role the poem takes on here as a marker, even (given its presumptive recognizability) an icon, of squareness—which is to say, of whiteness. This identification is reinforced later in the episode, when, for reasons which need not concern us, Geoffrey gets disguised in Afro and dashiki as "street poet" Raphael de la Ghetto. After reciting a poem that begins "Listen to the street beat" and ends "Listen, or I'll kill ya!' "

he responds to the cries of "Encore!" by launching into "The Charge of the Light Brigade," thereby blowing his cover and quickly losing the formerly rapt audience. The episode ends soon thereafter with Will's aunt reciting a poem by Amiri Baraka. Canon to the right of them, canon to the left of them, indeed.

"The Charge of the Light Brigade" is a good choice to play the role it plays in *The Fresh Prince* because its subject matter—a disastrous advance by British cavalry in the Crimean War—and perhaps, more subtly, its cadence (which contrasts with that of Will Smith's rapping, with which the episode opens) make the poem seem ludicrously removed from the experiences, interests, and expressive traditions of African Americans. What makes "The Light Brigade" an inspired choice, however, is not the self-evidence of this contrast but its history and historicity: there exists, in other words, a history of placing Tennyson's poem in relation to African American culture, and this history is one in which this relationship has been variously construed and vigorously contested. As I will show, from the moment it was published, "The Charge of the Light Brigade" was mobilized, especially though not exclusively by African Americans, as a site or tool to address the kinds of issues adumbrated by *The Fresh Prince*: the relationship of African Americans to the dominant cultural tradition; the nature and politics of interracial cultural rivalry, mimicry, and appropriation; and the role of poetry and the arts—and violence ("I'll kill ya!")—in the fight for racial empowerment and equality. This mobilization is part of a larger phenomenon whereby a surprising range of nineteenth-century British literature was taken up in often-unexpected ways by nineteenth- and early twentieth-century African American writers, editors, and intellectuals. The recovery of this tradition of interracial, transatlantic literary engagement illuminates the contours of early African American print culture, provides a new lens through which to view romantic and Victorian literature, and helps us to gain purchase on the cultural mobility and ideological malleability of literary texts more generally.

"Flat Burglary": "The Charge of the Light Brigade" in *Frederick Douglass' Paper*

"The Charge of the Light Brigade" was first published in the *London Examiner* on December 9, 1854, five weeks after the event it describes. Among the many places the poem was quickly reprinted was the Rochester, New York–based *Frederick Douglass' Paper*, the most prominent antebellum publication owned and edited by an African American. Douglass's reprinting of "The Light Brigade" (on January 12, 1855) might strike us as surprising, but it would not have surprised the *Paper*'s regular readers: new British literature was routinely reprinted on the last of the *Paper*'s four pages, where it appeared alongside cultural reporting and original work by African American and white American authors, as well as miscellaneous items from Dickens's *Household Words* and other British periodicals. While the American poetry and prose tended to be explicitly political or reformist, and often came from authors closely associated with the antislavery movement, the selections from British writers were more eclectic, with authors' prominence rather than their declared or perceived political commitments often decisive.[2]

The reprinting of a widely circulated poem by Britain's poet laureate—prestigious, popular, and not known as a political activist—would seem to fit this model, but in fact this is not simply a case of Frederick Douglass and his literary editor, Julia Griffiths, showing their fealty to the canon in front of them. Theirs is to reason why. The Tennyson that emerges over the years in *Frederick Douglass' Paper* has—or is ascribed—a politics, and a congenial one at that. The *Paper* first published his work in 1851, soon after it began publication, reprinting the "Ring out, wild bells" section of the previous year's *In Memoriam*. This selection's call to "Ring in redress to all mankind" holds clear appeal for a reform-minded newspaper—and indeed, the reprinting of the poem in the context provided by *Douglass' Paper* has the effect of giving specific content to the poem's vague utopianism. Two years later, this implicit enlistment of Tennyson in the *Paper*'s cause received confirmation of a sort when it was reported that Tennyson's wife was among the thousands of signatories of an abolitionist petition from "the ladies of England"; a brief item in the *Paper* wonders whether this will lead some supporters of slavery to refuse to read his work.[3]

To some extent, then, the *Paper*'s interest in "The Light Brigade" stems from its authorship by Tennyson the Poet Laureate/Fellow Traveler. Equally important, though, is the poem's subject matter: "The Charge of the Light Brigade at Balaklava"—to give the poem its full title as printed in *Douglass' Paper*—was one item among many the newspaper published about the Crimean War. This coverage treats the war not as a distant conflict between imperial powers but rather as a world-historical event and, more specifically, one front among several (including, of course, the antislavery movement itself) in the international battle for human rights and democracy. For example, one article celebrates the fall of Sebastopol to British and French troops

as a victory over "the great Autocrat of Europe" and criticizes "the hypocriti-
cal sympathies of American Republicanism in [Russia's] behalf."[4] Another
piece published the same day goes even further in forging this connection:
calling for a "convention of ideas," the paper's New York correspondent
writes that "Old Thomas Aquinas held such a meeting when he discovered
that 'all men are born equal.' . . . I rather think the general or public meeting
which Aquinas inaugurated, and at which Jefferson reported his celebrated
'Declaration,' is not yet adjourned: committees are out, which are yet to report, some at Sebastopol, some in Kansas."[5] In short, "The Charge of the
Light Brigade" was reprinted *because* of its topicality, not despite it; in fact, it
was not even the only Crimean War poem the *Paper* published. Nor were
these choices entirely idiosyncratic: another leading abolitionist journal, the
National Anti-Slavery Standard, also reprinted "The Light Brigade" the very
next day.

Yet while the appearance of "The Charge of the Light Brigade" in *Frederick Douglass' Paper* may have been unremarkable, the poem itself did not go
unremarked. In contrast to most of the poems and stories published in *Douglass' Paper*, which inspired no further comment,[6] "The Light Brigade" immediately became part of the discourse of the *Paper*, serving as a resource
in the ongoing dialogue among its African American contributors. Moreso
than the mere reprinting of Tennyson's work, this engagement, though brief,
casts the poem in a new light, radically recontextualizing and refunctioning
it. The first and most remarkable of these responses comes in the very issue
containing the poem. In fact, it comes in a piece located on the page *preceding* that on which the poem itself appeared, the recto to the poem's verso. As
we will see, this upsetting of priorities proves entirely apt.

This piece, headlined "From Our New York Correspondent" and bearing the specification "For Frederick Douglass' Paper," is by James McCune
Smith, the same writer who later aligns Sebastopol with Kansas. A regular
contributor to *Douglass' Paper* under the pseudonym "Communipaw," Smith
was the first African American to earn a medical degree and has been called
"the foremost black intellectual in nineteenth-century America."[7] His column's treatment of the "Light Brigade" takes the form of a dialogue with
"Fylbel," Smith's friend Philip A. Bell, himself a leading African American
editor and activist. Fylbel begins by asking Communipaw his opinion of the
first two lines of the poem, which he quotes approvingly. Communipaw responds with an appreciative formal analysis that takes the Western literary
tradition as its frame of reference: Tennyson's opening, he declares, "beats

Virgil's *'quatit ungula campum'*; for we have not only the sound of the horses' feet, as they begin with a canter, but the rush into the gallop."[8] However, when Fylbel next quotes the same four lines we saw Geoffrey the butler recite in *The Fresh Prince* ("Cannon to right of them . . ."), Communipaw abruptly withdraws his approval of the poem with the startling accusation, "Flat burglary! . . . Tennyson has stolen the sweep's blanket." He then goes on to advance an understanding of the poem diametrically opposed to that evoked by *The Fresh Prince*, where, as we saw, the poem's metrical form, historical referent, Englishness, and history as a recitation piece combined to signify whiteness. Here, by contrast, Smith declares that these lines are "a translation from the Congo, feebler than the original."

Elaborating on his surprising claim, Smith juxtaposes Tennyson's lines with a Congo chant "as old as—Africa":

> Canga bafio te,
> Canga moune de le,
> Canga do ki la,
> Canga li.

Communipaw does not know the meaning of the chant's words; what he is arguing, rather, is that Tennyson has "stolen" the chant as a formal construct— the anaphora, the stressed first syllable "can," the short line-length, and, roughly, the meter. As Smith explains, the chant was first transported beyond the site of its origination by enslaved Africans brought to the New World, and achieved wider dissemination via the circuits of cosmopolitan print culture. It is thus possible for Tennyson to have learned about the chant the same way Smith did: by reading about it in a French periodical. Smith even provides the citation ("Look in the *Revue des Deux Mondes*, Vol. 4th, page 1040.").[9]

Smith's claim of plagiarism may seem strained or hyperbolic. However, it is not outrageous by contemporaneous standards, for example in comparison to the best-known such charge, Poe's attacks on Longfellow. As Pierre Bourdieu might put it, Smith is playing the game of literary and cultural criticism according to its prevailing rules.[10] Or rather—like Poe—he displays his true mastery by playing *with* the game, pushing its rules to their limits. In particular, he pushes the question of relative originality and derivativeness to the extremes of an originality so absolute as to seem originless ("old as Africa"), on the one hand, and an indebtedness that is sheer repetition ("flat burglary"), on the other. At the same time, Smith expands the boundaries of the playing field, in two ways: first, by virtue of his own participation as an African American, and second, in his introduction of the idea of what we might call white-on-black plagiarism. Given prevailing beliefs in the fundamental imitativeness of members of the African race and the absence of cultural or aesthetic value in their artifacts and activities, the notion of influence and indebtedness running in this direction is virtually unthinkable at the time. What gives Smith's vision of a scandalous "Charge" its scandalous charge, then, is less its accuracy or even its plausibility than its very expression, its being put into discourse. Smith's claim of African influence introduces the possibility of such influence, even if his specific claim perhaps proves unpersuasive. For Smith, as for the Light Brigade, a wild charge can fail on one level and still succeed on another.

The overturning of discursive hierarchies is not the only form of subversion at issue here. As Communipaw informs Fylbel, the chant was used to call slaves to rebel in "St. Domingo." Quoting (and translating) his source, he reports that the chant helped transform "indifferent and heedless slaves into furious masses, and hurled them into those incredible combats in which stupid courage balked all tactics, and naked flesh struggled against steel." "Hurrah for our mother-land!" exclaims Fylbel. " 'Canga li!' Glorious war cry; it beats 'Volleyed and thundered,' out of sight." Tennyson's poem commemorates an advance against superior forces, whereas the chant is able to inspire such an advance—which, unlike the Light Brigade's, is ultimately successful. The relative "feeble[ness]" of "The Light Brigade" on which Smith insists is thus performative as well as aesthetic.

Thrilled by what he learns from Communipaw, Fylbel envisions using the Congo chant to reproduce the Haitian Revolution in the United States. Suggesting that " 'Canga li' must yet ring in the interior of Africa," he proposes renewing the African slave trade to import a million Africans a year for six years: "then, in six years," he reasons, "away down in the sunny South, these six millions of 'children of the sun,' restless under the lash, and uncontaminated, unenfeebled by American Christianity, may hear in their midst 'Canga li,' and the affrighted slave owners . . . will rush away North faster than they did from St Domingo." At this point, Communipaw cuts off Fylbel, telling him not to raise his voice—even as Smith puts it in writing.[11] Tennyson's depiction of the heroic but doomed actions of British soldiers thus not only derives from but also morphs into visions of equally heroic— but not always doomed—slave rebellions. What began as an appreciation of

Tennyson's artistry ends up a celebration—and bravura demonstration—
of African (American) agency and creativity.

Black Brigades: The Civil War "Light Brigade"

James McCune Smith's column inaugurates a tradition, discontinuous but
persistent, of using "The Charge of the Light Brigade" in particular, and the
work of Tennyson more generally, to think about race, culture, and violence.
It is important to note, however, that the most common form of African
American engagement with Tennyson's poem in the nineteenth century was
undoubtedly that which it takes in *The Fresh Prince*: recitation, in both
schools and public performances.[12] Such recitation demonstrated linguistic
and cultural competence—as defined, of course, by the dominant culture.
Yet absent anything like Smith's claim for an African role in the making of
this poem, or this culture, we might ask whether we should understand the
teaching and performance of Tennyson's poem as promoting an empower-
ing cultural literacy, on the one hand, or a deracinating cultural mimicry,
on the other—or, indeed, some combination of the two, with deracination
the price of empowerment? For young African Americans, what is the Crimea
to them, or they to the Crimea, that they should read and recite about it?
   Eventually, the teaching of Tennyson's poem will be criticized along
these lines. In a 1922 essay "Negro Literature for Negro Pupils," "The Charge
of the Light Brigade" is one of the few works Alice Dunbar-Nelson targets by
name as she decries the fact that "for two generations we have given brown
and black children a blonde ideal of beauty to worship, a milk-white literature to assimilate, and a pearly Paradise to anticipate, in which their dark
faces would be hopelessly out of place."[13] Arguing for the need to "instill race
pride into our pupils" by giving them "the poems and stories and folk lore
and songs of their own people," Dunbar-Nelson proposes dropping Tennyson's poem from the curriculum and replacing it with George Henry Boker's
1863 poem "The Second Louisiana" (also known as "The Black Regiment").[14]
This poem, while also by a white author, celebrates the pivotal role of an
African American regiment in the Civil War battle of Port Hudson, Louisiana. As in *The Fresh Prince of Bel Air*, "The Charge of the Light Brigade"
comes to represent that which must be cleared away to make room for black
history, experience, and expression. In a similar spirit, at around the same
time, when the Pan-Africanist Marcus Garvey attempted to purchase a ship

named the *Tennyson* for the Universal Negro Improvement Association's Black Star Line, he announced his plan to rechristen it the *Phyllis Wheatley*.[15]

No hint of such criticism or such a binary opposition is present in the 1860s reports in the African American press on the recitation of Tennyson's poem. What one finds in their place is not necessarily an indifference to the question of fit between text and student, nor an attempt to relocate both poem and reader to a realm of universality; instead, there are indications that Tennyson's poem has been selected with an eye toward its timeliness and felt relevance for these students, as a poem about war. Thus, "The Light Brigade" is reported being read at one high school exam along with a poem called "Restoration of the Flag to Fort Sumter."[16] In direct contrast to Dunbar-Nelson, another article reporting on a reading by graduates of the Institute for Colored Youth does not oppose Tennyson and Boker but instead aligns them: the evening's main performer, we learn, first came to prominence "as an orator . . . on the occasion of the organization of the Pennsylvania State Equal Rights League" two months earlier, "when he recited "Boker's Black Regiment,' in such an able and masterly style."[17]

It is not surprising that Boker's poem in particular gets paired with Tennyson's, since this pairing begins in Boker's poem itself: in celebrating the sacrifices of African American troops in the Civil War, "The Second Louisiana" takes "The Light Brigade" as its model. This African Americanization of Tennyson's poem indicates both the poem's continued resonance and its limitations. On the one hand, that is, the turn from "The Light Brigade" to "The Black Regiment" does not leave Tennyson's poem behind but instead maintains and affirms its presence, as resource or influence. On the other hand, the existence of a "black" version of "The Light Brigade" turns "The Light Brigade" into a "white" version of itself—that is, into the racially marked poem Dunbar-Nelson will see.

Boker's formal debt to Tennyson is evident, as his poem commemorates the martyrdom of a regiment in the distinctive dactylic dimeter of "The Light Brigade":

> Trampling with bloody heel
> Over the crashing steel,
> All their eyes forward bent,
> Rushed the Black Regiment.[18]

Boker also borrows Tennyson's use of anaphora—

"Freedom!" their battle-cry—
"Freedom! or leave to die!"
. . . .
Glad to strike one free blow,
Whether for weal or woe;
Glad to breathe one free breath,
Though on the lips of death.

His ending reworks Tennyson's, replacing the imperative to "Honor the Light Brigade" with a demand focusing on the survivors:

Oh, to the living few,
Soldiers, be just and true!
Hail them as comrades tried;
Fight with them side by side;
Never, in field or tent,
Scorn the Black Regiment.

Rather than the recitation of "The Charge of the Light Brigade" serving to demonstrate the humanity, equality, or artistry of African Americans, then, the poem gets adapted to describe—and increase—their own agency in securing that equality. Indeed, unlike the contributor to *Frederick Douglass' Paper* who fears a suicidal charge resulting in "the annihilation of the African Brigade, with no prospect of recruits,"[19] Boker celebrates a small-scale annihilation, and does so precisely to generate more recruits: "The Second Louisiana" was published by Philadelphia's Supervisory Committee for Recruiting Colored Regiments.

When Dunbar-Nelson proposes that "Negro pupils" read "The Second Louisiana" instead of "The Light Brigade," she suspends her essay's emphasis on black authorship.[20] Yet "The Light Brigade" also gets deployed in poems *by* African Americans—poems on the very same subject as Boker's.[21] The first such poem is likely James Madison Bell's 750-line "The Day and the War" (1864). Unlike Boker, Bell breaks from the metrical form of "The Light Brigade" in favor of a more conventional iambic tetrameter, usually in rhymed couplets; also unlike Boker, however, Bell openly thematizes his relationship to Tennyson, acknowledging the English poet's precedent while claiming an originality of his own:

Though Tennyson, the poet king,
Has sung of Balaklava's charge,
Until his thund'ring cannons ring
From England's center to her marge,
The pleasing duty still remains
To sing a people from their chains—
To sing what none have yet assay'd,
The wonders of the Black Brigade.[22]

Bell's characterization of Tennyson as "the poet king" is less unequivocal as praise than it might seem, for earlier in the poem he criticizes Britain for supporting the South in the Civil War and states that "kindred spirits there are none, / Twixt a Republic and a throne." This stance may have contributed to Bell's decision to present himself and the African American soldiers at the battle of Milliken's Bend as competing with Tennyson and the Light Brigade, rather than emulating them:

Let Balaklava's cannons roar
And Tennyson his hosts parade,
But ne'er was seen and never more
The equals of the Black Brigade![23]

Like James McCune Smith, Bell uses Tennyson's poem as a foil to assert the primacy of black freedom fighters. Superiority over the Light Brigade here takes the form of a more complete martyrdom—"*All* killed or wounded but the last!"[24]—which in turn portends the eventual triumph of the cause: "The Day and the War" was written to celebrate the first anniversary of the Emancipation Proclamation. Insofar as this outcome recalls that which Smith's insurrectionary Fylbel prophesies by way of *his* black "Brigade"—"Canga li"—it is fitting that the "Introductory Note" to "The Day and the War" was written by Fylbel's namesake, Philip Bell.[25]

Faded Glory: "The Light Brigade" at the Turn of the Century

The end of the Civil War did not end the use of "The Light Brigade" pioneered by "The Black Regiment" and "The Day and the War." However, the passage of time did change the poem's resonance. We see this in Paul Laurence Dunbar's 1895 poem "The Colored Soldiers," which again makes use of "The Charge of the Light Brigade" to celebrate the role of African American troops in the Civil War.[26] Dunbar's soldiers, like Tennyson's, valiantly storm "the very mouth of hell,"[27] and the final stanza of "The Colored Soldiers" tracks that of "The Light Brigade":

> When can their glory fade?
> O the wild charge they made!
>   All the world wondered.
> Honour the charge they made!
> Honour the Light Brigade,
>   Noble six hundred!
>   (Tennyson, "The Charge of the Light Brigade," 50–55)[28]

> And their deeds shall find a record
>   In the registry of Fame;
> For their blood has cleansed completely
>   Every blot of Slavery's shame.
> So all honor and all glory
>   To those noble sons of Ham—
> The gallant colored soldiers
>   Who fought for Uncle Sam!
>   (Dunbar, "The Colored Soldiers," 73–80)[29]

The unmistakable echo of the "Light Brigade" here derives not simply from the shared vocabulary—"honor," "glory," "noble"—and assertions of immortality, which are arguably generic, but from these features in combination with the similar syntax of the poems' final sentences, as Dunbar's concluding exclamation bestows the honor Tennyson's demands.

Crucially, however, unlike Tennyson's poem—and Boker's and Bell's—Dunbar's poem does not inhabit the moment it describes. Instead, "The Colored Soldiers" looks back three decades, and the poem takes as its topic the difference this temporal gap makes. As Jennifer Terry has noted, Dunbar is writing "against a backdrop of rising anti-black violence and the widespread collapse and reversal of political and legal gains made by African Americans during the post-war period."[30] He calls upon an earlier heroic moment and poetic model to counteract this backsliding, which is directly addressed in the poem: "They were comrades then and brothers, / Are they more or less to-day?" (57–58), "And the traits that made them worthy,—/ Ah! those virtues are not dead" (63–64). Tennyson's poem not only models a call for permanence but, forty years after its publication, models that permanence itself.

Yet there are poignant ironies in Dunbar's turn to "The Light Brigade," deriving from both the specific content of Tennyson's poem and its subsequent reputation. When Boker and James Madison Bell deploy Tennyson's poem, they pick up the theme of martyrdom but leave behind the poem's crucial attention to the fact that the charge it describes was also a mistake and a failure: a blunder. Dunbar argues similarly that the sacrifices he describes contributed to victory:

> Yes, the Blacks enjoy their freedom,
> And they won it dearly, too;
> For the life blood of their thousands
> Did the southern fields bedew.
> In the darkness of their bondage,
> In the depths of slavery's night,
> Their muskets flashed the dawning,
> And they fought their way to light.
>
> (49–56)

The problem, however, is that Dunbar's goal is precisely to dispel the idea that this mission failed—that these flashing muskets are no less glorious but also no more successful than the Light Brigade's flashing sabers. The turn to Tennyson thus implies exactly what "The Colored Soldiers" is intended to refute: that the colored soldiers "fought their way to light[-brigade status]" *as opposed to* the "light" of freedom. Instead of underwriting freedom, that is, glory and honor become consolation prizes in its absence. Even as "The Colored Soldiers" seeks to reclaim "The Light Brigade'"s triumphalism, then, it is haunted by the poem's negativity.

Another irony in Dunbar's use of "The Charge of the Light Brigade" to figure permanence is that the poem's currency has gotten debased over time. Both despite and because of its enduring place in the curriculum, "The Light Brigade" remains familiar throughout the second half of the nineteenth century but becomes increasingly subject to promiscuous, casual, and irreverent citation and appropriation. This is as true in the African American press as in the white press. The poem's decline is uneven, but we can get a sense of it from an 1882 article in the African Methodist Episcopal Church's widely read *Christian Recorder*. Mocking the supposed Negro love of titles, a reporter complains that a recent convention "to discuss the moral, social and political condition of the negro" devolved into a display of what he calls "titular twaddle": "Professors to right of us, professors to left of us, professors in front of us volleyed and thundered."[31] Thus does glory fade, not into oblivion but bathos.

It is perhaps not surprising, then, that although African American writers such as Alexander Crummell and Anna Julia Cooper continued to engage with Tennyson in significant and surprising ways in the period between the Civil War and the Harlem Renaissance, "The Charge of the Light Brigade" became a less prominent touchstone (with *In Memoriam* in particular taking its place). But "The Light Brigade" does appear in the most influential work produced in this period by an African American writer, W. E. B. Du Bois's *The Souls of Black Folk* (1903). Like Dunbar, Du Bois turns to "The Light Brigade" when grappling with the failed promise of Reconstruction.[32] True to Du Bois's more negative vision, however, it is precisely the poem's negativity that he calls upon. Whereas Dunbar asserts that "the Blacks enjoy their freedom," Du Bois counters that "despite compromise, war, and struggle, the Negro is not free," and he defines "the large legacy of the Freedmen's Bureau," which was established at the end of the Civil War to promote the rights and welfare of freed slaves, as "the work it did not do because it could not."[33] Defending nonetheless the efforts of the Freedmen's Bureau and its first commissioner, Oliver Howard, Du Bois writes:

> [N]othing is more convenient than to heap on the Freedmen's Bureau all the evils of that evil day, and damn it utterly for every mistake and blunder that was made.
>
> All this is easy, but it is neither sensible nor just. *Some one had blundered*, but that was long before Oliver Howard was born; there was criminal aggression and heedless neglect, but without some system of control there would have been far more than there was.[34]

As expansive as it is brief, this allusion transforms Tennyson's blunt characterization of a miscommunicated order into a tragicomic euphemism for one of the most momentous events in world history, the establishment of slavery in the New World. The victims of *this* "blunder" number in the millions, not the hundreds. This shift in scale has the effect of parochializing Tennyson's

concerns, even as Du Bois's unmarked allusion demonstrates the cosmopolitan sophistication of his own voice. This double movement is typical of the
tradition Du Bois caps, recalling in particular James McCune Smith's radical
reframing of the poem. In a development that Smith would applaud, moreover, the further passage of time has brought another twist: in the twenty-first
century, Du Bois's allusion serves less to enhance his own cultural capital than
to renew the poem's currency. In other words, "The Charge of the Light Brigade" now needs Du Bois more than Du Bois needs "The Charge of the
Light Brigade": the poem's very decentering in *The Souls of Black Folk* ensures
it a place in what is, for many latter-day readers (including many readers of this
essay), the canon in front of them.

CHAPTER 11

Another Long Bridge: Reproduction and Reversion in *Hagar's Daughter*

HOLLY JACKSON

A woman escapes at dusk from a slave pen in Washington, D.C., sprints across the Long Bridge toward the woods on the other side of the Potomac, finds herself caught between approaching captors on both sides, clasps her hands, lifts her eyes to heaven, and leaps into the river to her death in view of the White House and the Capitol building. This narrative was written by Seth M. Gates, a congressman from New York, and published under the headline "Slavery in the District" in the *New York Evangelist* on September 8, 1842.[1] The author presented it as an eyewitness description of an event that he had observed with a number of other onlookers. For at least sixty years, this scene circulated in American print culture as anecdotal evidence of the perversity of slavery and the desperate desire for freedom among the enslaved. It was reprinted in other periodicals, including 1845 issues of the *Herald of Freedom* and *Prisoner's Friend*.[2] It was retold in poems by Sarah J. Clarke and John Kemble Laskey, published in the *Liberator* in 1844 and 1845, respectively.[3] Frederick Douglass recounted the story in an address delivered in Boston on May 28, 1844.[4] Even after emancipation, this scene retained its appeal, resurfacing in diverse works including the autobiography *Half a Century* (1880) by journalist activist Jane Grey Cannon Swisshelm, Frances E. W. Harper's novel *Iola Leroy* (1892), and an 1897 history of African Americans by the Reverend Norman B. Wood.[5]

Of course, the position of this 680-word narrative in literary history was cemented eleven years after its original publication when William Wells Brown gave the woman on the Long Bridge a name, a backstory, and a Revolutionary genealogy, reproducing this excerpt verbatim as the climactic scene of the first known African American novel, *Clotel; or, The President's Daughter* (1853).[6] His rendering of this tale in the chapter "Death Is Freedom" has come to emblematize this foundational novel, serving as a revealing and pivotal image in the tradition of the African American novel that it inaugurated.

Conveying this magnetic narrative into the twentieth century, Pauline Hopkins reused it nearly in its entirety and original expression as the cornerstone of her first serialized novel, *Hagar's Daughter*, published in the *Colored American Magazine* from March 1901 to March 1902. From 1874, when Brown, by then a celebrity author and orator, awarded the fifteen-year-old Hopkins a ten-dollar prize for a high school essay, her literary oeuvre abounds with homage to this antecedent author, including a trail of unattributed quotations from Brown's fiction, drama and nonfiction.[7] In an excellent recent biography of Hopkins, Lois Brown holds that Hopkins's liberal and uncredited "borrowings" of these antecedent texts "raise the issue of plagiarism in *Hagar's Daughter*, even as they confirm the deep respect that Hopkins had for Brown's work."[8] Focusing on the striking reproduction of the Long Bridge scene, I argue that, far from unoriginality, this repetition marks an instance of intertextual suturing that contributed to the establishment of an African American literary tradition and typifies Hopkins's signature strategy as a writer of politically engaged historical romance. While this retelling itself serves as a bridge uniting the two novels in a tradition of African American literature spanning the century, Hopkins ultimately utilizes this duplication to foreground the failure of Reconstruction to facilitate a bridge into freedom for African Americans. Her repetition constructs a tragic loop, creating for readers the sense of déjà vu that Hopkins and her contemporaries describe as central to black experience at the turn of the twentieth century.

In Hopkins's novels, the struggles of post-Reconstruction African Americans indict the failed progress of racial equality after the Civil War. As she explains in the preface to *Contending Forces* (1900), "the atrocity of the acts committed one hundred years ago are duplicated today, when slavery is supposed no longer to exist."[9] She declares that the difference between the experience of antebellum slaves and African Americans at the beginning of the twentieth century "is so slight as to be scarcely worth mentioning."[10] Historical

recursivity, the duplication of the atrocities of slavery and the imperceptibil-
ity of any progress toward true equality and freedom for African Americans,
stands as Hopkins's primary characterization of the post-Reconstruction
nadir.

This disruptive mode of history informs her attention to sexual as well as
textual reproduction. In the social Darwinist racial discourse of this period,
notions of historical progress were inextricable from hereditarian theories of
inheritance and race survival. Hopkins strategically returns to antebellum
texts, manipulating a widespread white American cultural preoccupation with
black ancestral regression at the turn of the twentieth century. Responding to
white writers who forecast African American decline and even extinction in
the aftermath of emancipation, Hopkins portrays a fin de siècle culture in
which the inherited legacy of slavery enforces the immobility and even regression of African Americans, and an irrational clinging to the ancestral
past degrades white American families and the nation they represent.

This body of social scientific racism claimed that people of African descent had enjoyed a modicum of advancement under slavery but had failed
with freedom. As Charles Chesnutt explains in *The Marrow of Tradition* (1901),
"statistics of crime, ingeniously manipulated, were made to present a fearful
showing against the negro. Vital statistics were made to prove that he had
degenerated from an imaginary standard of physical excellence which had
existed under the benign influence of slavery."[11] Chief among these prophe-
cies of black extinction, Frederick L. Hoffman's 1896 *Race Traits and Tendencies of the American Negro* argues that since emancipation, "in vital capacity,
the most important of all physiological characteristics, the tendency of the
race has been downward."[12] Hoffman popularized the view that "the colored
population is gradually parting with the virtues and the moderate degree of
economic efficiency developed under the regime of slavery." He predicted
that in the near future, a combination of racial "traits and tendencies must in
the end cause the extinction of the race."[13]

Paul Brandon Barringer, chairman of the faculty at the University of Virginia at the time, agreed: "Every day of slavery seems to have counted for their
benefit."[14] He concluded that African Americans were "reverting through he-
reditary forces to savagery. Fifty centuries of savagery in the blood cannot be
held down by two centuries of forced good behavior if the controlling influ-
ences which held down his savagery are withdrawn as they have been in this
case."[15] These theories foreclosed the possibility that African Americans
might be safely integrated into American society because even the most re-

mote future generation would transmit the threat of return to a savage ancestral type.

The pages of the *Colored American Magazine* provided a forum for African American rebuttal to these theories of racial decline. A number of articles in the magazine flipped the accusation of reversion, positing white savagery and criminality in the nadir period as an inheritance from, or a return to, the conditions under slavery. A September 1901 article, which shares a page with an installment of *Hagar's Daughter*, explains that after the Civil War, the Southern people "immediately set to work with their great ability, influence and power, to defeat the emancipation act of the Nation, and return the Freedmen to a new and far more cruel slavery. They brought to their aid, those characteristics of cruelty and injustice, rooted and cultivated in them and their ancestors during slavery."[16] These characteristics, according to the author, manifested in a "system of barbarism, cruelty and injustice, in constant practice during the past thirty-five years; educating the children, the youth and young manhood of that white people, into the savagery of past ages."[17] In other words, the descendants of slaveholders were reverting to a savage ancestral condition. With similar outrage against barriers to black progress that amounted to a return to slavery, Hopkins's fiction seizes the biopolitical conceptual chain that connects family to race to nation to articulate a powerful antiracist response to popular theories of black reversion and decline.

Hopkins identifies a multivalent understanding of white kinship as a chief ideological structure impeding black advancement and deconstructs the white family as both sentimentalized private institution and politicized public phenomenon, the symbolic and biological building block of the nation and of a national identity founded in racial purity.[18] Intervening into the broader cultural preoccupation with theories of racial ancestry and national futurity, *Hagar's Daughter* interrogates women's role in the transmission of identity. The byzantine, multipart plot structure implements an abortive teleology that resists the linear, progressive conventions of the novel in its exploration of the relationship of family structures to national history.[19] The first chapter orients the reader in 1860, opening at a Confederate convention where we meet St. Clair Enson and a slave trader named Walker. The trader claims that he can help St. Clair resecure the inheritance that will pass from his brother to a newborn daughter and travels with him to Enson Hall in Maryland. Walker presents St. Clair's brother, Ellis Enson, with a bill of sale and claims his wife, Hagar, and their infant daughter as his "stolen property," supplying proof that Hagar had been a slave adopted by a rich white family and raised as their own child.[20]

Although Ellis Enson pays off Walker, he explains to Hagar that he must end their marriage not only to abide the law but to save his family: "I feel it my duty as a Southern gentleman, the representative of a proud old family, to think of others beside myself and not allow my own inclinations to darken the escutcheon of a good old name. I cannot, I dare not, and the law forbids me to acknowledge as my wife a woman in whose veins courses a drop of the accursed blood of the Negro slave" (59). His horror at the prospect that Hagar might "darken the escutcheon" of the "proud old family" of the Ensons (in other words, reveal as interracial an emblematic white family obsessed with its pure genealogy) proves to be the downfall of not only the Ensons but the nation that they represent.

The danger that Hagar poses to the Enson family highlights the position of women as both the cornerstone and the greatest threat to white racial purity. Perhaps not surprisingly, the discourse of black morbidity theorized racial identity as determined by maternal inheritance, so that the sexual license of white men held no consequences for racial integrity. William Benjamin Smith, for example, insists that white men who sire mixed-race children do not compromise white purity: "however degraded and even unnatural, they in nowise, not even in the slightest degree, defile the Southern Caucasian blood. That blood to-day is absolutely pure."[21] Underscoring his double standard for the transgression of interracial sex, he posits that "the offense of the man is individual and limited, while that of the woman is general, and strikes mortally at the existence of the family itself."[22] His indeterminate use of "family," seemingly to describe both the immediate kin relations of the woman in question and also the entire "racial family" of whites, positions white women as the safeguard of the survival of both inextricable formations.

Hagar's Daughter troubles the very idea of white womanhood, arguing that a woman of mixed racial heritage can function seamlessly as the white wife of an elite plantation owner and "would have remained in this social sphere all her life, beloved and respected by her descendants, her blood mingling with the best blood of the country if untoward circumstances had not exposed her ancestry" (62). In other words, Hagar's "one drop" of "black blood" would have circulated in the country's "white" gene pool, making no difference as long as it went undetected, as this passage implies that many other cases surely do. But in the white imagination, "the one drop of black blood neutralized all her virtues, and she became, from the moment of exposure, an unclean thing. Can anything more unjust be imagined in a republican form of government whose excuse for existence is the upbuilding of mankind" (62)? Rather than positively re-signifying black blood, Hopkins emphasizes instead that the discourse of racial blood is not only irrational but blatantly antidemocratic, a violation of basic republican principles.

At the end of this first plot, Ellis changes his mind and makes plans for a new life with Hagar abroad. However, the family is soon informed that Ellis has committed suicide, his disfigured body found at the edge of the property gripping a pistol. National history is again interspersed with family history, as St. Clair's usurpation of Enson Hall is coincident with the formation of the Confederate States of America, drawing on the traditional familial metaphor that cast the Civil War as a white fraternal schism.

Significantly, it is at the stark break between the two plots that Hopkins's extended near-verbatim reiteration of William Wells Brown's *Clotel* appears. When Hagar escapes captivity, the novel reverts to the language of Gates's 1842 Long Bridge narrative: "It was not far from the prison to the long bridge which passes from the lower part of the city, across the Potomac, to the forests of Arlington Heights. Thither the fugitive directed her flight" (73–74). Like Brown, Hopkins includes a description of "the hue-and-cry" of her pursuers and the "astonished citizens" that "poured forth from their dwellings" to join in the chase (Hopkins 74; Brown 205). Both novels declare, "her resolution was taken" and conclude, respectively, as follows: "[Clotel] raised her eyes toward heaven, and begged for . . . mercy and compassion . . . and then, with a single bound, she vaulted over the railings of the bridge, and sunk for ever beneath the waves of the river" (Brown 207)! In Hopkins's account, "[Hagar] raised her tearful, imploring eyes to heaven as if seeking mercy and compassion, and with one bound sprang over the railing of the bridge, and sank beneath the waters of the Potomac River" (75).

Why would Hopkins, writing in the first years of the twentieth century, revisit, indeed repeat, a novel published half a century earlier, that was itself a reproduction of a narrative published a decade before that? Hanna Wallinger has suggested that "since this leap and similar acts of mothers who would rather kill their children than have them grow up as slaves were most certainly familiar to her readers, Hopkins's repetition of such a well-known scene not only points out the longevity of the African American memory but also reminds the reader of the legacy of a past that will haunt the national memory."[23] While I agree that this repetition indicates the persistence of this narrative in cultural memory, I also see it as Hopkins's most striking formal tactic, both a refutation and an appropriation of pervasive socioscientific theories of black atavism.[24]

Dana Seitler has theorized the concept of atavism in fin de siècle America as "a 'reproduction' and a 'recurrence' of the past in the present . . . [bringing] the ancestral past into conjunction with the modern present."[25] According to Seitler, "atavism offers up a notion of time as multidirectional and of the body as polytemporal . . . atavism suggests not simply genetic continuity but historical and corporeal recursivity."[26] In this case, Hopkins represents this experience through textual recursivity, so "the gap between past and present, between history and prehistory, becomes bridgeable."[27] In bridging the 1850s and the twentieth century with the scene on the Long Bridge, Hopkins twists the phobic white preoccupation with black regression into a literary strategy that we might call textual atavism. Denying the narrative of national progress, Hopkins indicts a white cult of genealogy for catalyzing a reversion to the savage practices of slavery and disallowing black political evolution.[28]

In her essay in this volume, Lara Cohen models an analysis of intertextual citation focused on the relationship between content and formal practices. Reading another heavily circulated scene, Eliza Harris crossing the Ohio by leaping across ice drifts, Cohen writes, "the action of the scene also intimates something of how that practice might work: a textual strategy of leaping from fragment to fragment, cutting across the current's flow."[29] Along these lines, the Long Bridge narrative instructs us in the ways that images, anecdotes, and whole paragraphs circulate through print, bridging texts and serving as connective tissue to build discourses, movements, even identities. Although it seems to confirm our understanding of how literary traditions work, it shakes our reliance on traditional conceptions of this process as a progressive flow of inheritance and innovation. To wit, Hopkins's citation of Brown is not mere writerly homage but a rueful representation of stunted historical evolution. Bridging the 1850s and the twentieth century, this scene affirms African American literature as an intertextual tradition, but far from celebrating the continuity between these epochs in black experience, Hopkins presents it as a tragic impasse.

The projects of the Reconstruction period designed to aid the transition of the formerly enslaved into the full exercise of citizenship were imagined as "a bridge from slavery to freedom," as Charles Sumner described the Freedmen's Bureau in 1864.[30] In the pages of the *Colored American Magazine* surrounding the publication of *Hagar's Daughter*, there is frequent reference to the path or journey of progress that African Americans must complete. These accounts point to a variety of obstructions on this path of progress, making the bridge to freedom impassable. A July 1902 article denounces attempts "to blockade the Negro's road of progress with the frowning barriers of distinction and discrimination."[31] The passage to freedom can only be completed, this author declares, if Americans "batter down all walls and limitations— remove all obstructions from the Negro's thorny pathway of advancement."[32] A poignant example of this metaphor, Hopkins's retelling of the Long Bridge narrative modifies the meaning of its original incarnations, written before the abolition of slavery, so that Hagar's tragically foiled passage to freedom represents a failed transition between emancipation and her own early twentieth-century moment.

The break of twenty years immediately following this scene typifies Hopkins's disruptive narrative mode and its opposition to notions of linear, progressive national history.[33] Indeed, this interruption of the progress of the serialized plot, seeming to stop the forward action and start again with unrelated material, registers the failure of historical progress that, I argue, constitutes the subject of the novel as a whole.[34] Unlike Clotel, Hagar and her daughter are not granted the freedom of death but survive and resurface after the Civil War, representing the tragic survival of slavery in the post-Reconstruction United States.

The narrative reopens in 1882 with a conversation between two seemingly new characters, General Benson, the head of the Federal Treasury Department, and Major Madison. These characters introduce Senator Zenas Bowen, an unconventional western multimillionaire, his beautiful wife Estelle, his daughter from a previous marriage, Jewell, and her boyfriend Cuthbert Sumner, the son and heir of a wealthy New England family. They hatch a plot to gain both the Bowen and the Sumner family fortunes by breaking up the young couple, clearing the way for Madison's daughter, Aurelia, to marry Sumner and General Benson to marry Jewell. After a tangled courtship plot, Benson murders Elise Bradford, a woman working in his office and the mother of his illegitimate child, and pins the crime on Sumner, who is apprehended and jailed. Distraught, Jewell seeks the help of a detective, Chief Henson of the Secret Service. The ensuing trial reveals that nearly all of the characters have two identities. Madison is revealed as the slave trader Walker, and General Benson as St. Clair Enson, who is wanted as a conspirator in the Lincoln assassination. Chief Henson is actually his brother, Ellis Enson, and Estelle reveals herself as Hagar. Soon thereafter, Jewell, who Sumner had described as his "white angel of purity," is found to be Hagar's daughter, the interracial Enson heir who had apparently died with her mother in the jump from the Long Bridge (103).

In this second plot, the setting returns to the Enson plantation and social relations clearly revert to their antebellum structure. As Kristina Brooks observes, "There are just three characters whose names and racial identities remain constant over the twenty-year span of the novel, thus providing continuity between the two narratives."[35] She continues, "Aunt Henny, Marthy, and Isaac are static characters incapable of development. . . . Stuck in a time warp and in plantation culture, the mammy, wench, and buck are not subjects but objects for the reader's gaze."[36] While Brooks holds that these objectified caricatures offer a minstrel "sideshow" to the novel's "main act" of mixed-race characters, I argue that they signal the novel's central formal tactic, namely the uncomfortable persistence of the antebellum past in the post-Reconstruction present through the recurrence of ancestral literary types.

Through this double plot structure that folds back on itself, Hopkins slowly reveals that American society after Reconstruction is not a new society but at once the perpetuation and the repetition of the conditions under slavery, with only the names and surface details changed. Hopkins indicates that there has been no progress for African Americans, no successful crossing of the bridge into freedom and a new national era. The transformation of the Enson brothers into Benson and Henson signifies the splintering of the family identity so rigorously protected, even fetishized, in the first plot. Importantly, the disclosure of concealed identities reveals that none of the women in the novel are white. Even Aurelia Madison is revealed as an "octoroon," meaning that no matter which choice Cuthbert had made, he would not have married a white woman. All of the seemingly white families turn out to be interracial due to these mixed-race women's role as the transmitters of racial identity. This novel constructs maternal inheritance as ultimately inaccessible and mysterious, flouting the culture's obsession with white women as the safeguards and vessels of American national identity through white racial purity. Hopkins debunks the white woman at the center of the myth of the white family, whose sexual and racial purity served as the justification for the long campaign of racist terrorism in the nadir that garishly illustrated the failure of Reconstruction.

Shocked that Ellis Enson plans to remarry the recently widowed and racially revealed Hagar, Sumner asks, "ought we not, as Anglo-Saxons, keep the fountain head of our racial stream as unpolluted as possible?" (271). Enson points out that Sumner is willing to concede "every privilege but the vital one of deciding a question of the commonest personal liberty which is the fundamental principle of the holy family tie" (271). This exchange clarifies the novel's position that only the willingness to interracialize the family, or rather to accept the interracial character of the American family, will truly mean that African Americans are the acknowledged equals of whites. Hopkins refuses to concede sexuality as a private or purely "social" consideration, asserting instead a biopolitical analytics of reproduction as the controlling mechanism of a racially stratified society. *Hagar's Daughter* analogizes the "impassable social chasm" enforced between blacks and whites in the service of protecting the purity of "white blood" to an impassable bridge into freedom and a new historical era, suggesting that even in the twentieth century, African Americans were stuck in the hereditarily subordinate status that defined the condition of the enslaved.

Although Ellis and Hagar reunite, and the good brother regains possession of the patrimonial estate, seemingly restoring the order that the Civil War disrupted, the novel ends with a powerful symbol of the degraded future of the Enson family and the nation that it represents. The happy ending of this interracial couple is compromised by the fact that their child, the title character, has died prematurely of a sudden illness, foiling the marriage plot.[37] Hopkins rejects the heterofamilial teleology of novelistic conventions that would turn again to the institution of the family to represent narrative conclusion.

The only Enson child remaining symbolizes the degraded status of this fiercely protected white line: "Across the lawn of Enson Hall a child—a boy—ran screaming and laughing. . . . It was the child of St. Clair Enson and Elise Bradford, the last representative of the Enson family. . . . In him was embodied, a different form, a lesson of the degradation of slavery" (284). Hopkins describes this unnamed bastard with the Faulknerian epithet "the motherless and worse than fatherless child" (253). In Hopkins, this last white child, or "end son" that the family name itself seems to presage, exemplifies not the taint of interracialism perverting a white dynasty but rather the decay and corruption of whiteness, its failure to evolve and progress. The proud Enson line, so strenuously protected from the taint of blackness, continues only in illegitimacy and violence, hobbled by its own maniacal attempts to deny and exclude the blackness that it already contains. In a radical reversal of popular discourses of postbellum black decline, Hopkins depicts whites meeting that end instead. Far from extinction, "black blood is everywhere," plentiful, if unacknowledged, in the white families understood to constitute and represent the nation.

Hopkins rejects the white fixation on ancestry as irrational and stultifying but embraces her genealogical relationship to Brown and the narratives that precede her, seemingly offering print culture as an alternate vehicle for identity transmission and historical continuity in lieu of blood-based conceptions of lineage and reproduction tainted with socioscientific racism. The woman on Long Bridge seized the power over life and death, refusing to endure and pass on the condition of enslavement, but although she never makes it across in *Hagar's Daughter* or any other of the narrative's iterations, the medium nonetheless ensures her a kind of unquiet survival. It is tempting to think of print as a bloodless utopian space of continuity, inheritance, homage, and cooperative meaning making, but Hopkins's formal enactment of the recursive routes of print discourse expresses instead a galling sense of stasis, exemplifying the wrenching ambivalence with which narratives of slavery are reproduced and witnessed again in the African American novel. These works bear the tragedies of both remembering and forgetting, both dying and surviving, both silence and endless retelling.

CHAPTER 12

"Photographs to Answer Our Purposes": Representations of the Liberian Landscape in Colonization Print Culture

DALILA SCRUGGS

Perched on a lighthouse, Augustus Washington cast his gaze over the landscape of his newly founded and recently adopted country. Standing high above Liberia's capital city, Monrovia, Washington took a picture, capturing his point of view in a daguerreotype. This image remains only in the form of a wood engraving based on the photograph (Figure 12.1). The daguerreotype itself is unlocated. The print shows a vegetated landscape stretching into the horizon. The foreground is marked by palm tree fronds, which interrupt the sweeping vista of the town below. A cleared pathway winds along the center of the composition, drawing attention to the seemingly miniature buildings nestled in the forest. In the background, a river meanders toward the horizon, embracing the border of the settlement.

However, American Colonization Society (ACS) recording secretary Dr. James W. Lugenbeel was not impressed. Upon receipt of the daguerreotype taken from the lighthouse, he told Washington, "Unless you get a good, clear picture it will not answer our purpose."[1] Thus, this photograph was found insufficient and Washington was enjoined to send another picture, this one picturing the city from its anchorage. The result was a wood engraving that portrays Monrovia as a blossoming "city on a hill" (Figure 12.2). In the years that followed, this "view" was reproduced several times in ACS literature and elsewhere, eventually becoming an iconic representation of the capital of

Figure 12.1. "View from the Lighthouse," a wood engraving after a daguerreotype by Augustus Washington, ca. 1856. Courtesy of Harvard College Library, Widener Library, Widener Afr 7350.4.20; V.24.

Figure 12.2. "View of Monrovia from the Anchorage," a wood engraving after Augustus Washington, ca. 1856. Courtesy of Harvard College Library, Widener Library, Widener Afr 7350.4.20; V.24.

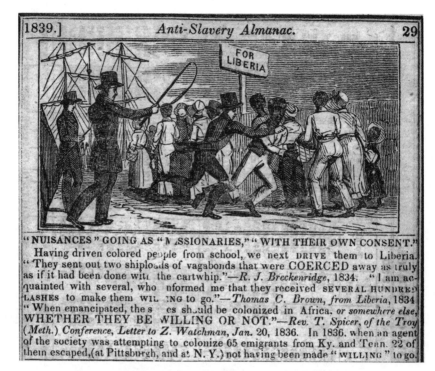

Figure 12.3. Illustration in *Anti-Slavery Almanac* (1839). Courtesy of the Library
Company of Philadelphia.

Liberia. Meanwhile, the view of Monrovia from the lighthouse was largely
rejected.

Lugenbeel's vexed reply underscores the stakes of pictorial representation
in the colonization debate. The American Colonization Society was the perennial villain in the abolitionist press. An illustration in the 1839 *Anti-
Slavery Almanac*, for example, depicted the society's mission to send blacks to
Africa as a second middle passage; its victims trudge toward a ship bound for
an unknown and undesirable destination (Figure 12.3). Scholars have ana-
lyzed abolitionists' savvy approach to visual propaganda, noting especially
their effective appropriation of proslavery imagery (such as runaway slave
advertisements), which was then redeployed in ways that satirically decon-
structed their original message.[2] But colonizationists also actively developed
a visual vocabulary to support their cause.

Augustus Washington seemed to offer colonizationists the perfect public
relations strategy: his images were thought to be backed by photographic

veracity and the authenticity of black settler testimony. In this respect, his photography's evidentiary claims resemble those of slave narratives, in which black eyewitness accounts and the facticity of black testimony were used to bolster white institutional power.[3] Harnessing Washington's photographs as evidence for publication proved elusive, however. Even as the society relied on newspapers to deploy their photographic evidence, the mechanics necessary to assimilate Washington's daguerreotypes into a newspaper image and the subsequent reprinting of the landscape images loosened rather than strengthened the society's grip on its visual messages. Washington's written testimony was no more easily drafted than his photographic evidence. To understand the American Colonization Society's efforts to manage the image of Liberia and to discern how that cause was both sustained and confounded by the processes of printing and reprinting, this essay will trace the production, dissemination, and textual framing of these two wood-engraved landscapes in colonization print culture.

Before retracing these pathways of circulation, some background about the American Colonization Society and the country of Liberia will provide context for the ACS's interest in representing the Liberian landscape. The ACS was founded in 1816 as a reform organization dedicated to promoting African "colonization," a movement dedicated to sending blacks to Africa. In 1821, the ACS procured land on the coast of West Africa and established a privately owned colony that would be known as Liberia. The land was a settlement for free African Americans and slaves manumitted on the condition that they go to Africa. In 1847, Liberia ceased to be an ACS colony and became a sovereign country. This change in status was in some measure pragmatic, as Britain and France questioned the legitimacy of a philanthropic organization's authority to curb their colonial ambitions in West Africa and the United States disavowed direct responsibility for the colony's protection. Although Liberia became an independent country, the American Colonization Society continued to support Liberia from the United States by promoting emigration among blacks and seeking financial support and political advocacy among whites.[4]

Colonization was a hot-button issue frequently mentioned in debates over the abolition of slavery. The ACS saw colonization as a moderate alternative to either perpetual slavery or immediate abolition. Colonizationists held that blacks were unable to be incorporated into American society and yet could be transformed into capable and industrious citizens by relocating to Africa. Equality (or likeness) of blacks with whites was predicated on the separation of the races and removal of blacks to Africa. Following scholars who observe this tension between sameness and difference in textual sources, this essay suggests that visual images of the Liberian landscape also articulated this colonization position.[5]

To promote African colonization, the American Colonization Society and its auxiliaries devoted a great deal of energy to constructing a Liberian landscape in text and image. The ACS needed pictures that would attract new settlers and encourage financial and political support from state and federal governments, as well as from the public at large. One of the first things the ACS wanted to do was to disabuse the American public of prevailing stereotypes that represented Africa as either "the arid desert with its burning sun and fiery atmosphere, or the tangled jungle with its putrid exhalations of deadly malaria."[6] Instead of some African wilderness, the ACS argued, Liberia was becoming a little America on the shores of Africa. Not only was Liberia a colonial "off-shoot of America," it was supposed to be a harbinger of the Christianization and civilization of Africa.[7] Liberia's ability to replicate American institutions and ways of life would be evidence of the viability of African colonization, suggesting that American values of Christianity, republicanism, and civilization were being exported to Africa. Clearly, ACS felt that the image of Monrovia, the capital of Liberia and its oldest settlement, would best represent this crucial progress of Western values in Africa for an American audience.

As African Americans did the actual work of colonizing West Africa, however, they faced tropical illnesses, met difficulties in establishing homes and farms, and encountered resistance from the indigenous inhabitants.[8] Although settlement of Liberia was fraught by these struggles for basic survival, the ACS's preferred visual representation of the Liberian landscape sublimated these issues by safely dividing clearing and bush, settlement and wilderness. By reproducing and circulating one favored image of Liberia in print, colonizationists sought to depict Liberia as a reforming place where African Americans could become capable citizens of a black republic while safely removed from white society. Thus, the contested representation of Liberia was not only about a small West African country but also spoke to a larger debate about race and citizenship in the United States.

ACS Reception

Prior to immigrating to Liberia, Augustus Washington (ca. 1820–75) operated a successful daguerreotype studio in Hartford, Connecticut. He took up daguerreotypy while he was a student at Dartmouth College in New Hampshire, turning to photography to help pay his school expenses. Succumbing to racial discrimination and financial debt, Washington withdrew from Dartmouth at the end of his freshman year in 1844.[9] He then opened a daguerreotype studio in Hartford, which he operated from 1846 until his departure for Liberia in late 1853.[10] Extant photographs from his Hartford practice indicate that he had a wide clientele, from Hartford's elite to those of more modest means.[11] During this time, Washington took the earliest known portrait of radical abolitionist John Brown.[12] In late 1853, Washington immigrated to Liberia and continued his daguerreotype practice in West Africa.[13] The photographer arrived in Liberia with commissions from colonization supporters for landscape views already in hand.

The ACS's commission of daguerreotypes views of Monrovia harnessed a popular nineteenth-century trend. Lithographic views of cities (Figure 12.4) were among the most widely consumed printed images in nineteenth-century America. These city views were used to promote and advertise the growth of American towns. Daguerreotypists also responded to the popular enthusiasm for landscape views. Many daguerreotype landscapes focused on western cities, like the bustling port city of San Francisco, California (Figure 12.5), in order to illustrate the progress of the city for folks back east.[14] Daguerreotype views were supposed to demonstrate that western cities were growing urban spaces, not just remote outposts. African Americans were among the myriad artists creating city views.[15] Likewise, views of Liberia were used to gather support for the colonization movement and encourage settlement in Liberia.

The American Colonization Society's expectations for Augustus Washington's daguerreotypes were likely shaped by preexisting conventions for representing Monrovia in colonization newspapers. From the earliest examples, views of Monrovia stress distinctions between clearing and wilderness, civilized and savage. "View of the Colonial Settlement at Cape Montserado" (Figure 12.6) was published in the April 1825 issue of ACS's *African Repository*, just three years after the first settlers arrived at the location that would be known as Monrovia. The landscape is shown in profile, depicting the city as seen from the mouth of the Mesurado River. Nearly two-thirds of the land is a forested landscape; one-third has been cleared. A handful of Western-style edifices are situated along the ridge of the cape. Set apart from and below these Western buildings are two cylindrical buildings with conical roofs, connoting native architecture. Territorial control is signified by the American

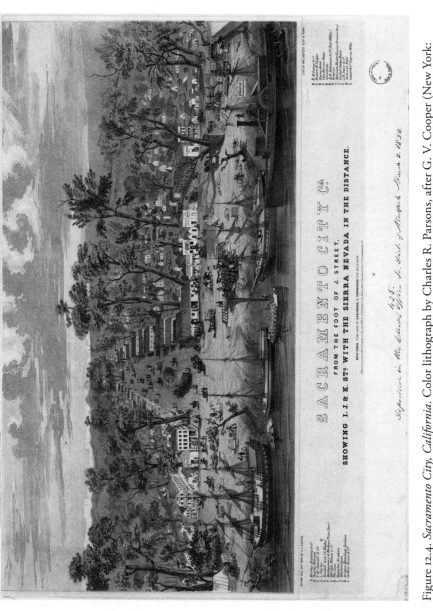

Figure 12.4. *Sacramento City, California*. Color lithograph by Charles R. Parsons, after G. V. Cooper (New York: Stringer and Townsend, 1850). Library of Congress Prints and Photographs Division, Washington, D.C. LC-DIG-pga-04015

Figure 12.5. *View of San Francisco Harbor* (1850 or 1851). Half-plate daguerreotype. Papers of the David D. Porter family, 1799–1899, Library of Congress, Washington, D.C. LC-USZC4-7421.

flags, one posted near the round tower, left of center, and the other at the summit of the promontory. Dozens of canoes glide along the water on either side of the sandbar, perhaps navigated by Krumen, an ethnic group known for their maritime expertise. These small craft are overshadowed by the American sailing vessel on the lower right.

The colonial transformations of the land imagined by colonizationists when Liberia was a fledgling settlement continued to shape the image of the Liberian landscape in colonization literature well after Liberia became a sovereign nation. The basic characteristics pictured in "View of the Colonial Settlement at Cape Montserado" are repeated in "View of Monrovia" (Figure 12.7), an image used in the February 1851 issue of the *African Repository*.[16] As in the 1825 view, land settlement is juxtaposed with vegetation. However, the scene is reframed so that the village occupies slightly more of the composition than the forested areas. Moreover, the artist eliminated details that would mark the landscape as specifically African; palm trees and cone-and-cylinder architecture are absent. The anchorage design has been elaborated to include several docks. Therefore, the illustration again stresses contrast between settlement and wilderness of Africa.

Emphasis on clearing and forest may have been designed to address health concerns of the tropical environment. White ACS agents and black

View of the Colonial Settlement at Cape Montserado.

Figure 12.6. "View of the Colonial Settlement at Cape Montserado," 1825. Engraving published in the *African Repository and Colonial Journal* 1, no. 2 (April 1825). Courtesy of Harvard College Library, Widener Library, Afr 7350 1, vols. 1–2 (1825–27).

Figure 12.7. "View of Monrovia," as published in the February 1851 issue of the *African Repository*. Harvard College Library, Widener Library, KF25518, V. 27, 1851.

settlers in Liberia alike died in great numbers due primarily to malaria, though yellow fever, typhus, typhoid, dengue were all present. According to some demographic studies, more than one in every five emigrants died from disease.[17] The parasite causes of malaria and its transmission by mosquitoes were not yet known.[18] Instead, "African fever," as it was sometimes called in colonization literature, was generally believed to be caused by miasma, or the effluvia of "bad air" (literally *mal aria*) given off by the environment. The believed causes were many, including foul smell emanating from swamps, wet vegetation, and decay from undergrowth in forests. The (popularly believed but misguided) solution to the miasma-plagued environment was to cut down tall trees to admit sunlight and cleanse the air.[19] While the alteration of the land was part of a fraught struggle for basic survival and territorial power, visual representations of the Liberian landscape suppress these issues by safely dividing clearing and bush, settlement and wilderness, civilized and savage.

The engraving based on Washington's view from the anchorage takes the composition of these earlier landscape representations one step further by focusing almost exclusively on the town, using surrounding foliage merely as a framing device (see Figure 12.2). The engraver most likely took interpretive liberties to give the view greater symbolic resonance. For example, atmospheric effects were difficult to capture in daguerreotypes; blue and violet rays overexposed the photographic plate, leaving the sky blank in many landscape daguerreotypes.[20] Here, however, the artist chose to bestow the church spire with a halo of clouds. This artistic intervention not only transcribes the presence of the building from the photograph into print but also interprets that structure as a symbol of Christianity.

This view embellished the front page of the New York State Colonization Society's newspaper the *New-York Colonization Journal* in January 1856.[21] The caption accompanying the woodcut advised the reader to take note of the church, high school, and market house, while observations about Monrovia's "substantial" and "commodious" stone buildings demonstrated the extent of the city's development. With this language, the article engages what Mary Louise Pratt has called a "rhetoric of presence."[22] Victorian "discovery" narratives assess landscape as "good" or "bad" based on what signs of high culture and Western institutions are present or lacking in the landscape. In other words, the narrator bases his aesthetic and ideological critique of a newly encountered land on the presence or absence of mosques, kiosks, palaces, gardens, and the like. Aesthetic deficiencies are understood as requiring the intervention of the narrator's home culture. By calling attention to the settlement's architecture and city planning, the ACS was trying to present proof that Liberia had already been transformed by the presence of American culture and civilization. The *New-York Colonization Journal* lauded Washington's daguerreotype of the anchorage as "the truest view yet obtained of Monrovia."[23]

In addition to discussing the wood engraving at hand, the newspaper also whetted the appetite of the audience by describing the "view from the lighthouse" in order to solicit funds to have the second daguerreotype made into a print: "We have another of his plates, giving a view of a large portion of Monrovia as observed from the lighthouse at the highest point of the Cape, a wood-cut of which would present Ashmun street, on which the church and school-house and market-house above described are located, as also Broad street and other streets parallel with it, extending nearly two miles along the hill. If any of our readers will furnish the $20 to defray the expenses, this shall appear in a future number of the Journal."[24] Here again, the city grid and signs of civilization (church and school) as well as economic prosperity (market house) are highlighted in the *Journal*'s description. While the editors may have had in hand a daguerreotype that fit this description of the outlook from the lighthouse, the resulting wood engraving did not convincingly produce this effect. Following this solicitation, the society must have received funds to have this second daguerreotype translated into a wood engraving.

Six months later, the *Journal* published the view from the lighthouse. This time, however, the paper addressed its engraved views apologetically. The editors had to concede that shrubbery obscured a clear view of the town. They asked their readers to remember that "small houses hid in gardens" are hard to see. If the buildings looked dwarfed by the tropical vegetation, it was because the "view was taken by the daguerreotypist at a distance of over half a mile from the nearest object, and presents a distant view of several miles."[25] Though the editors do not disavow the veracity of photography, they fault position of the photographer as witness to the landscape. A picture usually placed below the masthead of the newspaper was instead tucked away on the third page of the June issue. Perhaps there were problems with the photograph itself, but the textual anchoring of the wood engraving suggests that the image also raised anxiety about land.

The perceived failure of Washington's photographs is surprising since his strategy to photograph from the lighthouse conformed to contemporary practices for picturing the American city. Early nineteenth-century American city views were drawn from ground level or a slightly elevated position. By midcentury, however, the perspective from which the city was represented shifted from a frontal, eye-level view to an overhead vision of the landscape.[26] After the Civil War, town views took on an almost cartographic appearance as they were depicted from a vantage point thousands of miles above the city. Following the artistic conventions of lithographic city views, daguerreotypists set up their cameras on balconies and high hills to get a view wide enough to enclose the city into a unified whole.

Even though Washington followed the conventions for landscape photography, the medium itself posed its own challenges, especially in comparison to cityscapes pictured in lithographs. Lithographers were better able to construct and shape their view of the city, sometimes manipulating the city view by choosing imaginary viewpoints or adding details that illustrated future plans for the city rather than things as they actually were at the time. Daguerreotypists were restricted to points of view accessible to the camera operator. Furthermore, the indiscriminant gaze of the camera could register the disorder of the city with little room for corrective alterations once the view was taken.[27]

Since the original daguerreotypes are lost, it is impossible to determine what compositional infelicities or technical malfunctions may have appeared in the photograph. Perhaps Washington had inadequate lenses for taking "views" since his business was primarily in portraiture. Daguerreotype cameras used for taking landscape photographs required lenses that were corrected for sharpness of field, whereas lenses for portraiture sacrificed crispness of the image for a faster exposure time.[28] Blurring of the image could also have been caused by the camera shaking or movement in the landscape caused by wind blowing in the trees. Washington conceded failure as well. He spent his first several weeks convalescing from malarial infection; "I was never well enough to train around in the sun and take views," he later explained.[29] Even these failures, if they were in fact detrimental to the project, are symptomatic of difficulties experienced by settlers but nonetheless underplayed by colonizationists.

Beyond any technical difficulties Washington may have experienced while taking the photograph, the characteristics of the image were necessarily altered by the mechanics of translating the photograph into print. Daguerreotypes are unique images created by tiny droplets of mercury affixed to the shiny surface of a silver-coated copper plate. This process affords the daguerreotype an incredibly high image resolution. Thus, the daguerreotype may well have provided a vista of Monrovia's streets and homes. However, the technology for reproducing photographs in ways that retain their tonality in print would not be developed until the late nineteenth century. From the 1840s until the 1880s, wood engraving was the favored way of reproducing photographs for the illustrated press. The woodblocks used for wood engravings could be placed next to text blocks and run through the letterpress at the same time.[30] While the photograph conveys visual information through gradation of shade, wood engravings are composed by a matrix of lines.[31] Information is lost as an image is translated from one medium to the other. In photographs, icon, index, and symbol are seamlessly woven into a continuous field. The engraver's job is to use line to pluck out icons (a house, a street, a signpost) and assemble these disparate elements into a legible composition. Thus, even as wood engraving facilitated the appropriation of Washington's photograph for deployment in colonization newspapers, the mechanics of appropriation dictated a tenuous grasp on the information.

More than any possible mechanical failures, the loss of information as the engraver translated the scene from daguerreotype to wood engraving may have provoked psychological anxiety about the Liberian landscape as a potentially hostile environment, not only for the African American settler in Liberia but also for the viewer of the engraving in the United States. The artificial dichotomy between settlement and natural environment breaks down. Even if the taking a photograph from a lighthouse is a gesture of visual mastery of the landscape, the opaque ambiguity of the print rendered in dense hatching and swarming zigzags acts as a foil to the sweeping vista. Instead, the viewer is forced to submerge his gaze in the vegetation to pick out signs of settlement. I suspect that the ambiguity of the engraving came too close to unearthing the public's concerns about the relationship between the mortality rate and the natural environment in the West African settlement—negative press that the ACS spent a great deal of time combating.

Opposition in Press

Opponents of colonization seized on the difficulties of life on the African frontier and argued that colonizationists misrepresented the reality in Liberia. For example, black Northerner William Nesbit traveled to Liberia on the same voyage as Augustus Washington and registered his utter disappointment in a travel journal.[32] Nesbit's *Four Months in Liberia* contended that the land chosen by the ACS was unhealthy and the town settlements were dilapidated.[33] Nesbit wrote that Monrovia could not be compared to even the "meanest village" in the United States, with streets so shrouded in bush that "elephants might hide in perfect safety."[34] Not to put too fine a point on it, Nesbit's account claimed that "the face of the country [was] one magnificent swamp."[35] By describing Liberia as a land of swamps, colonization opponents drew on the swamp's association with disease, death, sin, and decay.[36]

Writing the introduction to Nesbit's travel journal, black nationalist and anticolonizationist Martin Delany suggested that the ACS purposely chose an unhealthy location as a death trap, a "national Potter's Field," for the black population in the United States.[37] His contention dovetails with the notion of swamps as a desert place, or no-man's-land.[38] Moreover, this assertion situates Liberia in relation to the United States not as a place of likeness but a place of abjection, a purging of black people from the American body politic.

A point-by-point rebuttal of Martin Delany's claims was offered in the September 1855 issue of the *New-York Colonization Journal*. The charges against the settlement to which the Society took greatest offense had to do with the characterization of the land, namely topography, water quality, timber availability, and farming activity. According to the author, Liberia was no swamp. To the contrary, "The country of Liberia partakes of the character of New England, as to *rocks*, and *hills* and *mountains*, and *streams*; and having repeatedly visited the whole coast . . . the salt meadows near New Haven are, in extent, equal to all the tide-covered lands of Liberia."[39] Their rebuttal was dependent on drawing a likeness between Liberia and the United States. These warring opinions pervaded the press coverage of Liberia for much of the century, from about 1820 to 1870.[40] Of course, descriptions of the Liberian landscape were not about the land per se but were designed to support or refute the viability and morality of the American Colonization Society's enterprise.

Whether espousing pro- or anticolonizationist views, eyewitness reports about Liberia hinged on a rhetoric of truthful representation, constituted by a professed transparent reportage and authentic testimony. Lugenbeel implemented this rhetorical and propaganda strategy in his own written descriptions of Liberia. He lived in Liberia from 1843 to 1849, serving as a physician and ACS agent. He recounted his travels in a scientific-sounding pamphlet entitled *Sketches of Liberia: Comprising a Brief Account of the Geography, Climate, Productions, and Diseases, of the Republic of Liberia*, published in 1850. In *Sketches of Liberia,* he stressed that his was not a historical account, but rather a transparent report of "utmost ingenuousness" that aimed to provide the unbiased reader with a "record of Liberia *as it is.*"[41] This rhetorical strategy resonates with the nineteenth-century discourse on photography rooted in positivism, where truth and knowledge could be acquired through observation.[42] Photography was touted as transparent representation of reality based on a mechanical and chemical technology that eliminated human intervention. The ethics of "objectivity" had been professed by journalists since the 1840s, some of whom overtly equated their practice with photography. Such evidence has led Dan Schiller to suggest that the idea of objectivity in the press is deeply intertwined with the development of nineteenth-century notions of photography's claim to unmediated realism.[43]

Since ACS literature rooted its propaganda in a rhetoric of direct and truthful representation, the society often published letters from African American settlers testifying to their health and happiness in Liberia. As historian Bell I. Wiley has observed, when the ACS published settlers' letters, it often edited them to portray the organization and its mission in a positive light.[44] Visual images by African American settlers in Liberia may have been proffered to the ACS's American constituency as a pictorial iteration of this propaganda strategy.

The archival record suggests that several of the ACS's landscape views were created by, or purported to be the handiwork of, African Americans. For example, a lithographic view of Bassa Cove (Figure 12.8), printed by Philadelphia lithographers Lehman and Duval, was issued by the Pennsylvania Colonization Society (PCS) in 1837. It was advertised in the society's newspaper the *Colonization Herald* as "a drawing made on the spot by Dr. Robert McDowall."[45] Robert McDowell, who was of African and Scottish descent, was the colonial physician and surgeon for the Pennsylvania Colonization Society's settlement at Bassa Cove. The lithograph shows a placid waterway that embraces a settlement, a small collection of homes separated into neatly partitioned lots with tidy fences. Such a quaint image was in keeping with the society's intention to establish a temperate colony; trading in rum, for example, was prohibited in this settlement. A figural group situated in the foreground alludes to the society's professed dedication to Christianizing natives. This picture of Bassa Cove was advertised for sale in the *Colonization Herald* for well over a decade, made available for purchase from the PCS office in Philadelphia, and also used as embellishment for the society's membership certificates.

The very idea of training McDowell as a colonial medical doctor was, at least in part, a public relations maneuver. Following a failed attempt to gain support from British abolitionists in England, Elliott Cresson, a Philadelphia colonization agent and favorite target of immediate-abolitionist derision, realized he would need black representatives in order to counteract the activism of black American abolitionists. British abolitionists saw black Americans as having authentic antislavery views because of their race.[46] Strategizing, Cresson suggested that McDowell could write letters testifying to the progress in Liberia that would "overturn all the machinations of our enemies."[47] Perhaps the lithograph was to serve as visual testimony to complement written accounts. In any case, the *Colonization Herald*'s claim that McDowell's drawing was "made on the spot" asserts its truthfulness based on direct observation, as the creator of this visual image reinforces this claim by virtue of his heritage and his presence in the very location being represented.

Immersed in this discursive contest over truthful reportage, Augustus Washington was aware of his instrumentalization by the ACS and took his role as eyewitness seriously, publishing several letters about Liberia shortly after arrival.[48] His first letters to the United States were glowing reports. After falling ill with malaria and observing the hardship of poorer immigrants,

Figure 12.8. *A View of Bassa Cove (in Liberia)*. Lithograph, after a drawing by Robert McDowell (Philadelphia: Lehman and Duval, lithographers, ca. 1836). Courtesy of the Library Company of Philadelphia.

his letters took a more critical turn.[49] Tellingly, Washington's commitment to photographic veracity led him to dismiss ACS talking points. "There is no use in covering up the dark parts of the picture," he wrote in a letter to John Orcutt, a traveling agent for the ACS.[50] Here, as elsewhere in his correspondence, Washington expressed an allegiance to fair and truthful representation in language informed by contemporary beliefs about photography.[51] After spending six months in the settlement, Washington set down a sober, almost scathing report of the state of Liberia. This would later be published in antislavery and anticolonization newspapers as an open letter entitled "Liberia as It Is."[52] "What has induced Washington to make such a slanderous, malicious thrust at this society and at his adopted home . . . ?" asked a dumbfounded Lugenbeel in a letter to a prominent Liberian resident.[53] The fact that Washington chose to publish his "censorious" letters in an anticolonization newspaper added insult to injury. Colonization newspapers tried to clean up a potential public relations meltdown, printing an apology on his behalf.[54] Perhaps because of Washington's opposition in the press, nearly two years intervened between the moment when Lugenbeel received the first of the daguerreotypes and the occasion when the two extant images attributed to Washington appeared in print.

While the society's reliance on eyewitness reportage may have led ACS agents to seek out the services of Augustus Washington, their rhetorical theory crumbled in practice. This explains why Washington became a problem when his words and images deviated from the society's expectations. Just as the wood engravings based on Washington's daguerreotypes became vexed by the circumstances of their production, the ACS's desires for and anxieties about the Liberian landscape resurface as the wood engravings were reprinted, circulating beyond the society's control.

Afterlife in Print

Following the publication of Washington's daguerreotypes in the *New-York Colonization Journal*, the wood engraving representing the view of Monrovia from the anchorage was reprinted in other periodicals and travel journals.[55] Meanwhile, the view from the lighthouse was largely neglected (see "The Neglected View," below). The circulation and recontextualization of imagery in colonization print media followed a larger trend of cross-editing in nineteenth-century American newspapers. Editors routinely filled their columns with articles culled from other regional, national, and international publications.[56] Attending to instances of reprinting, in which wood engravings based on Washington's photographs circulated in colonization publications and beyond, helps us understand the vision of Liberia that the ACS hoped to instill in their American audience. As Meredith McGill suggests, reprinting separates meaning from authors and instead "makes publication distinctly legible as an independently signifying act." For her, "reprinted texts call attention to the repeated acts of articulation in which culture and its audiences are constituted."[57] The afterlife of the wood engravings based on Washington's photographs suggests that reprinting not only unhinged the imagery from the photographer's authorial intent but also from colonizationists' desires, even as republication serves as its vehicle of appropriation and dissemination.

The degree to which Washington's images were assimilated into colonization print culture is exemplified by the appearance of the ACS's favored view of Monrovia in the March 1859 issue of a Methodist Episcopal Church periodical called the *Ladies' Repository*. The journal focused on issues of morality and religion, but also included two high quality prints at the start of every issue. The view of Monrovia from the anchorage appeared as a backdrop, only slightly modified, in a portrait of the Reverend Francis Burns (Figure 12.9). Burns was a missionary bishop of the Methodist Episcopal Church stationed in Monrovia. This illustration is typical of women's magazines of the antebellum era, which featured high quality steel-plate engravings that women could then clip, color, and use to decorate middle-class homes.[58]

In the *Ladies' Repository*, Burns's comely portrait is matched with an equally handsome portrait of a town. Commenting on the portrait, the editor suggested readers should check their initial reaction to the sitter's race: "The appearance of the portrait of a colored man may seem somewhat singular; but who that possesses the spirit of the philanthropist or the Christian will not welcome it . . . ?" Readers should instead look upon this picture as evidence of the oneness of all people in the eyes of God and "as a recognition of the glorious possibilities of Africa's redemption."[59] While Burns's blackness is understood as foreign to the readers, the landscape contains familiar trappings of an American city. Consequently, Burns's portrait positions him in the landscape, drawing on its message of all-Americanness.

That the Liberian landscape could enable white readers to revise their attitudes toward blacks is implied in the caption to "Ashmun Street, Monrovia," an illustration in the October 1858 issue of the Pennsylvania Colonization Society's newspaper the *Colonization Herald*.[60] The illustration (Figure 12.10)

Figure 12.9. J. C. Buttre, *Portrait of Rev. Francis Burns,* published in March 1859 issue of the *Ladies' Repository.* Courtesy of the American Antiquarian Society.

presents a wide thoroughfare receding into the background at an oblique
angle. Buildings situated along the tree-lined Ashmun Street share common
architectural features, such as pitched roofs, verandas, and chimneys. Regu-
larity and order of the urban design are implied through the trees and homes
that are spaced at regular intervals along the street. As the caption quickly
points out, the street is home to places of law and commerce. The order of the
town is matched by the regimented organization of its inhabitants. Liberia's
volunteer militia parades down the center of the road. Individual citizen-
soldiers coalesce into a cubic unit.

The caption quotes from Alexander M. Cowan's travel narrative *Liberia,
as I Found It*, wherein the author recounts his experience in Monrovia, a city
with orderly streets and orderly people:

> [H]ere, the town was laid out and improved. The race here presented
> themselves in an advanced state of improvement in every particular,
> of a distinct community. I had indescribable feelings, not of mis-
> trust of my personal safety, nor of disgust at the race claiming and
> expecting equality of social position with me, but at seeing them in
> their present position in the absence of white persons. Here was to
> be seen the moulding of their own body politic. I saw around me
> respectful manners, business habits, and their attendant conse-
> quences, good dwellings. . . . I was convinced I was in a well regu-
> lated town in its morals, its order, and cleanliness.

Cowan correlates the order of the city with the industry and morality of its
denizens, as did the newspaper's editor who paired Cowan's observations
with this illustration, itself reprinted from *Frank Leslie's Illustrated Newspaper*.[61] Cowan also expresses an "indescribable feeling" as he grapples with a
place where distinctions of color did not structure social relations. To Cowan's surprise, this was a town where blacks could be disciplined citizens absent the supervisory power of whites. Cowan's claims were perhaps addressed
to those who questioned blacks' capacity for self-government. For example,
in 1840 the governor of Alabama argued that, "If American slaves could be
colonized, they would descend to the condition of natives, instead of im-
parting the benefits of their limited information and civilization to them."[62]
Although the illustration posits the possibility of African American self-
discipline and civic participation, the composition reassuringly places the
American newspaper reader in the supervisory position. The reader's view is

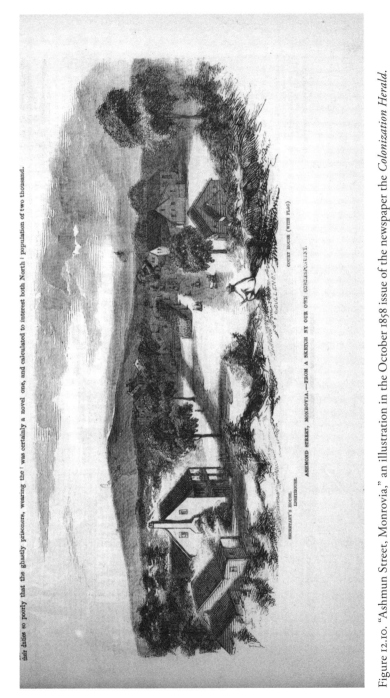

this duties so poorly that the ghastly prisoners, wearing the ¹ was certainly a novel one, and calculated to interest both North ¹ population of two thousand.

SECRETARY'S HOUSE.
LIGHTHOUSE.

COURT HOUSE (WITH FLAG)

ASHMOND STREET, MONROVIA.—FROM A SKETCH BY OUR OWN CORRESPONDENT.

Figure 12.10. "Ashmun Street, Monrovia," an illustration in the October 1858 issue of the newspaper the *Colonization Herald*. (For the sake of image quality, the image here is as it was originally published in the July 24, 1858 issue of *Frank Leslie's Illustrated Newspaper*.) Courtesy of the American Antiquarian Society.

elevated over the parade in the valley below, thus restoring racial hierarchies through empowered sight lines.

The Neglected View

While the ACS made extensive use of the representation of Monrovia's anchorage, the picture taken from the lighthouse was largely neglected.[63] When the view did appear, it belied the ACS's key message about the likeness of Liberia to the United States. For example, the image appeared in an article entitled "Negroland and the Negroes" in *Harper's New Monthly Magazine* in 1856.[64] The article repeated the colonization claim that Monrovia "presents an aspect not unlike that of American towns."[65] However, the magazine reproduced the view from the lighthouse with alterations that undercut that contention. Instead, the wood engraving supported the magazine's broader observation that Liberia was "a strange mingling of civilization and barbarism."[66]

The accompanying illustration crops the vignette around the "view from the lighthouse" so that it loses its wide panoramic view (Figure 12.11). In the original wood engraving, the palm trees and vegetated promontory that occupied the foreground afforded the viewer a sense of place within the landscape. Here the landscape is encapsulated in a rounder frame, as if there was a loss of peripheral vision; much of the foreground is eliminated along with the lateral extensions of the view. Although the original print failed to evince a sense of cartographic order typically found in city views, the engraver did manage to cut small pathways into the overall pattern of hatching. These faint pathways provided sight lines along which a viewer could make his way through the composition, allowing the townscape to emerge from the forest. These fine details are largely eliminated in the *Frank Leslie* reprint, subjecting the small efforts at organization present in the original print to myopic disorientation.

The representation of Monrovia was further removed from its association with American culture by its contextualization in the larger article. The primary emphasis of the article, as the title "Negroes in Negroland" crudely implies, is an attention to indigenous African architecture and the inhabitants of the African city. There are a few images of Western settlements, such as an illustration depicting Cape Coast Castle, a fortress built by the Portuguese for slaving, which was later converted into a seat of British governance. However, the rest of the images representing people and places in Liberian territory are representations of Kru villages. Reprinting the lighthouse view a time when it was a matter of debate whether the British vessels should not be withdrawn from the Slave Coast; and as he has been informed by a letter from Lord Palmerston, this pamphlet decided the question in favor of the continuance of the effort to put a stop to the Slave Trade.

Whoever may sneer at the labors of missionaries, the philosopher and the scholar will not. They have added more than all other men to our knowledge of the uncivilized portions of the human family. Of these we have no hesitation in pronouncing the negro races of Western Africa to be the most worthy of attention. They are the ones who present most promise of a future career of civilization and Christianity. It is morally certain that a century hence there will not exist upon the face of the globe an individual of the copper-colored aborigines of North America, or of the brown races of Polynesia. Indications are not wanting that the Cingalese and Hindus will pass away before the conquering white races. We believe that the Chinese have had their youth and their manhood—such as it was—and that they are to go the way of the builders of Babylon and Nineveh, of Copan and Palenque.

The negroes, on the contrary, have shown that they can live face to face with the whites. In the West Indies they have multiplied in a condition in which the aborigines became extinct in two generations. We know how they have thriven, physically, intellectually, and morally among us. However much slaveholder and abolitionist may differ in theory and conclusion, they both insist upon the essential fact, that the colored race among us have made great advances,

and are capable of and destined for still greater improvement. What the natives of the slave regions are at home, and what the country which they inhabit is, we may learn from the book of Mr. Wilson.

As we sail down the coast we pass the mouths of the great rivers Senegal and Gambia, winding through dense forests and thick jungles. Upon their banks grows the gigantic *baoba*, hugest of trees. The coast is under the control of the French and English, and is peopled by the Fulahs, Jalofs, and Mandingoes, the handsomest negroes of Africa, with tall elastic figures, woolly hair, and glossy black skins. The women, says one traveler, with a significant reservation, are as attractive as it is possible for black females to be. They are zealous Mohammedans, and are rapidly extending their faith among the tribes to the south.

At the flourishing settlements of Free-town and Monrovia we shall see a strange mingling of civilization and barbarism. The white man, rendered still paler by the wasting African fever, jostles the black emigrant from civilized countries, jauntily clad, and the sable denizen of the bush, with scarcely a rag to cover his nakedness. Free-town the chief settlement in the British colony of Sierra Leone, and Monrovia, the capital of Liberia, in spite of their unhealthy climate, may be fairly set down as successful experiments in African colonization. Monrovia, with its neat whitewashed dwellings and three or four churches presents an aspect not unlike that of American towns with a population of fifteen or eighteen hundred. Mr. Wilson makes the very sensible suggestion that the interests of both colonies would be materially advanced by the

MONROVIA.

in this context repositioned Liberia as an exotic locale rather than a familiar city transplanted in Africa.

By 1886, Washington's view from the lighthouse was wholly severed from its referent in Thomas McCants Stewart's *Liberia: The Americo-African Republic*.[67] Leading a varied life as an African American teacher, minister, and activist, Stewart published his book after a two-year sojourn in Liberia.[68] Both of the wood engravings after Augustus Washington's daguerreotypes are reproduced in Stewart's book.[69] Appearing near the beginning of the text, Washington's view from the anchorage remains the given view of Monrovia.[70] However, Stewart's book proffers the lighthouse view as "Settlement on the St. Paul's River" (Figure 12.12). Appearing near the end of the book, the image conveys Stewart's estimation of Arthington, an African American settlement in Liberia. "There is nothing about the place to describe. It is a settlement rather than a town," writes Stewart, underscoring the difficulties of colonial development in the interior.[71] Reframed as a picture of a settlement and not a metropolis, wilderness and few signs of civilization are to be expected. This is precisely the characterization of Monrovia the ACS had sought to avoid. The editorial choice suggests that ACS-sponsored images from the mid-nineteenth century continued to effectively control the image of Liberia, even as the ACS waged an increasingly losing battle to determine how these representations of the colony and its landscape signified.

Repercussions of Reprinting

Tracing the dissemination and textual framing of wood engravings based on Augustus Washington's photographs raises questions about the ways that instances of reprinting indexed colonizationists' appropriation of photographic evidence and instrumentalization of black testimony. Washington's very commitment to photographic veracity—to show, as he put it, "the shaded parts of the landscape, as well as our sunny founts"—meant that by the time he took his photographs of the Liberian landscape, he could no longer capitulate to colonization panegyrics about Americanized landscape and comfortable citizenry.[72] However, the photographer lost control over how his pictures could signify by sending them across the Atlantic, effectively putting them in a "white envelope."[73] Thus, theories of testimony and reprinting offer a note of caution for historians who critique ACS literature and yet reproduce colonization pictures as straightforward illustrations, ironically hewing more

SETTLEMENT ON THE ST. PAUL'S RIVER.

Figure 12.12. "Settlement on the St. Paul's River," an illustration in Thomas McCants Stewart's *Liberia: The Americo-African Republic*. Courtesy of the Library Company of Philadelphia.

closely to ACS desires for their images than nineteenth-century reprints.[74] Likewise, scholars of African American art history and studies of the "image of the black" risk assigning too much intentionality to black artists when they fail to attend to exigencies of print culture.[75]

Colonizationists mobilized Washington's pictures because of the authenticity accrued to the settler experience, and yet recruited the images for their own purposes. The American Colonization Society's preferred view of Monrovia constituted a reader (think of Cowan's "indescribable feeling") who was asked to imagine a place that could offer African Americans possibilities for uplift and citizenship. Orderly towns were proof of African Americans' ability to govern themselves. Thus, the ACS promoted an image of Liberia that portrayed the settlement as a place that replicated American values and yet was a distant, a "separate but equal" place where African Americans could conduct their parallel lives. In its Americanness, the Liberian landscape could rehabilitate black people and shape them into qualified citizens. Yet the view from the anchorage also places Liberia at a reassuring distance, as the ocean separates the black republic and the white reader.

In translating Washington's daguerreotypes into wood engravings, the ACS not only wrested authorial control away from Washington but also weakened its own grasp on the images' signification. Colonizationists may not have accounted for what scholars of both abolition imagery and the culture of reprinting have since argued: the loss of control over the testimonial properties of images inhered in the process of reprinting. As the images reappeared in popular periodicals like *Harper's*, they could be mobilized in ways that contradicted colonizationists' claims about Liberia's resemblance to the United States. Moreover, the ambiguity of the imagery resulted from the properties of the wood engraving itself, a technology necessary for reproduction and mass dissemination in the press. As Jonathan Senchyne explores in his essay (see Chapter 8), print consists of a binary matrix of marks and absences. Liberia's promise or peril lay nestled within a network of cross-hatching or hidden behind a mesh of zigzags. Even a finely delineated wood engraving breaks down as the carved lines of the woodblock degrade through reuse. Reprinting had the potential to empty images of meaning to the point where they come to stand for the very inability to testify.[76]

Networking *Uncle Tom's Cabin*; or, Hyper Stowe in Early African American Print Culture

SUSAN GILLMAN

What's in a network? For many who tout the new knowledge that will be unleashed by going or better yet being born digital, the past is an already discovered country. We can improve our access and have better recovery but the outer limits of that known world are fixed. Moreover, the supposed historical redundancy of the idea of "networks" stems from the mistaken ways this term is applied only to digital versions of earlier texts, especially those firmly anchored in the print culture of the eighteenth and nineteenth centuries. The general view is that new digital media will revolutionize the book by making it "networked," integrated with a potentially infinite set of other works in a variety of formats, thus transforming a static to a dynamic form, a finished work to one always in progress. But to assume that print, unlike other media, is a singular medium produces a misleading view of the book (or any print form).

What if we take as a case study that classic of multimedia adaptation, Harriet Beecher Stowe's nineteenth-century blockbuster *Uncle Tom's Cabin*? Her book's many afterlives are surely a species of networking, but with a slower temporal rate and a different spatialization (not electronic but physical) than those of today's digital age. When we understand the nineteenth-century book to produce the kind of proliferating references and cultural sprawl that many claim to be unique to the Internet age, then we relocate the question "What difference do digital media make?" from revolutionary to evolutionary grounds. A little less hype would allow for a more nuanced history of "networking."

How are models of interactive digital scholarship coextensive with African American traditions in print and performance? Stowe's novel may seem like an unlikely candidate in this context, but not because it wasn't a major presence in African American life and writing. Rather, to explore the ways in which African Americans cited or commented on *Uncle Tom's Cabin*, or the ways in which the novel (and the vast dramatic, popular, literary, and commercial culture it inspired) shaped perceptions of African Americans would be to hark back to an older model of the literary network, based in studies of influence and adaptation. This would not produce the kind of changed relationship to the literary past that we may forecast through connecting the new media to the historical construction of authorship and literature itself. How can we use the technology of digital editions and electronic archives to create more than a 3-D version of the flat world of print? Rather than relying on ties to print culture as stable and communication as a one-to-many enterprise, the newer generation of digital tools may be less prone to produce vast databases of previously unavailable digitized works and more characterized by a view of text making as dynamic and participatory and communication as a many-to-many undertaking. Smaller networks (plural), narrower and deeper, rather than singular, ever bigger and wider, may be put in intersecting relation with one another, as well as identified, named and half-spoken, by the texts and contexts themselves. Different "centers" means different concentric relations that reach across different spaces and times. In presiding over these kinds of open-ended, future configurations that are dependent on subterranean streams running through the past, this essay will argue that the networked history of *Uncle Tom's Cabin* in the context of early African American print culture suggests a way for the comparatively minded to straddle the bounds of comparison: to think both within and beyond compare.

As the ur-text of adaptation, *Uncle Tom's Cabin* is at the virtual center of a long-standing, well-developed, and highly regarded website and electronic archive, established in 1998, that is itself today's register and indicator of a nineteenth-century blockbuster complex. The University of Virginia website "Uncle Tom's Cabin & American Culture: A Multi-Media Archive, Directed by Stephen Railton" is an outstanding resource and conceptual guide, formatting the material temporally and generically: "Pre-Texts (1830–1852)" (includes minstrel shows), "Stowe's Uncle Toms" (various editions, as well as the texts of *The Key to Uncle Tom's Cabin* and the dramatization *The Christian Slave*), "Responses (1852–1930)," and "Other Media" (the biggest section, including "Uncle Tom's Cabin as Children's Book," "Tomitudes," "Songs and Poems," "Uncle Tom's Cabin on Stage," and "Uncle Tom's Cabin at the Movies").[1] While there are many more "Tomitudes" (decorative plates, snuffboxes, biscuit tins, mantelpiece screens, dolls, games, toys, and more objects, most manufactured in Europe) than editions, as material artifacts they are neither coextensive with nor equivalent to the novel and thus cannot be said to outweigh it, and the many stage and film versions have their own obvious ephemeral qualities. They are "ephemera," a category common to many collections and archives, of a most durable kind. The question of the "materiality" of the archive, both as buttress and challenge to its textuality, is thus brought into the picture almost from the start. This counterhistory begins with the traditional account of *Uncle Tom's Cabin* as a textual blockbuster that, if not less often read than performed, must be approached through its multiple avatars and afterlives. The multiple editions, dramatic scripts, publicity, and advertising tie-in materials for Stowe's blockbuster that are at the heart of the "Uncle Tom Complex" define one conception of the archive of "print culture." It consists paradoxically of all objects, textual and artifactual, print and performative, high and popular cultural that could be said to bear the Uncle Tom imprimatur. *Uncle Tom's Cabin* demonstrates that attempts to "network" early American print culture are both innovative and redundant.

More innovative and less redundant would be a consideration of how Stowe's novel could potentially relocate the spatiotemporal boundaries of "early African American print culture." As a classic by a famous white woman, known for a cross-cultural history of circulation, printed, visual, spoken, and digitized, *Uncle Tom's Cabin* works to question and potentially to redefine the limits of what counts as 'early African American print culture.' Taking these terms in order, first, the date and identity piece: if *Uncle Tom's Cabin* belongs in the early African American canon, then, to paraphrase Henry Louis Gates Jr. on Shelley Fisher Fishkin's "black" *Huck Finn*, isn't it great to discover, after all this time, that Harriet Beecher Stowe, one of our most canonical of other American Renaissance writers, may be "black," after all? (Other likely suspects for this honor have been Melville, nominated by Sterling Stuckey, and Poe, Toni Morrison's pick.)[2] Stowe's place in the decade of the 1850s speaks to the periodization question, where we draw temporal boundaries of early, middle, and late, and raises the corresponding question, a perennial one, of the "first" African American novel. The current top candidate, Williams Wells Brown's 1853 *Clotel*, has its own history of extensive networking, documented by Lara Langer Cohen in this volume (see Chapter 9, "Notes from the State of Saint Domingue"), that parallels and contextualizes Stowe's. The very question of first and seconds, of originals and copies, and their unexamined assumptions and potential uses, is key to any study of adaptation and translation (including such issues as the inequality of languages and digital conversion as an act of translation).

In turn, the print culture piece thickens the plot: if what some would call one of the most networked texts of the nineteenth century belongs to print culture, then what does this say to our assumptions about that critical sphere, especially the equation between the epoch and the medium? How do the modern concept of a social network and the interdiscipline of network science (generally associated with engineers, social scientists, and neuro- and evolutionary biologists rather than literary critics and historians) work in relation to nineteenth-century literature?[3] How should we use literature, particularly the nineteenth-century novel, to investigate the scientific and cultural roots of contemporary conceptions of the network, including computer information systems, the human nervous system, and communications technology? Why even assume the linearity, and implied priority, in the notion of nineteenth-century roots of twentieth-century fullness? Rather than presume that new media must signal new forms of literature, we may find through networking a literary past that is different from what we thought we knew and that has yet to materialize. Other than as an image or metaphor for the circulation of things and ideas, what does it mean to say that *Uncle Tom's Cabin* is perhaps the most networked text of the nineteenth century?[4]

Approached skeptically from both perspectives of African American and print culture, the novel encourages these kinds of questions. They are essential to the challenges made throughout this volume to our most familiar critical shibboleths about the primacy of authorship and the birth order of canon formation in black writing as well as the role of race, history, and the (para) textual condition, including the proliferating things now considered texts (verbal, visual, oral, and numeric data, in the form of music and maps, films, videos, and any computer-stored information).

Stowe thus provides an almost unparalleled case study of an author and object known for these kinds of circulation in print and performance cultures and histories across linguistic and national boundaries. A number of

scholars have traced the material citation history of *Uncle Tom's Cabin* in and
out of African American print culture, and my essay therefore takes a more
conceptual approach, thinking not just about borrowed images or words in a
thematic and representational sense but about the networks that enable this
borrowing in the first place.[5] Here, again, another larger conceptual question
would be to ask what it means to see as "networked" two texts with such
radically different circulation numbers as the longtime best seller *Uncle Tom's
Cabin* and the only recently reissued and canonized (in its own separate
"separate sphere") *Clotel*. Further, given that Stowe's networks and adaptations may not be fundamentally different from Brown's, just amplified in size
and effect, we may ultimately speculate that her novel simultaneously sets the
conditions of possibility for networking in the mid-nineteenth century and
offers a critique of the field of print networks in the period. In asking these
questions my essay joins several others in this volume that offer their own
qualified challenges to the familiar ideas that early African American print
culture "gives voice" to African American subjectivity, or expresses authorial
power, or recovers lost histories, or stages an intertextuality in the interest of
forming a canon or a countercanon.

Moreover, Stowe herself theorizes adaptation by way of what we might
call "maladaptation," an operation in which *Uncle Tom's Cabin* both wallows
and excels. Not only does a paradigmatic portrait of black George Washington hang on the wall of Tom and Chloe's cabin, but also there is St. Clare's
dizzying declaration of Topsy's imitativeness followed by his imitations of
her. Imitations of imitations, unexpectedly raced, gendered, and, to use a
term of Walter Mignolo's,[6] languaged: the metamoments of unspoken, interrupted, or incomplete translatability cement and unleash the complex of adaptations that make *Uncle Tom's Cabin* a good test case in even more ways
than those we've already enumerated. Questions of linguistic and cultural
translation raised by the Stowe archive (including foreign-language versions,
especially in Spanish, that are conspicuously absent from the University of
Virginia *Uncle Tom's Cabin* website) address broad issues of textual and performative circulation and possible links to translingual communities within
and beyond the United States. Within these texts the translatability of keywords for race, place, and ethnicity raises a different set of questions about
the limits and possibilities of intermedial and intercultural translation.
Mignolo's languaging makes the network scale, both expand and contract,
to the moment between speech and silence that allows us to hear and see

the role of language in culture, the ideology of monolanguage and national cultures.

Maladaptation: *Uncle Tom's Cabin* in African American Print Culture

Starting with all the media forms of *Uncle Tom's Cabin*, it's not easy to track the language of race, either in the novel or its afterlives. To be sure, there are studies of Stowe and race, but these tend toward the thematic and representational, focused on strategies of characterization or the figure of Uncle Tom himself, with the big questions phrased in either/or format: is Stowe's portrait racist, racialist, and/or feminized? Even if we say it's some combination of all of the above, the language of race in the novel is harder to pin down than we might think. It's not easy no matter how broadly we define "race" (either through the contemporary nineteenth-century terminology for racial classification, for example, mulatto/a, quadroon, octoroon, and so on, or via specific historical events, places, or figures that themselves have a historiography of "racial" associations and connotations, for example, Haiti, the history of New World slave rebellion, and black leaders). Neither indexical nor exhausted by its context, the language of race in *Uncle Tom's Cabin* is, to use Morrison's term, "a virtually unspeakable thing."[7] Following her lead, my term "racial maladaptation" focuses attention variously on how terms are used but don't quite fit their context, are conspicuously missing but implied, are, in short, mistranslated or untranslatable. Like Lara Langer Cohen's Brown with his "patchwork aesthetic," Stowe gives us a citational practice that tries to move away from the comfortable hermeneutics of metaphor, allegory, analogy, comparison, and historical contextualization. What does Stowe's battery of racial terms do, then, if it does not simply index historical events, or embody subjectivity, or figure the real and the true?

Whichever approach we take to tracing the language of race in *Uncle Tom's Cabin*, the outcome is that there is fairly skimpy evidence to follow, and what there is—clustered largely in the George Harris–Cassy subplots—tends to be most present not thematically *in* the text but in the matter at the edges of or outside the text. Symptomatically little of the George Harris story, other than the Eliza half that totally dominates, makes it into the many dramatizations on stage and in film. And the narrative attention, such as it is, to racially mixed characters (George Harris is a "mulatto," Cassy is a "quadroon") is itself part of the problem with defining the novel's racial politics. We get numerous histories of black-white interracial relations, where for better or worse so much dominant cultural attention has focused, yet the downplaying of the George Harris backstory translates into an ambivalent account of the history of sexuality under race slavery. "We remark, *en passant*," the narrator says symptomatically, "that George was, by his father's side, of white descent."[8] Mary Boykin Chesnut points to the missing link in one of the most famous lines of her *Diary*: "Mrs. Stowe did not hit the sorest spot. She makes Legree a bachelor."[9] Historian Barbara J. Fields has argued in two well-known essays that the persistent focus in American historiography on miscegenation and mulattoes reflects another kind of silence: "A telltale sign of the preoccupation of historians, sociologists, and others with a physical definition of race is the disproportionate concern of the field of comparative race relations with the incidence and treatment of mulattoes, as though race became problematic only when the appearance of the people concerned was problematic."[10] Although Fields's argument remains as controversial today as when she first made it in the 1980s, she points to the continuing problem that Toni Morrison took on (also, revealingly, in the 1980s), of talking about "race" in American history and culture. Today's debates about whether Obama's America is "post-race" can't help but resonate. Is Obama our "first black president," or has the fact of his presidency made obsolete the mention of "race" in political discourse? The chronological clarity of the "post" and the "first" may simply be inadequate to the task and irrelevant to the context. We need a way to pause at the "en passant," to language Mignolo's moment between speech and silence. In Morrison's terms: "invisible things are not necessarily 'not-there.' "[11]

That "race" should be such a virtually unspeakable thing (not only for Stowe then but also still for us, now) is not really surprising, given the ongoing challenge of defining Stowe's, and our, racial politics. (It's bad enough just to try to balance her often-contradictory stances on abolitionism, colonization, and antislavery). There are excellent new essays on Stowe and race, Stowe and the South in a recent edited collection that starts explicitly from the position that she should not be vilified as a racist but rather reconsidered in light of the racial thinking of the culture in which she lived.[12] Still George Fredrickson's term "romantic racialism" has stuck and, in my view, endured best. Frederickson reads *Uncle Tom's Cabin* as "the classic expression of romantic racialism" for its ethnological equation of racial differences with psychic and developmental characteristics (black as emotive, infantile, and white as rational, civilized).[13] Fredrickson wanted to draw a chronological and geographical distinction between the mainstream "Romantic Racialism in the North" of Stowe's era and the extreme "Southern Negrophobia at the Turn of the Century" (as he titled two of his chapters), but the literary-critical history of *Uncle Tom* studies has shown the difficulty of using the novel as a case study to fix such a divide, either spatially or temporally.

As a test case, on the other hand, *Uncle Tom's Cabin* has a few signal moments of racial maladaptation, places where, as I've suggested, the terms are used but don't quite fit their context, or where they're conspicuously missing but implied. In Morrison's diagnosis: these are moments in which "the mention of 'race' is either inevitable or elaborately, painstakingly masked. . . . Certain absences are so stressed, so ornate, so planned that they call attention to themselves; arrest us with intentionality and purpose."[14] In this way Stowe and her text invite thinking through adaptation, first, by thematizing and representing various adaptations, both overloaded and overdetermined, which are then interrupted, redirected—or maladapted. One paradigmatic example is the "portrait of General Washington [that] hangs on the wall of Uncle Tom's cabin, drawn and colored in a manner which would certainly have astonished that hero, if ever he had happened to meet with its like" (68). What a cryptic line. It is not necessary, or perhaps neither possible nor accurate, to say that this is a "black" George Washington. Instead the painting is said to be so "colored" that the nominal subject "would have" been astonished, "if" he "had happened" to meet with one like it. Written in the conditional tense that describes hypothetical scenarios, this statement is the conditional of might have beens: the past perfect (as past as tenses get) grammatically links a scenario that didn't happen in the past to the hypothetical outcome of conditions that are untrue in the present or unlikely in the future, but not impossible. Just so, *Uncle Tom's Cabin* ends, controversially, with its mulatto spokesman George Harris gesturing toward a separatist racial nationalism in the future: "I want a country, a nation, of my own" (610), he writes in a letter near the end. The novel's many references to the revolutionary legacy of the founding fathers, and how it might be extended to the slave, end abruptly, foreclosed in the vexed image of Liberia, where he announces he will disappear himself and his family (and thus Stowe engages the contemporary debate over colonization as a solution to black slavery if not freedom). If George Harris is George Washington's unnamed black alter ego, the colored liberator, who would have astonished that hero if ever he met with its like, then the portrait is a maladaptation with a counterfactual energy, a projection of alternative histories into possible futures.

Stowe's enigmatic portrait avoids the ready-made minstrelsy of a "blackface George Washington" that she willingly uses elsewhere in the novel. (For this reason it's probably misleading to call it "blackface.") Sam's "ludicrous burlesques and imitations" of political speechifying (136) and Sambo's "ludicrous imitation" of the "white niggers" at the slave auction (469) are immediately recognizable adaptations of the forms of minstrelsy that were popular in Stowe's nineteenth century and that are reflected in the minstrel songs and poems included on the University of Virginia website among both the pretexts and responses to *Uncle Tom's Cabin*. These loud and ludicrous imitations are not maladaptations, in the unspoken mode of the portrait or of Topsy's recursive imitation of Miss Ophelia that produces the co-constituent, St. Clare's imitation of Topsy. Unlike those unmistakable imitations, hallmark of the racial maladaptation is how easy it is to miss.

In the oft-read episode of Topsy's education at the hands of Miss Ophelia, Topsy exhibits a "talent" for "mimicry" and "imitating" that makes her at once a quick study of white domesticity (she performs Miss Ophelia, dressing up "in great style" in "her" clothes), an intractable reflection of what the slave child cannot know (learning the catechism from Miss Ophelia, she asks whether the "state" from which "our first parents" fell is "Kintuck"), and an unspoken condemnation of the unspeakable things in American slavery, Topsy's prideful line, her takeaway from Miss Ophelia's Sunday teachings, " 'I's so wicked!' "—always enclosed in at least single and sometimes double quotation marks—breaks free of that narrative enclosure and travels, first to ventriloquize Miss Ophelia and finally to infiltrate the voice of St. Clare (364–69). Laughingly pointing out to Ophelia the need "to give [Topsy] a meaning, or she'll make one," St. Clare both concludes his mockery and answers Miss Ophelia's reproaches of it, by quoting the pupil's own words: "as Topsy herself says, 'I's so wicked!' " Like Frederick Douglass's imbrication into his *Narrative* of the actual words of his master's injunction against learning to read ("Give a nigger an inch, and he will take an ell"), Topsy's language spirals out of the slave orbit into that of the master and from there to the world of words that is the novel itself.[15] Making Topsy's words St. Clare's own has the same destabilizing effect, reversing lines of ownership, as Douglass's quotation of his master's words within his own writing: it isn't clear any longer to whom the "I" of the "I's so wicked!" refers. St. Clare, speaking through Topsy, enacts a kind of minstrelsy in reverse, no blackface necessary. The first-person pronoun loses its special standing. In effect, Stowe's grammar mimics, both appropriates and repurposes, the available racial idioms.

When St. Clare speaks a little later of "Hayti" and "the San Domingo hour," his language is similarly unstable. This is another of the oft-quoted moments of the novel, when St. Clare and his brother (opposites in temperament and belief, like so many of Stowe's family pairs) argue about the history of republicanism and revolution among the "masses" in Europe. St. Clare's example of "the people of Hayti" introduces a racial valence, with his brother insisting that "the Haytiens were not Anglo-Saxons . . . the dominant race of the world" (292). St. Clare responds, unsurprisingly, with his own blood talk, a climatological version of romantic racialism and an implicit rebuke, a reminder of the historical reality of miscegenation, but what stands out is the future threat embedded in the very names he uses. There is "a pretty fair infusion of Anglo Saxon blood among our slaves, . . . enough of the African to give a sort of tropical warmth and fervor to our calculating firmness and foresight. If ever the San Domingo hour comes, Anglo Saxon blood will lead on the day" (392).

"Hayti" and "the San Domingo hour": the two names do not reflect Stowe's confusion about what to call the only black republic in the New World but rather are symptomatic of a broader archival pattern, the use or absence of the very term "Haiti." Haiti was the name given to colonial Saint Domingue (to use the French as opposed to the Spanish Santo Domingo), after independence in 1804, and was based on the indigenous Arawak-Taino name for the island, meaning mountainous or high lands. Historian Ada Ferrer notes that in Cuba and in the Spanish-speaking world in general, metropolitan and colonial authorities made only scattered use of the name, as though, she says, to use it routinely and officially would be to recognize the victory of slaves and the defeat of European rule.[16] Stowe's own language used in the 1852 United States reflects the same disconnect that Ferrer identifies in the Spanish-speaking world between "the categories and the names deployed by narrators and the complex and unprecedented realities on the ground."[17] The force of the Haitian example is registered not only in Stowe's dual names but also in the strange absence of Haiti in the novel. Following St. Clare's threatening note, other than one brief allusion in George Harris's farewell letter at the end of novel, dismissing "Hayti," home of "a worn-out, effeminate" race (609), as a location for his racial nation, there is no further languaging of Haiti.

So, too, with all the adaptations of *Uncle Tom's Cabin*, the plays and films as well as Stowe's *The Key to Uncle Tom's Cabin*. The George Harris plot is not a major driver in the novel's performance history (Linda Williams comments that the George Harris ending in a future Africa was not amenable to either visual or dramatic representation), and Haiti is not referenced at all in the *Key*.[18] All of the adaptations repeat the same signal silence on and of Haiti, in its own way as loud and roaring as the unspeakable things unspoken of *Beloved*'s 124. As such, they provide an opportunity to trace the "unthinkability" of Haiti, to use Michel-Rolph Trouillot's oft-quoted term for the construction of a powerful historiographical silence around the Haitian Revolution, its relative absence in historical knowledge. Compared to other world revolutions, Haiti is, Trouillot wrote in 1995, "the revolution the world forgot."[19] This is a silence in which the archive itself is implicated, in a process of archival power that selects and orders the documents and facts to underwrite and legitimize the power inherent in the historical act itself. Trouillot's influential argument about the inability of contemporary observers to understand and narrate the events of the revolution, especially from the slave perspective, with the language and categories available then, or even now, still stands but has been rethought and revised. Historian Ferrer and others working on the cultural legacies of the Haitian Revolution in the Atlantic world approach the archive as itself containing traces of that process of silencing, so that we can track how certain narratives and silences are created, reconstructed, maintained, and abandoned. Morrison, too, underscores the role of the double negative in producing racial discourse: invisible things are not necessarily not there, just as unspeakable things, unspoken, are not necessarily unheard. Challenging the emphasis on the material text in the context of traditional print culture, this approach to the mutually transformative relations of African American literature and print culture is concerned less with "repressed" or "silenced" texts, and more with events and nonevents, realized and unrealized relations.

The figure of Haiti thus functions as the privileged site of Stowe's racial maladaptations, precisely because she names it rarely and equivocally (as "Hayti" at times and as "the San Domingo hour" at other times) and because as a name in several different languages, it carries the burden of multiple slave revolts across historical periods and geographical locales. So when we ask "Where's Haiti?" the Stowe archive provides an unexpected answer: everywhere yet nowhere, Haiti in many pieces but no Haiti whole. In *The Key to Uncle Tom's Cabin* (1854), Stowe answered charges against the validity of her indictment of slavery by asserting that the novel is a "mosaic of facts" and then providing her sources, keyed to the chapters, to demonstrate the documentary evidence on which she based her accounts. The novel was assembled "in the same manner that the mosaic artist groups his fragments of various stones into one general picture. His is a mosaic of gems—this is a mosaic of facts." Earlier, in her preface to the 1852 European edition, Stowe had defended the novel on the same aesthetic grounds: "It has been said that the representations of this book are exaggerations! and oh would that this were true! would that this book were indeed a fiction, and not a close wrought mosaic of facts!"[20] Stowe's "mosaic of facts" points to where and how Haiti circulated in the nineteenth-century United States and perhaps also beyond: in the paratexts—citations, footnotes, and documentation, complete and incomplete—of works devoted to other issues and causes, and at the narrative edges of the texts themselves. Haiti locates the outer edge of the possible.

In linguistic terms, Haiti's multiple names point to one last example of the languaging of racial maladaptation in the novel. Stowe's term "Creole Spanish" brings into her text the disparate uses, between speech and silence, of "creole" in New Orleans and the Caribbean in the nineteenth century.[21] This is a characteristically minor episode that, like the others I have discussed, has received critical attention disproportionate to its size, and, also like the others, it has a distinct racial valence. When Stowe uses the term "Creole Spanish," it stands out both in the U.S. race-slavery context of the novel and in the hemispheric history of slavery in the New World. In Spanish America *criollo* refers to a person of European descent born in the Americas (and later extended to anywhere outside Europe). In contrast to this broad usage, Stowe reserves both "Spanish" and "Creole" for her mixed-race characters only. The "mulatto" George Harris effects the first stage of his escape from slavery by disguising himself as a "Spanish-looking fellow" (182), "with a dark Spanish complexion" (180), and, near the end of the novel, the "quadroon" Cassy carries out her escape from the Legree plantation by impersonating a "Creole Spanish" lady (597). Stowe's "Creole Spanish" is thus another one of her oddly, unevenly, and only semirecognized racialized terms.

For us today "Creole" is protean, an adaptable, all-purpose term for "blood" (heredity, identity) and language (culture) that derives from two primary disciplinary locations, anthropology and linguistics. Stowe's Creole Spanish does not refer to language, but is probably meant to distinguish culturally from the usual identification in the U.S. context, especially in the regional context of New Orleans and Louisiana, of Creole with French. But George Harris's "Spanish masquerade" produces misleading historical implications, including the suggestion of an alternative to the one-drop rule of U.S. race relations in the fantasy of "Spanishness as a world elsewhere."[22] (The novel ends with another fantasy, which has been soundly criticized over the years, of a black world elsewhere in Liberia.) In historical terms this representation of Spanish Creole in New Orleans is misleading because it ignores the geography of the Spanish Empire in the New World, where the term in Spanish, *criollo*, would have meaning.

Instead Stowe's "Creole Spanish" has no particular linguistic connotations at all and, further, is racially nonspecific, a generalized marker of difference, ethnic, national, social. A brief look at the two examples shows the terminological anomalies of "Creole" and "Spanish" in Stowe's race-slavery context. First, George Harris, almost always identified as a mulatto, is here disguised with "a dark, Spanish complexion" (180); he "had metamorphosed . . . into the Spanish-looking fellow he then appeared" (182). Second, Cassy, usually called a "quadroon" (her life history is told in a chapter entitled "The Quadroon's Story"), is here "dressed after the manner of the Creole Spanish ladies,—wholly in black. A small black bonnet on her head, covered by a veil thick with embroidery, concealed her face. It had been agreed that, in their escape, she was to personate the character of a Creole lady. . . . Brought up, from early life, in connection with the highest society, the language, movements and air of Cassy, were all in agreement with this idea; and she had still enough remaining with her, of a once splendid wardrobe, and sets of jewels, to enable her to personate the thing to advantage" (597). In both cases Stowe's Creole Spanish appears unlocated and unmoored, associated with concealment, disguise, and "personation" rather than identification. An amorphous term, "Creole" is, moreover, notably absent where we'd expect to find it, at the end of the novel, when the dispersed slave families are reunited, and the French Madame de Thoux is revealed as George Harris's sister, raised in the West Indies. So Stowe's "Spanish Creole" points to a historical anomaly: while the term "Creole" is common in the U.S. French context (as a nineteenth-century marker of language, culture, and society), oddly enough in the Stowe lexicon and usage, it doesn't seem to work as well for the Spanish New World, either for the Spanish imperial period in the Southwest or more broadly as a term identifying the Spanish-speaking people of the United States. It's certainly not as omnipresent as it is in "Spanish America."

Stowe's "Creole Spanish," then, pointedly doesn't travel or translate equally in all times and locations and as such points to another instance of maladaptation in the form of mis- or untranslatability. Among the many translations over time of *Uncle Tom's Cabin*, there have been comparatively few in Spanish, especially in relation to those in French or German (understanding the latter as counted among the world's prestige languages). So I'd like to follow the trail of Stowe's clue in her anomalous Spanish Creole to a place at once seemingly distant and yet proximate, the 1884 novel of Indian reform known as the "*Uncle Tom's Cabin* of the Indian," *Ramona* by Helen Hunt Jackson. The model for my approach is poet-patriot José Martí, who conceived of the hemispheric pan-nationalism of his famous essay "Our America" (1891) during his longtime exile from his native Cuba in New York City. It is especially Martí's role as translator, particularly of one of his favorite books in English, Jackson's *Ramona*, itself a work known for its long life on stage and in film, with extraordinary abilities to translate and be translated, that makes Martí such an emblem for the method and project of (mal)adaptation. Martí's translation of the "*Uncle Tom's Cabin* of the Indian" will provide a kind of provisional closure appropriate to the network that is emerging through Stowe to Jackson and Martí, connecting multiple points on the hemispheric space-time map and serving as an exemplum of the way that the encounter of Europe with the Americas occasioned modernity and the colonial system.[23]

Maladaptation: *Ramona*, the "*Uncle Tom's Cabin* of the Indian"

If *Uncle Tom's Cabin* is the ur-text of adaptation, in both conventional and unconventional senses, it is yet "another," "second" *Uncle Tom's Cabin*, *Ramona* by both Jackson and Martí, that provides an unlikely model for rethinking early African American print culture. The intertexuality that *Uncle Tom's Cabin* practices and in which it is implicated does not lend itself to traditional theories of adaptation. We might, however, understand its mode of circulation as a "text network." As Kirsten Silva Gruesz and I have written elsewhere,

> "Text-network" is one term for this kind of circulation, used in studies of the ancient novel, where it refers to a characteristic and central type of Hellenistic world literature, such as the "Alexander

romance." Bodies of prose composition with no definitive origin
and no telos in their dissemination, no known "author" and no definitive form, they exist only as a multiplicity of different versions, in
a wide variety of different languages, retailored to fit a host of different cultural contexts, diffused in a multiplicity of directions over
much of the Asian-African-European land mass. One way to describe them would be as translations without an original.[24]

If we think of Stowe's *Uncle Tom's Cabin*, Jackson's *Ramona*, and Martí's
translation as networked in this way, then we can approach them not as individual texts that refer to one another indexically or contextually, but rather as
a set of iterations independent of their birth order and the priorities dictated
by country or language of origin. Gruesz and I elaborate:

When José Martí called his version of Helen Hunt Jackson's *Ramona*
(1887) "otra *Cabaña*" (another *Uncle Tom's Cabin*), proposing that
it spoke out in favor of the Indians as "la Beecher" did for the Negroes, he signaled that his was more than a literal translation:
rather a *transculturation* (anticipating Cuban anthropologist Fer-
nando Ortiz's 1940s term), the product of more than one author,
belonging to more than a single national literary tradition, that
elevates the role of translation to active participant in, rather than
mere footnote to, the production of literary and cultural meaning.

Thinking in this way through adaptation allows us to account for a spectrum
of modes and genres, across print and performance, in which national histories are explicitly translated and implicitly compared as models of other
nations' histories. Such a translingual approach to the Stowe-Jackson text
network builds on and goes beyond the conventional intertextual pairing
that Jackson herself famously initiated when she said that she did not dare to
think she had written "a second Uncle Tom's Cabin."[25]

Just so Jackson lives on in Stowe's shadow, playing second to Stowe's first
lady, much as *Uncle Tom's Cabin* is the gold standard, the first term in the
many comparisons that follow in its wake. Comparison both generates and
reflects the fame of the "original" and continually draws critical attention
back to it. Following the author's lead, many *Ramona* readers, including
Martí and his "otra *Cabaña*," likewise make the comparison but few follow
up on the gesture. One Stowe critic sees the novel as such a prototype of the

protest novel that virtually every writer who has approached her league has been credited with producing "'The *Uncle Tom's Cabin* of' her or his cause." Jack London even paid tribute to Upton Sinclair's *The Jungle* (1906) as "the 'Uncle Tom's Cabin' of wage slavery."[26] Given how strikingly often the old saw "a second *Uncle Tom's Cabin*" is invoked and just as quickly passed by, it's as though the initial comparative gesture alone is enough, the fact of comparison assumed and forgotten.

In light of these problems, how do we compare? How can we avoid the pitfalls of simple juxtaposition without analysis or, perhaps worse, the hierarchy of original and copy? Alternatively, in lieu of assuming equivalence between the objects of comparison, how do we incorporate the historical unevenness and asymmetry that is either denied or poorly accommodated by the method of (com)pairing? We need a self-conscious, self-critical comparativism, aware of both the fact of and assumptions about comparison, both the limits and the possibilities.

In the Stowe-Jackson case, the basis of the comparison itself has not been questioned or reflected on. While both novels have individually produced their own substantial performance and adaptation histories (stage and film versions, translations, publicity and newspaper materials, and an array of authenticating documentation) as well as critical studies of them, the two have not been systematically or self-consciously compared. Instead, while the extensive performance history, across media and languages, of the globetrotting *Uncle Tom's Cabin* is well known, in contrast, the *Ramona* archive, smaller in scale, is studied more locally as a Southern California phenomenon. The much-touted adaptation history of *Uncle Tom's Cabin* dominates, approached from multiple historical and disciplinary perspectives, most recently in the form of a "transatlantic Stowe." An explicitly traveling figure, this latest Stowe tracks the nineteenth-century stage adaptations, including minstrel shows and songs, in what one London newspaper called the "Tom-Mania" of the United States and Europe (with a nod to Russia and another nod to translations, folded within the broad concept of an adaptation). Like most Stowe adaptation studies, the new transatlantic Stowe takes a slice of the whole history, divided by period, genre, language, and/or national location. In short no comprehensive critical comparativism of the self-conscious kind invited by Jackson-Stowe and company, thinking about how their performance/print cultures/histories develop, diverge, and intersect across time in relation to national and linguistic traditions, has yet been done. Neither has a metacritical view been taken of the limits and possibilities of comparison itself.

What cultural work is done, for them and us, then and now, by pairing the two blockbusters? Why compare/pair any two texts, not to mention their contexts? What do we get out of comparison? Stowe provides a ready route into what is probably the largest and most significant complex of texts and contexts in the nineteenth century. In so doing she gives us license to challenge "material text" readings with theories of networks, defined both textually and digitally. Clearly, the classical idea of a text network would be altered by the rise of print, the flourishing, by Stowe's time, of a recognized social space for the author as professional and as celebrity, and by our time, of digital archives, the multimedia and interactive websites that make nineteenth-century books available through electronic networks. Nevertheless, the text-network model has the advantage of denaturalizing these potent modern ideologies surrounding the author and the original, and privileging *circulation* over the post-Romantic fetishization of *composition*. It makes translation both a material practice and a metaphor for the constant and multidirectional movement of texts through channels that are often not officially sanctioned or legitimated with an acknowledgment, like so many invisible translators. Within the texts the translatability of keywords for race, place, and ethnicity raises a different set of questions about the limits and possibilities of intermedial and intercultural translation.

How do we delimit and define the object of study, when the objects not only include the multiple editions, translations, authenticating documents, dramatic scripts, films, and publicity materials for both Stowe's and Jackson's blockbusters, but also extend to the histories, languages, and cultures of the contexts in which they circulate? Taking special interest as the concept of the text network does in texts whose adaptive lives cross generic and linguistic boundaries encourages sustained thinking about the interrelations between print and performance cultures and histories. Better yet, the starting point has to acknowledge lack of fit in that these networks do not produce a seamless set of interconnections. A text network starts with a series of negative propositions: not attributable to a single author, iterations are not necessarily translations but clearly derivative of each other in some way, although there exists no "original" from which to measure the distance of derivation. Further there's the question of whether and how this can apply to modern works, after the rise of the author. So, too, when we systematically put together "print culture" and "African American": the result is a suggestive emphasis on the instability of such conceptual workhorses as authorship and audience, identity and print, text and context. Lara Langer Cohen and Jordan Alexander Stein define this anticanon by its "unknown authors, limited audiences, baffling narratives, and dubious claims on identity and plausibility . . . understood to be artless, immature, desultory, partial, unreadable, fraudulent, fragmentary, or, simply, unstable" (see Introduction). "Unstable" is exactly the term for the *Uncle Tom* text network or better yet for the comparative conjuncture of performative hemispheric antislavery reformism, forms of citation or adaptation, or even more generally something like repurposing past literary productions into and for present ones.

What is the relationship between the logic of racial maladaptation that is so generative for Stowe-Jackson and company, and the idea of a text network? Does the instability of racial discourse itself provide the model for that logic, or is it reflected in or as, the network of texts? It's a bit of a chicken-and-egg problem: which came first, or which is on first, the unstable racial discourse or the text network? Does the network reflect, make visible, or produce those instabilities? If the latter, then multiple languages and translations are required to name them. Thinking of texts as and through networks, as dynamic entities that cannot be rigorously separated from one another and that are composed of relations of force, movement, and intensity allows us to see how these works are being themselves "worked," as entities that function at once on multiple scales and in multiple times. The paratexts (prefaces, afterwords, footnotes, and other authorizing materials "outside" the text proper) that are so often dismissed as marginal and minor come into view more fully, so that the special relation between the "bookish realm" of paratextuality and the "larger realm of racialized power" may be better understood. The text network enables us to see how race relates to the "(para)textual condition," starting but not ending with the ways that African American cultural production has long made use of the paratext, often mobilized by white editors and prefacers, as a space for confronting white power.[27] To rethink the parameters of print culture, we need a way to conceptualize it beyond the text that dominates now, despite the assumption, for example, that illustrations belong in the mix. We lack a name, a concept, and a methodology for including all adaptations, visual as well as verbal, as well as a way to account for circulation, like that of William Wells Brown's *Clotel*, that exceeds actual sales.

Finally, text networks defy any of the author- or character-centered ways that scholars have continued to approach the criteria by which texts become "black." The links between Stowe's novel and Martí's translation of Jackson cannot be articulated within traditional models of authorial influence or within comparative mappings of the way that specific genres migrate from one nation to the next. As network studies have discovered in cell biology, in online social networks, and in phonemes: stuff spreads in mysterious, often counterfactual ways.[28] Networking *Uncle Tom's Cabin*, in all possible ways, literal and metaphoric, social and digital, virtual and actual, points to the necessity of finding multidirectional lines of transnational contact, characterized by unanticipated geographical and temporal contiguity across far-flung spatial, national, and linguistic contexts—including, finally, our own present conditions.

PART IV

Public Performances

CHAPTER 14

The Lyric Public of *Les Cenelles*

LLOYD PRATT

The acknowledged first anthology of African American literature is a collection of Francophone poetry titled *Les Cenelles: Choix de poésies indigènes*. It was published in New Orleans in 1845. Over the course of its history, a single recurring question has pursued this collection: what are its politics? The revision of the African American literary canon during the 1980s and 1990s offers a concentrated example of this approach to literary history conceived of as political connoisseurship. The perceived assimilatory stance of the *Les Cenelles* poets, all of whom were free men of color, troubled many of the canon makers of these decades. In the estimation of Henry Louis Gates Jr. and Michel Fabre, for instance, the poetry in *Les Cenelles* is notable primarily for its stylistic debts to the French romantics, its departure from the vernacular tradition, its failure to mount a sustained antislavery critique, and, of course, its primogeniture.[1] As these and other influential critics acknowledge, the *Les Cenelles* poets did borrow from the politicized models of the French romantics, but in the estimation of the field, the New Orleanians in question tamed those models in the process of reproducing them. Fabre asks, for example, "why so few of these works offer a critique of the social and racial system" that defined antebellum New Orleans.[2] More recent studies by critics and historians set out in search of just such a clearly demarcated critique.[3]

Yet neither of these two generations of critics and historians has attempted to "lyricize" the *Les Cenelles* poems. This should come as something of a surprise. If, as Virginia Jackson influentially argues, lyric reading has dominated the academic study of European and Anglo-American (white) poetry in the United States since the nineteenth century, then one would expect the legitimating efforts of later twentieth-century African American canon makers to take up this particular practice of reading as well. This is to say that *Les Cenelles* and Emily Dickinson's poetry share a rough chronology in common, one in which the way to make the case for the significance of a poem is to demonstrate its lyrical qualities. As Jackson argues, "lyric reading" tries to read all poetry as if it was lyric poetry. As she explains, moreover, lyric reading determines that all legitimate poetry (that is, all lyric poetry) issues from a self in conversation with itself. [4] It argues that poetry is a spontaneous and transcendent effusion of this self and is therefore ahistorical, and it proposes that poetry worthy of the name is addressed not to specific persons but to a general audience of future readers. Importantly, those who obey these impulses of lyric reading also assume that all real literature of any kind is or should be lyric. Lyric reading of this kind has played a definitive role in credentialing the modern canons of poetry, as well as the canons that define literary study more generally. Yet you would be hard-pressed to find a fully elaborated lyric reading of any of the poetry in *Les Cenelles*.

Here are a few easy ways to explain this absence: One might point to the long-held racist supposition that writers of color had no coherent self worth expressing. Then there is the fact that some specific poems in *Les Cenelles* are difficult to fit into the model of lyric reading that has dominated academic criticism; it is challenging (although certainly not impossible, as one of the *Les Cenelles* poets, Pierre Dalcour, shows) to associate acrostics with lyricism. It is also arguable that the standards of taste that covertly govern most academic criticism have determined that these are simply bad poems. The fact that their authors are Francophone rather than properly French probably does not help matters, nor does the fact that they are not written in English. Given that these poems predate the rise of lyric reading as Jackson describes it, these poems might also be said to have a historically predictable deficit of lyricism.

However, all of these are ultimately unsatisfactory explanations for why so little lyric reading has been performed on these poems, especially given the historical conditions that make them ripe for such a reading. As Jackson explains, one of the main factors that made Dickinson susceptible to the lyric reading project was the long-standing myth of her personal inaccessibility, historical irretrievability, and social isolation. A similar forced amnesia around the lives, cultural productions, and sociality of people of color is characteristic of any racist society. When it comes to *Les Cenelles*, this manufactured amnesia has been in full effect. The *Les Cenelles* archive has been made to seem smaller and more scattered than it is. It would be easy to strip this poetry of its history in the way that Jackson shows has been done to Dickinson as a predicate to the practice of lyric reading.

I want to suggest that certain formal and material features of *Les Cenelles* permit a kind of sociality—a mode of being in common with others—that is generally unavailable to nineteenth-century readers and that offers rewards alternative to those of lyric reading. I am especially interested in this volume's dependence on apostrophe and its intratextual citational practices. These factors in many respects foreclose the practice of lyric reading and the problematic dependency on a lyric self associated with liberal individualism: the reigning principle of lyric reading dictates that all legitimate poetry must underwrite a process of substitutive identification with the other—a process in which the reading subject comes to identify with and substitute herself for the voice of the poem. *Les Cenelles* forestalls this lyric project of substitutive identification. In so doing, it also cuts against the sentimentalist ethos with which this project is allied and which dominates much ostensibly antiracist mid-nineteenth-century Anglophone American writing. Unlike either sentimentalism or the lyric reading project, this collection predicates a humanistic community of strangers organized around an ongoing process of mutual self-revelation that forecloses substitutive identification with the other. The tendency of the sentimental novel to encourage what Jackson calls the "fallacy of an identity between self and other" has been discussed at length in the criticism on this topic. [5] For its part, the project of lyric reading is, as I have suggested, to generate the fantasy of a lyric writing subject being overheard—a fantasy that in turn offers a model for the reading subject's own self-organization that also turns on what Jackson terms a "figurative logic of self-projection."[6]

In the following pages, I want first to explain how I think the recent spatial turn in literary studies prevents us from accounting fully for the particular mode of sociality that *Les Cenelles* inscribes. In the predominating logic of the spatial turn, identification is an either-or choice: either nation or the transnational, either the African American or the black Atlantic. I suggest that the first step toward understanding where *Les Cenelles* permits us to go in terms of being in common with others is to acknowledge the ways in which literature functions to support several different modes of identification at once without resolving them into a single point of coherence. This first claim in turn makes it easier to see how the *Les Cenelles* poets pursue smaller and less readily recognizable forms of identification and community. In the final section of this essay, then, I turn to the question of what sort of heretofore-unacknowledged modes of sociality emerge in the pages of *Les Cenelles*. Rather than offering this mode of sociality as a definitive alternative to nationalism, say, or blackness, I want instead to provide a template for thinking these different modes of sociality—nation, blackness, and what I will call a lyric public—at the same time. One might ask: How might a lyric public interfere with the pull of nationalism? What alternatives to race-based belonging are these poets offering us? And, of course, why?

After the Spatial Turn

Lyric reading and sentimental fiction share a project of overwriting difference with similitude that privileges the dominant same over the minor difference. *Les Cenelles* demurs from participating in that project. It is rather part of a broader African American print cultural engagement with the problematic of sentimental identification. Although it counted as a discovery in the 1980s and 1990s when scholars determined that perhaps there were problems with substitutive identification, its primary objects—African Americans, in particular—have been questioning this project's protocols since at least the mid-nineteenth century. We see that interrogation at play in *Les Cenelles*'s coordination of frequent deployments of the literary figure of apostrophe alongside internal citations to this poetry's conditions of composition and circulation. As I explain in more detail below, the net effect of orchestrating these figurative and commemorative tendencies is not to cross a divide of understanding but rather to preserve one. This volume makes possible a community of the human whose members exist in a milieu of ongoing encounter rather than a scene of mutual substitutability. And in this sense it anticipates what we might call a "lyric public." In the idiom of nineteenth-century U.S. political history, it holds out the possibility of a version of community that caters neither to Jacksonian individualism, nor to older republican ideals of communitarianism, nor even to emerging notions of African American communalism. Whether *Les Cenelles* ever actualized this version of community remains a vexing question. As Michael Warner cautions, "[i]t is very difficult to hybridize [lyric address and public address] without compromising lyric transcendence," and any effort to generate a public of whatever kind is conditioned by material circumstance.[7] Yet I want to speculate that this collection facilitates precisely a "compromise[d] lyric transcendence," and that this might be the source of its greatest interest. I also want to suggest that this pursuit of a lyric public constitutes one answer to Alexander G. Weheliye's recent query regarding the category of the human and its continued salience as an axis of affiliation: "[W]hat different modalities of the human come to light," Weheliye asks, "if we do not take the liberal humanist figure of 'man' as the master-subject but focus on how humanity has been imagined and lived by those subjects excluded from this domain?"[8]

To see the contribution of *Les Cenelles* to a different measure of the human, however, our first order of business must be a detour into and around the reigning approach in the humanities to the question of human collectivities. I am referring, of course, to the spatial turn. It is by now a standard gesture to suggest that the recent turn in literary and cultural studies away from the nation and toward new and different scales of affiliation presents a unique opportunity to address in a more satisfactory way such long-standing issues as the politics of *Les Cenelles*. Over the last fifteen years, we have been introduced (or reintroduced) to (among others) the transatlantic, the circum-atlantic, the black Atlantic, the trans-American, the hemispheric, the global, the planetary, the oceanic, and the global American South. Although there has been salutary work done in each of these different scales of analysis, the increasingly plangent dream of a perfect scale evidenced by their proliferation can have two occlusive effects. On the one hand, the spatial turn as enacted in the context of U.S.-based literary and cultural studies has often advocated a false choice: between the region and the nation, the nation and the transnational, the local and the global, the hemisphere and the oceanic basin, or some other propositional binary. As postcolonial critics, critical geographers, and more sensitive Americanists and African Americanists have recognized, this logic of the either-or choice ignores how one is always simultaneously embedded in many different and asymmetric scales of belonging, each one of which requires political attention and the sum of which constitutes a given historical subjectivity.[9] On the other hand, the growing empiricist historicism that has come to define the spatial turn—an archivalism that often takes the objectivity of the archive for granted—can obscure those scales of affiliation that have no state-sanctioned or recognizable "material" correlative and thus no self-evident archival depository. These scales often emerge from utopian political longing. The spatial turn has encouraged us, I am suggesting, to ignore those scales of affiliation that have only oblique relationships to the boundaries defined by "state institutions, laws, formal frameworks of citizenship, or preexisting institutions such as the church."[10] These are scales of affiliation that exist only (and always) in the space of address.

Quoting Michael Warner, these are the "kind[s] of public[s] that come into being only in relation to texts and their circulation."[11]

In her introduction to *The Traffic in Poems: Nineteenth-Century Poetry and Transatlantic Exchange* (2008), Meredith McGill usefully reminds us that despite the fanfare around the recent shift in literary studies, this field is already a latecomer to the spatial turn and to transatlantic studies in particular. McGill recalls how "early modern historians have been engaged in an often contentious reframing of their subject since the mid-twentieth century, when postwar enthusiasm for NATO and other alliances, combined with the ambitious scope of *Annales*-school history, made the Atlantic community newly visible as a political, economic, and cultural unit." The relatively slow response on the part of literary studies to the spatial turn, she continues, has much to do with "the considerable dragweight provided by the nationalist orientation of literary studies." Although this "dragweight" might seem finally to have lifted with the "explosion of interest in transatlantic literary study in the past decade," McGill also cautions that this amplification of interest in transatlantic literary study has been "[g]enerally biased toward prose[,] produc[ing] readings that are thematic in nature, keyed to authors' engagement with transatlantic subjects, or . . . conducted at a scale of analysis too broad to attend to questions of literary form." McGill's comments suggest that the sense of novelty surrounding transatlantic literary studies often follows from a willful forgetting of intellectual and procedural debts to disciplines (especially history) and genres (especially prose narrative) whose priorities and trajectories dictate in an unacknowledged way the structure of the transatlantic studies project. The same might be said for the spatial turn more generally. As McGill contends, "despite their strong efforts to think beyond the nation, most of these studies leave national literary histories more or less in place."[12] In McGill's account, an undertheorized expansion or axial rotation of a scale of analysis not only fails to challenge the rule of the nation; such efforts reinforce the integrity of the thing they claim to oppose. I would add that many recent attempts to dilate and/or reorient the scale of literary and cultural studies have in effect substituted a different set of hegemonic scales for the scale of the nation, while at the same time they argue for the defamiliarizing force of these new scales and their power to render visible what were previously invisible economic and social inequities. It is questionable whether this replacement of the nation as a unit of analysis with spatial and/or affiliative scales defined by the slave trade, the borders established by (non-Anglo) European colonists, or the market revolution amounts to a generative transformation in thought and politics. It is also important to consider how these replacement scales eclipse past and present alternative accounts of the human.

Of course, since at least the mid-nineteenth century, the issue of affiliative scale, in particular, has been a central preoccupation of the African American intellectual and political traditions. From Martin Delany's vision of an extra-national revolution, to W. E. B. Du Bois's interest in the Black Belt, to the arguments of *Négritude*, to the various Afrocentrisms, the question of which scale of affiliation most capably meets the political, material, and existential needs and experiences of African-descended peoples has been an intellectual and a political lodestar. It comes as no surprise to scholars adequately versed in the African American tradition to hear that how you draw the line marking who stands within and who without the circle is a deeply political issue. Yet the African American tradition has also anticipated with a difference the more recent spatial turn dominating the humanities at large. In the context of the African American intellectual tradition, the either-or tendency around the question of scale has also predominated, but it has emerged less from any reflexive empiricism than it has from an almost compulsive return to the normative question of which scale of affiliation best nurtures the political aspirations of African and African diasporic people by palliating the historical crime of natal alienation. In other words, African American intellectual history has its own habit of formulating the question of scale as a choice that is not a choice: either *Négritude* or the nation within a nation, either diaspora conceived as a permanent unfolding of difference or diaspora conceived as the preamble to spiritual and political return. Here the explicit rejection of the idea that the choice of scale is a neutral choice has led to a restrictive sense of which scales of affiliation pertain to the lives and cultural labors of African-descended peoples.

If counterhegemonic efforts to shift the scale of analysis often beget old hegemonies in a new disguise, and if both the spatial turn and African American thinking have often rejected the overlap of belonging that defines any historical subjectivity, then what alternative modes of framing are available? I want to answer this question by recourse to another: what would happen if we were to set aside for a moment the dream of a perfect scale and to indulge instead in an elaboration of scales of affiliation articulated in and through nothing more than the space of address emerging from poetry? How might such a practice of reading permit us to see how nineteenth-century works such as *Les Cenelles* allow affiliation not only with others of one's state-sanctioned "kind," but also with those from whom one has been legally segregated?

Les poésies indigènes

Les Cenelles is, of course, low-hanging fruit for an analysis that emphasizes transnational and global connections. As the history and criticism on this poetry and its authors often tell the story, the free Creoles of color in New Orleans were a cosmopolitan crowd whose identification with the United States was tenuous at best. Many were the children of enslaved women of African descent and men of the white planter class who frequented New Orleans to engage in the system of *plaçage*. Inheritors of property and Francophiles to a person, the young men of this class were schooled in Paris, and its young women were educated in New Orleans by schoolmasters who were Parisians. They formed a separate class in the city, one neither white nor black, but with certain privileges all their own. With the arrival of the American administration in Louisiana in the first decades of the nineteenth century, these privileges declined and reached their nineteenth-century nadir in the 1840s and 1850s. From the perspective of this twice-told tale of the Creoles of color of New Orleans, the scale of the (U.S.) nation is inapt for understanding this community's self-conception and the terms according to which it imagined and inhabited the world. Henry Louis Gates Jr. has written of this volume: "*Les Cenelles* argues for a political effect—that is, the end of racism—by publishing apolitical poems, poems which share as silent second texts the poetry written by Frenchmen three thousand miles away. We are just like the French—so, treat us like Frenchmen, not like blacks."[13] In this account, as in those more recent arguments that emphasize this writing's French republican, Catholic universalist, or romantic humanist origins, the (U.S.) nation plays a bit part in how these writers conceive their politics and their selfhood.

The subtitle of this collection of poetry, *Choix de poésies indigènes*, complicates any such direct replacement—as opposed to supplementation—of the scale of the nation with a transnational or circumatlantic one. There are in particular several salient ways to think about the issue of the indigenous referenced in the subtitle. According to the *Grand Robert*, in its adjectival form *indigène* is a botanical and biological term designating flora and fauna. It can also describe a nationally internal local practice or custom; a person who is native to a particular part of the nation; or a person who is a native of a colonial outpost. In its noun form, *indigène* can also signify a local resident native to a region of the nation or a person native to a colonial outpost. The literary criticism and historical writing on *Les Cenelles* and its authors has paid surprisingly little attention to this volume's subtitle, with the first of these definitions—the botanical designation of native flora—especially neglected. That neglect is peculiar, for the title of the collection, *Les Cenelles,* directly cites the indigenous flora of the bayous and the river bottoms that circle and thread through New Orleans. Although *Les Cenelles* has often been translated as "The Holly Berries," the term more specifically refers to the mayhaw berry. As the historian Jerah Johnson explains, moreover, the mayhaw berry played a central role in the heterosexual courting rituals of New Orleans's community of free Creoles of color. Creole men of color ventured out in mayhaw-gathering parties, and Creole women of color then invited those men to join them in their kitchens as they turned mayhaw berries into mayhaw preserves. According to Johnson, the specificity of the term helps to explain the volume's dedication to the "beautiful women of Louisiana."[14]

Indigenousness might at first seem to have little to contribute to U.S. nation formation: the "indigenous" summons the "local." Moreover, the European colonists of North America tried hard to disarticulate nation formation from the claim of indigenousness. Yet the mayhaw's connection to U.S. nationalism emerges more clearly when we identify *Les Cenelles* as in dialogue with the antebellum Anglophone poetry of writers such as William Cullen Bryant. Throughout his poetry, Bryant uses his meditations on indigenous North American flora to caption his own literary project as a nationally specific venture. In "The Painted Cup," "The Yellow Violet," "The Prairie," and other similar poems, he figures the landscape of North America as largely empty of human civilization and as instead a terrain of virgin flora that only a new and specifically American national literature can capably document. In this sense, he suggests that his specific poetic practice does not merely reflect an already-existing nation. It conjures that nation into being by confusing the indigenous qualities of the flora with the defining qualities of the (white) American frontiersman. With his choice of the title *Les Cenelles* and the subtitle *Choix de poésies indigènes*, Armand Lanusse, the volume's editor, strikes a similar pose but plants the roots of America in the soil of southeast Louisiana. Where Bryant associates American flora and thus America with a countryside stripped of human presence, especially in a poem like "The Prairie," the title *Les Cenelles* metonymically links the indigenous flora of America to a practice of affiliation specific to free Creoles of color. To the extent that the title references an indigenous plant that played a central role in the social world of Creoles of color, this poetry identifies the practices of affiliation that defined free Creoles of color as the indigenous precedent to (and for) the nation. Lanusse asks his reader to take his compass points for the nation from the practices of New Orleans's Creoles of color: this collection frames extant Creole of color circuits of affiliation as the indigenous and therefore preferred model for practices of U.S. nation formation.

It might seem like a stretch to suggest that the *Les Cenelles* poets were explicitly interested in establishing their own (local) practices of affiliation as a model for the project of stabilizing larger scales of affiliation such as the nation—or even that they were engaged in a self-conscious dialogue with writers such as Bryant. It appears to be much less so after one discovers that the poetry of *Les Cenelles* was part of a second ongoing conversation among Francophone New Orleanians, many of whom did not strictly disidentify with the U.S. nation. They instead sought to lay claim to it and redefine its meaning. In venues for "indigenous" literature such as the biweekly column titled "La littérature indigène," published in one of New Orleans's "white" Francophone newspapers, *La Réforme* (a newspaper to which some of the *Les Cenelles* poets also contributed), as well as in the more pointedly editorial columns of other Francophone outlets, Creoles of all shades responded to the growing Anglophone American know-nothing nativism of the 1840s and 1850s with a claim to the nation routed through their own account of the indigenous. Although the *Les Cenelles* poets and their white Francophone compatriots did set out to define a *littérature indigène* that contested Anglophone American literary nationalism, in other words, they remained American cultural nationalists.

It will perhaps come as no surprise to learn that this reading of the term *indigène* as a deforming species of U.S. cultural nationalism has little currency. This is due in part to the ingrained reluctance of (amateur and professional) archivists to permit the *Les Cenelles* poets their claim on the nation. One reason we have the level of access to *Les Cenelles* that we do, for example, is the essential collecting work of the dedicated (if racist) early twentieth-century bibliophile Edward Larocque Tinker, whose extensive archive of Francophone and Anglophone Louisiana is now housed mainly at the American Antiquarian Society and the University of Texas's Harry Ransom Center. One item of note in the Antiquarian Society's collection is the book sleeve that Tinker manufactured for his copy of *Les Cenelles*. In a striking woodcut image that Tinker created and that illustrates both his book sleeve and a pamphlet Tinker wrote about *Les Cenelles*, Tinker adopts many of the familiar tropes of nativist modernism, the combination of which goes some way toward obscuring this anthology's link to Louisiana's indigenous flora and reattaching the term *indigène* to the poets themselves, effectively reframing them as colonial African natives. From the perspective Tinker offers with his book sleeve, these poems have no legitimate claim on the scale of the (U.S.) nation, despite the title's placement of this poetry at the center of an indigenously American tradition. Where the original reference to the indigenous mayhaw defines New Orleans's Creole of color community as the template for the (U.S.) nation, Tinker redraws the circle to reattach these poets to the presumptively presocial and clearly prenational European imperial enterprises in Africa and the Americas.

Enter the Stranger

I have gone to some length to map out two different scales of affiliation supported by this poetry: that of New Orleans's Creoles of color and that of the nation. At the same time, I have tried to suggest their interarticulation through the term *indigène*, which serves as a kind of switching point that permits these two seemingly exclusive scales of affiliation to support each other and to live simultaneous lives. I want now to pursue even further my question of what would happen if we were to set aside for a moment the dream of a perfect scale and to indulge instead in identifying and elaborating scales of affiliation articulated in and through nothing more than the space of address emerging from African American poetry. To answer this question in more detail, it makes sense to begin with the issue of the heavy reliance of the *Les Cenelles* poets on the literary figure of apostrophe—if for no other reason than that apostrophe has long been the go-to literary figure for discussions of lyricism and the politics or poetry. *The New Princeton Encyclopedia of Poetry and Poetics* offers this definition of apostrophe: "A figure of speech which consists of addressing an absent or dead person, a thing, or an abstract idea as if it were alive or present."[15] As this definition would suggest, one clear indication that apostrophe is in effect is the presence of the rhetorical "O": "O, muse"; "O, Wild West Wind," and so on. Apostrophe can target objects of adoration and respect, recipients of desire and loathing. It also dominates the writing in *Les Cenelles*. These poets address their prolific apostrophes to the gods, to the one God, to teachers and patrons, to a disdainful public, to each other, and to the many avatars of nature.

Jonathan Culler famously argues that apostrophe has two significant imaginative effects. First, it animates its inanimate or absent objects of address. In familiar Anglophone examples such as Shelley's "Ode to the West Wind," the object of address achieves a subjective ontology that it otherwise lacks. What was previously mute and inactive becomes active and begins to speak. As Culler writes, "the function of apostrophe [is] to make the objects of the universe potentially responsive forces. . . . The apostrophisizing poet identifies his universe as a world of sentient forces."[16] This apostrophizing poet, in other words, arrogates to himself the right of world making—the ability to transform objects into subjects. Second, apostrophe works in a counterintuitive way to animate the voice of the poem, and in turn to empower the poet. In this reading, the voice of the poem, from which the figure of apostrophe emanates, has no a priori force of its own. The poem's voice requires an answer from the world in order for it to achieve some measure of subjective coherence. For Culler, then, "apostrophe is a device which the poetic voice uses to establish with an object a relationship which helps to constitute him. The object is treated as a subject, an *I* which implies a certain type of *you* in its turn. One who successfully invokes nature is one to whom nature might, in its turn, speak."[17] Here the poetic voice achieves its significance by establishing a relationship to the world of the inanimate that paradoxically animates both the voice of the poem and its inanimate addressee.

Anyone familiar with the history of literature and literary criticism will know that it is not news that apostrophe has a certain political charge when taken up in specific contexts. To find apostrophe emerging from New Orleans's community of free people of color is to discover, for example, a literature making broad claims for itself and its authors. These poems claim the right to address the inanimate and thereby to animate the world. Even more significantly, they engage in a process of self-animation. If Culler is right that apostrophe is the primary figure of self-sufficiency, then these poems are proclaiming the self-sufficiency of New Orleans's free people of color. More important than this surface gesture toward self-sufficiency, however, is the way that this poetry simultaneously obviates the kind of self-sufficiency associated with what Saidiya Hartman calls "burdened individualism" while raising the possibility of something like what Hannah Arendt points us toward as a politics of plurality.[18]

This process of turning away from one version of self-sufficiency and toward another is not self-evident on a first reading of this poetry. As I suggested just a moment ago, one more conventional perspective would focus on the fact that apostrophe collapses the distinction between self and other upon which a politics of plurality depends. As Jackson demonstrates, apostrophe encourages a narcissistic confusion of self and other, especially when it comes in the anodyne format of the postromantic codex collection of poetry. This particular book format tends to strip away all contextualizing references. This anonymizing of the poem and its voice makes it easier for the reader to identify with the apostrophizing voice. In other words, it encourages a problematic sort of substitutive identification. Consider, for example, these lines from Camille Thierry's poem "Toi," which was not included among the poems he published in *Les Cenelles*, but which dates from the same period:

> Tu ne murmuras point quand l'heure était venue,
> L'heure de nos adieux . . .
> Tu t'envolas tranquille à travers chaque nue,
> Comme un ange des cieux.
>
> Enfant, nous te suivrons au delà des nuages,
> Où l'âme trouve un port,
> Où l'on n'entend jamais le grand bruit des orages,
> Òu l'ouragan s'endort.
>
> [When the time came, you muttered not a sound—
> The time for our goodbyes . . .
> Calm, you flew off, like angel heaven-bound,
> Over the shrouded skies.
>
> Follow I shall, child, past the clouds, to reach
> A port of soul's safekeeping,
> Where never brawls the tempest's blare and screech,
> And hurricane lies sleeping.] [19]

In one familiar account of lyric poetry, the reader does not recognize herself as "toi" but rather as the "je" implied in the "nous" of line 5. The apostrophic address to "toi" is *so* private as to seem privative. It refers to no specific addressee, and it appears to emanate from no specific place or time. The "je" here is abstract enough to be perceived as *any* "je." Rather than Thierry or even the voice of the poem (the poem's "je") traveling to the heavens with the object of address, it is the reader who ends up taking that imaginative journey—and the reader takes it alone. The soul that "trouve un port" is the reader's own, and the "port" turns out to be the reader's soul itself. Although the figure of apostrophe appears to require the poem's "je" and its "toi" to travel toward each other and toward a moment of encounter, it actually encourages an inward turn that enfolds both the agent and the object of address into the reader's "je." The reader's "je" is reinforced, but in the process the poem's "je" and its "toi" disappear.

Although this is one standard reading of apostrophe, J. Douglas Kneale offers a counterpoint that suggests how a "third position" may be read out of this "structure of address."[20] This third position is neither the voice of the poem nor the position of the reading subject, but what we might call the position of the stranger—and it is this position of the stranger that these and other nineteenth-century African American writers will increasingly pursue and cultivate. In "Apostrophe Reconsidered," Kneale charges Culler with a basic definitional error. He suggests that Culler's influential discussion of apostrophe mistakes apostrophe for direct address in general. According to Kneale, apostrophe involves more than just an address to an inanimate or absent thing. Apostrophe involves a *turning aside* from the primary object of address to a new and different addressee. As the etymology of the word "apostrophe" and its origins in the classical context of the Roman senate chamber would suggest, apostrophe is a form of interruption with at least three witnesses: the agent of address, its original target, and its secondary target. Quoting Kneale: "By describing apostrophe as turning from an original . . . addressee to a different addressee, from the proper or intended hearer to another, we emphasize the figure as a *movement* of voice, a translation or carrying over of address. This understanding is crucial if we are to distinguish simple direct address from the turning aside of address, from the rhetorical and temporal movement of apostrophe."[21] Kneale reminds us here of the performative quality of apostrophe: in the moment of apostrophe, the primary object of address is made secondary and placed at a remove.

Kneale's reading would appear to disqualify many lines from *Les Cenelles* from counting as apostrophe, because they do not clearly turn away from a prior addressee. This is the case because several of these poems *open* by addressing muses, deceased friends, inanimate objects. Valcour B.'s "A Hermina" begins:

Amour, écoute un amant qui t'implore,
O Cupidon, le plus puissant des dieux!

[Hear O God of Love a lover's prayer,
Cupid, most powerful god of all!] [22]

His "A Malvina" opens:

Belle de grâce et belle de jeunesse,
O Malvina, tu parus à mes yeux

[Aglow with grace and youth, O Malvina
In all your beauty to my eyes you appeared] [23]

He is even so fond of the figure of apostrophe as to turn it upon the hat of his beloved in these first lines:

Chapeau chéri,
De celle que j'admire

[Cherished hat,
Of the one I admire] [24]

And Louis Boise animates spring with these first lines:

Tendre Printemps, viens rendre à la Nature
Et ses trésors et ses puissants attraits.

[Tender Spring, render to Nature
Her treasures and her enchanting lures.] [25]

In each of these cases, and in many of the others in *Les Cenelles*, it would be natural to assume that there is no former addressee. Is it not impossible to interrupt an address that has not yet begun? However, these are in fact instances of apostrophe, even in Kneale's more restricted sense, to the extent that they "turn aside" from—*and in so doing animate*—the intimate stranger whom modern print culture will come to imagine as its primary addressee. Warner follows Georg Simmel and other classic social theorists in arguing that in modernity, "strangerhood is the necessary medium of commonality."[26] He proposes further that modern forms of print culture involve an experience of stranger relationality wherein we have a feeling of in some way being in common with those whom we do not know—what Simmel in "The Stranger" describes as an experience of the "unity of nearness and remoteness."[27] The poetry of New Orleans's Francophone free people of color reminds us of what Warner also suggests about the emergence of stranger relationality: stranger relationality is in significant measure produced in formally specific acts of publication. A poem that opens with apostrophe would, in Kneale's formulation, amount to "simple direct address." But in the context of modernity, these opening addresses involve a performative turning aside that figures the primary addressee of this poetry as an audience of human strangers.

A Lyric Public

The apostrophizing poets of New Orleans in this sense not only arrogate to themselves the right to animate their inanimate or absent objects of address, acquiring in the process a subjective significance of their own. They also claim the right to participate in stranger relationality—that is, the privilege to remain substantively unknown and the right to grant that privilege to others. These poets in this way reset the terms of encounter according to which New Orleans's Creole free people of color will make their case at home and abroad. These poets do not engage in a form of direct address that is much more familiar to those of us who read mainly in the Anglophone African American literary tradition. This poetry is not a form of petition. It does not directly petition its reader for sympathy, nor does it petition a constitutionally exclusive legislature for the right simply to be human. In this sense, it is neither sentimental in the terms that have been said to define Anglophone sentimentality, nor does it display the standard gestures of the lyric. It instead opens a space into which its authors and their readers can emerge together as a new kind of human. In this space of literary affiliation among strangers, any human's experience is specific and not immediately knowable, but the specificity of that experience is not an exclusively racial, national, or regional specificity. These poems describe a line of demarcation separating each of us from all the rest of us. They preserve mutual opacities, and they do so in a way that summons a scale of human affiliation predicated on the unexchangeability of any one human for another. They also seek to foreclose the privative sort of "burdened individualism" often held up as the alternative to social disenfranchisement. *Les Cenelles* positions the free person of color as an intimate stranger whose specificity is his alone, in other words, and in so doing it draws a circle of affiliation accessible to anyone willing to acknowledge that specificity as a shared condition of being human.

In this sense, *Les Cenelles* goes some way toward presenting apostrophe in a format that does not immediately conduce to the more familiar operations of lyric reading. As Jackson explains, lyric reading compromises both the author/voice of a poem and its reader in a wash of narcissistic cross-identification. For Warner, this is one reason why lyric address and public address are at odds. As Warner explains, public address seeks to draw a wide circle of affiliation, and so it is predicated on its being self-consciously addressed to strangers and marked as such. As he also suggests, public address imagines and engenders a very specific kind of stranger. In premodern contexts, Warner explains, strangers are always on their way to being something else, but in modernity strangerhood is a privileged and permanent condition. He writes:

> Strangers in the ancient sense—foreign, alien, misplaced—might of course be placed to a degree by Christendom, the *ummah*, a guild, or an army, affiliations one might share with strangers, making them seem a bit less strange. Strangers placed by means of these affiliations are on a path to commonality. Publics orient us to strangers in a different way. They are no longer merely people whom one does not yet know; rather, an environment of strangerhood is the necessary premise of our most prized ways of being. Where otherwise strangers need to be on a path to commonality, in modern forms strangerhood is the necessary medium of commonality. The modern social imaginary does not make sense without strangers.[28]

As Warner indicates, to be a fully licensed citizen in modern society is to be *permanently* a stranger, someone granted the privileges of what Erving Goffman calls "civil inattention"—a form of recognition that is both the sign and the entry card to the sphere of modern civic life.[29] *Les Cenelles* does less to encourage understanding, or sympathy, or identification than it does to acquire strangerhood and preserve it.

Yet it does so in a way that runs counter to our commonsense expectation of what it means to be a stranger. Here, to be a stranger is not to be an abstract persona stripped of any specificity. It is rather to be a self whose social specificity forms the ground of his human specificity. This stranger is indeed different from all others, as more conventional idioms of individualism imagine is the case. But his difference derives from his sociality rather than from some prefabricated rights-bearing personhood. One does not retreat to a pond to discover one's individuality. One preserves the bonds of sociality formed in, say, one's writing circle. Indeed, *Les Cenelles* retards the dissolution of the generative "third position" of the stranger. It does so by enfolding within itself the residue of a sociality that lyric reading and sentimentalism seek to deny. As Jackson explains in her account of Dickinson's figures of address, most lyric readings hinge on the emptiness of a book form, the poetry collection, that offers the delusory sense that real poetry (which is to say lyric poetry) is written for no one in particular and from nowhere in particular. One of Jackson's central critical gestures is to reattach Dickinson's poems to their specific living historical addressees.

It is significant that *Les Cenelles* does much of that work for us. We are provided not only the given names of specific addressees in poems such as "A Hermina." We also have poems such as Valcour B.'s "Épître à Constant Lépouzé, en recevant un volume de ses poésies." There is also his "L'ouvrier louisianais (Imité de Béranger), à mon ami Armand Lanusse." In addition to these explicit addressees, members of this community are cited and honored in other ways. Armand Lanusse offers this epigraph to his poem "La prêtre et la jeune fille": "Paix sur terre aux mortels de froid tempérament. / Malheur à qui du ciel reçut un coeur aimant!"[30] It comes from Alfred Mercier, a fellow New Orleanian whose writing was in circulation in the city during this period. Lanusse's "Besoin d'écrire" is dedicated "à mon ami, Nelson D." And so forth. These practices make it difficult to imagine these and other poems in this volume as the product of a self in conversation with itself. The reader might wish to occupy the position of the lyric reader who overhears a solitary self, but instead must finally admit to listening in company with the dozen or so others addressed, named, and honored in *Les Cenelles*. Here the reader listens "dans un société." Introducing his poem "La foi, l'espérance et la charité," Pierre Dalcour writes:

Dans une société, où l'on jouait aux Jeux innocents, il fut ordonné à un jeune homme, pour racheter son gage, de faire une déclaration d'amour à la dame de son choix. Il s'avança aussitôt auprès d'une jeune personne qui passait pour être un peu dévote, et s'en acquitta ainsi.

[At a gathering where they were playing *Jeux innocents* (innocent games), a young man, in order to redeem a wager, was ordered to make a declaration of love to a lady of his choice. He immediately approached a young lady who had the reputation of being rather devout, and acquitted himself in this manner.] [31]

Les Cenelles discourages us from reading this as a fictionalized opening gambit, permitting us to imagine instead the actuality of the scene as the site of origin for the poem that follows. In a similar gesture, Dalcour subtitles another poem, "Caractère," with the deictic account of the origin of the poem: "Mot donné par mon ami Armand L." (Word proposed by my friend Armand L.).[32] Dalcour thus identifies the lyric and apostrophizing poem that follows as the product of an exchange between two people who retain the specificity of their names:

Moi qui fais des vers par caprice,
Aujourd'hui je suis condamné
Par un ami, Dieu, quel supplice!
A rimer sur un mot donné.
   Allons, ma muse,
   Un peu de ruse,
Il faut m'aider à sortir de ce pas;
   Vite, on me presse,
   Quelle détresse!

[I who write verses for pleasure
Today I am condemned
By a friend, God, what torture!
To rhyme upon a given word.
   Let's go, my muse
   A little ruse

> You must help me to get out of this;
> Quickly, the pressure is on,
>   What distress!] [33]

The title, the subheading, and the poem locate this work in a scene of Creole sociality. Although an indefinite article opens the title of Lanusse's poem "Un frère au tombeau de son frère," the parenthetical addition to the title of "(25 Septembre 1836)" offsets that indefiniteness of person and place. In many of the poems, the "air" that is to accompany it is specified. Often those airs are from Béranger, whose fame precipitated the formation of Béranger societies across France and in New Orleans. These references to Béranger suggest a lyric society—a lyric with public origins.

It is perhaps this lyric public that Armand Lanusse seeks to address in the opening lines of *Les Cenelles*. His introduction includes an epigraph from Félicité de Lamennais: "Toute conviction sincère mérite le respect, et la conscience de l'homme est un sanctuaire sacré pour l'homme, un asile où Dieu seul a le droit de pénitrer comme juge" (Every sincere conviction deserves respect, and a man's conscience is his hallowed sanctuary, a haven where God alone has the right to enter and judge).[34] This epigraph identifies the primary possession of any individual as his unassailable private soul, and it does so in the public forum of the published book. It is perhaps for this reason that Régine Latortue and Gleason R. W. Adams translate the first lines of the introduction, "Afin de prévenir les personnes dans les mains desqelles ce livre pourra tomber en faveur de ceux d'entre nos amis en poésie qui ont répondu franchement à notre appel et qui ont daigné contribuer à la production de ce volume, nous pensons qu'il nous suffira d'exposer dans cette introduction, d'un manière brève et précise, les motifs qui nous ont fait enterprendre la publication de ce recueil," as "In order favorably to predispose the reader toward the poets who have contributed voluntarily to this volume, we believe that a brief, precise exposition of the reasons for existence might be helpful."[35] As Latortue and Adams understand them, these lines constitute an address to "the reader" that puts the lyric writing subject's abstract "asile" before "the reader" and permits "the reader" to imagine his own "asile" to be one and the same with that of "l'homme." In the original French, however, the lines that open this volume stand in a tempering relationship to the epigraph. Rather than addressing "the reader," those lines reference instead "les personnes dans les mains desqelles ce livre pourra tomber." Rather than the solitary reader, we have instead "les personnes." Where the translation emphasizes the relationship of "the reader" to "the poets," the original highlights the relationship between "les personnes" and "ce livre."

In the world of *Les Cenelles*, the most poignant expressions of individual selfhood emerge from, preserve, and extend a tightly woven social matrix— a relationship among "les personnes." The lyric self of *Les Cenelles* always comes with a citation. This citationality is one of the potentials of not only "ce livre," but of any "livre." In this sense, this collection of poetry—or really, this way of collecting poetry—extends an invitation to strangers to join in the work of constructing a lyric self without conceding the sociality that makes such efforts possible.

CHAPTER 15

Imagining a State of Fellow Citizens: Early African American Politics of Publicity in the Black State Conventions

DERRICK R. SPIRES

This essay examines the *Proceedings of the Black State Conventions* of the 1840s as political documents central to our understanding of early African American print culture and the role of print circulation, as metaphor and as medium, for defining participatory politics more generally in the early United States.[1] Just as the struggle against slavery and kidnapping generated the national conventions of the 1830s, activism for political rights, especially the suffrage, fueled the state conventions in the 1840s. The very acts of organizing and holding conventions to petition for voting and other rights created a public black civic presence, demonstrating that black citizens could and did conduct themselves as people fully capable of self-determination in a republican government. Moreover, the texts the conventions produced—printed proceedings (including minutes, addresses, petitions, and reports) aimed at state institutions as well as black and white audiences—extended, circulated, and concretized this civic presence via the periodical press and pamphlets.[2] The *Proceedings of the Black State Conventions*, then, are important not only because of the arguments they make for and about suffrage, but also for the work they do *as* texts, as performative speech acts that seek to manufacture the very citizenship practices from which the delegates had been excluded.[3]

While many scholars quote from these texts, few have treated the state convention proceedings as distinct and important political and cultural phenomena, as important as the black press, the slaves' narratives, and the national conventions to our understanding of early African American print culture and U.S. print culture more generally.[4] As literary historian John Ernest argues about the more familiar national conventions, these proceedings are "important historical texts not simply in content but in their mode of presentation"; they are "collective performances designed to be a representative embodiment of an imagined African American community."[5] Framed by one convention as a "fair representation of our people in the State," the proceedings displayed to black men and women around the state and to white politicians the breadth and depth of the leaders of this people and, more specifically, demonstrated the irrationality of excluding this qualified and rational segment of the civic body.[6]

My argument here is not necessarily that the black conventions do anything particularly different from other like gatherings, but rather, that the choice of this public form—the convention and circulated proceedings—signifies in certain recognizable and performative ways that addresses (without the accompanying frame) could not. The petitions, conventions, meetings, parades, and other nongovernmental forms of citizen participation during the 1830s and 1840s were not, from the antebellum citizen's view, ancillary or symbolic demonstrations of protest. Rather, these unofficial modes of participatory politics were a viable, visible, and a potentially revolutionary mode of direct intervention in a civic sphere in which voting was just becoming accessible to masses of white men.[7]

Black State Conventions of the 1840s: Background

Maintaining a public and civic presence as an explicitly political community was crucial to the conventions' overall project, because even as suffrage served as one of the primary political and cultural points of identification for white manhood, it became an even more powerful symbol of disidentification and political and legal alienation for African Americans and women.[8] In the age of the "common man," an age in which the nation celebrated the popular election of the president and when states nationwide were voting on constitutional revisions that had fundamental effects on state governance, exclusion from this process symbolized a forcible removal from the civic imaginary itself and served as a legal precedent for further restrictions.[9] Suffrage, then, perhaps equal to antislavery in the 1840s, was a particularly key

point of attack for black activists on the state level.[10] The "colored inhabitants" of New York were the first to organize a statewide convention expressly
addressing franchise rights in 1840. Michigan, Pennsylvania, Indiana, and
Ohio all held at least one state convention during the 1840s. After the passage
of the Fugitive Slave Act of 1850, black citizens would hold similar conventions in other states focused on new threats of reenslavement in addition to
local issues.[11]

More than a single event, the conventions were a constellation of events
and texts ranging from debates, initial meetings, and advertisements to select
delegates, to the convention itself and the circulation and public reading of
"Proceedings" afterward. Conventions began in print with the convention
calls, issued months before the meetings, which usually included a list of
grievances and asked potential attendees to gather statistical information on
black populations.[12] Indeed, part of the effectiveness of the black state conventions was the highly publicized nature of the organizing process: numerous calls in newspapers, local meetings with their voting on resolutions,
printing these resolutions in papers like *Colored American, Pennsylvania Freeman, National Anti-Slavery Standard,* or *New York Tribune,* and the articles
against the conventions. During the convention, delegates passed resolutions
on staple topics such as education, economic development, temperance and
other moral reforms, and general resolutions encouraging the community to
continue to work toward its own elevation.[13] During open evening sessions,
attendees offered speeches on issues like education, temperance, and economic
development.

Finally, delegates issued the "Proceedings" or "Minutes" of the convention, including two or three addresses, one to the white "voters" or "people of
the state," appealing to them for constitutional amendments and general support. The other, addressed to "colored fellow citizens," requested their continued support of uplift programs and their participation in the statewide
petition drive. The addresses, if not the entire proceedings, were reprinted in
newspapers.[14] Some conventions, however, strategically delayed reprinting
the proceedings in newspapers to maximize the distribution of pamphlets.
Convention organizers could then cite this consumption as a sign of public
approval.[15] These conventions, then, began and ended in print, producing and
circulating documents at each juncture in a way that kept their civic claims
constantly in the public eye. This proliferation of documents, a veritable
cacophony of voices, and constant agitation created a politicized space—
different from a periodical, pamphlet, fair, or other form of publicity, yet

combining elements of each—that resonated with recognizable events and texts ranging from the Continental Congress and the U.S. Declaration of Independence to contemporaneous states' conventions.[16]

The rest of this essay focuses on the Convention of the Colored Inhabitants of the State of New York in 1840 and the 1848 State Convention of the Colored Citizens of Pennsylvania as models for reading other black state conventions. The New York convention was the first state-based convention and provides a model for how black activists used the form. The attention the New York convention gives to documenting its proceedings is useful for analyzing the formal structure and circulation of these documents, particularly the addresses and calls for a convention, and how the process forced black and white activists alike to grapple with the meaning of "color" and "condition" in constructing political communities. As the discussion below suggests, the conventions confronted these racial formations long before the first delegates set out for the meeting halls. The 1848 Pennsylvania convention suggests a potentially revolutionary practice. In the tradition of David Walker's *Appeal*, the convention calls for citizens to take responsibility for a state constitution that, they argue, has substituted arbitrary standards for republican principles of self-government. Linking the two conventions shows the synergy between early African American print culture and civic practice in offering alternative modes of political participation even as official channels continued to close.

Calling a Convention: Doing Politics Through a "Different Medium"

How convention organizers shaped the political communities of "colored" citizens the delegates claimed to represent was integral to the convention process. Delegates needed to define colored citizens as a group with shared political claims against the state while not reinforcing the sense that they were a separate people. And the debate about this framing began well before the first delegates set off for Albany, New York, in 1840. White and black activists alike were often ambivalent toward the conventions' "complexional" nature. William Whipper, James McCune Smith, and others opposed the 1840 New York convention because of the expense, the possible diffusion of labor, and their sense that the suffrage movement would be better served by an interracial coalition under the umbrella of human rights.[17] After the convention,

William Whipper famously penned a set of three letters to the *Colored American* that critiqued the emphasis on color in the convention's documents, arguing that such language was "in direct opposition to the 'rights of humanity.' "[18] White antislavery activists like Nathaniel Rogers, editor of the *National Anti-Slavery Standard*, accused the organizers of repeating the prejudices of white men in addressing their call to colored citizens. Rogers's June 18, 1840, editorial addressed itself to the organizers as a "friend," arguing: "We oppose all exclusive action on the part of the colored people, except where the clearest necessity demands it."[19] "[T]ime should be taken," the editorial continued, "to discuss the measures to be employed deliberately; and the people should be made distinctly to understand that *our* country is *your* country; our God your God."[20] The language implies that at the very least the black conventioneers' actions were too hasty, showing a lack of rational deliberation; at worst, it implies that this deliberation could only occur with their (white) presence and guidance.

Defending the convention against such criticisms forced supporters to grapple with the meaning of "color" as an organizing principle, questions of agency vis-à-vis fracturing antislavery organizations, and the tensions between presenting African Americans as autonomous individuals and the public's tendency to read their political actions as the result of white patronage.[21] One such defender, "Sidney," responded to William Whipper's letters in one of the clearest articulations of a pragmatic political black nationalism in early African America: "Whenever a people are oppressed, peculiarly (not complexionally), distinctive organization or action is required on the part of the oppressed, to destroy that oppression. The colored people of this country are oppressed; therefore the colored people are required to act in accordance with this fundamental principle."[22] In much the same vein, Samuel Ringgold Ward responded to Rogers's *Standard* editorial by pointing out white abolitionists' racial privilege and myopia: their inability "to see a colored man when in the company of other whites necessitates such a convention."[23] Ward upbraids Rogers: "had you worn a colored skin from October '17 to June '40, as I have, in this pseudo-republic, you would have seen through a very *different medium*."[24] Sidney and Ward connect being "colored" to a historical experience of oppression and to a mode of seeing this oppression as an issue of political power and representation. Being colored in this instance signifies in the same way as being propertyless might in other circumstances. To have a "colored skin," their analysis suggests, is to be without property in whiteness, a property worth about $250 in New York.[25] This material and experiential position gave Ward and Sidney a theoretical framework for articulating a "colored" civic identity at the intersections of racial, economic, and political particularities, while maintaining the connection to the platform of human rights that concerned critics like Whipper and Rogers.

Ward's "different medium" also offers a particularly apt description of how Charles B. Ray used this debate to position the *Colored American* against the *Standard* and antislavery organizations more broadly. The debate over the convention coincided with the shift of editorial duties from Samuel Cornish to Ray at the *Colored American*. Indeed, the debate provided an opportunity for Ray to assert the paper's new direction even as he and others used the *Colored American* to frame the convention's public presence. He installs the paper as "the organ of the colored people," a representative of black public opinion, and as a watchdog (and preserver of black rights of oversight) "to reprove all parties" in anti-slavery activism.[26] Ray and Ward also registered the growing sense among black abolitionists that antislavery organizations had little interest in allowing black members to set the agenda or to be in positions to do so. This division, for Ray, was evident in antislavery conventions in which the black participants were "looked upon as playing second fiddle," sitting as "passive as 'dumb dogs'" in the presence of the white leadership.[27] "If we act with our white friends" under such conditions, one response to Rogers concludes, "the words we utter will be considered theirs, or their echo."[28] Black abolitionists could lecture and even preside over the meetings, but the decisions would always come down from the white leadership, and the public would always see it that way.

As they argued against the *Standard*, Ray and others outlined their sense of the relation between popular perception, political agency, and the power of narration—that is, the power of constructing a narrative of black citizenship authentically "written by itself." The convention welcomed white attendance—even needed the approbation of whites—but Ray maintained that any political progress would require the kind of publicity that only a gathering arranged by an autonomous black political collective could provide. Such an event, a "different medium," would demonstrate to the state that, rather than operating as puppets to abolitionist organizations or guaranteed votes for a Whig establishment, black citizens desired the franchise for their own and the state's benefit, "that as citizens we should possess the privileges and immunities of citizenship: and . . . we are as capable of appreciating and exercising those rights as others."[29] It would position them as *political* actors rather than objects of legislation. The publicity from holding this convention, in other words, was just as important as the subject for discussion.

New York: Franchise as Circulation, Deliberative Politics as Stagecraft

With this debate through newspapers and dozens of local meetings as a prelude, the 1840 Convention of the Colored Inhabitants of the State of New York convened in Albany, from August 18 to 20; approximately 140 delegates represented counties across the state.[30] Building on petition drives begun in the late 1830s by Henry Highland Garnet, Charles Lenox Remond, George T. Downing, and others, the convention was organized to create auxiliary county committees to facilitate statewide petition efforts.[31] Delegates proposed and voted on resolutions mostly concerned with the significance of suffrage and the most practical means of convincing the state assembly to abolish property requirements. In subsequent years, Henry Highland Garnet, James McCune Smith, and other delegates would submit the convention's proceedings and 2,093-signature petition to the state assembly and would later represent black citizens in committee hearings on the franchise during the 1846 state constitutional convention.[32]

Central to the convention's argument for removing property restrictions was its interpretation of suffrage as the life force or blood of the state.[33] The trope of circulating blood illustrates how the suffrage creates commonality without requiring homogeneity. In a passage calibrated to demonstrate the importance of franchise rights to the convention's black readers, the "Address . . . to Our Colored Fellow Citizens" argues: "the possession of the franchise right is the life blood of political existence. It runs through all the convolutions of our civil state. It connects itself with our literary immunities, enters into our ecclesiastical associations, and blends with our social and domestic relations."[34] The franchise protects public discourse ("literary immunities") and links all the interest-based civic and social institutions that could otherwise atomize a community, and it creates a common network, a circulatory system, through which differences can be mediated. Figured as blood, the franchise displaces the biological bases for fellow citizenship; fellow citizens become "related" through their joining of civic power under the auspices of shared political channels, documents like the Declaration of Independence and the U.S. Constitution providing "the connecting chain that runs through the whole mighty mass of humanity . . . the common sympathies and wants of the race," that is, the human race.[35]

By framing political participation as generative of, rather than requiring, a unified civic body, the 1840 New York convention attempted to uncouple the formal structures of consent and deliberative politics from their racially ascriptive underpinnings and to situate the state's franchise restrictions as the *cause* rather than the result of "black condition."[36] The franchise is, as the convention's form petition put it, an "instrument of their elevation," not a goad or reward for it.[37] Blocking access to the franchise "is like extracting the living principle from the blood of the system."[38] "Is it any wonder," they ask, "that our energies have been relapsed, that our powers have been crippled, our purposes nerveless, our determinations dead and lifeless?"[39] "From this" outside repression, the convention tells its fellow colored citizens, "proceeded our degradation. This has been the source of our suffering and oppression."[40] The cultural and political advantages of the franchise open access to political and economic opportunities—"those resources of pecuniary and possessional emolument, which an unshackled citizenship does always ensure"— inaccessible to the disfranchised.[41] Where the framers of New York's 1821 constitution argued that blackness signified immutable inferiority (either biologically or as a result of enslavement), the 1840 convention argues that the state's policy had functioned to create an ontological and teleological signification of black skin that was not there before.

Even as the 1840 New York convention presented a reasoned argument for suffrage rights, however, its success depended on the performance and presentation of these arguments to the public in a way that conformed to a deliberative style of politics.[42] While the convention, the event itself, produced arguments for civil rights, the documents surrounding the convention—the calls and debates leading up to the event and the proceedings and reports following the event—circulated this performance, producing a black civic presence aimed at gathering the public approval needed for constitutional change. As Ray observed, the impressions the convention left on the attending audience—"many of the leading men in Albany of the Whig political party, and of public matters"—and readers of the convention's proceedings were at least as important to the delegates as the outcome of the debates and their theoretical soundness.[43] The Whig onlookers provide a moment of Hegelian recognition, but with an ever-present caveat of difference— "as one of their own class said to us"—that reemphasized the power differential between the convention delegates (since many could not vote) and the white voters and legislators who made up part of its audience.[44] The need for formal recognition exposes tensions within these conventions. They were at once immanent practices in and signs of citizenship, and at the same time, they were stagings adhering to certain stylistic conventions and dependent on voter affirmation for validation.[45]

Ray's comments also reveal the measure of aesthetic judgment and persuasion always attendant to deliberative politics, especially in lieu of a civic space fraught with inequity.[46] The organizers of the 1840 New York convention were keenly aware that the convention's legitimacy depended as much on how well the proceedings showed it executing its business as a deliberative body (or at least how well it presented this execution to the public) as it did on what the convention actually decided. Ray reiterates that the "Proceedings" represent the convention's "respectable and noble" character, revealing the delegates' ability to conduct business without "angry debate," settling differences "amicably and yet without compromise."[47] Indeed, the *form* these debates and resolutions take in the proceedings carried at least as much weight as their content because the text could confirm Ray's claim that the convention adhered to a notion of deliberative politics. And, because audiences would read any sign of disorder as confirmation of black difference, the minutes needed to be especially scrupulous on this point.

The minutes for the New York convention include the substance of disagreements (no matter how heated), but not the actual back and forth, in a way that frames it as a democratic process of revision. For example, when some delegates (C. B. Ray, T. S. Wright, E. P. Rogers) supported a resolution encouraging black citizens to buy property to meet the franchise requirements, others (H. H. Garnet, U. Boston, A. Crummell) opposed it because the resolution implied consent to the current requirement. The minutes recount the exchange: "A very spirited debate arose on this resolution, owing to the exception taken to that part of it which asserted that the obtainment of a certain amount of property, *'elevates us to the rights of freemen.'* . . . The discussion on the resolution, continued till near the close of the session, when Mr. Ray introduced an amendment, which was strongly opposed, owing to its containing . . . the same objectionable feature as the original resolution." The minutes exclude the actual back and forth, instead offering the procedural commentary: "spirited debate," "discussion," introduction of an amendment, opposition to the amendment, and so on. They adjourn without a resolution and return to the question later, but "after some further discussion . . . laid [it] indefinitely upon the table."[48] This presentation offers enough description to give readers a sense of the stakes involved in the resolution's language, the delegates' astute attention to this language (mirroring similar debates about semantics during constitutional conventions), and the democratic process through which the convention negotiated this impasse. Without the messy details of individual arguments, however, even this clearly divisive issue (it consumes the better part of two sessions after all) reads relatively smoothly.

The minutes do not mention the debate again, but later that evening, after several reports, two resolutions appear that resolve the tensions around the original proposal: "Resolved, That we recommend to our people to become possessors of the soil within the limits of this State" and "Resolved, That in recommending our people to possess themselves of the soil, we no less protest against that clause in the Constitution of the State which requires a property qualification of us . . . considering it wrong in principle, sapping the foundation of self government, and contrary to all notions of natural justice."[49] These two resolutions register and synthesize the primary disagreements over the original proposal as dialectical progression. Like other resolutions, the proceedings do not record the vote count, nor do they give the names of who proposed which parts of these adopted resolutions. Where the debate account registers the political fault lines, the new resolutions appear as if none of the earlier exchange and deadlock had occurred. In its linear progression, this presentation functions dialectically to meld discordant voices into a, coherent representative civic voice. But the differences themselves do not disappear. The proceedings present an "institutionally heteroglossic" structure,[50] at once ephemeral—the record of a singular event, situated in a particular political moment—and at the same time "compiled" and "collected" as a record of the political moment. Internally, the resolutions relate to each other dialogically in a call-and-response sequence mediated, as it were, by the "third party" of the overall corporate author as a product of public democratic exchange.[51] The pieces of the proceedings also dialogue with each other: the preamble with the resolutions, the resolutions with the addresses, the resolutions with each other, and so on. This formal structure, at once a dialectical progression through compromise and at the same time a dialogic interplay between distinct voices and sections, no less than the resolutions' content demonstrates the deliberative politics that opponents claimed were beyond black citizens' mental capacities or social conditions. The convention proceedings show the delegates doing the work of the republican citizenship, modeling how official civic institutions ought to channel citizens' civic energy.

How these convention proceedings frame their interactions with the state and their various audiences should nuance the way we read black constructions of publics and counterpublics. We can read the New York convention and its proceedings as manifestations of the print counterpublic formations scholars have identified within African American, African Atlantic, and subaltern traditions more broadly. Even as such counterpublics shaped their own discursive and cultural communities and practices, they aimed for more than simple inclusion.[52] The black state conventions demonstrate that, as a politics, this strategy could be directed outward, changing the tenor of official public discourses in a way that could be radically transformative for both. If counterpublics, following Nancy Fraser, "are parallel discursive arenas where members of subordinated social groups . . . formulate oppositional interpretations of their identities, interests, and needs," then these texts oscillate between and bridge these parallel arenas as neither counter nor official, but rather as temporary mesopublic spaces.[53] Just as the New York convention's theory of suffrage emphasizes circulation, a system of interstitial connections between citizens and between citizens and the state, these texts operate within the spaces between publics. As the next section suggests, the conventions' staging reaches full effect when the proceedings first acknowledge and then transgress these boundaries.

Pennsylvania: Sublime Appeals to Revise the Civic Compact

More than the 1840 New York convention, the 1848 State Convention of the Colored Citizens of Pennsylvania explicitly cited the creation and movement of collective texts as a tool for joining politically separate communities. That is, in enlisting public support for their claims against the state, these conventions could fundamentally change the public's political identity, displacing the power of whiteness in managing political interests. The convention issued an "Appeal to the Colored Citizens of Pennsylvania" and an "Appeal to the Voters of the Commonwealth of Pennsylvania" with the original proceedings.[54] Though the appeals addressed different audiences, both audiences had direct access to both addresses under the auspices of the state convention report and in newspapers that tended to reprint them side by side.[55] In this way, the appeals mirror the dialectic-dialogic model of deliberative politics presented in the debate-to-resolution sequence during the convention itself, grafting white voters and black petitioners into a single civic body. Just as the lines separating newspaper columns signal that each article belongs to the same institutional structure, the 1848 proceedings' heteroglossic structure connected its separate audiences as fellow citizens.

Where the New York conventions addressed themselves primarily to the state's legislature and Whig elite, the 1848 Convention of the Colored Citizens of Pennsylvania appealed to the voters, at once as sovereign citizens with the power to overturn the gross injustice of the 1838 state constitution and at the same time as complicit with politicians who pandered to their racial prejudices. In rhetoric that prefigures Frederick Douglass's Fourth of July "Oration," the "Appeal to the Voters" reviews the state's history of republicanism through its own documents, "the sublime appeals of her distinguished statesmen": "We only ask the favor of the application of your own principles to your civil code. . . . You claim that your own Independence Hall is the sacred spot where your republicanism was born, cradled and received a national baptism, and from whence the same vestal fire of freedom is encompassing the globe."[56] The delegates situate Pennsylvania as the preeminent exemplar of republicanism to the world. The proliferation of documents (quotes from the state constitution, the Declaration of Independence), monuments (Independence Hall), and events within the "Appeal to the Voters" form the basis of a covenant between the state and its citizens. The use of "you" throughout the "Appeal to the Voters" punctuates the voters' responsibility for their own laws and how these laws violate the state's self-proclaimed republican principles.[57] As outside witnesses, the "we" of the "Appeal to the Voters" excoriates the "you," the appeal's audience. The emphasis on the contractual or covenant nature of republicanism in the "Appeal to the Voters" shifts the argumentative burden from the meaning of blackness and ostensible material and ontological differences between types of citizens to the principles of republicanism as applied to *all* citizens.

While the "Appeal to the Voters" engages the voters' responsibility and patriotism, suggesting that the current voters risk forsaking the legacy of their forebears, the "Appeal to the Colored Citizens" excoriates these same voters for breaking their state's republican contract for personal gain. In so doing, the appeals offer an incisive analysis of how electoral politics structured through racial hierarchies worked to limit democratic citizenship even as it appeared to create a more democratic public sphere. The "Appeal to the Colored Citizens" argues that racism functioned as a "*passport* to power" that allowed white citizens to limit potential political opposition as much as they could. It suggests that the state's elite and white citizens more generally have deliberately refused to base their decisions on the very standards they themselves claim to use and have instead used suffrage restrictions not only to suppress republican governance and to disfranchise citizens who could not vote, but also to control more easily those citizens who could. As the "Appeal to the Colored Citizens" argues with chagrin: "They [delegates to the Reform Convention] were cunning logicians, and well knew that no argument founded on *condition* would meet the *false prejudices* of *their* constituents. They knew that the period had long since passed when it would be *possible* to *frame* a standard of *condition* that would separate the *white* from the *colored* people. . . . So they disfranchised us . . . assuming *condition* as their *reason*, and *complexion* as their standard."[58] The 1837–38 convention based the franchise requirements on social and economic condition only to make whiteness the standard for measuring them in a way that smoothed over differences between white men.[59] Race was never an indicator of civic worth, but rather, the "Appeal to the Colored Citizens" argues, the "*capital*" funding a shell game in which race substituted for republican principle, giving the sense that all white citizens were abstractly equal, when the delegates were actually trying to maximize their own political power. Many of those who supported the suffrage restriction "would not only have *disfranchised us*, but the *poor* of *every nation*, and whole *political* parties, that were opposed to them in the bargain."[60] By focusing voters' attentions on protecting their shared interests in whiteness against incursions from a black mass or any easily isolated "others," those in power could more easily mask their maneuvering for more control.[61]

For the appeals' black readers, giving an account of racial oppression that indicts white duplicity and arbitrariness instead of black condition or behavior eliminated improvement-then-rights tactics even as it provided reasons for continuing to support moral and material uplift as good in and of itself. Though the delegates to the constitutional convention were guilty of pandering to racial prejudices, white voters were equally guilty for holding and acting on their own "false prejudices."[62] So long as white voters gave ontological, normative, and moral value to skin color, black citizens would never become "elevated" enough. And, because racialized suffrage requirements made the state vulnerable to manipulation and antirepublican control, the 1848 convention appealed to citizens, black and white, to revise the existing contract.[63]

With this more general threat to republicanism foregrounded, the convention asked white voters to join them in producing new texts: "Our object in assembling is not only to petition the Legislature *ourselves*, but also to

solicit *you to petition* . . . to instruct [legislators] in a course of action."[64] Together, the appeals sought to build an interracial coalition of petitioners around
voting rights. If petitioning and holding conventions offered the otherwise
disenfranchised limited participation within the political system, and thus
limited membership within the civic community, then joining in petition
efforts could also create a different, potentially more powerful political community. The petition campaign, coming from black and white citizens, could
reenact the drafting of state documents as a contract between the two. The
act of petitioning—not simply signing a preformulated petition, but actively
creating and circulating these documents in conjunction with the convention's work—could realign the terms of community affiliation in a way that
would match the boasted efforts to spread republicanism abroad and establish consensus about a more egalitarian notion of republican government.

This sense of appeal, with its framing through a convention of representative citizens and its resonances with the Continental Congress's Declaration allowed the delegates to "reframe the meaning of popular sovereignty"
by invoking a ritual of consensus that would supersede any existing government.[65] The invocation of "the sublime appeals of [Pennsylvania's] distinguished statesmen," particularly the Declaration of Independence, through
the structure of a convention that calls its own addresses to the public "appeals" directly links the 1848 convention to a national tradition of government by consent and continuing revolution.[66] This approach shifts voters'
attention away from a systems-off citizenship in which the would-be citizen
must attain a certain standard before earning full rights to a systems-on citizenship in which, according to the state and nation's founding contracts, all
governed citizens receive all the rights of citizenship until they "[forfeit] their
rights" by committing a crime.[67]

Yet, even as the Pennsylvania convention calls on these founding documents of a U.S. political tradition, its more confrontational style reads less
like the theoretical explication of the franchise from the 1840 New York addresses and more like a manifesto in the tradition of David Walker's *Appeal*
(reprinted in 1848 by Garnet with a biography of Walker and Garnet's 1843
"Address to the Slaves") and the 1837 "Appeal of Forty Thousand Citizens,"
respectfully asking voters for redress, but maintaining the moral and legal
high ground and an allegiance to an explicitly political black community.
Invoking this tradition in their title and tone, the Pennsylvania convention's
appeals call for black citizens to work toward their own political liberation
with or without popular support, even as they argue that the Constitution

secures black citizens' rights: "Slaves have but learned to lick the dust, and stifle the voice of free inquiry; but we are not slaves—our right to natural liberty, and qualified citizenship, is guaranteed to us by the Constitution."[68] The 1848 "Appeal to the Colored Citizens" dismantles the racial illogic by which black citizens had been disfranchised as a part of a larger call to black citizens to take control of their own political fates. In this way, the proceedings of the 1848 convention may begin with notes of deference, but they have elements of the manifesto at their core: an articulation of a new political position and policy for black Pennsylvanians and an ultimatum directed at the state that these citizens will no longer equivocate about their political rights as citizens.

If the voters do not overturn the legislature's ruling, it will not be a verdict on the "condition" of the colored citizens, but rather, an admission that the state cannot hold up to its own professed standards. Where New York's Charles Ray emphasized the recognition of Whig onlookers, the Pennsylvanians situate themselves as the state's judges and arbiters of their own destiny. "We shall live and labor in the glorious anticipation of success," they begin, "but if it should prove otherwise, and you should not consent to repeal the sentence you have passed on Providence, we shall derive the rich consolation that in making this appeal we have discharged a duty we owe to *ourselves*, to freedom, and republicanism—to posterity and to God."[69] Even though black Pennsylvanians need the voters' support to regain the suffrage, they do not depend on these voters for political identity. If the voters rejected the "Appeal," then the voters would have failed, ultimately usurping the natural order and rendering their constitution invalid via its own logic. The declaration echoes the warning in the "Appeal of Forty Thousand Citizens": "no amendments of the present Constitution can compensate for the loss of its foundation principle of equal rights, nor for the conversion into enemies of 40,000 friends."[70] Ultimately, black citizens will be justified in separating from a state that refuses consent from its whole people.

More than the "Appeal to the Voters," the "Appeal to the Colored Citizens" directly confronts voters' criminal negligence in accepting truncated republicanism; but, because the two appeals were printed side by side as a part of the same proceedings, the "Appeal to the Colored Citizens" speaks to these voters even as it ostensibly addresses a black audience. The result is that while the "Appeal to the Voters" acknowledges white voters as the sovereign people, inheritors of the state's revolutionary heritage, and responsible for the progress of republican governance, the "Appeal to the Colored Citizens" accuses these same voters of gaining and maintaining this power through usurpation. This doubling allows the convention to request even as it condemns, to ask for judgment even as it dispenses its own judgment, and to approach the voters as nonthreateningly as possible even as it shapes a unified black political community through a sense of righteous indignation. Each instance represents an algorithm depending on audience reception, a step-by-step protocol leading to either citizenship practices in the United States that are more democratic on one end or grounds for disassociation on the other.

This is not a narrative of triumphs or happy endings, however. In states that either refused to extend voting rights or instated racial restrictions, black citizens did not regain the suffrage until after the Civil War. But, this is not a narrative of failure either. Even if state assemblies rejected their petitions, the conventions forced the states to debate about whether or not to enter the documents into official records and to revisit continually the meaning of not only black citizenship but citizenship more generally.[71] In this way, the conventions helped create an African American civic presence in the absence of formal representation, a presence active throughout state records despite efforts to remove it. Indeed, the legacy of these documents continued beyond the confines of the conventions that produced them and the issues they explicitly raised. Commentary on the 1848 Pennsylvania convention, for instance, appeared in the December 22, 1848, issue of *North Star* alongside an article on caste in Europe and excerpts from the new French constitution, linking early African American politics to global struggles for liberty. Ward reprinted the 1848 appeals almost a year later in *Impartial Citizen* with an article on "Progress Among Colored Men" amid a spirited debate with Douglass over the pro- or antislavery nature of the U.S. Constitution and the need for explicitly political activism. And it is no coincidence that prominent figures in the conventions of the 1840s—Garnet, Alexander Crummell, and Delany—would later argue that if the nation continued to be unresponsive, then black Americans should take their civic power elsewhere.

CHAPTER 16

"Keep It Before the People": The Pictorialization of American Abolitionism

RADICLANI CLYTUS

Engravings are employed to enforce arguments [against slavery], to illustrate facts, to give an energy to language, and life to the form of words, to bring before the "mind's eye" more vividly than the arbitrary signs of the Alphabet can, the reality of things of which we speak.—They are used to bring home to the bosom of the reader a full conception of the wrongs and sufferings of his fellow-men, that he may *look on* them as well as *read of* them, and that he may feel as though he were among them and of them, an eye-witness and partaker of their woes.

—Joseph Horace Kimball, "Pictorials"

If to our bodily eyes could be presented evidences of the suffering caused by every act of selfish will,—if, in the careless moods of our minds, we could be surprised into a clear view of what we have inflicted by even the very slightest breach of the golden rule,—the sight might make the best of us shudder. To do this,—to exhibit to the conscience of the oppressor the injuries of the oppressed,—is *your* work, friends of the slave! Persevere! Never relax! Heed not the testy command, "Otez-moi ça!" Withdraw the picture only to present it again, assured that in the retirement of the chamber, in the silence of solitude, the disturbed conscience must, sooner or later, make the avowal, "cette vue me fait frémir;" and the victims will ere long be let go.

—Harriet Martineau, "Persevere"

Historians of early nineteenth-century American visual culture are hard-pressed to identify a phenomenon as iconographic as the promotional efforts of the American Anti-Slavery Society's (AASS) pamphlet campaign of 1835. Within two years after its December 4, 1833, debut, the AASS attempted to nationally distribute (by way of the federal postal system and a network of northern colporteurs) an unprecedented 1,100,000 pieces of antislavery tracts and ephemera, of which over half would be illustrated.[1] Consequently, not only does the AASS's archive include a superabundance of graphic prints that detail the sordid horrors of the peculiar institution, but many of the society's rhetorical expositions single out the visual medium as uniquely suited for creating an incontrovertible semblance of slavery's cruel and inhumane realities. As the epigraphs above demonstrate, both British and American abolitionists understood the "cognitive signification of pictorial imagery" as constituting a more natural and unmediated form of representation than the printed word.[2] For the AASS, in particular, images were intended to supplement "written and spoken argument[s]," which the society regarded as deficient in "fix[ing] the attention" and "gain[ing] the judgment" of potential converts. Motivated by "their belief that revelation was superior to reason," the AASS maintained that "reform either of individuals or communities, [could] never be accomplished without excitement, [or] without enlisting passions" that would move "the mind to diligent and earnest investigation."[3]

Notwithstanding this visualist sensibility among antebellum audiences, there has been little scholarly effort to understand the historical privileging of sight as contributing to abolitionism's ocularcentric ethos.[4] Rarely do we encounter a concern for antislavery pictorial rhetoric in relevant cultural histories of vision. Although texts such as David Freedberg's *The Power of Images: Studies in the History and Theory of Response* (1989), Jonathan Crary's *Techniques of the Observer: On Vision and Modernity in the Nineteenth Century* (1992), W. J. T. Mitchell's *Picture Theory: Essays on Verbal and Visual Representation* (1994), Peter Burke's *Eyewitnessing: The Uses of Images as Historical Evidence* (2001), and Susan Sontag's *Regarding the Pain of Others* (2003) are in many ways conceptually attuned to the philosophical and historical contours that might explain the motivations behind abolitionist visual culture, their studies barely speculate on what is perhaps one of the most provocative vision-centered moments in the history of nineteenth-century mass media. What is more, while the recent antislavery scholarship of Michael Chaney and Marcus Wood considers the socio-aesthetic function of abolitionist iconography (for example, how these images can be read and what they signify rhetorically), the scope of their research ultimately forgoes an analysis of those structural conditions that underwrite the AASS's use of graphic illustrations.

Such lack of engagement with the society's ocularcentric ethos is quite surprising since transatlantic abolitionism's penchant for the printed image is undeniably rooted in the eighteenth century's cult of humanitarian sensibility and its treatment of sympathy as an emotion "stirred primarily through sight."[5] That is, transatlantic abolitionism's belief that it could effect greater benevolent intervention on behalf of slaves by pictorially representing them in graphic scenes of corporeal distress was not so much a matter of its own making as it was a function of the period's moral-sense philosophy, which viewed, as Karen Halttunen suggests, "ethics as a matter of sentiment, sentiment as a matter of sympathy, and sympathy as a matter of spectatorship."[6] In contrast to the pessimistic predisposition of puritanical doctrine and the rational cynicism of Thomas Hobbes, reform-minded ethical theorists deemed human nature "instinctively sympathetic" and "naturally inclined to virtuous action."[7] This emerging critique of cruelty, observes Halttunen, redefined the meaning of human suffering for English and Anglo-American culture and transformed a "pre-modern acceptance of the inescapability of pain" into the need for its eradication.[8] Accordingly, moral-sense philosophers who embraced this vision-centered "psychology of sensation," in particular the third Earl of Shaftesbury, David Hume, and Francis Hutcheson, "steadily broadened the arena within which humanitarian feeling was encouraged to operate, extending compassion to animals and to previously despised types of persons including slaves, criminals, and the insane."[9] But while the intellectual origins of this compassionate theology hark back to the liberalizing influence of mid- to late seventeenth-century nonconformists and their rejection of Calvinist dogma, the iconophilia of transatlantic abolitionism, observes Elizabeth B. Clark, owes a great deal more to the process of cathartic empathy outlined in Adam Smith's Enlightenment treatise *The Theory of Moral Sentiments* (1759):[10]

How selfish soever man may be supposed, there are evidently some principles in his nature, which interest him in the fortune of others, and render their happiness necessary to him, though he derives nothing from it except the pleasure of seeing it. Of this kind is pity or compassion, the emotion which we feel for the misery of others, when we either see it, or are made to conceive it in a very lively manner. . . . As to love our neighbour as we love ourselves is the great law of Christianity, so it is the great precept of nature to love ourselves only as we love our neighbour, or what comes to the same thing, as our neighbour is capable of loving us.[11]

Although these views hardly implicate Smith as a dyed-in-the-wool abolitionist—he speaks only peripherally to the condition of enslaved Africans throughout *The Theory of Moral Sentiments*—one can appreciate how such logic both encourages and affirms the use of pictorial representations in the promotion of benevolent action.[12] This is precisely because Smith regards the disembodied perspective of the mind's eye (and not the bodily experience of eyewitnessing) as responsible for stimulating empathy between a compassionate spectator and his subject. For it is by "the imagination," contends Smith, that "we place ourselves in [the sufferer's] situation . . . and become in some measure the same person with him, and thence form some idea of his sensations, and even feel something which, though weaker in degree, is not altogether unlike them."[13] From such reasoning it follows that pictorial and textual stimuli, when presented in a "lively manner," are equally capable of rendering information about "what other men feel." Notwithstanding those ideological and social practices that contribute to the process of meaning making, Smith's model of the imagination functions as both a conduit and generative agent of phenomenological knowledge. His notion of spectating is not only synonymous with perception but it also exposes the perversely subjective truth about the nature of how and what things really are. As Smith asserts, "It is the impression of our own senses only, not those of [the sufferer] which our imaginations copy."[14] Furthermore, if our sensory apprehension of graphic representations, as W. J. T. Mitchell claims, cannot be wholly distinguished from those mental images that we acquire through our mind's eye, it stands to reason that a corollary of Smith's charge is a belief in the transpositive power of pictorial imagery.[15] Such a rationale, I argue, was perfectly suited for a radical evangelical Protestant organization that employed the

slogan "KEEP IT BEFORE THE PEOPLE" and whose official treatise on "Pictorials" affirmed that "[e]ngravings . . . are used to bring home to the bosom of
the reader a full conception of the wrongs and sufferings of his fellow-men."[16]
Moreover, that Smith's theory of spectatorial sympathy has its roots in the
Judeo-Christian precept of the Golden Rule sheds further light on the AASS's
visual strategies, which likewise drew on a Christian visualist paradigm,
wherein the blindness of slaveholders and the dark sins of slavery respectively
warranted enlightenment and revelation. Through a consideration of ephemera distributed by the AASS during its 1835 pamphlet campaign, this essay will
investigate how the AASS's starkly coded schema both contributed to its
presumption that "the eye" was indeed "an avenue to the nation's heart and
conscience" and encouraged the pictorial representation of slavery as part of
its means to effect immediate abolition.[17]

"The Truth Shall Make You Free"

The pamphlet campaign of 1835 was not the first occasion when abolitionists
would find motivation in Christianity's dualist visual metaphors and their
respective associations in order to demonize slaveholding and to promote
Christian benevolence. Early British antislavery advocates also argued as much
when they too proclaimed that

> borrowed beams illume our way
> And shed a bright and cheering ray
> So Christian Light dispels the gloom
> That shades poor Negro's hapless doom.[18]

The AASS inherited such sentiments from Britain's Society for Effecting the
Abolition of the Slave Trade (SEAST) as it began to adopt that organization's
innovative publication and distribution methods.[19] Besides the AASS's appropriation of Josiah Wedgwood's 1788 iconic kneeling slave motif and slogan
"Am I Not a Man and a Brother" (see Figure 16.1), the AASS also understood
the society's own evangelical impulses according to those reform-minded
decrees that required British Christians "to go out into all the earth, preaching deliverance to the captives, giving light to them that are sitting in darkness, and pouring the balm of consolation into every wounded heart."[20]

Figure 16.1. "Am I Not a Man and a Brother," after Josiah Wedgwood, in James Field Stanfield's *Observations on a Guinea Voyage* (London: Printed by James Phillips, 1788). Courtesy of the Library Company of Philadelphia.

Despite these similarities, there is a material link between the AASS's use of pictorial images and visual metaphors that we do not find in SEAST's rhetorical initiatives. The AASS became invested in ocularcentric tropes at the very moment when advancements in print technology enabled the society to cheaply produce illustrations at unprecedented rates, suggesting that the AASS's exploitation of a vision-centered discourse resulted from the unique historical context that was transforming the world of antebellum publishing.[21] We need only to consider Kimball and Martineau's declarations in the opening epigraphs to comprehend how the incentive to use antislavery imagery germinated alongside those visual tropes of revelation and enlightenment, and the AASS's newfound capacity to produce illustrated mass media. In both instances, seeing graphic images of slavery is not only tantamount to bearing witness to the "injuries of the oppressed" but it also provides the most effective means to enable spectatorial sympathy among those who were physically barred from investigating the peculiar institution and thus unable to grasp "the suffering caused by every act of selfish will."[22]

Under these circumstances, it is important to realize that even the figuratively graphic language used by the society to describe slavery should be considered part of the AASS's overall visual strategy. As example, let us bear in mind Nathaniel Southard's editorial comments for *The American Anti-Slavery Almanac for 1838*, wherein his notion of offering a "picture" of slavery is clearly attuned to the power and presence of the AASS's pictorial representations:

> I have given a great variety of "pictures of slavery by slaveholders." These, with only two or three exceptions, I cut with my own hands from the southern papers in which they first appeared. As my opportunity for examining such publications has been very limited, it will at once be understood, that the reader here sees only a small part of those portraits which slaveholders have hung up in the vestibule of slavery's prison-house. Of the mad havoc which riots unchecked in her dark and secret caverns, we can have no conception, which shall bear any near relationship to reality, until the iron has entered our own souls.[23]

Southard's references to "pictures of slavery by slaveholders" should not be taken literally; the "portraits" he cuts with his "own hands" refer to the motley collection of anecdotes that the editor systematically appropriated from southern newspapers and transformed into antislavery copy.[24] To this end, Southard's deployment of pictorial expressions exemplifies the extent to which the AASS believed visual metaphors to enhance the experience of readers. That is, in order to make slavery experientially real, as it were—in order to enable the sensational effects necessary to apprise readers of their moral obligation to the enslaved—the AASS privileged those rhetorical methods that conveyed the idea of slavery as a series of perceptual images based on reliable documentary evidence. Moreover, the fact that Southard's graphic troping of slavery is articulated in conjunction with a Christian metaphorics of light and darkness, not only illumes the figurative "vestibule of slavery's prison-house" within the mind's eye of readers but it also suggests that antislavery literature (not unlike antislavery imagery) could potentially manifest states of vision akin to eyewitnessing.

The notion that visual imagery could play a primary role in facilitating the spiritual or moral conversion of a viewer is of course commonplace throughout the history of Western aesthetic theory as well as Judeo-Christian thought. As David Freedberg demonstrates in *The Power of Images*, motifs of human suffering in religious paintings more than confirm the sixteenth-century Italian painter Giovanni Battista Armenini's observations on the dynamic nature of the visual: "when the beholders see very grave tortures present and apparently real," explains Armenini, "they are moved to true piety, and thereby drawn to devotion and reverence—all of which are remedies and excellent means for their salvation."[25] That we find this vision-centered rhetoric of conversion structuring the parable of the Apostle Paul—a proselytic archetype for reform-minded Protestants—is perhaps one of the most useful clues linking the spectatorial culture of evangelical abolitionism to the dynamic interplay between bodily sight and the spiritual enlightenment found in the New Testament. As I will demonstrate below, the AASS's rhetorical sensibility is modeled on the moment in Acts 26.18 when Paul, after seeing the light of God, also receives his evangelical warrant "to open [the Gentiles'] eyes so that they may turn from darkness to light and from the power of Satan to God, so that they may receive forgiveness of sins and a place among those who are sanctified by faith in me."[26] In other words, Paul's conversion by divine luminescence is indicative of the salvation that will be afforded those nonbelievers who were deemed blind to the light and hence the will of Christ.

Such a triangulation of vision, truth, and the power of conversion finds its graphic expression in Patrick Henry Reason's "The Truth Shall Make You Free," an allegorical frontispiece commissioned by the Boston Female Anti-Slavery Society for its literary annual, *The Liberty Bell* (1839; Figure 16.2). Reason, an African American engraver best known for his portraits of Granville Sharp and other notable abolitionists, appears to have drawn artistic inspiration for his tableau's strident optimism from the masthead of William Lloyd Garrison's antislavery newspaper the *Liberator* (Figure 16.3). In each of these views, the "deliverance" of African Americans from bondage (both metaphysical and literal) is signified by a foreground image of instruction while a background scene depicts unfettered industrious black workers laboring to establish the nation anew. But whereas Garrison's masthead is primarily evocative of how emancipation would enable the benefits of free labor, Reason's illustration of the power of Truth attempts to negotiate the metaphysical consequences of salvation for Anglo- and African Americans alike.

Figure 16.2. "Truth Shall Make You Free," Patrick Henry Reason, *The Liberty Bell* (1839). Courtesy of the Library Company of Philadelphia.

Compositionally, Reason's engraving posits two distinct yet related narratives of redemption. In the first instance, the magisterial gesturing of Truth—personified here in typical nineteenth-century angelic form—invites us to examine the black figures grouped in the left foreground. While we are initially drawn into this intimate visual exchange between the divine apparition and the standing mother, the tableau's triangular arrangement just barely allows our gaze to linger on the latter's visage before it is directed downward onto the body of a reclining unshackled slave and then eventually outward toward a praying supplicant. That Reason facilitates this endpoint away from the male's body and literally into the bosom of prayer not only satisfies the golden mean of proportion but also activates the composition's narratological thrust of redemption through conversion. In this right-

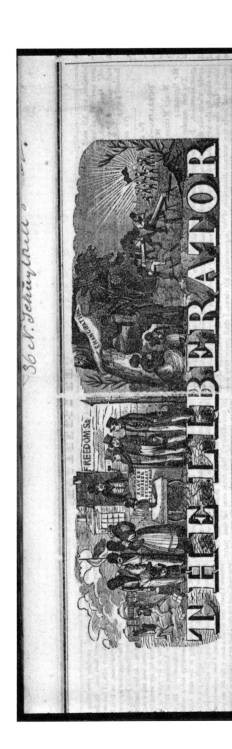

Figure 16.3. Masthead detail, *The Liberator* (1838). Courtesy of the Library Company of Philadelphia.

triangulated scene, where all eyes and prayers are fixed upon Truth, spiritual awakening is rendered synonymous with rebirth and the liberation from physical bondage. However, we must be careful not to read the fate of Reason's former slaves too literally. As Jon Cruz reminds us, religious conversion "was irrelevant to the legal force of slavery. Converted or not, slaves by civil law were property . . . not subjects."[27] It is far more productive, then, to interpret Reason's slave as a metaphor for the universality of humankind's unfailing enslavement to sin, or as a proxy to be contemplated by Anglo- and African Americans. To do so corresponds with the second-person scriptural imperative that is the engraving's title and reinforces modern abolitionism's claim that the benighted soul of the republic necessitated salvation and deliverance.

Nonetheless, the idea of redemption takes on a very different meaning when we consider Reason's engraving from the right foreground. Again, African Americans are presented as the composition's primary subjects, but unlike the adjacent view, it is instructional literacy and not scripture that enables the contemplative countenances on Reason's black youth. While this scenario is intended to remind African Americans to persevere in their struggles to obtain literacy, it is also bound up with evangelicalism's democratic impulses, given that literacy was both the obstacle and means toward salvation for many unlettered Americans following the Second Great Awakening. In this way, it's possible to read the explicit parallelisms between Truth and the analogously positioned white male figure as symbolically reinforcing such ideals. However, considering Reason's emphasis on the universality of Christ's message, it is not improbable that the engraver is offering white viewers commentary on the beneficent effects of sympathy. If the Truth is expected to free Anglo-Americans, they must first work to "elevate the character and condition of the people of color, by encouraging their intellectual, moral, and religious improvement."[28] Yet, Reason's left foregrounding of three sovereign black subjects undermines this seemingly paternalistic point of view. The ecology of deliverance, which begins with the regenerative image of the erect mother and eventually settles on the praying supplicant, overwhelms the intermediary concerns of those beneficent white Christians operating in the right foreground. So while Reason's engraving clearly speaks to the racial egalitarianism typical of AASS rhetoric, it nonetheless posits a potentially subversive counterdiscourse of black self-reliance.

Despite such inherent tension, both foreground views are reinforced by the elliptical composition's explicitly ocular structure. This allusion arguably brings to mind the notion of an omniscient eye surveying the various scenes

of secular and spiritual redemption within the engraving while simultaneously peering outward at potential converts and viewers. Supporting this interpretation is the browlike arch of the engraving's title and the bulbous
hatching effect that is intended to signify the eye's vitreous humor. But while
the book held by Truth offers no textual reference to the Bible, its privileged
placement within the tableau's ray-emitting iris all but establishes its divine
provenance. Thus, as the focal point of Reason's engraving, Truth's illumi-
nated embodiment readily accords with the vision-centered metaphorics of
light that is elaborated throughout John 1:5–7: "This is the message we have
heard from him and proclaim to you, that God is light and in him there is no
darkness at all. If we say that we have fellowship with him while we are walking in darkness, we lie and do not do what is true; but if we walk in the light
as he himself is in the light, we have fellowship with one another, and the
blood of Jesus his Son cleanses us from all sin." Further attesting to this affirmation of Christian ideality is the engraving's allusion to two powerful
antislavery symbols: the plantation overseer and the middle passage. Here,
both the redeemed overseer, who dons a pliant smile and flaccid whip, and
the ship at sea, an ostensible referent to the transatlantic slave trade, are no
longer encoded with the perverse associations they are customarily afforded
through antislavery iconography. Instead, each of these tropes corroborates
the AASS's unwavering conviction that the future of the nation's social and
economic prosperity depended upon the immediate abolition of slavery. By
composing such scenes of futurity within an ocular framework, Reason essentially qualifies the goals of abolitionism within the sight-based conver-
sionary rhetoric of evangelicalism: in other words, seeing becomes believing.

Although antislavery scholarship is generally cynical about the antiracist
sensibilities espoused by evangelical abolitionists, much of the AASS's rhetorical efforts to end slavery were as concerned with alleviating the psychic
ills of white prejudice as they were preoccupied with abolishing the peculiar
institution. Throughout the first year of the pamphlet campaign, the *Anti-
Slavery Record* dedicated a significant portion of its editorial space to exposing the impolitic attributes of northern racial animus. Anecdotes and sketches
with such titles as "Natural Equality," "Colorphobia," and "Illustration of the
Strength of Prejudice," with their critiques of caste and color's ideological
imperatives, challenged readers to reevaluate their own relationship to the
persecution of African Americans, whether they were nominally free or in
chattel bondage.[29] In addition, the *Slave's Friend* instructed children through
a bevy of verse and parables as to how they might remember the slave and

"banish" "Mr. Prejudice."[30] Under the perceptive editorial skills of Lewis Tappan and Elizur Wright, the juvenile magazine broached the issue of black subjectivity at the level of nomenclature in an effort to abolitionize the consciences of its readers: "Instead of saying that man of color, say that *colored American*. Instead of saying, I have been to a *colored school*, say, I have been to a school of *colored Americans*. Instead of saying, I have been to a meeting of *colored people*, say, I have been to a meeting of *colored Americans*."[31] Moreover, the AASS would structure this antiprejudice campaign, like its vision-centered appeals to end slavery, according to a Manichaean trope that privileged light over darkness or, perhaps more specifically, sight over blindness. Drawing on the visualist sensibility structuring Paul's conversion parable, abolitionists codified racial prejudice as an irreligious concept hopelessly intent on subverting God's luminous will. As two black Philadelphia abolitionists, Grace and Sarah Douglass attest in a May 27, 1839, letter to William L. Garrison: "O, the enemy of all good is busy blinding the eyes and hardening the heart of many! But those who are fixed on the Rock of Christ Jesus need not fear force nor fraud."[32]

Ironically, this trope of slavery's obstructive effects would find its most eloquent and sustained articulation in the writings of the reluctant abolitionist and Boston Unitarian minister William Ellery Channing. In his 1835 essay "Slavery," which was composed in direct response to the tumultuous debate surrounding the AASS's aggressive condemnations of slaveholding, Channing manages to give moral clarity to the nature of racial prejudice, though all the while remaining somewhat of an apologist:

> A man born among slaves, accustomed to this relation from his birth, taught its necessity by venerated parents, associating it with all whom he reveres, and too familiar with its evils to see and feel their magnitude, can hardly be expected to look on slavery as it appears to more impartial and distant observers. Let it not be said that, when new light is offered him, he is criminal in rejecting it. Are we all willing to receive new light? Can we wonder that such a man should be slow to be convinced of the criminality of an abuse sanctioned by prescription, and which has so interwoven itself with all the habits, employments, and economy of life, that he can hardly conceive of the existence of society without this all-pervading element? May he not be true to his convictions of duty in other relations, though he grievously err in this? If, indeed, through cupidity

and selfishness, he stifle the monitions of conscience, warp his judgment, and repel the light, he incurs great guilt. But who of us can look into his heart? To whom are the secret workings there revealed?[33]

Notwithstanding these early equivocations—for Channing ultimately casts his lot with New England's radicals following the martyrdom of the abolitionist printer Elijah P. Lovejoy on November 7, 1837—his metaphorical representation of slavery's blinding effects would continue to be cited as part of abolitionism's transatlantic graphic initiatives. As late as 1848, the British reformer Wilson Armistead would appropriate the Unitarian minister's ocularcentric rhetoric in order to give credence to his *Tribute to the Negro: Being a Vindication of the Moral, Intellectual, and Religious Capabilities of the Colored Portion of Mankind; with Particular Reference to the African Race*. Quite revealingly, Armistead's voluminous illustrated tome, which attacks racial prejudice by memorializing notable African Americans through the genres of biography and portraiture, transmogrifies Channing's formulation of the blindness of slaveholders into a far more radical antislavery visual appeal:

> "Men," [Channing] continues, "may lose the power of seeing an object fairly, by being too near as well as by being too remote. The Slaveholder is too familiar with Slavery to understand it. To be educated in injustice is almost necessarily to be blinded by it more or less. To exercise usurped power from birth, is the surest way to look upon it as right and as good." Alas! then, for the unfortunate Negro;—his oppressor, swallowing the gilded bait of commerce, advancing rapidly to fame and fortune, beholds his victim through a very imperfect and defective lens.
>
> The Slavery Optic Glass is not famed for developing all the wonders of creation; on the other hand it disfigures and disparages the Almighty's most glorious work, Man, made after the image of his Maker. The atmosphere of Slavery freezes, as it were, the current of sympathy. . . . The blight which falls on the soul of the wrongdoer, the desolation of his moral nature is a more terrible calamity than he inflicts. In deadening his moral feelings, he dies to the proper happiness of a man: in hardening his heart against his fellow-creatures, he sears it to all true joy: in shutting his ear against the voice of justice, he turns the voice of God within him into rebuke. . . .

While our tenderest sympathies are awakened for the victims of
their tyrannical barbarity, we should mourn deeply over their oppres-
sors; our aspirations ought daily to ascend before Him, who can
unstop the deaf ear, and open the eyes of those "who are blind," that
He would, in His mercy, show them the awful situation in which
they stand.[34]

The logic of both Channing and Armistead's critiques is at once provocative
and vexing. On the one hand, their reasoning challenges the very idea that
slaveholders possessed the moral aptitude to grasp the unethical dimensions
of their inhumane practices. In true sensibilist fashion, Channing and Armistead regard those profiting from slavery as insensible to the protocols of
sympathy. Their charge that the self-interested pursuit of mammon by slaveholders rendered them figuratively impaired and therefore incapable of dis-
cerning right from wrong is an apt extension of how moral-sense philosophy
theorized the insensibility of the blind. Much like those sightless persons
who Denis Diderot presumed lacked a sense of sympathy owing to "[t]heir
abstract manner of experiencing others' pain," slaveholders simply could not
comprehend the nature of their depravity.[35] On the other hand, this business
of being "too familiar with Slavery to understand it" or "too near" to refer
objectively to matters that required a sentimental response also threatens to
undermine the authorial integrity of those fugitive slaves who were expected
to offer up their life stories as documentary proof of slavery's inherent perver-
sion.[36] While many of the legitimating epistles which frame ex-slave autobiographies are perhaps best described as overly concerned with validating
the authenticity of their narrator's claims, an alternative perspective might
include a consideration of the former slave's ability to speak objectively. This
is certainly true of the prefatory remarks posited by a Mr. Fisher, who served
as the amanuensis for Charles Ball's *Slavery in the United States* (1837):

Many of [Ball's] opinions have been cautiously omitted, or carefully
suppressed, as being of no value to the reader; and his sentiments
upon the subject of slavery have not been embodied in this work.
The design of the writer, who is no more than the recorder of facts
detailed to him by another, has been to render the narrative as simple, and the style of the story as plain, as the laws of the language
would permit. To introduce the reader, as it were, to a view of the
cotton fields, and exhibit, not to his imagination, to his very eyes,

the mode of life to which the slaves on the southern plantations must conform, has been the primary object of the compiler.[37]

Arguably, if there was ever a subject too close to slavery, it was the professional ex-slave.

It's no wonder that abolitionists understood themselves as duty bound to remove the obstructive veil of racialist thinking from the minds of proslavery sympathizers by either ironizing their anti-abolitionist reactions to pictorial images or explicitly acknowledging the heuristic import of the AASS's use of visual metaphors (Figure 16.4).[38] Common throughout the society's proceedings is the rather presumptuous notion that through the promulgation of antislavery literature "[p]rejudice has been removed, light has been shed, love has been kindled and thousands have been brought to see in our growing cause the dawn of a brighter day for our dishonored country, and her millions of enslaved children."[39] However, such declarations of success should give us pause when we recall that the majority of abolitionist ephemera sent to the South was confiscated and destroyed by mobs of local elites who were intent on prohibiting mass distribution, or that the galvanization of northern antislavery support for the pamphlet campaign was primarily motivated by a desire to protect the First Amendment rights of white American citizens.[40] For these reasons, there is far more to the fact that evangelical abolitionists began to systematically reference the phraseology "hardening of the heart" as part of their explanation of the moral and intellectual obtuseness that they believed so defined racial prejudice.[41] While this conception of obstinacy recurs throughout biblical scripture, where it has its basis in both human failing and divine intervention, it seems without question that abolitionists drew from popular Old Testament usage, in which the hardness of the Pharaoh's heart toward the enslavement of the Israelites is reflective of God's will and not the Pharaoh's own. This treatment is rather fitting for antislavery pundits not only because it is contextually relevant, owing to its regard for the nature of prejudice and its relationship to the chattel slavery of the Israelites and the notion of conversion, but also because it evokes an analogous sense of obduracy, as evidenced through Armistead's anticipation that only God can "open the eyes of those 'who are blind,' [. . . and] show them the awful situation in which they stand."[42] Certainly, the fact that Armistead's comments are articulated more than a decade after the AASS initiated its publication campaign problematizes any direct association between the two. But even so, the intractability of which Armistead speaks appears germane to the muted

12   RECEIPTS.   [84

Who bids?

"INCENDIARY PICTURES."

Owing to the absence of the Editor no "incendiary picture" was prepared for this number of the Record. We have, however, procured and placed above a little one—"inflammatory, incendiary, and insurrectionary in the highest degree"—which is in common use at the South. The cast from which it was taken was manufactured in this city, for the southern trade, by a firm of stereotypers, who, on account of the same southern trade, refused to stereotype the Record, *because* it contained just such pictures! Now, how does it come to pass, that this said picture when printed in a southern newspaper is perfectly harmless, but when printed in the Anti-Slavery Record is perfectly incendiary? We have nothing further to say about it till this question is answered.

Figure 16.4. "Incendiary Pictures," *Anti-Slavery Record* (1836). Courtesy of the Library Company of Philadelphia.

skepticism surrounding the AASS's coercive tactics. More specifically, we might consider the society's decision to direct a significant portion of its marketing efforts toward the socialization of children as an indirect commentary on the (in)effectiveness of moral-suasion propaganda with targeted adult audiences.

"Keep It Before the People"

Regardless of such metaphysical quandaries, the AASS could not afford to be so circumspect in the heuristic narratives that it compiled for the likes of those readers who had fallen under the spell of "Slavery's optic glass."[43] As suggested earlier, the Anti-Slavery Society was well aware of the challenges it faced while courting an ambivalent adult audience, despite having made unusually optimistic claims in its annual reports during the height of anti-abolitionist reactions to the pamphlet campaign.[44] This concern is especially apparent in the parable "The Generous Planter," which appears to be the AASS's most comprehensive heuristic representation of spectatorial sympathy. Published in the August 1835 edition of the *Anti-Slavery Record*, the account outlines in detail those factors that the AASS believed might favorably disturb the consciences of potential southern converts as well as mollify any society members who may have had reasons to doubt the plausibility of the campaign's pictorial schemes.

In short, "The Generous Planter" tells the story of a wealthy slaveholder who unwittingly encounters the manumitted family of his favored male slave, Ben, during an excursion to a local boardinghouse. As a result of this chance meeting, the planter is able to gain access to their "miserable hovel" and becomes privy to the family's attempts to finance the purchase of their beloved patriarch.[45] Consequently, the sight of their frugality in the face of "abject" (90) poverty compels the planter to free Ben and ultimately the remaining slaves on his estate.

For a parable that attempts to demonstrate the manufacture of spectatorial sympathy for heuristic purposes, "The Generous Planter" reduces much of its pivotal plot construction to coincidence or providential circumstances. To begin, the planter's encounter with Ben's family, which enables the narrative's initial development, is attributed entirely to God's will. So too is the planter's decision to manumit his slaves (90). As the narrator reveals, "There was no longer any doubt on [the generous planter's] mind as to the course which it was his duty to pursue. The voice of conscience was clear in its decisions, and conscience was '*obeyed as God's most intimate presence in the soul*'" (95–96). Such a sense of the exceptional is also extended to each of the tale's characters. If not eponymically, the generous planter is presented as a slaveholder of uncommon distinction. Described as having "inherited his slaves from his father" (93) and being ever mindful of continuing their "comfortable" (96) treatment under his own supervision rather than employing "the arbitrary control of despotic deputies," he is the proverbial "good" master and is thus afforded a "generous mind" and "heart" (91) to boot. Similarly, Ben's family functions as inimitable types in inasmuch as the planter "could not of course suppose that all his slaves, still less the general mass, were as well fitted for emancipation as Ben and his family were" (95).

On some level, "The Generous Planter's" reliance on Providence and the exceptional appears to subvert the AASS's heralding of pictorial propaganda as essential to inducing spectatorial sympathy in its potential converts. How

can such a visual pedagogy be effective if so many preconditions are necessary on the part of the observer and his subject? For evangelical abolitionists,
this question is perhaps resolved by their unerring belief in the mysteries of
Providence. That is, the conscience of the potential convert—like the very
obduracy of proslavery ideologues—was not a theological matter to be pon-
dered, save for what measures would be the most expedient in bringing about
their soul's salvation, thereby laying the groundwork for Christ's Second
Coming. In this way, we might best understand the premise of the AASS's
pamphlet campaign as a means for its members to fulfill the dictates of God's
will in expectation of his favorable judgment. For this much is also assured
the generous planter, whose own acts of manumission elevate him not only in
the sights of his former slaves but also in the eyes of God: "The sight of their
happiness, with the blissful reflection, that, under Providence, he was the author of it, was, to the good planter, a rich reward for every sacrifice, whether
real or imaginary, which he had made. How is it any slave-holder can refrain
from an act which brings so high a recompense! Surely this is the slaveholder's appropriate *compensation*, and a beautiful one it is" (96).

Accepting, then, that such divine interventional measures are nominally
facilitative, let us consider those moments in which the vision-centered logic
of "The Generous Planter" is employed by the narrative, beginning with the
planter's observation of the slave family's quarters:

> The slave-holder was still speechless. Think you he was touched by
> the scene before him?
>
> "Has the slave-holder a heart?" some uncharitable abolitionist
> may reply, for, strange paradox, abolitionists are sometimes unchari-
> table. Yes, our slave-holder had a heart, and it was touched, deeply
> touched. His mind had been for some time previous preparing for
> such a scene to have its full effect on him. Here in this miserable
> hovel, in a family of slaves, the wife and children of one of his own
> bondmen, was a degree of moral energy and of self-denial beyond
> what he had ever dreamed of. To the outward eyes all was low,
> mean, abject; but he saw the beauty and sublimity of the fountain of
> virtue within, as he had never seen it before. The proud, the wealthy,
> the hospitable, the humane planter, as he had been called, when he
> compared himself with these poor slaves, felt himself sunk to the
> very depths of littleness.
>
> "Is master sick?" said Lucy.

"Yes, good woman," he replied; "yes, sick, sick of myself, sick of slavery, sick of every thing." . . . "Lucy, your husband has been worth more to me than all the money you have in that box. I have no right to any of it. Keep it for yourselves. Your husband is free from this moment. May you all be as happy as you deserve to be." He then darted out of the house (91).

The message for readers could not be clearer; it is perhaps a bit too clear and too readily resolved, given the planter's seemingly instantaneous conversion as demonstrated by the graphic illustration that adorns the cover of the *Anti-Slavery Record* (see Figure 16.5). But capturing the planter's immediate affectation of sympathy also helps to redouble the heuristic potential of the conversion at hand. If this pictorial representation reveals the moment in which the planter's sympathetic feelings were aroused, then, a similar expectation is proposed on behalf of the reader/viewer who is concurrently undergoing instruction in the very same act of contemplation. Significantly, while it is difficult not to read this scene as reaffirming the passage's ocularcentric ethos (especially considering the undefined light that illuminates the planter's realization), there is some indication that the tableau also references the deliberation of the planter's conscience as an auditory phenomenon. The cocked hand gesture of the planter, though likely a sign of his waving off the anguish of guilt, could reasonably be read as an aural allusion, in which case his conversion is delivered by the "the voice of conscience," which was "obeyed as God's most intimate presence in the soul." To embrace this possibility, however, does not disturb the integrity of the parable's vision-centered approach. Regardless of the fact that conversion in evangelical Christianity is also effected through the preaching of the gospel, the very idea of the conscience, as it evolves out of Adam Smith's theorization of spectatorial sympathy, is codified primarily as a visual metaphor: "But though man has, in this manner, been rendered the immediate judge of mankind, he has been rendered so only in the first instance; and an appeal lies from his sentence to a much higher tribunal, to the tribunal of their own consciences, to that of the supposed impartial and well-informed spectator, to that of the man within the breast, the great judge and arbiter of their conduct."[46] So it is not surprising that the generous planter is described as a man whose "mind had been for some time previous preparing for such a scene to have its full effect on him" ("The Generous Planter," 91). Indeed, it is revealed that while the planter and his wife were engaged in planning "Sunday schools and other modes of

THE

ANTI-SLAVERY RECORD.

VOL. I.   AUGUST, 1835. [SECOND EDITION.]   No. 8.

(See page 91.)

THE GENEROUS PLANTER.

Susan. Oh how I wish I could help you, my dear mother!
Mother. You do help me, my dear Susan.
S. How do I help you, mother?
M. I will tell you. When you are good, and do as I bid you, it makes my work go on easier. That is one way you help me. And you are able to do many little things which I should have to leave off to do, that helps me. Besides, I can speak to you of your father, and that is pleasant to us both, and so makes my work pleasant.
S. But, mother, it seems as if you could never get money enough to pay for father's freedom, they ask so many, many dollars, and you can hardly get one dollar in a day, even when you have work

Figure 16.5. "The Generous Planter," *Anti-Slavery Record* (1835). Courtesy of the Library Company of Philadelphia.

instruction, in the hope of improving [the] moral condition" of their slaves, "anti-slavery publications came into their hands" (94) and "his eyes began to be opened. It was a slow process, yet he never willfully turned from the truth" (93). What makes the disclosure of these events significant for our analysis goes beyond the fact of the planter's encounter with antislavery ephemera if we consider that "[a]fter quitting the house [of Lucy], he walked rapidly up and down several streets for an hour or two, then shut himself up in his room for decision and for action" (93).

While the planter's exposure to antislavery literature and his subsequent behavior enact those prescribed tropes of spectatorial sympathy, his retreat into his lodgings in order to contemplate the manumission of his remaining slaves reveals that there is also an architectural dimension to the AASS's rhetoric of conversion. More specifically, the planter's spiritual and moral enlightenment, like that of those readers/viewers who bear witness to his redemption, appears to be contingent upon the space of the parlor as an ideal setting for the presentation and consumption of antislavery sentiment. A brief consideration of William Ellery Channing's conversion to radical abolitionism, as documented by Harriet Martineau in her essay "The Martyr Age of the United States" (1839), all but confirms the importance of understanding the nature of spectatorial sympathy as bound up with those devotional practices associated with the domestic interior:

Next followed the virtual accession of a great northern man to the cause; for though Dr Channing continued to censure the abolitionists for two years after this, it was in the autumn of 1834 that his mind's eye was fixed upon the question on which he has since acted a brave part. It was at the close of this summer, in the parlour of his Rhode Island retreat, that the memorable conversation with Mr. [Edward Strutt] Abdy took place, by which Dr Channing's attention was aroused to the wrongs of the coloured race. . . . As soon as Mr Abdy had quitted him, he applied himself to learn the truth of the case, and in the month of October preached a thorough-going abolition sermon, as to its principles at least, though many months elapsed before he learned fully to recognize the merits of the men who were teaching and practising them at the hazard of all that ordinary men most value. But the ray of doubt which was thus carried into the country retreat has now brightened into the sunshine of perfect conviction.[47]

Although it is Abdy's reasoned debate that ultimately brings Channing around, and not the use of actual pictorial imagery, such a circumstance in no way restricts Channing's conversion to an aural impetus. That the convert fixes "his mind's eye" upon "the wrongs of the colored race" as a means to arrive at his "brave part" is concisely indicative of the AASS's "visual culture of belief." Given the implicit visual nature of reflection, it is impossible to divorce the act of remembering from the idea of envisioning. As both the generous planter and Channing "learn the truth of the case" in their respective quarters, they are each enabled by images, whether they be the actual graphic ephemera produced by the AASS or the effects of memory. With respect to memory, as Richard Terdiman asserts, it is both "the modality or our relation to the past" and the agent that constructs our present sense of the world through the objects and ideas that appear and are therefore *recalled* to us.[48] For memory operates beyond "the rationalist segmentation of chronology into 'then' and 'now'" because it "functions in every act of perception, in every act of intellection, in every act of language." Moreover, as Terdiman concludes, "[m]emory thus underlines the possibility of intelligibility as its precondition. Cognition cannot be divorced from the *re*-cognition of memory: no memory, no meaning."[49] The fact that two of the most popular antislavery slogans, "Am I not a man and a brother?" and "Remember them that are in bonds as bound with them" (Hebrews 13:3), not only encourage states of attentiveness but also link cognition to imagery—both literally (through Wedgwood's actual emblem) and imaginatively (given the two concepts' respective spectatorial modes of reflection)—qualifies the importance of reconsidering the role of reflection as a visual phenomenon (Figure 16.6).

However, if remembering, as Susan Sontag posits, "is, more and more, not to recall a story but to be able to call up a picture," the above account of Channing's conversion within the contemplative space of the parlor also collapses the cognitive sensations that are derived from envisioning slavery through descriptive narrative and pictorial graphics into an all-inclusive mimetic discourse, wherein memory is "coincident with *representation*" or "the function by which symbols, or simulacra, or surrogates, come to stand for some absent referent."[50] Contemporary thinkers have largely regarded this crisis of representation as a destabilizing proposition, owing to the sense of relativism suggested by memory's "present past" formulation.[51] And, yet, it is this temporal and phenomenological dissonance that enables the empathic transposition of the self into the other.

Figure 16.6. "Am I Not a Woman and a Sister," *Slave's Friend* (1836). Courtesy of the Library Company of Philadelphia.

But what indeed are we to make of the parlor's spatial significance in light of Martineau's claim that it is "in the retirement of the chamber" and "in the silence of solitude" that viewers would most likely be moved to introspection and thus influenced by graphic representations of human suffering? The answer isn't simply the most obvious, which is that such a space might be ideally suited for sustained bouts of contemplation. The significance of the parlor also appears to correspond with the social logic of the sitting room as it was understood within the broader antebellum cultural imagination. According to John F. Kasson, not only was the parlor the primary space where middle-class families received guests and displayed "objects of cultural attainment and personal association," but it was also a site where "a carefully elaborated social statement" could be established via "well-stocked bookcases, homemade artworks such as needlepoint and painted china, and personal collections of . . . engravings" that were "exhibited on walls, parlor tables, . . . and mantelpieces." In other words, "[t]he parlor became a kind of

Figure 16.7. Edward W. Clay, *The Fruits of Amalgamation* (1839). Courtesy of the American Antiquarian Society.

PRACTICAL AMALGAMATION.

Figure 16.8. Edward W. Clay, *Practical Amalgamation* (1839). Courtesy of the Library Company of Philadelphia.

'memory palace' of culture, a miniature museum thick with meaning, an artful declaration of its owner's sensibility."[52]

It is rather fitting, then, that both Channing and the generous planter would retreat into this politicized interior. For the antislavery parlor, in addition to its domestic articles "covered . . . with devices and mottos reminding the users of the poor slaves," also contained an assortment of ephemera, which the AASS had designed specifically for consumption by the fireside.[53] That political caricaturists often satirized the pictorial culture of this setting attests to the general awareness of the parlor as a profound site of ideological and material contestation (see Figures 16.7 and 16.8). Although the pride of placement allotted antislavery ephemera in Edward Clay's *Fruits of Amalgamation* (1839) and *Practical Amalgamation* (1839) appears visually overwhelmed by the illicit commingling of white women with black men, it is imperative that we keep in mind that these lithographs, through their inherent nature as prints that comment about an emerging print culture, are first and foremost a response to the AASS's pamphlet campaign. This is not to say that white women weren't crucial to the propagation of abolitionism's ocularcentric ethos, or, that they are somehow inconsequential to Clay's immediate satirical objectives; after all, who but women organized the antislavery bazaars, donned apparel with cameos of Wedgwood's kneeling supplicant, and painstakingly reproduced the iconic message of cross-racial compassion on household wares, handkerchiefs, needlepoint, and pincushions. If the moral center of the nation was indeed the home, as normative cultural values dictated, then, the parlor, as Elise Virginia Lemire argues, "serve[d] as "a woman's 'cultural podium' from which she could exert her moral beneficence on American society."[54]

And yet literally behind these scenes in which Clay vilifies white abolitionist women, we find on the walls as well as in the hands of his reclining black dandy the essence of his satirical motivations: the intrusion of politics into the domestic sphere via antislavery mass media. The fact that Clay enables viewers to comprehend the titles of his abolitionist portraits (Arthur Tappan, William Lloyd Garrison, Daniel O'Connell, and John Quincy Adams) along with Thomas Paine's *The Age of Reason* (1795) and the masthead of the *Emancipator* ultimately signals the unprecedented potency of the AASS's publishing initiatives.

While the trend has been to historicize the AASS's pamphlet campaign as a resounding failure given the outbreak of anti-abolitionist sentiment following its initiation, abolitionists' belief in the power of pictorial images and the efficacy of visual culture hardly faltered during the twenty-five-year pe-riod leading up to the Civil War.[55] Instead, it appears that the nature of the AASS's initial printing enterprise engendered a proliferation of new forms of antislavery visual expression. By midcentury, not only would antebellum au-diences find themselves attending antislavery theatrical productions, moving panorama exhibitions, and lectures where fugitive slaves bore their naked torsos in order to expose the corporeal consequences of the lash, but they would also consume novels and short stories by abolitionist authors who claimed that their sole "vocation" was that of a "painter" and that their primary objective was "to hold up [slavery] in the most lifelike and graphic manner possible."[56] Arguably, this need to "see what we can, and tell what we see" also has it origins in those visualist ideals that attended the concurrent rise of sociology and anthropology as scientific disciplines.[57] When we con-sider the second-person pronominal experiments in transatlantic antislavery travel narratives or the flaneuristic prose of black correspondents writing for *Fredrick Douglass' Paper*, particularly those urbane sketches by William J. Wilson and James McCune Smith, it becomes clear that the antebellum vogue for vision is undoubtedly attuned to the ocular sensibilities that were manifest from the Enlightenment onward. Nevertheless, scholars of anti-slavery visual imagery must always be mindful of those epistemologies of vision that the AASS used to govern so much of what antebellum audiences saw. For such preconditions were not only foundational to that era's socio-aesthetic practices, but they also determined the next half-century's "visual culture of belief."[58]

CHAPTER 17

John Marrant Blows the French Horn: Print, Performance, and the Making of Publics in Early African American Literature

ELIZABETH MADDOCK DILLON

Performing Conversion

Sometime late in the year of 1769, John Marrant walked into an evangelical meeting in Charleston, South Carolina, where the famous Reverend George Whitefield was holding forth: Marrant's intention was to blow his French horn in the midst of the meeting in order to disrupt the sermon of the controversial Methodist preacher. Marrant, then fourteen years old, was a free black young man of tremendous musical talents who had been incited to this prank by a companion. However, as he lifted the French horn off of his shoulder, jostling for room among the throng of bodies gathered to hear Whitefield, Marrant was suddenly struck down by the religious exhortation of Whitefield: rather than lifting the horn to his lips as he had intended, he abruptly found himself lying speechless and senseless on the ground. His revival from this stupor, which occurred over the course of the next several days, unfolds as a tale of religious awakening, culminating in the moment when "the Lord was pleased to set [his] soul at perfect liberty."[1] This account of Marrant's conversion, which appears in *A Narrative of the Lord's Wonderful Dealings with John Marrant, a Black* (1785), is striking for a number of reasons. First, it is one of the earliest documents in print that is authored by an African American. Second, it places us within a familiar scene (religious revival) before a famous white man (George Whitefield), but the scene is narrated from the unfamiliar perspective of a free black youth. Third, central to the scene is an unusual and somehow excessively present material object: namely, the French horn.

The French horn is an object that we are unlikely to readily place in the hands of the eighteenth-century black youths of our historical imagination. But precisely the thingly, material quality of the French horn (an object that attracts attention to itself—one with sinuous curves, reflective ambit, deep and penetrating tones within) and its striking presence at the center of the scene lends a certain allure and potency to the conversion narrative.[2] Indeed, in a dismissive review of Marrant's narrative, which appeared in a London periodical, the role of the French horn is the specific subject of mockery: the review reports that Marrant "had strolled into a meeting house where Mr. W. was preaching, in order to disturb the meeting by blowing a French-horn; but was himself struck to the ground by a blast from the spiritual trumpet."[3] The mirroring relation between the literal French horn and the figurative spiritual trumpet is presented here as *de trop*—a sign that the narrative as a whole is too "glibly" constructed, too "enlivened by the *marvellous*" to be of serious interest to readers. The French horn is too much of a scene stealer, according to this review, and its presence turns Marrant's conversion narrative into an orchestrated performance of Methodist drama rather than a legitimate account of religious experience.

Given the oddity of the French horn as an object with a starring role in a conversion narrative as well as the difficulty of interpreting this object as a sign of the force of the narrative, or the opposite—that is, of the narrative's originality or its excessively codified nature—it seems worth asking: why is there a French horn in the middle of John Marrant's conversion narrative? Further, were one to begin by placing this object—the French horn—rather than the subject—John Marrant—at the forefront of an analysis of this text, might such a move enable a new reading of the *Narrative* and of its stature as one of the first texts of early African American print culture? My aim in this essay is to propose such a reading of Marrant's *Narrative*, as well as, more broadly, to propose a new account of the public sphere by way of an analysis of the performative dimensions of early African American print culture. Specifically, I aim to delineate the workings of an *embodied* public sphere in contrast to existing accounts of a print public sphere characterized by rational critical thought and disembodied authorship.[4] Ultimately, I will argue, it is not possible to understand early African American print culture according to existing models of the print public sphere: an account of the embodied scenes of performance that inform print production, however, significantly augments and shifts our understanding of the public sphere such that texts such as Marrant's *Narrative* no longer hover at the illegible edges of the print public sphere, but reveal central dynamics of race, embodiment, and performance in relation to the social and political belonging that characterizes the public sphere.

Making Sense, Making Music, Making Noise

Perhaps it is worth looking, then, at the scene of Marrant's conversion (French horn in hand) with greater attention. Here is the account offered in the *Narrative*:

> One evening I was sent for in a very particular manner to go and play [music] for some Gentlemen, which I agreed to do, and was on my way to fulfil my promise; and passing by a large meeting house I saw many lights in it, and crowds of people going in. I enquired what it meant, and was answered by my companion, that a crazy man was hallooing there; this raised my curiosity to go in, that I might hear what he was hallooing about. He persuaded me not to go in, but in vain. He then said, "If you will do one thing I will go in with you." I asked him what that was? He replied, "Blow the French-horn among them." . . . So we went, and with much difficulty got within the doors. I was pushing the people to make room, to get the horn off my shoulder to blow it, just as Mr. Whitefield was naming his text, and looking around, and, as I thought, directly upon me, and pointing with his finger he uttered these words, "PREPARE TO MEET THY GOD, O ISRAEL." The Lord accompanied the word with such power, that I was struck to the ground and lay both speechless and senseless near half an hour. When . . . something more recovered, every word I heard from the minister was like a parcel of swords thrust into me, and what added to my distress, I thought I saw the devil on every side of me. I was constrained in the bitterness of my spirit to halloo out in the midst of the congregation, which disturb-

ing them, they took me away . . . as far as the vestry. . . . When the people were dismissed Mr. Whitefield came into the vestry, . . . and the first word he said to me was, "JESUS CHRIST HAS GOT THEE AT LAST."[5]

When Marrant sets out on this particular evening, he is planning to perform as a musician before a group of "Gentlemen," presumably at a dance or an informal concert of some sort. His intention, then, is to make music with his French horn. But he is waylaid, first by the sight of a gathering crowd, and then by a noise—the noise that Whitefield is said to make, described as that of "hallooing." Eager to hear this noise—perhaps in order to understand what leads so many people to attend to this "hallooing"—Marrant seeks to persuade his companion to join him in entering the meeting. His companion agrees on one condition: that Marrant use his French horn to create *noise* in the midst of Whitefield's meeting. What is the difference between making music with the French horn and making noise with it? What is the difference between the forceful words of Whitefield's sermon (which later strike Marrant down) and the noise of *hallooing*? And why does Marrant, ultimately, end up disrupting the meeting, not with his French horn (which makes neither noise nor music), nor with his own words, but with a "halloo" of his own that he is "constrained in . . . bitterness" to emit?

What I mean to point to with this line of inquiry are the shifting definitions and registers of sound that constitute verbal communication, music, and noise in the passage. Initially, it is Marrant's skill as a musician that brings him into a community of meaning; his ability to create music with the French horn causes him to be sought out by a companion and ushered toward a social event, an event at which Marrant will likely be paid to perform and be received with pleasure. In contrast, the community gathered around Whitefield is initially construed as senseless; it is characterized by Whitefield's status as a "crazy man" and the imputed lack of meaning of his speech. Whitefield's "hallooing" is, then, a meaningless noise, worthy of being derided by the prank of noisemaking that Marrant's companion contrives. But when Marrant enters the meeting, the meaning of each of these sounds shifts dramatically: the sound that issues from Whitefield's lips is anything but noise—rather, it is a sentence whose meaning is so palpable to Marrant as to assume physical force. Rather than entering a community of nonmeaning, then, Marrant has unwittingly entered a community in which sense seems directed at him and directly affects him. And as a result, a sound that formerly seemed to have meaning for Marrant (his own voice) becomes itself a bitter noise—a disruptive "halloo" that intrudes upon the Christian meaning that informs and organizes a new community of sense making around him.

Borrowing a phrase from Jacques Rancière, one might say that the "distribution of the sensible" (*partage du sensible*) shifts dramatically during the course of this single paragraph of text. According to Rancière, the sharing of sensibility among a people—or more specifically, the sharing of meaning making—is a fundamentally aesthetic matter that is, in its collective nature, also inherently political. Insofar as a group of people consents to find meaning in a shared set of sense data (an aesthetic decision), they constitute themselves as a political community. Significant, as well, for Rancière are the limits of meaning making—that is, the kinds of sense information (noises, halloos, and so on) that are not collectively understood as meaningful signifiers and, as such, constitute the *limits* of a political community. Rancière defines these terms as follows: "I call the distribution of the sensible the system of self-evident facts of sense perception that simultaneously discloses the existence of something in common and the delimitations that define the respective parts and positions within it."[6] The distribution of the sensible thus defines both what is included and what (or who) is excluded from the community as well. To change the "distribution" of sense will change the boundaries of the political community. With respect to Marrant's *Narrative*, one can clearly see Marrant's own movement from an aesthetic and political community in which the sounds issuing from Whitefield's mouth are mere noise (excluded from the *sensus communis*) to a community in which the same sounds are deeply meaningful and serve as the central organizing language of the community.

But Rancière's argument is actually a bit more subtle than what I have just indicated, and, I would suggest, it is also a bit more useful to our understanding of Marrant's text than I have thus far indicated. Rancière writes:

> The "distribution of the sensible" refers to the implicit law governing the sensible order that parcels out places and forms of participation in a common world by first establishing the modes of perception within which these are inscribed. The distribution of the sensible thus produces a system of self-evident facts of perception based on the set horizons and modalities of what is visible and audible as well as what can be said, thought, made or done. Strictly speaking, distribution therefore refers both to forms of inclusion and to forms of

exclusion. The sensible of course, does not refer to what shows good sense or judgment but to what is *aistheton* or capable of being apprehended by the senses.[7]

In this passage, Rancière points out that the communal decision as to what constitutes meaning—as to wherein the sensible lies—is not one that is collectively adjudicated by means of rational critical debate as one might suppose within a Habermasian framework. Rather than a matter of "good sense or judgment," the sensible is *aistheton*, or what is "capable of being apprehended by the senses." We might note that much hinges here on the word "capable": on the one hand, a *capacity* for apprehension would seem to be a matter of physiology if we are in the realm of the senses. And yet, Rancière's claims rely upon an insistence that what can be heard and seen is not simply a matter of biology but one of aesthetics and politics. The "self-evident facts of perception"—the seemingly unmediated operations of sense apprehension—are, Rancière contends, structured in relation to political communities of meaning in which certain sounds *can* be heard as collectively meaningful and others cannot.

The implications of Rancière's account of a *sensus communis*—a collectivity, a public sphere—defined in relation to the distribution of the sensible rather than in relation to rational critical debate are significant with respect to considerations of early African American print. According to Jürgen Habermas's influential account of the public sphere, when people are free to express their ideas, these ideas compete with one another on the basis of their self-evident logic and rationality rather than on the basis of the prestige or power of their speakers: the impersonality of print, or, alternatively, the rules of public sphere engagement, ideally guarantee the triumph of reason and its Enlightenment corollary, justice. And yet, to what extent is the logic of "self-evidence"—the free competition of rational ideas in the open space of the public sphere—politically circumscribed in advance? In contrast to Habermas's account of articulate political subjects debating within a public space or sphere, Paul Gilroy has proposed a model of diasporic African Atlantic culture that he describes as a "counterculture of modernity." He identifies both the form and history of this culture as antithetical to norms of Habermasian communicative reason and print publicity. Instances of the counterculture Gilroy describes include music and memory—aesthetic forms that are "not reducible to the cognitive." Gilroy explains that "the extreme patterns of communication defined by the institution of plantation slavery dictate that we recognise the anti-discursive and extra-linguistic ramifications of power at work in shaping communicative acts."[8] Gilroy thus suggests that because slaves within an Atlantic plantation culture were forbidden from self-expressive, rational communication, an alternative, counterculture of expression developed, characterized by its resistance to the form and content of Western Enlightenment and rationality. Indeed, the knowledge regime that enforced a system of racial oppression was precisely what slaves sought to evade. As such, then, meaning might profitably be lodged, for the enslaved, in the locations where a plantocratic *sensus communis* ended—in sites and sensations that were precisely not self-evident to the master class. Moreover, the nonparticipation of African American voices in an Enlightenment public sphere might be understood as more than a matter of self-camouflage or protective secrecy: the very fact of race slavery contradicted the premises of Enlightenment humanism and the liberal equality allegedly embedded (proceduralized) in a public sphere of rational critical debate. As such, slaves occupied a position that gave the lie to the epistemology of the public sphere and its "logic." From the point of view of the enslaved, communicative norms based on such a logic could only be understood as epistemologically unsound—namely, illogical.[9]

Gilroy's account of a counterculture of modernity linked to the Atlantic slave trade points toward a political history that is linked to differential distributions of the sensible.[10] In terms that render this racialized history of the sensible even more pointed Édouard Glissant writes, "For Caribbean man, the word is first and foremost sound. Noise is essential to speech. Din is discourse. . . . Since speech was forbidden, slaves camouflaged the word under the provocative intensity of the scream. . . . This is how the dispossessed man organized his speech by weaving it into the apparently meaningless texture of extreme noise."[11] In the case of John Marrant, the cusp between music, noise, and sense-bearing language seems particularly uncertain and unstable, as we have seen. And in light of the claims that I have just rehearsed by Rancière, Gilroy, and Glissant, I would argue that it is no accident that this is the case. Gilroy's emphasis on music as an alternative to the language of Enlightenment "logic" and Glissant's discussion of noise as a form of communicative speech indicate the historical position of African Americans as participatory members in a public sphere that operates in terms that differ dramatically from those proposed by Habermas.

How might we define the shape and terms of participation in a public sphere *not* grounded in critical rationality, *not* grounded in an abstractive, negative relation to embodied presence? Further, how might we understand such a public sphere in terms that are not merely oppositional with respect to existing, dominant accounts of the public sphere—that is, not simply defined in terms of illogic, nonspeech, nonsense, or sheer physical presence? Again, reference to Rancière's work proves useful here: according to Rancière, a politics of radical equality occurs not in the center of the traditionally conceived public sphere (as Habermasians would have it) but at its fringes. Specifically, the possibility of equality is mobilized in moments of *dissensus*—moments when the limitations and exclusions of existing framings of the public sphere are rendered visible rather than naturalized under the guise of the self-evident, under the guise of the sensible. Rancière writes: "A dissensus is not a conflict of interests, opinions, or values: it is a division put in the 'common sense' a dispute about what is given, about the frame within which we see something as given. . . . This is what I call a dissensus: putting two worlds in one and the same world. A political subject, as I understand it, is a capacity for staging such scenes of dissensus."[12] Notably, Rancière employs a theatrical language here: he refers to the device of framing, much as a theatrical event is framed by a stage and a proscenium arch for apprehension and consumption by an audience. What occurs beyond the frame of a staged performance is defined as outside or beyond the meaning conveyed by a theatrical scene—as unworthy of registering as sensible data. Yet Rancière suggests that politics occurs precisely when a disruption of the frame becomes visible or intrudes upon existing distributions of the sensible. This jarring at the foundations of meaning making—a rendering disjoint of the frame of meaning—is dissensus. What registers as political in this account is not the voice of a subject who presents a persuasive argument to other subjects; rather, it is the movable line drawn between sense and nonsense—the aesthetic and political break between what constitutes common sense (in any given setting, at any given historical moment) and what constitutes its exterior.

Rancière's dissensus—viewed historically in relation to the world of early African American print—bears a relation to the *break* identified by Fred Moten as central to a history of African American aesthetics. More specifically, Moten describes a black aesthetic tradition of performance that operates "in the break," offering material resistance to structures of exchange value and meaning: "There occurs in such [black] performances a revaluation or reconstruction of value, one disruptive of the oppositions of speech and writing, and spirit and matter. It moves by way of the (phono-photo-porno-)

graphic disruption the shriek carries out." [13] Here, Moten invokes the "din" or "noise" of black (non)speech—the noise of the scream, the cut, or the shriek at the disrupted edge of one regime of meaning and the beginning of another. And Moten underscores, as well, the meaning-making (political) possibilities of performing in this break. Consider, with respect to Marrant's conversion scene, Moten's discussion of this break as a "radically exterior aurality that disrupts and resists certain formations of identity and interpretation by challenging the reducibility of phonic matter to verbal meaning or conventional musical form." [14] Marrant's French horn is an instrument for the production of just such a "radically exterior aurality": it is, within Marrant's conversion scene, productive of music, of noise, and of stunned silence. Each shift in the form of aurality the horn embodies enacts a disruptive distribution of the sensible—a challenge to *sensus communis*, the din of dissensus.

In viewing the public sphere through the lenses offered by Rancière and Moten of the theatrical, performative dimensions of a radical politics/aesthetics we are able to see the limits of normative accounts of the public sphere *subject*—a subject who is typically seen as fully formed and endowed with a wholly functioning (and comprehensible) voice prior to his or her entry into the public sphere. The human subject, in an Enlightenment tradition, is defined by this capacity for reason and self-expression, thus Habermas tends to presume that all humans will find their place (and voice) within the charmed circle of the public sphere. A somewhat less sanguine line of thought has pointed out that barriers of access to the public sphere in the eighteenth century may inhere in the technologies of literacy and printing. Michael Warner thus argues that blacks were unable to participate in the print public sphere because of a prohibition on access to literacy as well as lack of access to the resources of printing: "Printing constituted and distinguished a specifically white community," writes Warner. [15] If we follow this view, however, a form of racial redlining around the print public sphere assumes the shape of a historical infelicity or injustice that does not, fundamentally, eclipse the democratic possibilities of the print public sphere. But here let me propose that we reverse this account and imagine a political subject who is formed not *prior* to entry into the public sphere but in the moment of assuming substance (or conversely, lapsing into nonsensibility) within the modalities of self-evidence generated by the *sensus communis* in any given staging or embodiment of the public. On this account, the public sphere would look less like a bounded circle that preexisting subjects seek to enter from the outside than like the formation of particulate matter into crystals or molecules moving from soluble disassociation into nucleated, aggregate form. Pursuing this image, we might imagine a public sphere in which the force of meaning radiates outward from a nucleus, instantiating and giving form to a set of meanings (and subjects) that do not formally preexist this assemblage. Dissensus (politics) might thus be seen to arrive not when debate occurs within a bounded sphere, nor when individuals seek to enter such a redlined circle, but when a new distribution of the sensible crystallizes a community into an assemblage, thereby reconstructing the very terms of political subjectivity.

The "assemblage" model of a public sphere that I invoke here draws, in no small measure, on the increasingly prevalent theoretical imagery of the network—an imagery that seems particularly germane to accounts of African American publishing and performance in early America.[16] And, too, I mean to invoke Bruno Latour's work on actor network theory insofar as this work describes power and politics in terms of provisional assemblages of subjects and objects—assemblages that form the substance of the Latourian social world.[17] In what follows, I want to play out some of this imagery—networks, assemblages, crystallizations— in relation to John Marrant's *Narrative* and the specific scenes or performances of sense making, noisemaking, and music making that occur in that text. Let us return, then, to the *Narrative* and to the French horn that led John Marrant into the assembly gathered around George Whitefield.

Transitional/Translational Objects: A Horn, a Fiddle, a Bible

In 1773, the Boston lawyer Josiah Quincy visited Charleston, South Carolina, and reported that he attended a dinner at which he heard "six violins, two hautboys and bassoon, with a hand-taber beat excellently well." After dinner, he was treated to a performance of "six French horns in concert—most surpassing musick! Two solos on the French horn by one who is said to blow the finest horn in the world: he has fifty guineas for the season from the St. Cecilia Society."[18] Quincy, visiting from Boston, reckoned himself a superb judge of cultural value and, while preserving a general degree of disdain for Charlestonians and their habits, Quincy bestows upon the French horns he hears on this evening the highest degree of approbation to be found in his journal. As such, we might conclude that Charleston boasted an unusually accomplished cohort of French horn performers in the late eighteenth century. Note, as well, the relatively elite company the French horn keeps in this passage: violins, hautboys, and bassoons appear in the group of instruments assembled with the French horn. In addition, Quincy refers to the St. Cecilia Society in which one of the French horn players performs. This private concert society was formed in 1766, just one year prior to John Marrant's arrival in Charleston.[19] The society was supported by a group of subscribers culled from the city's economic and social elite who underwrote a series of concerts throughout the year. While it is unlikely that Marrant performed as a member of the St. Cecilia orchestra, it is clear that he participated in a Charlestonian music culture that would have included the French horn players of the St. Cecilia Society.

How then, did Marrant join this select company of musicians? In the description of his entry into the world of French horns and fiddles, Marrant relates that he became interested in music when, out walking in Charleston one day, he "passed by a school, and heard music and dancing, which took [his] fancy very much."[20] He persuaded his mother to have him apprenticed to the owner of the music and dance school, thereby locating himself at the center of Charleston's musical economy. Marrant writes:

> The first day I went to [the school owner] he put the violin into my hand, which pleased me much, and applying close, I learned very fast, not only to play, but to dance also; so that in six months I was able to play for the whole school. In the evenings after the scholars were dismissed, I used to resort to the bottom of our garden, where it was customary for some musicians to *assemble* to blow the French-horn. Here my improvement was so rapid, that in a twelve-month's time I became *master* both of the violin and of the French-horn, and was much respected by the Gentlemen and Ladies whose children attended the school, as also by my *master*. This opened to me a large door of vanity and vice, for I was invited to all the balls and *assemblies* that were held in the town, and met with the general applause of the inhabitants.[21]

Two aspects of Marrant's language in this passage are worth underscoring: First, his rapidly acquired skill in playing the fiddle and the French horn position him in a location of mastery: he becomes, as he states, "master" of these instruments. While mastery is constitutively denied to him by the racialized structure of Charleston society, he finds another form of mastery here—one that competes (linguistically) in this passage with the master status of the school owner to whom he is apprenticed.[22] Second, Marrant's mastery of the French horn, in particular, serves to embed him in assemblages (scenes he explicitly defines as "assemblies") including the cohort of musicians (some, if not most, of whom were probably white) who blow the French horn together in the garden in the evening and at the elite society balls and concerts at which he is invited to perform.

Although Marrant's language here appears to be casually descriptive of his early musical career prior to his conversion, it is worth noting that the participation of blacks in assemblies in Charleston in the late eighteenth century was a matter of no small political import: indeed, the assembling of blacks was expressly forbidden by law. The most extensive regulations concerning black assembly were codified in the Negro Act of 1740: the act not only fixed the permissible ratio of blacks to whites on plantations at ten to one, but it also prohibited more than seven blacks from traveling together on a road without a white person and authorized all justices to keep order by "dispers[ing] any assembly or meeting of slaves which may disturb the peace or endanger the safety of his Majesty's subjects."[23] In addition, the 1740 law states that "all due care [must] be taken to restrain the wanderings and meetings of negroes and other slaves, at all times, and more especially on Saturday nights, Sundays, and other holidays, and their using and carrying wooden swords, and other mischievous and dangerous weapons, or using and keeping of drums, horns, or other loud instruments, which may call together or give sign or notice to one another of their wicked designs and purposes." Further, masters were forbidden by the act to allow "public meetings or feastings of strange negroes or slaves in their plantations."[24]

Of particular interest in the phrasing of the 1740 law is the connection it draws between the specter of black gatherings and music, feasting, and weaponry. Enacted directly following the Stono rebellion, the law is clearly written in response to the events that unfolded in the environs of Charleston in 1739 when roughly twenty slaves gathered and began attacking white warehouses and killing whites in order to acquire weapons. According to an account of the events printed in London's *Gentleman's Magazine* in March 1740, the Stono rebellion began as slaves "calling out Liberty, marched on with Colours displayed, and two Drums beating, pursuing all the white people they met with. . . . They increased every minute by new Negroes coming to them, so that they were above Sixty, some say a hundred, on which they halted in a field, and set to dancing, Singing and beating Drums, to draw more Negroes to them, thinking they were now victorious over the whole Province, having marched ten miles & burnt all before them."[25] Accounts such as this evidently engendered fear among whites about the activities of groups of blacks "dancing, Singing, and beating Drums"—that is, groups of slaves performing a black cultural *sensus communis* and thereby displaying and giving voice to their political power as a collectivity. As Richard Cullen Rath reports, slave colonies in the Caribbean had repeatedly enacted legislation to outlaw drumming and blowing horns among slaves: white planters were concerned that horns and drums might function as calls to arms among slaves.[26] With the Negro Act of 1740, South Carolina followed in the footsteps of such efforts—efforts that aimed to prevent the communicative function of horns and drums. Further, such legislation points to the fact that dance and music were cultural forms with particular power and persistence that were exercised in the face of a system that sought to eradicate the communicative and collectivizing (that is, social and human) capacities of New World Africans in order to more efficiently extract their labor for profit. Recalling Gilroy and Moten's terms, we might say that white slave owners recognized that something more than noise issued from New World African instruments, but were often at a loss to characterize and thus regulate what occurred in the "break" beyond the *sensus communis* of the plantocracy.

In addition to regulating assembly and music making, the 1740 law also aimed to prohibit literacy among slaves. Specifically, the law criminalized the teaching of writing to slaves. Yet as compared to the skills that literacy comprises, those of music making are somewhat more difficult to regulate: that is, if reading and writing are fairly identifiable acts, the act of performing music (horn blowing, drumming, creating din, making noise, shrieking) and the meanings attached to such music are less so. And indeed, the broader question of the meaning of music and dance among slaves and free blacks in South Carolina is quite complex. As Rath demonstrates, drumming and horn playing in particular were viewed as threatening and were banned by planters in the Caribbean and the Carolina low county. However, as Saidiya Hartman shows, planters were often interested in having slaves play the violin and dance in ways that demonstrated (to a planter audience), "contentment" and fitness for slavery. Thus, as Hartman reports, it was not unusual for planters to provide slaves with fiddles and encourage certain forms of dance.[27] Similarly, Rath argues that fiddles largely replaced drums after 1740 as the instrument of slave music in the low country: "the [fiddle] was not thought of as a threat, as drums were." However, Rath also points out that the ways in which the fiddle was used by slaves were not entirely controlled by white intentions: "While drums were banned, the violin functioned well for quietly representing African drumming traditions that were so feared, but little understood, by planters. The polymeter rhythms of banned drums were stored in the distinctive pulse of the stick knockers and the fiddler's three- or four-note rhythmic pattern."[28] In related terms, Hartman documents the ways in which—in contrast to the efforts of slave owners to generate "simulated jollity" among slaves—musical forms of patting juba carried countermeanings of New World African autonomy, cultural production, and rebellion against white oppression: "Juba was a coded text of protest. It utilized rhythm and nonsense words as cover for social critique."[29] The accounts of the Stono rebellion suggest the power of music in articulating a new epistemic framing—a new assemblage—that challenged plantocratic power. The Negro Act of 1740 demonstrates that whites were fully aware of the challenge to their power that such assemblages implied and sought to eradicate both the assembling of collectivities of blacks and the communicative possibilities that writing and music enabled for those collectivities. However, music, in particular, remained in a zone of indeterminacy with regard to assemblage and communication, precisely because its meaning does not lie in rational expression and thus potentially evades the episteme of the plantocratic public sphere.

Significantly, attempts to stop the gathering of black collectivities in South Carolina in the eighteenth century failed; despite laws to the contrary, blacks gathered at a variety of sites in Charleston, including the street, the marketplace, the racetrack, and in private spaces as well. Further, extant evidence demonstrates that whites were ineffectual in their efforts to eradicate large gatherings of blacks unmonitored by whites at which dancing, music, and festivity occurred during the eighteenth century. Consider, for example, a newspaper account from 1772, complaining about the lack of enforcement of laws against slave gatherings in Charleston:

> The [author of the letter] had once an opportunity of seeing a Country-Dance, Rout, or Cabal of *Negroes*, within 5 miles distance of this town, on a Saturday night; and it may not be improper here to give a description of that assembly. It consisted of about 60 people, 5–6th from Town, every one of whom carried something, in the manner just described: as, bottled liquors of all sorts, Rum, Tongues, Hams, Beef, Geese, Turkies and Fowls, both drest and raw. . . . Moreover, they were provided with Music, Cards, Dice &c. The

entertainment was opened, by the men copying (or *taking off*) the manners of their masters, and the women those of their mistresses, and relating some highly curious anecdotes, to the inexpressible diversion of that company. Then they *danced, betted, gamed, swore, quarrelled, fought,* and did everything that the *most modern* accomplished gentlemen are *not ashamed of*. . . . They had also their private committees; whose deliberations were carried on in too low a voice, and with so much caution, as not to be overheard by the others. . . . Whenever or wherever such nocturnal rendezvouses are made, may it not be concluded, that their deliberations are never intended for the advantage of the white people?[30]

The gathering is initially described as a "Country-Dance, Rout, or Cabal"—a series of terms whose definitions, while equated with one another in this passage, cover a wide range of meanings, beginning with the social and recreational resonances of the term "dance," moving to the legal/military implications of the term "rout" (one definition of the word that seems germane in this instance is "an assembly of people who have made a move towards committing an illegal act which would constitute an offence of riot"),[31] and concluding with the politically resonant term "cabal." Dancing and feasting are thus closely associated with military and political engagement. Further, the parody of white masters mobilizes a collective understanding of and disdain for the codes of performance that structure white and black behavior in daily life and that inform white subjugation of blacks. Moreover, as the conclusion of the passage makes clear, for the white observer of this event, the gathering of blacks into a collectivity can only imply an assault upon the white power structure.[32]

It is intriguing to speculate that John Marrant might have performed at exactly this kind of gathering or "rout" in Charleston. Only four years before the event described above, Marrant was in the service of a carpenter in Charleston, but spent more time engaged in playing music than in carpentry: "Every evening I was sent for to play on music, somewhere or another; and I often continued out very late, sometimes all night, so as to render me incapable of attending my master's business the next day; yet in this manner I served him a year and four months, and was much approved of by him."[33] Marrant does not specify, in this instance, what kinds of gatherings he attended, but one might suppose that there were a variety of kinds, from the sort for which his first master trained him—that is, balls and concerts for the white slaveholding class—to the sort of informal gatherings that occurred within the black community such as that described above. What is clear is that Marrant's skills as a performer were in immense demand; he indicates, as well, that he was well paid for his musical performances and his master's approbation of his musical career indicates that he received a degree of respect for his musical skills.

Thus, while the "using and keeping of drums, horns, or other loud instruments" was forbidden to slaves by the Negro Act of 1740, Marrant was apprenticed in order to be taught to use and keep a French horn and to play it loudly and frequently.[34] Why this apparent contradiction? I would suggest that the significance of the horn, and the meaning of the sounds it emits, is wholly conditioned by the assemblage formed around it. For this reason, a French horn would seemingly bear no relation to the implicitly African horn (the abeng, for instance) blown to signal slave rebellion or to communicate among slaves. The French horn, as we have seen, is understood as a European, rather than an African horn, and one that is sounded in the performance of European orchestral, dance, and military music. An advertisement appearing in the *South Carolina Gazette* in 1784 makes the status of the French horn particularly evident: books of instruction for the French horn are included in a lengthy enumeration of luxury goods on sale at the store of Charles Morgan in Charleston—goods "just imported from London" that include sheet music; instructions on playing the violin, flute, harpsichord, piano forte, guitar, clarionet, bassoon, German flute, hautboy, and fife; books of poetry, divinity, and philosophy; stationery; maps; jewelry; teapots; gilt watch chains; gold and silver lace; and sword knots (among other items). We might read this particular list of objects as a significant assemblage: each of the items on the list confers with it the status of wealth and luxury that form the network of power, display, and performative abilities of the white planter class of Charleston. Notably, at the end of the advertisement a short addendum appears: "N.B. WANTED to hire for two or three month, from 10 to 20 Negroe Men."[35] The "Negroe Men" who are sought here are, on the one hand, marked as typographically separate from the luxury goods advertised above, and yet, the advertisement as a whole assembles the labor of these men in close proximity to the luxury goods enumerated in the larger advertisement.

As such, the possible conclusions that we might draw from reading this advertisement as an assemblage point in opposing directions: on the one hand, the "10 to 20 Negroe Men" mentioned at the close of the advertisement would seem to have little relation to the goods enumerated earlier. On the other hand, their proximity suggests some kind of metonymic relation, one that we might identify in terms of the economy of surplus that is on display in the advertisement itself. The labor of the "10 to 20 Negroe men" literally subtends or underwrites the presence of English luxury goods in Charleston. The bodies of these men are both written out of the display of erudition, pleasure, and consumption that is signaled in the list of goods, and their presence is quite literally required ("WANTED") to make such a display possible.

John Marrant, both a Negro man and a French horn player, does a remarkable job of navigating the assemblage on view here to his own advantage. On the one hand, he is a figure of black labor—not enslaved, but apprenticed and called upon to perform labor for the white master class. Yet while Marrant may be subject to laws that regulate black bodies in Charleston, his French horn is not subject to such regulation, and by associating himself with the French horn and the world assembled around it, Marrant becomes a part of a variety of disparate publics, including the public of the dancing school, the public of white balls and concerts, possibly the public of black assemblies or "routs," and certainly the public gathered around George Whitefield. The French horn thus becomes something of a transitional object for Marrant: the French horn, in the hands of John Marrant, performs the relation between white luxury and black labor, but does so in a setting that seeks to erase the relation of interdependence—that seeks to exclude black persons from public meaning.[36]

In the contradiction between a legal system designed to prevent blacks from attaining forms of citizenship and belonging associated with the public sphere and John Marrant's own experiences at the center of social assemblies in Charleston—in the contradictory status of the sound that emanates from a horn blown by a black person in Charleston in the eighteenth century—we can see evidence of the complex and movable nature of the rules of assemblage. For instance, we can see the way in which networks of association crystallize the meaning of a black body or a French horn in differential terms in any given instance, thus shifting the contours of publics and the subjects found within them. In advancing this argument, I do not mean to suggest that Marrant's French horn was, in fact, an abeng of sorts (an interesting, but eminently speculative claim). Rather, I would suggest that Marrant's experience with the French horn gave him mastery not only of music but of the unstable and mobilizing force of performance and assembly, particularly for African Americans whose performances achieved radical force from the position of the "break"—that is, from the position of epistemic dissensus or the

site of frame disjuncture and by means of catalyzing or crystallizing the possibility of new assemblages emerging from such disruption.

As I argued at the outset of this essay, Marrant's conversion scene can be
read as the performance of just such a dissensus. The sense data generated by
the French horn shifts from music, to noise, to silence and generates, with each
term, a different assemblage or *sensus communis* in relation to this sense data.
I want to suggest that Marrant is able to use precisely this methodology—
that of disruptive assemblage—in repeated performances across the *Narrative*, up to and including the performance of the sermon that is the basis for
the *Narrative*'s appearance in print. Let me sketch, here, the brief outlines of
such a reading of the remainder of the *Narrative*.

Following his conversion to Methodism, Marrant wanders into the
woods, befriends a Native American hunter, and is later taken prisoner by the
Cherokee who have seemingly marked him for execution. In a long scene
that unfolds as Marrant is ushered toward the moment of his impending
death, Marrant is able to successively convince a series of members of the tribe
to convert to Christianity: ultimately, the king of the tribe is converted as well
and Marrant is heralded as a tribal prince rather than executed as an inter-
loper. The signal features of Marrant's labor of conversion (and thus his salvation from death) include dramatic prayer and the singing of hymns. When he
is first imprisoned by the Cherokee, and at several points in the subsequent
narrative of his captivity, Marrant prays volubly—an act that elicits queries
from his Indian captors as to whom his interlocutor is in these verbal exchanges. Marrant writes:

> And truly this dungeon became my chapel, for the Lord Jesus did
> not leave me in this great trouble, but was very present, so that I
> continued blessing him, and singing his praises all night without
> ceasing: The watch hearing the noise, informed the executioner that
> somebody had been in the dungeon with me all night; upon which
> he came in to see and to examine, with a great torch lighted in his
> hand, who it was I had with me; but finding nobody, he turned
> round, and asked me who it was? I told him it was the Lord Jesus
> Christ but he made no answer, turned away, went out, and fastened
> the door.[37]

In this instance, Marrant emphasizes that his song—which he engages in all
night—is the sign of an assemblage: Marrant is singing because Christ is

present to hear his song. Interestingly, the executioner and the watch assume as much as well: hearing his song as a form of address, they search for the person to whom Marrant's song has been directed. Moreover, Marrant encourages just such an interpretation when he insists to the executioner that Christ is present. Accordingly, the executioner is hailed, so to speak, as a member of the assemblage—as someone who has participated in the *sensus communis* of Marrant's song. Moreover, Marrant insists that this song is generative of a public—that it is a sensible form of address that the executioner, too, should be capable of hearing. In similar terms, Marrant repeatedly performs (in this same scene) the shock of dissensus—the shock of unexpected communication—of noise refigured as sense. Thus, for instance, he stages another scene of prayer as he is led to his execution, and in this case, before those who are gathered to listen, he shifts suddenly from speaking in English to the Cherokee language: "About the middle of my prayer, the Lord impressed a strong desire upon my mind to turn into their language, and pray in their tongue. I did so, and with remarkable liberty, which wonderfully affected the community."[38] Following this scene of communal translation— which for a Cherokee listener might be experienced as a transition from the noise of English to the sense of the Cherokee tongue—members of his audience are jarred into a new community of meaning, namely, a Christian assemblage.

One might read the famous "talking book" incident in this scene in similar terms. Marrant, as we have seen, performs his religious faith as dispersed across bodies and things, including Jesus Christ and the Bible. Christianity is thus a network of sorts for Marrant, and it is this network that the king's daughter expresses interest in when she laments that the Bible will not talk to her. The king's own conversion occurs, finally, on the heels of his daughter's illness brought on by her exile from Christian community: in other words, the growing assemblage of converts and the shared *sensus communis* among them ultimately convinces the king that meaning inheres in Marrant's words, songs, and performances—a meaning that the king chooses, finally, to endow with political value. Marrant, in turn, becomes a recognized and celebrated member of the Cherokee community.

What Marrant seems to be particularly skilled at is creating a sense of community (an assemblage) in locations where sense itself does not initially seem to be shared between Marrant and those around him. This occurs not only when he is captured by the Cherokee, but again when he begins preaching to the slaves on the plantation where he is employed as a carpenter, and it occurs, as well, when he delivers the ordination sermon that serves as the basis of the *Narrative*. We might say, then, that Marrant has a marked ability to *make publics* around him by means of performance, and for this reason, it is perhaps not an accident that he is among the earliest African Americans to appear publicly in print. As such, then, we might view Marrant's accomplishment less as that of entering into the public sphere (crossing the boundary from outside to inside the redlined circle of the print public sphere) than that of generating a public around the nucleus of his own performative interaction with other subjects and objects (including the French horn, Christ, and the Bible). As Cedric May notes, the *Narrative* is in fact a transcribed version of a sermon that Marrant preached on the occasion of his ordination as a minister in the Huntingdon Connexion at a chapel in Bath, England, in 1785.[39] Two amanuenses published versions of the sermon: the first, the basis for the *Narrative* cited in this essay, was "arranged, corrected, and published" by the Reverend William Aldridge; another version of the sermon appeared in print as a poem titled *The Negro Convert, a Poem: Being the Substance of the Experience of Mr. John Marrant, a Negro, as Related by Himself, Previous to His Ordination* (1785), authored by Samuel Whitchurch.[40] The fourth edition of the Aldridge version (cited in this essay) was evidently reedited by Marrant himself; the title page announces that the *Narrative* has been "Enlarged by Mr. MARRANT, and Printed (with Permission) for his Sole Benefit."[41] Notwithstanding the evidence of Marrant's hand in the editing of the fourth edition of the *Narrative*, critics have been wary of attributing the full force of authorship to Marrant in a text that is prefaced with Aldridge's comment that he has "always preserved Mr. Marrant's ideas, tho' [he] could not [preserve] his language; no more alterations, however, have been made, than were thought necessary."[42] Given that the words of the *Narrative* may not be those of Marrant, how is it possible to attribute to this text the status of African American authorship? How is it possible to read the text as conveying the voice of Marrant rather than that of Aldridge?

One mode of reading such a text consists in searching between the lines in order to excavate an authentic black voice beneath the cover of Aldridge's white voice—to find, in the words of John Sekora, the black message sealed within a white envelope.[43] Sekora, for one, is not optimistic about the possibility of finding an authentic voice within such a packaged product. And yet, if one shifts away from the notion of a Habermasian, preconstituted subject who generates expressive truth upon entering into print, a different understanding of the printed text of John Marrant emerges. Consider, instead, the meaning of the text as an assemblage. Precisely because Marrant has generated such an assemblage—created a *sensus communis* through acts of performance—he has found both an audience and a conduit for a new distribution of the sensible. The fact that Marrant's sermon generated two print versions by two separate amanueses might, on this account, be viewed less as evidence that an impassable screen shields the authentic voice of Marrant from view than evidence of the force of Marrant's sense-making capacities—sense making demonstrated by the fact that his performances generated a sense of meaning, communication, and significance among a community of audience members. This community, crystallizing outward from Marrant, was, in turn, augmented by its intersection with the Huntingdon Connexion and the impulse of members of that network to turn to print as a means of distributing the sensible. Again, what strikes me in this case is Marrant's consummate skill in the generation of new communities—namely, his ability to frame a *sensus communis* such that it becomes "common sense" for an evangelizing Christian network to publish his narrative. To cite the work of Daphne Brooks, it seems clear that Marrant enters print precisely because he has "mastered the art of spectacle, (representational) excess, and duality" in a manner that is crucial to the history of African American cultural meaning making: that is, he has marshaled an array of networked relations that are often contradictory in order to position himself as the bearer of meaning rather than as a figure subject to death and erasure.[44] I do not mean, in the least, to attribute nefarious or a-religious intentions to Marrant in making this argument; rather, I would suggest that Marrant infused a particular Christian community with a new "common sense" according to which his narrative was profoundly valuable and worth sharing widely.

We have known for a very long time that publication in print is not transparently linked to individual authorial interiority. Ongoing work in the history of the book has demonstrated repeatedly that the printed book is the result of a series of collective interchanges (performances of sorts) involving authors, editors, printers, publishers, consumers, booksellers, reviewers, and readers not to mention technologies related to such matters as paper production, printing presses, typefaces, and transportation infrastructures.[45] Books are the products of networks of peoples and technologies. However, to my mind, there remains a disconnect between the implications of this work in the field of history of the book and the stubborn insistence on a politics of expressive individualism that is implied in dominant accounts of the print public sphere. This fallback position renders a mediated narrative such as

Marrant's marginal if not altogether discredited; as such, it also tends to posit a resolutely white public sphere as an inevitable (if regrettable) historical truth. The alternative account of a performance-based, embodied public sphere that I have traced in this essay makes visible the participation of New World Africans in networked early American and transatlantic public spheres that are both interracial and intraracial. In his mastery of performance, John Marrant produces a new *sensus communis* at the limits of an Enlightenment reason that holds a contradictory racial politics at its core. Performing in and through this contradiction, Marrant demonstrates the power of reassembling the social by means of language, noise, music, performance, and print.

NOTES

INTRODUCTION

1. On *Freedom's Journal*, see Jacqueline Bacon, *"Freedom's Journal": The First African-American Newspaper* (Lanham, Md.: Lexington Books, 2007). On early African American periodicals more generally, see Penelope L. Bullock, *The Afro-American Periodical Press, 1838–1909* (Baton Rouge: Louisiana State University Press, 1981); Armistead S. Pride and Clint C. Wilson II, *A History of the Black Press* (Washington, D.C.: Howard University Press, 1987); Frankie Hutton, *The Early Black Press in America, 1827–1860* (Westport, Conn.: Greenwood Press, 1993); James P. Danky, ed., *African American Newspapers and Periodicals: A National Bibliography* (Cambridge, Mass.: Harvard University Press, 1998); and Todd Vogel, ed., *The Black Press: New Literary and Historical Essays* (New Brunswick, N.J.: Rutgers University Press, 2001). Though more celebratory than descriptive, Irvine Garland Penn's *The Afro-American Press and Its Editors* (Springfield, Mass.: Willey, 1891) remains an invaluable trove of information.

2. See Elizabeth McHenry, *Forgotten Readers: Recovering the Lost History of African American Literary Societies* (Durham, N.C.: Duke University Press, 2002), chap. 1; and John Ernest, *Liberation Historiography: African American Writers and the Challenge of History, 1794–1861* (Chapel Hill: University of North Carolina Press, 2004), chap. 5.

3. Leon Jackson, "The Talking Book and the Talking Book Historian: African American Cultures of Print—The State of the Discipline," *Book History* 13 (2010): 252.

4. Numerous works have contributed to destabilizing these concepts, but the following have been particularly influential, at least for us: D. F. McKenzie, *Bibliography and the Sociology of Texts* (Cambridge: Cambridge University Press, 1986); Margreta de Grazia, *Shakespeare Verbatim: The Reproduction of Authenticity and the 1790 Apparatus* (Oxford: Oxford University Press, 1991); Meredith L. McGill, *American Literature and the Culture of Reprinting, 1834–1853* (Philadelphia: University of Pennsylvania Press, 2003); Jody Greene, *The Trouble with Ownership: Literary Property and Authorial Liability in England, 1660–1730* (Philadelphia: University of Pennsylvania Press, 2005); Leah Price, *The Anthology and the Rise of the Novel: From Richardson to George Eliot* (Cambridge: Cambridge University Press, 2005); Leon Jackson, *The Business of Letters: Authorial Economies in Antebellum America* (Stanford, Calif.: Stanford University Press, 2007); and Trish Loughran, *The Republic in Print: Print Culture in the Age of U.S. Nation Building, 1770–1870* (New York: Columbia University Press, 2007).

5. Jackson, "The Talking Book," 254.

6. Anna Brickhouse, *Transamerican Literary Relations and the Nineteenth-Century Public Sphere* (Cambridge: Cambridge University Press, 2004); Kirsten Silva Gruesz, *Ambassadors of Culture: The Transamerican Origins of Latino Writing* (Princeton, N.J.: Princeton University Press, 2002); Rodrigo Lazo, *Writing to Cuba: Filibustering and Cuban Exiles in the United States* (Chapel Hill: University of North Carolina Press, 2005); Matt Cohen, *The Networked Wilderness: Communicating in Early New England* (Minneapolis: University of Minnesota Press, 2010); Jeff Glover and Matt Cohen, eds., *Early American Mediascapes* (Lincoln: University of Nebraska Press, forthcoming); Andrew Newman, *On Records: Delaware Indians, Colonists and the Media of History and Memory* (Lincoln: University of Nebraska Press, 2012); Birgit Brander Rasmussen, "Negotiating Peace, Negotiating Literacies: A French-Iroquois Encounter and the Making of Early American Literature," *American Literature* 79 (September 2007): 445–73; and Phillip H. Round, *Removable Type: Histories of the Book in Indian Country, 1663–1880* (Chapel Hill: University of North Carolina Press, 2010).

7. Frances Smith Foster, "A Narrative of the Interesting Origins and (Somewhat) Surprising Development of African American Print Culture," *American Literary History* 17 (Winter 2005): 714–40; Xiomara Santamarina, "'Are We There Yet?': Archives, History, and Specificity in African-American Literary Studies" *American Literary History* 20 (Spring–Summer 2008): 304–16; Jackson, "The Talking Book."

8. Sarah Blackwood, "Fugitive Obscura: Runaway Slave Portraiture and Early Photographic Technology," *American Literature* 81 (Spring 2009): 93–125; Michael Chaney, *Fugitive Vision: Slave Image and Black Identity in Antebellum Narrative* (Bloomington: Indiana University Press, 2007); Jeannine Marie DeLombard, *Slavery on Trial: Law, Abolitionism, and Print Culture* (Chapel Hill: University of North Carolina Press, 2007); Marcy J. Dinius, "'Look!! Look!!! at This!!!!': The Radical Typography of David Walker's *Appeal*," *PMLA* 126 (January 2011): 55–72; Ernest, *Liberation Historiography*; Eric Gardner, *Unexpected Places: Relocating Nineteenth-Century African American Literature* (Jackson: University Press of Mississippi, 2009); Beth A. McCoy, "Race and the (Para)Textual Condition," *PMLA* 121 (January 2006): 156–69; McHenry, *Forgotten Readers*; Edlie Wong, *Neither Fugitive nor Free: Atlantic Slavery, Freedom Suits, and the Legal Culture of Travel* (New York: New York University Press, 2009).

9. Janet Duitsman Cornelius, *When I Can Read My Title Clear: Literacy, Slavery, and Religion in the Antebellum South* (Charleston: University of South Carolina Press, 1993); David Waldstreicher, "Reading the Runaways: Self-Fashioning, Print Culture, and Confidence in Slavery in the Eighteenth-Century Mid-Atlantic," *William and Mary Quarterly* 56, no. 2 (April 1999): 243–72; Heather Andrea Williams, *Self-Taught: African American Education in Slavery and Freedom* (Chapel Hill: University of North Carolina Press, 2005).

10. Grey Gundaker, "Give Me a Sign: African Americans, Print, and Practice" in *An Extensive Republic: Print, Culture, and Society in the New Nation, 1790–1840*, ed. Robert A. Gross and Mary Kelley, vol. 2 of *A History of the Book in America* (Chapel Hill: University of North Carolina Press, 2010), 483–95; Jeannine Marie DeLombard, "African

American Cultures of Print," in *The Industrial Book, 1840–1880*, ed. Scott E. Casper et al., vol. 3 of *A History of the Book in America* (Chapel Hill: University of North Carolina Press, 2007), 360–73.

11. Vincent Carretta, *Equiano the African: Biography of a Self-Made Man* (Athens: University of Georgia Press, 2005). See also John Bugg, "The Other Interesting Narrative: Olaudah Equiano's Public Book Tour," *PMLA* 121 (October 2006): 1424–42.

12. Daphne Brooks, *Bodies in Dissent: Spectacular Performances of Race and Freedom, 1850–1910* (Durham, N.C.: Duke University Press, 2006); Tavia Nyong'o, *The Amalgamation Waltz: Race, Performance and the Ruses of Memory* (Minneapolis: University of Minnesota Press, 2009).

13. See also Lloyd Pratt's "The African American Romance Theory of History" (paper presented at the meeting of C19: The Society of Nineteenth-Century Americanists, State College, Pa., May 20–23, 2010).

14. Kenneth W. Warren, *What Was African American Literature?* (Cambridge, Mass.: Harvard University Press, 2011), 17.

15. For a useful overview of the major (and contradictory) senses in which the term "print culture" is used, see Harold Love, "Early Modern Print Culture: Assessing the Models," *Parergon* 20, no. 1 (2003): 45–64.

16. Henri-Jean Martin, *The History and Power of Writing*, trans. Lydia G. Cochrane (Chicago: University of Chicago Press, 1988), 329.

17. Lucien Febvre and Henri-Jean Martin, *The Coming of the Book: The Impact of Printing, 1450–1800*, trans. David Gerard (1958; repr., London: Verso, 1997), 172; Jürgen Habermas, *The Structural Transformation of the Public Sphere: An Inquiry into a Category of Bourgeois Society* (1962), trans. Thomas Burger, with the assistance of Frederick Lawrence (Cambridge, Mass: MIT Press, 1989); Benedict Anderson, *Imagined Communities: Reflections on the Origin and Spread of Nationalism*, rev. ed. (London: Verso, 1991),

18. Anderson, *Imagined Communities*, 44.

19. Barbara Christian, "The Race for Theory," *Cultural Critique* 6 (Spring 1987): 57.

20. Peter Stallybrass, "Against Thinking," *PMLA* 122 (October 2007): 1584.

CHAPTER 1. THE PRINT ATLANTIC

I would like to acknowledge the helpful feedback of James N. Green, Carrie Hyde, Dawn Peterson, and the participants at the "Early African American Print Culture in Theory and Practice" conference (Philadelphia, March 2010), especially Edlie Wong, who responded to this essay, and Jordan Alexander Stein and Lara Langer Cohen, conference organizers.

1. David Waldstreicher, "Reading the Runaways: Self-Fashioning, Print Culture, and Confidence in Slavery in the Eighteenth-Century Mid-Atlantic," *William and Mary Quarterly* 56, no. 2 (April 1999): 247.

2. William Robinson identifies the first advertisement as the one to which Susanna Wheatley likely responded; *Phillis Wheatley: A Bio-Bibliography* (Boston: G. K. Hall,

1981), 1. The book advertisement is reprinted in Phillis Wheatley, *Complete Writings*, ed. Vincent Carretta (New York: Penguin, 2001), 167. For these epigraphs I have consulted the typography of the original advertisements.

3. Ignatius Sancho, *The Letters of the Late Ignatius Sancho*, ed. Vincent Carretta (New York: Penguin, 1998), 111–12. Throughout this essay I have relied on Carretta's heavily researched Penguin editions of both Wheatley and Sancho, the latter of which remains unjustifiably out of print.

4. Paul Gilroy, *The Black Atlantic: Modernity and Double Consciousness* (Cambridge, Mass.: Harvard University Press, 1993). Book historians have amply demonstrated print's connective role in the Atlantic world in this period. For a recent case, see *Early American Studies* 8, no. 1 (2010), ed. James N. Green and Rosalind Remer, a special issue entitled "The Atlantic World of Print in the Age of Franklin." See also relevant volumes in the multivolume projects on the history of the book in Britain, Scotland, and America: John Bernard, David McKitterick, and I. R. Willison, eds., *The Cambridge History of the Book in Britain*, 6 vols. (Cambridge: Cambridge University Press, 1999–2009); Bill Bell, ed., *The Edinburgh History of the Book in Scotland*, 4 vols. (Edinburgh: University of Edinburgh Press, 2007–9); and David Hall, ed., *A History of the Book in America*, 5 vols. (Chapel Hill: University of North Carolina Press, 2000–2010). There is much more scholarship on Wheatley than Sancho. For important recent discussions, see Paula Bennett, "Phillis Wheatley's Vocation and the Paradox of the 'Afric Muse,'" *PMLA* 113 (January 1998): 64–76; Max Cavitch, *American Elegy: The Poetry of Mourning from the Puritans to Whitman* (Minneapolis: University of Minnesota Press, 2007), 180–95; Katy Chiles, "Becoming Colored in Occom and Wheatley's Early America," *PMLA* 123 (October 2008): 1398–1417; Markman Ellis, "Ignatius Sancho's *Letters*: Sentimental Libertinism and the Politics of Form," in *Genius in Bondage: Literature of the Black Atlantic*, ed. Vincent Carretta and Philip Gould (Lexington: University Press of Kentucky, 2001), 199–217; Betsy Erkkila, *Mixed Bloods and Other Crosses: Rethinking American Literature from the Revolution to the Culture Wars* (Philadelphia: University of Pennsylvania Press, 2005), 62–101; Astrid Franke, "Phillis Wheatley, Melancholy Muse," *New England Quarterly* 77 (June 2004): 224–51; Henry Louis Gates Jr., *Figures in Black: Words, Signs, and the "Racial" Self* (New York: Oxford University Press, 1987), 61–79; Felicity Nussbaum, "Being a Man: Olaudah Equiano and Ignatius Sancho," in Carretta and Gould, *Genius in Bondage*, 54–71; Eric Slauter, "Neoclassical Culture in a Society with Slaves: Race and Rights in the Age of Wheatley," *Early American Studies* 2 (2004): 81–122; and Frank Shuffelton, "On Her Own Footing: Phillis Wheatley in Freedom," in Carretta and Gould, *Genius in Bondage*, 175–89. The only important discussion of Wheatley from a print culture perspective is Kirstin Wilcox, "The Body into Print: Marketing Phillis Wheatley," *American Literature* 71 (March 1999): 1–29.

5. In emphasizing the importance of format, I follow Matthew Brown's discussion of the phenomenology of reading in *The Pilgrim and the Bee: Reading Rituals and Book Culture in Early New England* (Philadelphia: University of Pennsylvania Press, 2007).

6. Erkkila, *Mixed Bloods*, 78.

7. My count includes individual titles, not all imprints. The most comprehensive bibliography of early black imprints is Dorothy Porter, "Early American Negro Writing: A Bibliographical Study," *Papers of the Bibliographical Society of America* 39 (1945): 192–268.

8. The 1770 catalog of the Library Company of Philadelphia, for example, subdivided alphabetical groupings by size. Bigger books also cost more to borrow; according to the catalog, nonmembers paid by the week to rent out books: 8p for folios; 6p for quartos; 4p for octavos, duodecimos, and pamphlets. See *The Charter, Laws, and Catalogue of Books, of the Library Company of Philadelphia* (1770), 37. Thanks to James N. Green for discussing library catalogs with me.

9. Bradin Cormack and Carla Mazzio, *Book Use, Book Theory: 1500–1700* (Chicago: University of Chicago Library, 2005), 8.

10. I offer the first edition of Marrant's London-published *Narrative* as a comparison here to correct for other factors that would determine type size and layout. Printers in North America often conserved paper by squeezing more words on a page, as in the first American edition of Wheatley's *Poems* (1786). Furthermore, subsequent London editions of a text would often use smaller, unleaded type and thus have fewer pages, as the third edition of Sancho's *Letters* (1784) demonstrates.

11. Thomas Wooldridge to the Earl of Dartmouth, November 24, 1772, quoted in *Critical Essays on Phillis Wheatley*, ed. William Robinson (Boston: G. K. Hall, 1982), 20–21.

12. Benjamin Rush, *An Address to the Inhabitants of the British Settlements in America Upon Slave Keeping* (Philadelphia, 1773), quoted in Robinson, *Critical Essays*, 24.

13. Richard Nisbet, *Slavery Not Forbidden by Scripture* (Philadelphia, 1773), quoted in Robinson, *Critical Essays*, 32. Eric Slauter mentions Nisbet's revision in "Neoclassical Culture in a Society with Slaves." For a discussion of responses to Wheatley, especially in Rush and Nisbet, see Gates, *Figures in Black*.

14. *Monthly Review*, November 1775, 409.

15. *Gentleman's Magazine*, January 1776, 27–29.

16. *Monthly Review*, October 1774, 457–59.

17. Sancho, *Letters*, 4.

18. Thomas Jefferson, *Notes on the State of Virginia*, in *The Portable Thomas Jefferson*, ed. Merrill D. Peterson (New York: Penguin, 1975), 189.

19. Ibid.; Joseph Woods, *Thoughts on the Slavery of Negroes* (London, 1784), 14; George Gregory, *Essays Historical and Moral* (London, 1785), 300; Thomas Clarkson, *Essay on the Slavery and Commerce of the Human Species* (London, 1786), 108–12; Thomas Burgess, *Considerations on the Abolition of Slavery and the Slave Trade* (Oxford, 1789), 131; George Buchanan, *An Oration Upon the Moral and Political Evil of Slavery* (Baltimore, 1793), 10; John Stedman, *A Narrative of Five Years' Expedition Against the Revolted Negroes of Surinam*, vol. 2 (London, 1796), 259–60.

20. Clarkson, *Essay*, 108.

21. Richard Nisbet, *The Capacity of Negroes for Religious and Moral Improvement* (London, 1789), 31; like the others quoted above, Nisbet mentions "The Letters of Ignatius Sancho" in the same breath as Wheatley.

22. Full documentation of the books Thomas Jefferson sold to the Library of Congress in 1815 is available in a modern edited text of the original manuscript catalog: *Catalogue of the Library of Thomas Jefferson*, ed. E. Millicent Sowerby, 5 vols. (Washington, D.C.: Library of Congress, 1952–59), online at http://www.loc.gov/rr/rarebook/coll/130 .html. The *Catalogue* reveals that Jefferson owned the 1773 London edition of Wheatley's *Poems* and the 1784 Dublin reprint of Sancho's *Letters* (see vol. 4, pp. 491–92, for Wheatley; and vol. 5, p. 11, for Sancho).

23. Sancho, *Letters*, 9.

24. For all three variants see Wheatley, *Complete Writings*, 128–29, 130–31, 39–40.

25. The *New-York Journal* may have printed this poem because of new interest in Wheatley following the recent announcement of her departure for London. See the *New York Gazette*, May 27, 1773, for notice of Wheatley's travels. On the publishing history of the poem to Dartmouth, see Mukhtar Ali Isani, "Early Versions of Some Works of Phillis Wheatley," *Early American Literature* 14 (1979): 149–55.

26. *New-York Journal*, June 3, 1773.

27. Wilcox, "The Body into Print," 18.

28. Samuel Johnson, *A Dictionary of the English Language* (London, 1755–56), s.vv. "peruse" and "read." In Noah Webster, *A Compendious Dictionary of the English Language* (New York, 1806), s.v. "peruse," the definition is "to read over, examin [*sic*], observe."

29. For his secondary definition of "to peruse" Johnson chooses from half a dozen instances when Shakespeare uses the word to describe the examination of persons, as in *Henry VIII*, when in an aside the Lord Chamberlain declares of Queen Anne: "I've *perus'd* her well" (Johnson, *Dictionary*, s.v. "peruse").

30. Wheatley, *Complete Writings*, 5.

31. For a seminal discussion of the effect of white institutions on black-authored texts, see John Sekora, "Black Message/White Envelope: Genre, Authenticity, and Authority in the Antebellum Slave Narrative," *Callaloo* 32 (Summer 1987): 482–515.

32. In a recent essay I discuss this tendency in early black Atlantic scholarship to privilege a biographical approach over one that would seriously consider media; see Joseph Rezek, "The Orations on the Abolition of the Slave Trade and the Uses of Print in the Early Black Atlantic," *Early American Literature* 45, no. 3 (2010): 655–82.

CHAPTER 2. THE UNFORTUNATES

1. I realize that nominating the "early black book" as a category of book and "early black book history" as a particular thread of book history may raise questions for some readers. I do not mean to suggest that books written by authors of African descent in the eighteenth and early nineteenth centuries existed in a sphere separate from books written by authors of European descent. I utilize these terms only as functional analytics. If we can identify books authored by individuals of African descent and identify within this group differentiable patterns of authorship, publication, and sales, then we can, I believe, talk usefully about early black book history.

2. Cathy Davidson, "Olaudah Equiano, Written by Himself," *Novel* 40 (Fall 2006/ Spring 2007): 18–51.

3. Matthew Brown, *The Pilgrim and the Bee: Reading Rituals and Book Culture in Early New England* (Philadelphia: University of Pennsylvania Press, 2007), 206.

4. Ranajit Guha, "The Prose of Counterinsurgency," in *Selected Subaltern Studies*, ed. Ranajit Guha and Gayatri Spivak (New York: Oxford University Press, 1988), 55.

5. Joanna Brooks and John Saillant, ed., *"Face Zion Forward": First Writers of the Black Atlantic, 1785–1798* (Boston: Northeastern University Press, 2002), 55.

6. Ibid., 95.

7. Norma Myers, *Reconstructing the Black Past: Blacks in Britain, 1780–1830* (London: Frank Cass, 1996), 35; Peter Fryer, *Staying Power: The History of Black People in Britain* (London: Pluto, 1984), 72, 75; Paul Edwards and James Walvin, *Black Personalities in the Era of the Slave Trade* (London: Macmillan, 1983), 18–19.

8. Vincent Carretta, *Equiano, the African: Biography of a Self-Made Man* (Athens: University of Georgia Press, 2005), 275.

9. Ibid., 295.

10. Walter Wilson, *History and Antiquities of Dissenting Churches*, vol. 4 (London: Printed for the author, 1814), 320.

11. *Universal Magazine* 90 (1792): 398.

12. Carretta, *Equiano, the African*, 301.

13. See John Howard, *An Account of the Principal Lazarettos in Europe* (London: T. Cadell, J. Johnson, C. Dilly, and J. Taylor, W. Eyres, 1789); Samuel Ogden, *Extracts, in Illustration of the Probationary Sermons Preached at the Asylum, on Sunday, March ——— 1789* (London: Printed at the Logographic Press; sold by J. Walter; and J. Taylor, 1789); Daniel Defoe, *The Life and Most Surprising Adventures of Robinson Crusoe*, 16th ed. (London: Printed for J. Taylor, 1789); Lady Mary Wortley Montague, *Letters of the Right Honourable Lady M——y W——y M——e* (London: Printed for J. Taylor, 1790); John Pearson, *A Plain and Rational Account of the Nature and Effects of Animal Magnetism* (London: Printed and sold by W. and J. Stratford . . . ; Taylor and Co . . . ; and Couch and Laking . . . , 1790); William Love, *The Ability of Jesus Christ to Save Sinners: A sermon, preached in the Chapel of Newgate, on Sunday November 21st, 1790, at the request of the friends of Francis Fonton, (who was executed on the Wednesday following, . . . for forgery* (London: Sold by W. Ash . . . ; Messrs. Taylor and Co.; G. Terry, J. Potts; by the author, 1791).

14. William Robinson, *Phillis Wheatley and Her Writings* (New York: Garland, 1984), 336 n. 1.

15. Donald Franklin Joyce, *Gatekeepers of Black Culture: Black-Owned Book Publishing in the United States, 1817–1981* (Westport, Conn.: Greenwood Press, 1983), 171; Donald Franklin Joyce, *Black Book Publishers in the United States: A Historical Dictionary of the Presses, 1817–1900* (Westport, Conn.: Greenwood Press, 1991), 14–19.

16. Joyce, *Gatekeepers*, 9; Joyce, *Black Book Publishers*, 23–28.

17. Harriet Wilson, *Our Nig*, ed. Henry Louis Gates Jr. (New York: Random House, 1983), 3.

18. Ranajit Guha, "Some Aspects of the Historiography of Colonial India," in *Selected Subaltern Studies*, ed. Ranajit Guha, and Gayatri Spivak (Oxford: Oxford University Press, 1988), 40.

19. William St. Clair, *The Reading Nation in the Romantic Period* (Cambridge: Cambridge University Press, 2004), 31; Manuel Castells, *The Informational City* (Oxford: Blackwell, 1989), 147; Lisa Gitelman, *Always Already New: Media, History, and the Data of Culture* (Cambridge, Mass.: MIT Press, 2006), 7.

CHAPTER 3. FRANCES ELLEN WATKINS HARPER AND THE CIRCUITS OF ABOLITIONIST POETRY

I am grateful to Jay Cook, David Hall, Tricia Lootens, Andrew Parker, and Edlie Wong for their generous readings of drafts of this essay. Audiences at the University of Toronto, Miami University, Radcliffe Institute for Advanced Study, Texas Christian University, the McNeill Center, and the Historical Poetics Group's "Crossing the Bar" conferences helped me sharpen and extend my argument.

1. Important exceptions to this general trend include Joan Shelley Rubin, *Songs of Ourselves: The Uses of Poetry in America* (Cambridge, Mass.: Harvard University Press, 2007), and Angela Sorby, *Schoolroom Poets: Childhood, Performance, and the Place of American Poetry, 1865–1917* (Durham: University of New Hampshire Press, 2005), both of which, however, focus on the post–Civil War United States.

2. Virginia Jackson, *Dickinson's Misery: A Theory of Lyric Reading* (Princeton, N.J.: Princeton University Press, 2005), 48.

3. For a concise description of the problem of defining "format" and a bibliographer's solution to proliferating uses of the term, see G. Thomas Tanselle, "The Concept of Format," *Studies in Bibliography* 53 (2000): 68–117.

4. Frances Smith Foster has collected these three serialized novels, initially published in 1869, 1876–77, and 1888–89 as *Minnie's Sacrifice, Sowing and Reaping, Trial and Triumph: Three Rediscovered Novels by Frances E. W. Harper* (Boston: Beacon Press, 1994).

5. In this essay, I will use "Harper" to refer to experiences and practices that were specific to her post-1864 career, to cite the body of writing published under her married name while she was still alive, and to refer to the corpus that has been assembled by late twentieth-century scholars as the work of an author. I will use "Watkins" to refer to her career and writing before 1860, and "Watkins Harper" to refer to experiences and practices that were common to her antebellum and postwar careers. I hope that the awkwardness of using multiple names for this author and orator will keep readers alive to the historical and political differences that helped shape her career, to differences internal to the corpus, and to a certain incommensurateness or excess that characterizes a body of writing that was so intimately bound up with performance.

6. The easy rescalability of digital images and the difficulty of representing a book's thickness on the screen remain obstacles to the apprehension of the historical significance of format for scholars who work primarily with digitally mediated printed texts.

7. It is important to note that Harper continued to publish her work in chapbook format until late in her career; the shift from "Watkins" to "Harper" doesn't index a corresponding shift in format. Indeed, printed evidence suggests that she continued to publish her postwar poems in small batches for distribution on her Southern lecture tours. Despite the shift in ambition signaled by the turn to blank verse, and the recasting of her name on the title page as "Mrs. F. E. W. Harper," her long poem *Moses: A Story of the Nile* (1869) was published as a forty-eight-page pamphlet (with a four-page prose piece, "The Mission of the Flowers," rounding out the volume). The copy of the 1870 edition held by the New-York Historical Society indicates on the cover that it is the third edition, but, judging from the date (1869) and edition (second) printed on the title page, the publisher simply pasted a new paper cover onto an older text block, a common strategy for reissuing unbound sheets and unsold texts.

8. William Wells Brown's abolitionist songster *The Anti-Slavery Harp* (Boston: B. Marsh, 1848) was also published as a forty-eight-page pamphlet. For a bracing assessment of how much of early African American writing was published in cheap and ephemeral formats, see Chapter 2 in this volume, Joanna Brooks's "The Unfortunates: What the Life Spans of Early Black Books Tell Us About Book History."

9. See, for example, Frances Smith Foster's indispensible anthology *A Brighter Coming Day: A Frances Ellen Watkins Harper Reader* (New York: Feminist Press, 1990), especially section 3 of the introduction (35–39), which offers a concise description of the complexities attending the creation of a comprehensive Harper bibliography, and the appendix dedicated to the "Contents of Frances E. W. Harper's Books" (401–8), which gives the most accurate, but still incomplete, information available on Harper's published volumes. Foster's main concern in this appendix is to document additions, deletions, and changes to the sequence of poems in the various editions she consulted. Like most African American authors, however, Harper still awaits thorough and exacting bibliographical study. Jean Fagan Yellin and Cynthia D. Bond's *The Pen Is Ours* (New York: Oxford University Press, 1991) provides an alphabetical list of Harper's individually published newspaper poetry, letters, and anthology pieces as well as her published volumes, but also includes a number of errors, most notably repeating the attribution to Harper of an 1854 volume, *Eventide: A Series of Tales and Poems* (Boston: Ferridge [*sic*], 1854), published under the pseudonym "Effie Afton." This misattribution sticks like a burr to Harper bibliography and cataloging records, but goes largely unremarked in the criticism—one mark of the indefinite edge of the Harper corpus (Joan R. Sherman's early survey of the poet's career and writing is a notable exception; see *Invisible Poets: Afro-Americans of the Nineteenth Century* [Urbana: University of Illinois Press, 1974, 1989]). Melba Joyce Boyd, *Discarded Legacy: Politics and Poetics in the Life of Frances E. W. Harper, 1825–1911* (Detroit: Wayne State University Press, 1994), includes a helpful "Bibliographical Commentary"

(76–78), noting that many of the later volumes, which include the poet's address on the title page, were apparently self-published.

10. Titles published in chapbook format by Watkins's Boston publisher, James B. Yerrinton (who also published *The Liberator*), include *Argument of Wendell Phillips, Esq., Before the Committee on Federal Relations (of the Massachusetts Legislature)* (Boston, 1855), 43 pp.; and Charles K. Whipple, Committee of the Anti-Sabbath Convention, *Sunday Occupations* (Boston, 1849), 60 pp. Titles published in this format by Watkins's Philadelphia publisher, Thomas E. Merrihew (and his various partners), include *Speech of Hon. Horace Mann, of Massachusetts, on Slavery and the Slave-Trade in the District of Columbia* (Philadelphia, 1849), 48 pp.; *The Proceedings of the Woman's Rights Convention, Held at West Chester, Pa.* (Philadelphia, 1852), 38 pp.; William Henry Furness, *Christian Duty: Three Discourses Delivered in the First Congregational Unitarian Church of Philadelphia* (Philadelphia, 1854), 42 pp.; F. B. Meek, *Descriptions of New Species and Genera of Fossils Collected by F. V. Hayden in Nebraska Territory* (Philadelphia, 1857), 34 pp.; John Hancock, *The Great Question for the People! Essays on the Elective Franchise; or, Who Has the Right to Vote?* (Philadelphia, 1865, 40 pp.; and Rachel L. Bodley, *Introductory Lecture to the Class of the Women's Medical College of Pennsylvania* (Philadelphia, 1868), 20 pp.

11. Frances Smith Foster astutely notes that Harper did not need to be rescued from obscurity so much as from a long tradition of condescension to her work; see "Gender, Genre and Vulgar Secularism: The Case of Frances Ellen Watkins Harper and the AME Press," in *Recovered Writers / Recovered Texts*, ed. Dolan Hubbard (Knoxville: University of Tennessee Press, 1997), 46–59. Landmark early histories of African American achievement—such as William Wells Brown's *The Black Man: His Antecedents, His Genius, and His Achievements* (New York: Thomas Hamilton, 1863); William Still's *Underground Rail Road* (Philadelphia: Porter and Coates, 1872); and W. E. B. Du Bois's *The Gift of Black Folk* (Boston: Stratford, 1924)—kept Harper's reputation very much alive, though often as a token, minor, or transitional figure.

12. Mill elaborates: "Eloquence supposes an audience; the peculiarity of poetry appears to us to lie in the poet's utter unconsciousness of a listener. Poetry is feeling confessing itself to itself, in moments of solitude" ("Thoughts on Poetry and Its Varieties," quoted in Jackson, *Dickinson's Misery*, 129). See also Jackson's call to rethink nineteenth-century poetic genres in the context of their circumstances of address in "Bryant; or, American Romanticism," in *The Traffic in Poems: Nineteenth-Century Poetry and Transatlantic Exchange*, ed. Meredith L. McGill (New Brunswick, N.J.: Rutgers University Press, 2008), 185–204.

13. *A Brighter Coming Day*, 58. Unless otherwise noted, references to Harper's poetry (cited parenthetically by page number) are to this volume.

14. For a reading of "The Slave Mother" similar to my own (although one that assimilates Harper's poetry to a bardic tradition based in part on the presumption of its oral delivery), see Keith D. Leonard, *Fettered Genius: The African American Bardic Poet from Slavery to Civil Rights* (Charlottesville: University of Virginia Press, 2006), 44–46.

15. Many critics claim that Harper recited her poems as part of her antislavery lectures, but I have yet to find hard evidence of this practice and I worry that this might be

a critical back-projection of a familiar twentieth-century cultural phenomenon, the poetry reading. Indeed, William Still's 1872 biographical sketch suggests that Harper's
postwar declamation of her long, verse epic *Moses: A Story of the Nile* was an exception
to the rule of selling volumes of poetry after her orations. Summing up Harper's "seven-
teen years of public labor" pleading "the cause of her race," Still writes: "Fifty thousand
copies at least of her four small books have been sold to those who have listened to her
eloquent lectures. One of these productions entitled 'Moses' has been used to entertain
audiences with evening readings in various parts of the country" (*The Underground Rail
Road*, 779). Such evening readings would be consonant with the nineteenth-century
tradition of delivering long poems as lyceum lectures or as part of commencement cer-
emonies and not evidence that she featured or incorporated poetry into her antislavery
lectures. Harper did, however, write antislavery verse to be recited or sung at gatherings
such as William C. Nell's March 5, 1858, commemoration of the Boston Massacre, discussed below.

16. One copy of *Poems on Miscellaneous Subjects* (Philadelphia: Merrihew and Thompson, [1864]), currently owned by the New-York Historical Society, includes the following
note on the paper wrapper: "Mrs. F. E. Harper, a colored lady of culture and refinement
from Baltimore, Md. Spoke at Bridge St. Me. Ep. Church."

17. See *Weekly Anglo-African*, June 30, 1860; *National Anti-Slavery Standard*, July 7,
1860; and *Liberator*, July 20, 1860.

18. See "Speech of Parker Pillsbury," *Liberator*, July 20, 1860, [113].

19. Frances Ellen Watkins, "To Charles Sumner," *Liberator*, July 20, 1860, 116.
Harper made subtle changes to this poem when she collected it for publication in the
1871 *Poems*, translating markers of the occasional nature of the poem into a more simple
past tense: the conditional "for thou hast spoken" becomes the historical "that thou has
spoken;" "the lightning of thy lips has smote" becomes "did smite;" the speaker's fearful
present-tense apprehension of continuing losses, "That. . . . faithful friends/ Were dropping" is rekeyed as a temporary setback, "As . . . faithful friends/ Were dropping" ("Lines
to Charles Sumner," in *A Brighter Coming Day*, 173). I thank Edlie Wong for alerting me
to the significance of these revisions.

20. One of Harper's earliest printed poems, "To Mrs. Harriet Beecher Stowe" was
first published in *Frederick Douglass' Paper* on February 3, 1854, and reprinted in all subsequent editions of *Poems on Miscellaneous Subjects*. Although presented as a simple declaration of thanks, the poem nonetheless arrogates the privilege of assuring Stowe that she has
been accorded an irrevocable "place" in the hearts of her black readers and that she will
find future fame in "the blessing of the poor" (*A Brighter Coming Day*, 57).

21. "Correspondence," *Provincial Freeman*, March 7, 1857, accessed through Accessible Archives. For evidence that some of Watkins's auditors doubted her originality, see
a letter published in the *Bangor Daily Whig and Courier*, March 7, 1856, which avers
"The clearness of logic, the elegance of diction, and exuberance of imagination displayed by her, so far surpassed our expectations that some among us were strongly dis-
posed to set the production down to the credit of one of the Beechers, or some other
writer of equal note. I confess to having shared in this opinion but am now convinced

from personal acquaintance that she is fully capable of writing the remarkable lecture she delivered."

22. W. L. G., "Preface" (August 15, 1854), in *Poems on Miscellaneous Subjects*, by Frances Ellen Watkins (Boston: F. B. Yerrinton and Son, 1855), 3–4. For Watkins's "border-state heritage," see Sherita L. Johnson, "'In the Sunny South': Reconstructing Frances Harper as Southern," *Southern Quarterly* (Spring 2008): 70–85, quote at 81.

23. For Harper's travel on the lecture circuit in the summer of 1857 along with William Wells Brown, see William Edward Farrison, *William Wells Brown: Author and Reformer* (Chicago: University of Chicago Press, 1969), 287–88.

24. The locus classicus for the sexual stigma borne by formerly enslaved women is Harriet Jacobs (who published under the pseudonym Linda Brent partly for protection), *Incidents in the Life of a Slave Girl* (1861). Given that all women orators faced accusations of impropriety for breaking the prohibition against their speaking in public, it is not surprising to find so few African American women on the antislavery lecture circuit. As Shirley J. Yee has detailed, noted abolitionist speakers such as Maria Miller Stewart, Mary Ann Shadd Cary, and Sarah P. Redmond shared with Frances Ellen Watkins Harper a measure of economic and educational privilege that helped insulate them against attack; see *Black Women Abolitionists: A Study in Activism, 1828–1860* (Knoxville: University of Tennessee Press, 1992), 112–35. For a public attack on Frances Ellen Watkins that casts her very presence on the lecture platform as an instance of miscegenation, see the *New York Herald* report on the 1856 meeting of the Massachusetts Anti-Slavery Society: "Mrs. Maria Weston Chapman, Abby Kelley Foster, and other white women, meet upon the same common platform of abolition philanthropy and amalgamation with Box Brown, the eloquent humbugging fugitive slave, 'Miss Frances E. Watkins, a young colored woman of Baltimore,' and those hoary old infidel sinners, Lloyd Garrison and Wendell Phillips. 'Mingle—mingle—mingle'" (reprinted in the *Liberator*, February 8, 1856).

25. For evidence that Frances Ellen Watkins used her inability safely to return to Maryland as a centerpiece of her antislavery lectures, see the sympathetic report in the *Wilmington Republican*, reprinted in the *Liberator*, December 19, 1856: "she was a native of Baltimore, and there clustered all the remembrances and attachments of her infantile years, there reposed the ashes of her mother, and though no costly cenotaph or imposing marble marked her resting place, the spot was dear to her; yet she was debarred the privilege of visiting it, by a statute which disgraces the land and marks with shame and infamy those who enacted it." The *New York Herald*'s hostile account of the May 1857 antislavery convention similarly suggests that her appeal turned on the drama of a thwarted homecoming: "even the pathetic speech of Miss Ellen Frances [*sic*] Watkins (black woman) of Baltimore, who was afraid to go back there that she might weep over her mother's grave, had no effect on the hardhearted spectators from whom only thirty thousand dollars were wanted to keep up steam for the coming year" (May 17, 1857).

26. Harper frequently referred to her solidarity with the enslaved as a matter of both choice and compulsion, as in her brief prose piece "The Colored People in America": "Identified with a people over whom weary ages of degradation have passed, whatever

concerns them, as a race, concerns me" (*A Brighter Coming Day*, 99). Her most ambitious poem, the blank-verse *Moses: A Story of the Nile*, reads like an allegory of her own vocational crisis, beginning with the long drawn out spectacle of Moses' "strange election" (139), his decision to "cast [his] lot among the people of [his] race" (149). For an astute reading of *Moses* and of Harper's postwar poetry more generally, see Mary Loeffelholz, "A Difference in the Vernacular: The Reconstruction Poetry of Frances Ellen Watkins Harper," in *From School to Salon: Reading Nineteenth-Century American Women's Poetry* (Princeton, N.J.: Princeton University Press, 2004), 94–127.

27. Quoted in Still, *The Underground Rail Road*, 779–80. Still's citation indicates with asterisks that some of Greenwood's text has been omitted, although critics who cite Still have ignored the fact that something is missing from this text. Interestingly, the missing passage offers a more nuanced account of Harper's style, suggesting both that her genteel composure is a carefully constructed pose and that the long history of mistaking her persona for her person begins with Still: "Yet, after all, Mrs. Harper's greatest power lies in her wit and humor. There is something very peculiar about her here. She makes her best points, utters her keenest satire, with a childlike simplicity, a delicious *naïveté* I have never seen surpassed. She is arch, yet earnest; playful, yet faithful. She shoots sin with a fairy shaft; she pierces treason through the joints of his armor with the bodkin of a woman's wit." For the complete text of Greenwood's account, see "Lectures in Philadelphia: A Letter from Grace Greenwood," New York *Independent*, March 15, 1866. A selection from this letter to the *Independent*, which reported on the entire lecture series, was reprinted as "Mrs. Harper—Colored Lecturer" in the Philadelphia monthly *Arthur's Home Magazine*, June 1866, 401.

28. For the centrality of vicarious feeling to poetess poetics, see Tricia Lootens, *Lost Saints: Silence, Gender, and Victorian Literary Canonization* (Charlottesville: University of Virginia Press, 1996); and Virginia Jackson and Yopie Prins, "Lyrical Studies," *Victorian Literature and Culture* 27 (1999): 521–30.

29. Tavia Nyong'o, *The Amalgamation Waltz: Race, Performance and the Ruses of Memory* (Minneapolis: University of Minnesota Press, 2009), 118.

30. William Nell, *Boston Massacre, March 5th, 1770: The Day Which History Selects as the Dawn of the American Revolution; Commemorative Festival, at Faneuil Hall, Friday, March 5, 1858; Protest Against the Dred Scott Decision* (Boston: E. L. Balch, 1858), 2. For an account of the performative nature of early African American history writing, and a more detailed description of the Commemorative Festival, see John Ernest, *Liberation Historiography: African American Writers and the Challenge of History, 1794–1861* (Chapel Hill: University of North Carolina Press, 2004).

31. Frances Ellen Watkins, "Freedom's Battle," in Nell, *Boston Massacre*, 3

32. For an influential early assessment of Harper's poetry in these terms, see Patricia Liggins Hill, "'Let Me Make the Songs for the People': A Study of Frances Watkins Harper's Poetry," *Black American Literature Forum* 15, no. 2 (Summer 1981): 60–65.

33. For an account of revolutionary messianic time in African American literature more generally, and its production of a "radically sustaining relationship to the future,"

see Lloyd Pratt, *Archives of American Time: Literature and Modernity in the Nineteenth Century* (Philadelphia: University of Pennsylvania Press, 2010), quote at 23.

CHAPTER 4. EARLY AFRICAN AMERICAN PRINT
CULTURE AND THE AMERICAN WEST

The author wishes to thank Jodie Gardner, the Saginaw Valley State University Braun Fellowship program, Mary Hedberg, and the organizers of and participants in the Early African American Print Culture Conference—especially Lara Langer Cohen, Leon Jackson, Jordan Stein, and Edlie Wong.

1. Foster's work has been germinal on these concerns; see, e.g., Foster, "A Narrative of the Interesting Origins and (Somewhat) Surprising Development of African American Print Culture," *American Literary History* 17 (Winter 2005): 714–40; and Foster, introduction to *Nellie Brown; or, the Jealous Wife, with Other Sketches*, by Thomas Detter, ed. Frances Smith Foster (Lincoln: University of Nebraska Press, 1996). DeLombard's chapter on African American "cultures of print" offers an excellent introduction to black print culture studies; see Jeannine Marie DeLombard, "African American Cultures of Print," in *The Industrial Book, 1840–1880*, vol. 3 of *A History of the Book in America*, ed. Scott E. Casper et al. (Chapel Hill: University of North Carolina Press, 2007), 360–73. Todd Vogel's collection *The Black Press: New Literary and Historical Essays* (New Brunswick, N.J.: Rutgers University Press, 2001) and Jacqueline Bacon's *"Freedom's Journal": The First African-American Newspaper* (Lanham, Md.: Lexington Books, 2007) offer key studies of black periodicals building from bibliographic work like Penelope L. Bullock's *The Afro-American Periodical Press, 1838–1909* (Baton Rouge: Louisiana State University Press, 1981) and compendiums like Irvine Garland Penn's *The Afro-American Press and Its Editors* (Springfield, Mass.: Wiley, 1891). Elizabeth McHenry's *Forgotten Readers: Recovering the Lost History of African American Literary Societies* (Durham, N.C.: Duke University Press, 2002) is also required reading.

2. Houston Baker, *Long Black Song: Essays in Black American Literature and Culture* (Charlottesville: University of Virginia Press, 1972), 2.

3. Quoted in William Loren Katz, *The Black West* (New York: Harlem Moon/Broadway, 2005), xi.

4. In terms of the study of print culture in the American West, for example, even the best works—e.g., Barbara Cloud's efforts—devote little time or attention to African Americans. See Barbara Lee Cloud, *The Business of Newspapers on the Western Frontier* (Reno: University of Nevada Press, 1992); and Cloud, *The Coming of the Frontier Press: How the West Was Really Won* (Evanston, Ill.: Northwestern University Press, 2008).

5. The eastern black press clearly labeled Indiana as "West"; John Mifflin Brown's salutatory in the *Repository* hoped the journal would "soar not above the humble cabins of

thy own native West" without visiting "the frontier settler" therein; see J[ohn] M[ifflin] B[rown], "Salutatory," *Repository of Religion and Literature and of Science and Art* 1 (April 1858): 1. Also see Eric Gardner, *Unexpected Places: Relocating Nineteenth-Century African American Literature* (Jackson: University Press of Mississippi, 2009), 56–91. The expected dividing lines—e.g., the Mississippi River—and the expectation of the West as "rural" don't always signify across cultures and time periods.

6. Black textual presences in and from California appeared concurrently with initial print discussion of the Gold Rush: Frederick Douglass's periodicals, for example, reported extensively on the black West through texts like Abner Francis's letters from both California and Oregon and a dozen later letters on black California from William Newby published under the playful pseudonym "Nubia." On African Americans in California, see especially Rudolph M. Lapp, *Afro-Americans in California* (San Francisco: Boyd and Fraser, 1987) and *Blacks in Gold Rush California* (New Haven, Conn.: Yale University Press, 1977); and Douglas Henry Daniels, *Pioneer Urbanites: A Social and Cultural History of Black San Francisco* (Philadelphia: Temple University Press, 1980); see as well as the relevant sections of Katz, *The Black West*; and Quintard Taylor, *In Search of a Racial Frontier: African Americans and the American West, 1528–1990* (New York: W. W. Norton, 1998). Philip Montesano's work on black San Francisco, though harder to obtain, is crucial: see Montesano, *Some Aspects of the Free Negro Question in San Francisco, 1849–1870* (San Francisco: R. and E. Research Associates, 1973). Delilah L. Beasley's pioneering efforts in *Negro Trail Blazers of California* (Los Angeles: Times Mirror, 1919), though riddled with errors, are also important.

7. Many bibliographies erroneously list the paper's start date as 1857; some even list 1855. The surviving issues are from August 22 and December 12, 1857. I should also note the exceedingly short-lived four-page monthly founded in 1862 by John J. Moore, the *Lunar Visitor*, of which only two issues survive; while an interesting early California effort, because the *Visitor*'s impact on the three papers I consider was limited, in the interest of space, it is not discussed here.

8. See Philip S. Foner and George E. Walker, eds., *Proceedings of the Black National and State Conventions, 1840–1865*, 2 vols. (Philadelphia: Temple University Press, 1979–80), 2:126.

9. The 1856 convention offered "expressions of thanks" to the "ladies" of Sacramento and San Francisco for supporting the struggling paper; see ibid., *Proceedings*, 2:150, 157.

10. Ibid., 154.

11. Ibid., 153–54. Later accounts of the *Mirror*'s founding—several of which appeared in Anderson's *Pacific Appeal*—depict him as more friendly; see, e.g., the June 7, 1862, *Appeal*.

12. Foner and Walker, *Proceedings*, 2:156–59.

13. Ibid., 154–55, 159.

14. See Peter K. Cole, *Cole's War with Ignorance and Deception* (San Francisco: J. H. Udell and R. P. Locke, 1857). I discuss this in more depth in Gardner, *Unexpected Places*, 95–97.

15. Some bibliographers and historians—seemingly building from a brief description of California periodicals in Penn's *Afro-American Press*—have erroneously suggested that the *Appeal*, founded in 1862, represented a continuation or even a simple renaming of the *Mirror*.

16. This break was foreshadowed in a short piece Bell wrote for the first issue of the *Appeal*—published April 5, 1862—titled "Selfishness and Monopoly" and depicting the "Editor" choosing to "light our segar" with a submission, "much to the chagrin of our Proprietor." Bell actually grew close to state leaders quickly; by 1865, he was their choice over Anderson.

17. See Bell's "Stop My Paper," *Appeal*, June 7, 1862, which details an editor's woes in dealing with subscribers with diametrically opposed views and in which Bell asserted that the paper had to attend "to the good of the whole people, not to indulge in individual idiosyncrasies."

18. The feud became deeper after 1867 negotiations to unite the papers—in the words of the *Christian Recorder*, May 18, 1867—"got into a 'snarl.'" Still, the fact that— even after Bell left the *Appeal*, founded the *Elevator*, and traded barbs with Anderson in print—the pair could consider reunion suggests their depth of commitment to the black California press.

19. John Ernest, *Liberation Historiography: African American Writers and the Challenge of History, 1794–1861* (Chapel Hill: University of North Carolina Press, 2004).

20. Bell referred to himself in the series in ways that confirm his authorship; already known in the black press under this pseudonym, Bell also signed a contemporary *Appeal* piece with his real name and then added "aka Cosmopolite." After his May 23, 1863, introduction, Bell considered Thomas M. D. Ward in the June 6, 1863 issue, and followed with pieces on Newby (June 20, 1863), Abner Francis (July 4, 1863), E. R. Johnson (July 18, 1863), William Yates (August 1, 1863), D. D. Carter (August 15, 1863), William Hall (August 29, 1863), and Isaac Sanks (November 28, 1863).

21. Bell's sense of representativeness was clearly male; that said, he did comment on the wives of his subjects—offering heavily gendered praise—and these comments challenged many public sphere depictions of black women.

22. On Sanks, see *Appeal*, November 28, 1863; on Newby, see *Appeal*, June 20, 1863. The description of Francis appeared in the *Appeal*, July 4, 1863, just before a piece addressing black engagement in the Civil War; Bell was surely aware of the equation between Francis's color, the public service embodied in an "alderman," and the patriotism of the article's date.

23. Meredith L. McGill, *American Literature and the Culture of Reprinting, 1834–1853* (Philadelphia: University of Pennsylvania Press, 2003).

24. See, e.g., "Journalistic Magnanimity," in the *Christian Recorder*, May 16, 1878, as well as accounts like the laudatory biography of Bell in Penn, *Afro-American Press*.

25. While I have mixed feelings about the various "black Atlantics" that have entered our discussions—and share some of the critiques Sandra Gunning advances in her

perceptive "Nancy Prince and the Politics of Mobility, Home, and Diasporic (Mis)Identification," *American Quarterly* 53 (March 2001): 32–69—this subfield has urged further and useful consideration of mobility as one of the central issues surrounding nineteenth-century blackness.

26. Leon Jackson, "The Talking Book and the Talking Book Historian: African American Cultures of Print—The State of the Discipline," *Book History* 13 (2010): 251–308.

CHAPTER 5. APPREHENDING EARLY AFRICAN
AMERICAN LITERARY HISTORY

I am particularly grateful to Leon Jackson for his contribution to my thinking about this chapter.

1. Paul Gilroy, *The Black Atlantic: Modernity and Double Consciousness* (Cambridge, Mass.: Harvard University Press, 1993), 19. Even in the absence of a self-identified, pre–Civil War African American literature, the canon and its attendant literary history remain as products of African Americanist inquiry; see Kenneth W. Warren, *What Was African American Literature?* (Cambridge, Mass.: Harvard University Press, 2011).

2. See Joanna Brooks and John Saillant, eds., *"Face Zion Forward": First Writers of the Black Atlantic, 1785–1798* (Boston: Northeastern University Press, 2002), 47–176; Vincent Carretta, *Equiano the African: Biography of a Self-Made Man* (Athens: University of Georgia Press, 2005).

3. Frederick Douglass, *Narrative of the Life of Frederick Douglass, an American Slave, Written by Himself* (1845; reprint, New York: Penguin, 1982), 18.

4. Vincent Carretta and Philip Gould, eds., *Genius in Bondage: Literature of the Early Black Atlantic* (Lexington: University Press of Kentucky, 2001), 1.

5. Abraham Johnstone, *Address of Abraham Johnstone, a Black Man* (Philadelphia: Printed for the purchasers, 1797), 2; Cotton Mather, *Tremenda: The Dreadful Sound with Which the Wicked Are to Be Thunderstruck* (Boston: Printed by B. Green, for B. Gray and J. Edwards, 1721), 38.

6. See Adam Potkay and Sandra Burr, eds., *Black Atlantic Writers of the Eighteenth Century: Living the New Exodus in England and the Americas* (New York: St. Martin's Press, 1995); Henry Louis Gates Jr. and William L. Andrews, eds., *Pioneers of the Black Atlantic: Five Slave Narratives from the Enlightenment, 1772–1815* (Washington, D.C.: Civitas, 1998); Brooks and Saillant, *Face Zion Forward*; the exception is Vincent Carretta, ed., *Unchained Voices: An Anthology of Black Authors in the English-Speaking World of the Eighteenth Century* (Lexington: University Press of Kentucky, 1996). See also Dickson D. Bruce Jr., *The Origins of African American Literature, 1680–1865* (Charlottesville: University Press of Virginia, 2001); Philip Gould, *Barbaric Traffic: Commerce and Antislavery in the Eighteenth-Century Atlantic World* (Cambridge, Mass.: Harvard University Press,

2003); Carretta and Gould, *Genius in Bondage*; Gesa Mackenthun, *Fictions of the Black Atlantic in American Foundational Literature* (New York: Routledge, 2004); Rafia Zafar, *We Wear the Mask: African Americans Write American Literature, 1760–1870* (New York: Columbia University Press, 1997).

7. Edgar J. McManus, *A History of Negro Slavery in New York* (1966; reprint, Syracuse: Syracuse University Press, 2001), 98; G. S. Rowe, "Black Offenders, Criminal Courts, and Philadelphia Society in the Late Eighteenth-Century," *Journal of Social History* 22 (Summer 1989): 697; Shane White, *Somewhat More Independent: The End of Slavery in New York City, 1770–1810* (Athens: University of Georgia Press, 1991), 64–65.

8. Frances Smith Foster, *Witnessing Slavery: The Development of Ante-bellum Slave Narratives* (Westport, Conn.: Greenwood, 1979), 36.

9. William L. Andrews, *To Tell a Free Story: The First Century of Afro-American Autobiography, 1760–1865* (Urbana: University of Illinois Press, 1986), 33.

10. Ronald A. Bosco, "Early American Gallows Literature: An Annotated Checklist," *Resources for American Literary Study* 8 (1978): 81; see Richard Slotkin, "Narratives of Negro Crime in New England, 1675–1800," *American Quarterly* 25 (1973): 3–31. Estimates were reached by collating these two checklists with the thirteen additional works attributed to the black condemned encountered in my own research.

11. Cotton Mather, *Warnings from the Dead* (Boston: Printed by Bartholomew Green, for Samuel Phillips, 1693), 74, 72.

12. Cotton Mather, *Pillars of Salt: An History of Some Criminals Executed in This Land, for Capital Crimes* (Boston: Printed by B. Green, and J. Allen, for Samuel Phillips, 1699), 71.

13. Andrews, *To Tell a Free Story*, 41.

14. Louis P. Masur, *Rites of Execution: Capital Punishment and the Transformation of American Culture, 1776–1865* (New York: Oxford University Press, 1989), 25–49; Stuart Banner, *The Death Penalty: An American History* (Cambridge, Mass.: Harvard University Press, 2002), 9–13.

15. Banner, *The Death Penalty*, 25–32.

16. Daniel A. Cohen, *Pillars of Salt, Monuments of Grace: New England Crime Literature and the Origins of American Popular Culture, 1674–1860* (New York: Oxford University Press, 1993), 6.

17. Ibid.

18. Ibid., 4–5.

19. Ibid.

20. Thaddeus McCarty, *The Power and Grace of Christ Display'd to a Dying Malefactor* (Boston: Printed and sold by Kneeland and Adams, 1768), 20.

21. Gould, *Barbaric Traffic*, 74, 72–73; Gould does not address gallows texts.

22. *Boston Gazette*, May 1–8, 1721; Mather, *Tremenda*, 27.

23. Mather, *Tremenda*, 27

24. Foster, *Witnessing Slavery*, 39.

25. Andrews, *To Tell a Free Story*, 44, 43.

26. Ibid., 43, 44.

27. "Chronological Checklist" is part of Slotkin's "Narratives of Negro Crime in New England, 1675–1800."

28. Sentencing Project, "Felony Disenfranchisement Laws in the United States," http://www.sentencingproject.org/doc/publications/fd_bs_fdlawsinusMar11.pdf, 1.

29. Pew Center on the States and the Public Safety Performance Project, "One in 100: Behind Bars in America 2008," http://www.pewcenteronthestates.org/report_detail .aspx?id=35904, 3.

30. Sentencing Project, "Felony Disenfranchisement Laws in the United States."

31. Angela Y. Davis, *The Angela Y. Davis Reader*, ed. Joy James (Malden, Mass.: Blackwell, 1998), 62; see Saidiya V. Hartman, *Scenes of Subjection: Terror, Slavery, and Self-Making in Nineteenth-Century America* (New York: Oxford University Press, 1997), 76–78.

32. Steven Wilf, *Law's Imagined Republic: Popular Politics and Criminal Justice in Revolutionary America* (Cambridge: Cambridge University Press, 2010), 6, 10.

33. Olaudah Equiano, *The Interesting Narrative of the Life of Olaudah Equiano, or Gustavus Vassa, the African* (London: Printed for and sold by the author, 1789), 2:242, 239.

34. Brooks and Saillant, *Face Zion Forward*, 94.

35. John Joyce, *Confession of John Joyce, Alias Davis, Who Was Executed on Monday, the 14th of March, 1808* (Philadelphia: Printed at No. 12, Walnut-Street, for the Benefit of Bethel Church, 1808), title page.

36. See H. Bruce Franklin, *Prison Literature in America: The Victim as Criminal and Artist* (New York: Oxford University Press, 1989); Susanne B. Dietzel, "The African American Novel and Popular Culture," in *The Cambridge Companion to the African American Novel*, ed. Maryemma Graham (Cambridge: Cambridge University Press, 2004), 162–63.

37. Nick Chiles, "Their Eyes Were Reading Smut," Op-Ed, *New York Times*, January 4, 2006, http://www.nytimes.com/2006/01/04/opinion/04chiles.html; Gerald Early, "What Is African American Literature?" February 5, 2009, http://www.america.gov/st/peopleplace-english/2009/February/20090210134821mlenuhreto.1840784.html.

38. "Representatives and direct Taxes shall be apportioned among the several States which may be included within this Union, according to their respective Numbers, which shall be determined by adding to the whole Number of free Persons, including those bound to Service for a Term of Years, and excluding Indians not taxed, three fifths of all other Persons" (U.S. Const., art. I, sec. 2).

39. James Madison, Alexander Hamilton, and John Jay, *The Federalist Papers* (1788; reprint, New York: Penguin, 1988), 332.

40. Colin [Joan] Dayan, "Legal Terrors," *Representations* 92 (Autumn 2005): 80.

41. Davis, *Angela Y. Davis Reader*, 62.

42. John L. Brooke, "Consent, Civil Society, and the Public Sphere in the Age of Revolution and the Early American Republic," in *Beyond the Founders: New Approaches to the Political History of the Early American Republic*, ed. Jeffrey L. Pasley, Andrew W. Robertson, and David Waldstreicher (Chapel Hill: University of North Carolina Press, 2004), 230.

43. Joanna Brooks, "The Early American Public Sphere and the Emergence of a Black Print Counterpublic," *William and Mary Quarterly* 62 (January 2005): 67–92; Richard S. Newman and Roy E. Finkenbine, "Forum: Black Founders in the New Republic: Introduction," *William and Mary Quarterly* 64 (January 2007): 91.

44. Edlie L. Wong, *Neither Fugitive nor Free: Atlantic Slavery, Freedom Suits, and the Legal Culture of Travel* (New York: New York University Press, 2009), 7.

45. Henry Box Brown, *Narrative of the Life of Henry Box Brown, Written by Himself* (Manchester: Lee and Glynn, 1851), frontispiece.

46. Cohen, *Pillars of Salt*, 79.

47. Frederick Douglass, *Life and Writings of Frederick Douglass*, ed. Philip S. Foner (New York: International Publishers, 1950), 1:363.

48. Teresa Goddu, "The Slave Narrative as Material Text," in *The Oxford Handbook to the African American Slave Narrative,* ed. John Ernest (Oxford: Oxford University Press, forthcoming).

49. Andrews, *To Tell a Free Story*, 35.

50. Bruce, *Origins of African American Literature*, 65.

51. Ibid., xi, 32; John Sekora, "Red, White, and Black: Indian Captivities, Colonial Printers, and the Early African-American Narrative," in *A Mixed Race: Ethnicity in Early America*, ed. Frank Shuffleton (New York: Oxford University Press, 1993), 103.

52. Hartman, *Scenes of Subjection*, 94.

53. Toni Morrison, *Playing in the Dark: Whiteness and the Literary Imagination* (Cambridge, Mass.: Harvard University Press, 1992), 5–6.

54. Arthur, *The Life, and Dying Speech of Arthur, a Negro Man; Who Was Executed at Worcester, October 10, 1768; for a Rape Committed on the Body of One Deborah Metcalfe* (Boston: Printed and sold [by Kneel and Adams] in Milk-Street, 1768).

55. Although cited, the broadside receives no sustained analysis in Slotkin, "Narratives of Negro Crime," 20; Foster, *Witnessing Slavery*, 36; Andrews, *To Tell a Free Story*, 41; for historical analysis, see T. H. Breen, "Making History: The Force of Public Opinion and the Last Years of Slavery in Revolutionary Massachusetts," in *Through a Glass Darkly: Reflections on Personal Identity in Early America*, ed. Ronald Hoffman, Mechal Sobel, and Frederika J. Teute (Chapel Hill: University of North Carolina Press, 1997), 67–95.

56. Aaron Hutchinson, *Iniquity Purged by Mercy and Truth* (Boston: Published by desire of some of the hearers, 1769), 19.

57. Isaac Frasier, *A Brief Account of the Life, and Abominable Thefts, of the Notorious Isaac Frasier* (New London: Printed and sold by Timothy Green, 1768), 15.

58. Internal evidence does not always distinguish between the enslaved, indentured servants, and quasi slaves under gradual emancipation schemes. For references to Arthur as a slave, see Andrews, *To Tell a Free Story*, 41; Cohen, *Pillars of Salt*, 125; Breen, "Making History," 77.

59. George S. Sawyer, *Southern Institutes* (Philadelphia: J. B. Lippincott, 1859), 313.

60. Gould, *Barbaric Traffic*, 148.

61. Mather, *Tremenda*, 32.

62. Ibid., 38.
63. Ibid., 26.
64. Ibid., 33, 32.

CHAPTER 6. BLACK VOICES, WHITE PRINT

1. For another account of *Invitation*, see David Waldstreicher, *In the Midst of Perpetual Fetes: The Making of American Nationalism, 1776–1820* (Chapel Hill: University of North Carolina Press, 1997), 337.

2. My understanding of the placement and use of *Invitation* is based on discussions of American broadsides and street literature as described in Georgia B. Bumgardner, *American Broadsides: Sixty Facsimiles Dated 1689 to 1800* (Barre, Mass.: Imprint Society, 1971), and Leslie Shepard, *The History of Street Literature: The Story of Broadside Ballads, Chapbooks, Proclamations, News-Sheets, Election Bills, Tracts, Pamphlets, Cocks, Catchpennies, and Other Ephemera* (Detroit: Gale Group, 1973), respectively, as well as the firsthand account by Hosea Easton, *A Treatise on the Intellectual Character, and the Civil and Political Condition of the Colored People of the U. States; and the Prejudice Exercised Towards Them: With a Sermon on the Duty of the Church to Them*, in *To Heal the Scourge of Prejudice: The Life and Writings of Hosea Easton*, ed. George R. Price and James Brewer Stewart (Amherst: University of Massachusetts Press, 1999), 107.

3. On racist jokes, see Robert K. Dodge, *Early American Almanac Humor* (Bowling Green, Ohio: Bowling Green University Popular Press, 1987); Robert Secor, "Ethnic Humor in Early American Jestbooks," in *A Mixed Race: Ethnicity in Early America*, ed. Frank Shuffleton, 163–93 (New York: Oxford University Press, 1993); and John Wood Sweet, "Bodies Politic: Colonialism, Race and the Emergence of the American North" (Ph.D. diss., Princeton University, 1995), 436–521.

4. For example, see Joanne Pope Melish, *Disowning Slavery: Gradual Emancipation and "Race" in New England, 1780–1860* (Ithaca, N.Y.: Cornell University Press, 1998), 163–94; John Wood Sweet, *Bodies Politic: Negotiating Race in the American North, 1730–1830* (Baltimore: Johns Hopkins University Press, 2003), 353–92; Waldstreicher, *Perpetual Fetes*, 333–44; and Graham White and Shane White, *Stylin': African American Expressive Culture from Its Beginnings to the Zoot Suit* (Ithaca, N.Y.: Cornell University Press, 1998), 106–16.

5. My sense of "practice" is indebted to Michel de Certeau, *The Practice of Everyday Life*, trans. Steven Rendall (Berkeley: University of California Press, 1984), xi–xxiv; and Annemarie Mol, *The Body Multiple: Ontology in Medical Practice* (Durham, N.C.: Duke University Press, 2002).

6. My focus on race and figuration emerges from a matrix of scholarship including but not limited to Michel Foucault, *The History of Sexuality*, vol. 1, *An Introduction* (New York: Vintage Books, 1978); Donna J. Haraway, "Situated Knowledges: The Science Question in Feminism as a Site of Discourse on the Privilege of Partial Perspective," *Feminist Studies* 14, no. 3 (1988): 575–99; Saidiya V. Hartman, *Scenes of Subjection: Terror,*

Slavery, and Self-Making in Nineteenth-Century America (New York: Oxford University Press, 1997); Toni Morrison, *Playing in the Dark: Whiteness and the Literary Imagination* (Cambridge: Harvard University Press, 1992); Edward Said, *Orientalism* (New York: Pantheon Books, 1978); and Carroll Smith-Rosenberg, *This Violent Empire: The Birth of an American National Identity* (Chapel Hill: University of North Carolina Press, 2010).

7. See Eric Cheyfitz, *The Poetics of Imperialism: Translation and Colonization from "The Tempest" to "Tarzan"* (Philadelphia: University of Pennsylvania Press, 1997), 196; Mol, *The Body Multiple*, 78–85; Bruno Latour, *The Pasteurization of France*, trans. Alan Sheridan and John Law (Cambridge, Mass.: Harvard University Press, 1993); and John Law, *Organizing Modernity: Social Ordering and Social Theory* (Oxford: Wiley-Blackwell, 1994).

8. The term "material-semiotic" is most often associated with Donna Haraway, who writes, "Discourses [and figures] are not just 'words'; they are material-semiotic practices through which objects of attention and knowing subjects are both constituted." Donna J. Haraway, *Modest_Witness@Second_Millennium.FemaleMan©_Meets_OncoMouse™: Feminism and Technoscience* (New York: Routledge, 1997), 218, and see esp. 8–14 and 217–18; see also John Law, "Actor Network Theory and Material Semiotics" (version of April 25, 2007), accessed May 18, 2007, http://www.heterogeneities.net/publications/Law2007 ANTandMaterialSemiots.pdf.

9. On "congealed labor," see Karl Marx, *Capital: A Critique of Political Economy*, vol. 1, trans. Ben Fowkes (New York: Vintage Books, 1977), 142.

10. The principle of "irreduction" is most insistently articulated in Latour, *Pasteurization of France*, but is also a primary concern in Haraway, "Situated Knowledges."

11. The phrase "performative and pedagogical" is from Homi Bhabha, "Dissemi-Nation: Time, Narrative and the Margins of the Modern Nation," in *The Location of Culture* (New York: Routledge, 1994), 221–22.

12. My notion of a visual and literary mode of ordering draws from the notions of "literary technologies" as described by Steven Shapin and Simon Shaffer, *Leviathan and the Air Pump: Hobbes, Boyle, and the Experimental Life* (Princeton, N.J.: Princeton University Press, 1985), 22–79; and "mode of ordering" as described by Law, *Organizing Modernity*, throughout.

13. On "rowdy" celebrations and celebrants, see Susan G. Davis, *Parades and Power: Street Theater in Nineteenth-Century Philadelphia* (Philadelphia: Temple University Press, 1986), 159–63.

14. David Hackett Fischer, *The Revolution of American Conservatism: The Federalist Party in the Era of Jeffersonian Democracy* (Chicago: University of Chicago Press, 1965), 33.

15. On the convention of disinterestedness, see Gordon Wood, "Interests and Disinterestedness in the Making of the Constitution," in *Beyond Confederation: Origins of the Constitution and American National Identity*, ed. Richard R. Beeman, Stephen Botein, and Edward Carlos Carter (Chapel Hill: University of North Carolina Press, 1987), 223–27; and Steven Shapin, *A Social History of Truth: Civility and Science in Seventeenth-Century England* (Chicago: University of Chicago Press, 1994), 237–38. On the Federalists' political stance during the early nineteenth century, see Linda Kerber, *Women of the Re-*

public: Intellect and Ideology in Revolutionary America (Chapel Hill: University of North Carolina Press, 1986).

16. On "national manhood," see Dana D. Nelson, *National Manhood: Capitalist Citizenship and the Imagined Fraternity of White Men* (Durham, N.C.: Duke University Press, 1998).

17. On the "rhetoric of pretense," see David Waldstreicher, "Reading the Runaways: Self-Fashioning, Print Culture, and Confidence in Slavery in the Eighteenth-Century Mid-Atlantic," *William and Mary Quarterly* 56, no. 2 (April 1999): 243–72.

18. W. E. B. Du Bois, *Black Reconstruction in America, 1860–1880* (New York: Free Press, 1998), 700–701; and David Roediger, *Wages of Whiteness: Race and the Making of the American Working Class* (New York: Verso, 1991), 12.

19. *Poulson's American Daily Advertiser*, January 1, 1808, 3.

20. *American Citizen*, October 8, 1807, 3; *Republican Watch-Tower*, October 9, 1807, 4.

21. *Independent Chronicle*, January 4, 1808, 3; *Republican Spy*, January 13, 1808, 3.

22. See Jon Hall, "Social Evasion and Aristocratic Manners in Cicero's 'De Oratore,'" *American Journal of Philology* 117 (Spring 1996): 95–120; and Ryan Patrick Hanley, "David Hume and the 'Politics of Humanity,'" *Political Theory* 39, no. 2 (2011): 205–33.

23. *Public Advertiser*, October 10, 1807, 2.

24. Hartman's *Scenes of Subjection* inspired this phrase.

25. This quote and those in the next two paragraphs are taken from *Grand Bobalition of Slavery: Grand and most helligunt Selebrashun of de Bobalition of Slabery . . .* (Boston, n.d., ca. 1820).

26. On "rotation in office," see Gordon Wood, *The Creation of the American Republic, 1776–1787* (Chapel Hill: University of North Carolina Press, 1969), 140–41; Fischer, *Revolution of American Conservatism*, 161; and J. G. A. Pocock, *The Machiavellian Moment: Florentine Political Thought and the Atlantic Republican Tradition* (Princeton, N.J.: Princeton University Press, 1975), 382–83, 393–94, 407, 414, 473, and 519.

27. The quotations appearing in this and the next paragraph are cited from *Dreadful Riot on Negro Hill* (Boston, 1816). On intercepted letters and the epistolary format generally, see Lennard Davis, *Factual Fictions: The Origins of the English Novel* (New York: Columbia University Press, 1983), 174–92.

28. Daniel A. Cohen, *The Female Marine and Related Works: Narratives of Cross-Dressing and Urban Vice in America's Early Republic* (Amherst: University of Massachusetts Press, 1997), 28 and 43.

29. On republicanism, see Bernard Bailyn, *The Ideological Origins of the American Revolution* (Cambridge, Mass.: Belknap Press, 1967); Wood, *Creation of the American Republic*; and Pocock, *Machiavellian Moment*. On virtue's gendered character, see Ruth Bloch, "The Gendered Meaning of Virtue in Revolutionary America," *Signs: Journal of Women in Culture and Society* 13, no. 1 (1987): 37–58.

30. For the most detailed discussion of "mob" action, see Paul Gilje, *Rioting in America* (Bloomington: Indiana University Press, 1996).

31. On gender and citizenship, see Kerber, *Women of the Republic*; and Mary Beth Norton, *Liberty's Daughters: The Revolutionary Experience of American Women, 1750–1800*

(Boston: Little, Brown, 1980). On race and gendered citizenship, see Pauline Schloesser, *The Fair Sex: White Women and Racial Patriarchy in the Early American Republic* (New York: New York University Press, 2002). Angela Y. Davis, "The Legacy of Slavery: Standards for a New Womanhood," in *Women, Race, and Class* (New York: Vintage, 1983), 3–29, provides a nuanced account of the impact of slavery, labor, and gender.

32. The quotations in this and the next paragraph are taken from *Reply to Bobalition of Slavery* (Boston, 1819).

33. Lord Chesterfield was Philip Dormer Stanhope (1694–1773), author of *Principles of Politeness, and of Knowing the World,* an etiquette manual published in several editions on both sides of the Atlantic during the Revolutionary era until well into the Jacksonian period.

34. See Wood, *Creation of the American Republic.*

35. On "mimetic corruption," see Michael Meranze, *Laboratories of Virtue: Punishment, Revolution, and Authority in Philadelphia, 1760–1835* (Chapel Hill: University of North Carolina, 1996), 8 and 87–127.

36. Clarence S. Brigham, *Journals and Journeymen: A Contribution to the History of Early American Newspapers* (Philadelphia: University of Pennsylvania Press, 1950), 62.

37. Frank Luther Mott, *American Journalism: A History, 1690–1960* (New York: Macmillan, 1962), 168–69.

38. On William Duane, see Richard Rosenfeld, *American Aurora: A Democratic-Republican Returns* (New York: St. Martin's Press, 1997); and Jeffery Pasley, *"The Tyranny of the Printers": Newspaper Politics in the Early American Republic* (Charlottesville: University of Virginia Press, 2002).

39. *Tickler,* October 21, 1807, 1; March 23, 1808, 2; May 23, 1810, 2; May 30, 1810, 3; and July 11, 1810, 3.

40. *Scourge,* November 30, 1811, 3.

41. *Satirist,* March 21, 1812, 2.

42. *Satirist,* April 20, 1812, 2.

43. *Tickler,* July 19, 1809, 3. For more on the "African Tammany Societies," see Philip J. Deloria, *Playing Indian* (New Haven, Conn.: Yale University Press, 1998), chap. 2.

44. *Tickler,* August 23, 1809, 4.

45. *Tickler,* September 6, 1809, 3; October 25, 1809, 2; February 14, 1810, 2; February 21, 1810, 4; and February 28, 1810, 4.

46. *Satirist,* February 29, 1812, 3, and March 1, 1812, 3; and *Scourge,* October 19, 1811, 3.

47. On popular punishment and politics in the Anglo-American political tradition, see Alfred F. Young, "English Plebeian Culture and Eighteenth-Century American Radicalism," in *The Origins of Anglo-American Radicalism,* ed. Margaret Jacob and James Jacob (London: Allen and Unwin, 1984), 184–212.

48. *Tickler,* September 16, 1807, 1; *Scourge,* August 10, 1811, 1; and *Satirist,* January 16, 1812, 1.

49. *Tickler,* October 18, 1809, 4.

50. Reprinted in *Tickler*, January 24, 1810, 4.

51. Richard Steele, *Tatler* no. 144, March 11, 1709, in *The Tatler, Complete in One Volume: With Notes, and a General Index* (London: Jones and Company, 1829), 286.

52. Pasley, *Tyranny of the Printers*, 429, n. 65.

53. William C. Dowling, *Literary Federalism in the Age of Jefferson: Joseph Dennie and "The Port Folio," 1801–1812* (New York: Columbia University Press, 1999).

54. On "a speaking aristocracy and a silent democracy," see Fischer, *Revolution of American Conservatism*, 4, 17; and Christopher Grasso, *A Speaking Aristocracy: Transforming Public Discourse in Eighteenth-Century Connecticut* (Chapel Hill: University of North Carolina Press, 1999).

CHAPTER 7. SLAVERY, IMPRINTED

1. William Grimes, *Life of William Grimes, The Runaway Slave. Written by Himself* (New York, 1825), 68. All subsequent citations will refer to the recently republished edition of Grimes's 1855 revision: William Grimes, *Life of William Grimes, the Runaway Slave*, ed. William L. Andrews and Regina Mason (New York: Oxford University Press, 2008).

2. William L. Andrews, *To Tell a Free Story: The First Century of Afro-American Autobiography, 1760–1865* (Urbana: University of Illinois Press, 1986), 81.

3. The strongest claim to authorship of the first American slave narrative would likely be that of Venture Smith (1729?–1805). First published in 1798, his thirty-two-page narrative was narrated to Elisha Niles, a schoolteacher and Revolutionary War veteran. As is discussed later in this essay, the *New Haven (Conn.) Daily Palladium* reports that an additional chapter appended to the end of Grimes's 1855 edition was dictated by Grimes to Samuel H. Harris, a prominent printer in New Haven.

4. Under the terms of the 1790 Copyright Act, in order to register a copyright for an initial term of fourteen years, one had to deposit a copy with a state clerk to be delivered to the secretary of state within six months of publication and publish a copy of the clerk's certificate of title-page deposit in a newspaper for four weeks. Copyright registration was thus a significant undertaking and it is unclear whether or not Grimes followed up on all the requisite steps to fully claim, much less later renew, his copyright. A handwritten copy of the actual title-page deposit claim completed by Charles A. Ingersoll, clerk of the District of Connecticut, can be found in the Library of Congress. That does not mean, however, that any of the later steps were followed. Many copyright claimants (likely including Grimes) were actually invoking "scarecrow copyright" inasmuch as they were often filing claims prepublication and then affixing the claim onto their publications but not following through with the necessary postpublication deposit or the four-week run of a public newspaper claim. By 1855, when Grimes came out with a second edition, the law had been revised and made even more complicated. It demanded that three copies be deposited: one to district court (for transmittal to the secretary of state), one to the

Smithsonian, and one to the Library of Congress. There are no records for any deposit of the 1855 edition and it is unlikely Grimes attempted to copyright this edition. For an excellent overview of copyright, see William F. Patry, *Copyright Law and Practice* (Washington, D.C.: Bureau of National Affairs, 1994). See also George Thomas Tanselle, "Copyright Records and the Bibliographer," *Studies in Bibliography* 22 (1969): 77–124.

5. It wasn't until the *Dred Scott* decision of 1857 that the U.S. Supreme Court emphatically declared that black people were not U.S. citizens and that states could not define citizenship on their own terms. Up until that point, the notion that free blacks might be citizens with some attendant legal rights was variously recognized throughout the northern states and territories with free jurisdiction. For a good overview of the case, see Austin Allen, *Origins of the Dred Scott Case: Jacksonian Jurisprudence and the Supreme Court, 1837–1857* (Athens: University of Georgia Press, 2006).

6. The first copyright given to an African American, slave or free, in the United States was likely the shared rights given to Absalom Jones and Richard Allen, who received a copyright in 1794 for their twenty-eight-page pamphlet *A Narrative of the Proceedings of the Black People, During the Late Awful Calamity in Philadelphia*. See Richard Newman, Patrick Rael, and Phillip Lapsansky, eds., *Pamphlets of Protest: An Anthology of Early-American Protest Literature, 1790–1860* (New York: Routledge, 2000). Since the 1790 law covered only books, maps, and charts, the pamphlet was evidently considered a "book." However, at roughly 8,500 words, this pamphlet was not really book-length as we understand the notion today, nor was it close to the length of Grimes's 1825 narrative, which was roughly 32,000 words.

7. The son of a white man, Grimes had skin fair enough to pass as white in the evenings but never mentions being able to pass during the daytime.

8. The next likely claimant to the title of African American copyright holder to a book-length narrative would probably be Richard Allen, the same man who registered the first black copyright with his 1794 pamphlet. His life narrative, *The Life, Experience, and Gospel Labours of the Rt. Rev. Richard Allen; To Which Is Annexed the Rise and Progress of the African Methodist Episcopal Church in the United States of America; Containing a Narrative of the Yellow Fever in the Year of Our Lord 1793: With an Address to the People of Colour in the United States*, was published in Philadelphia by Martin and Boden in 1833 and was duly registered under what had by then evolved into the 1831 Copyright Act.

9. Jeremiah Nyhuis discovered this *Liberator* obituary notice for me and also several other hitherto unknown references to Grimes in local Connecticut papers. I am very grateful to him for selflessly sharing his discoveries.

10. In later years Grimes had certainly become involved in the abolition movement, for on May 21, 1842, the *New-England Weekly Review* snidely noted his absence from an abolitionist meeting by remarking, "Seigneur Grimes and his accomplished son were not present to take the chair."

11. The 1825 version opens with the following:

DISTRICT OF CONNECTICUT, ss. BE IT REMEMBERED, That on the twenty-eighth day of January, in the forty-ninth year of the Independence of the United States of America, WILLIAM GRIMES of the said District, hath deposited in this Office the title of a Book, the right whereof he claims as Author, in the words following, to wit: "The Life of William Grimes, the Runaway Slave. Written by Himself." In conformity to the Act of the Congress of the United States, entitled, "An Act for the encouragement of learning, by securing the copies of Maps, Charts, and Books, to the Authors and Proprietors of such copies, during the times therein mentioned." CHARLES A INGERSOLL, Clerk of the District of Connecticut. A true copy of Record, examined and sealed by me. CHARLES A. INGERSOLL, Clerk of the District of Connecticut.

12. See note 4 for details on how Grimes should have fulfilled all the steps. Furthermore, since his 1855 edition was not published with a title deposit claim, it seems likely that even if he had properly fulfilled all of the requisite steps for the 1825 edition, he never bothered to renew his rights, which presumably would have expired some fourteen years after the 1825 edition appeared. The records of the Connecticut District Court of 1834 (fourteen years after he had registered his first claim) show no renewal registered to Grimes.

13. I have searched incomplete editions of various Connecticut and New York papers of the 1850s for such an advertisement and have not located one, but I'm convinced that the advertisement exists, since so many other details of Grimes's life check out.

14. Mysteriously, his 1855 edition was printed in New York, not in Connecticut where he was living at the time.

15. Grimes refers to a "Mr. Wolhopter" in his memoirs, but the printing byline of the works coming from the Savannah press spells the name as "Woolhopter."

16. Grimes had nothing to lose by asserting any possible pressroom skills in his later life but since he neither describes them specifically nor mentions them generally by saying, for example, that he sought work in a northern print shop when in dire financial straits, it seems safe to speculate that either the skills were not there or—equally likely— the print trade in the North was closed to him because of his race and low social status. Nonetheless, while we cannot know for certain what work he did for Woolhopter and what skills he might or might not have had, his experiences there cannot be discounted when we recall both his invocation of bookish metaphors and his abilities to finance and somehow publish two different editions of his life narrative without official sponsorship or prior subscriptions. He may not have been a printer, but he certainly knew how to go about producing a book. As he explains at the end of his narrative, he could both read and write: "I have learned to read and write pretty well; if I had opportunity I could learn very fast. My wife has tolerable good education, which has been a help to me" (103). Thus there is no evidence to suggest that his 1825 story was transcribed or edited in any significant way by anyone other than himself. It would not be surprising, of course, if one of his Yale or

Litchfield friends reviewed his work for him in some way, and we do know that his addenda in his 1855 edition were dictated.

17. On December 12, 1797, Philip D. Woolhopter was admitted as a junior partner to a printing firm to be known as Seymour and Woolhopter. In 1802 Francis Stebbins joined as another partner and the firm became Seymour, Woolhopter, and Stebbins. Stebbins and Seymour eventually withdrew from the firm, and Woolhopter continued it under his name until 1817. Indeed, it was during the summer of 1809, when Grimes began work with Woolhopter, that Woolhopter took over the entire printing business.

18. One telling example was the case of Prudence Crandall, who was prosecuted for educating out-of-state African American girls at her Canterbury academy in violation of Connecticut law. The 1833 court case hinged upon the argument of whether or not African Americans were citizens of states within which they resided and indeed if African Americans were citizens at all. Crandall was tried and convicted, but in 1834 the case was reversed on a technicality, frustrating the hopes of activists who had sought a precedent-setting case concerning citizenship. See *A Statement of Facts, Respecting the School for Colored Females in Canterbury, Ct.: Together with a Report of the Late Trial of Miss Prudence Crandall* (Brooklyn, Conn.: Advertiser Press, 1833).

19. Joanna Brooks, "The Unfortunates: What the Life Spans of Early Black Books Tell Us About Book History" (Chapter 2 in this volume).

20. "Old Grimes" was a title of a Mother Goose rhyme popular in the eighteenth century and ran, in its most simple version, as follows:

Old Grimes is dead, that good old man,
　We ne'er shall see him more;
　He used to wear a long brown coat
　All buttoned down before.

By 1822, poet Albert Gordon Greene, a recent graduate of Brown University in Providence, had added several other comic verses to the initial stanza and published it in the *Providence Gazette*, January 16, 1822. While William Grimes claims the song was originally written about his paternal grandfather, Greene likely based his version upon a notorious con man and counterfeiter named Grimes, who may have embroiled Brown University authorities in a fraudulent roofing scheme. It is tempting to speculate that William Grimes himself could have been involved in such an incident, for he does admit to living in Providence, Rhode Island, at just about the period an infamous roofing scam was hatched, but the Greene poem makes no reference to the race of "Old Grimes," and it may all be a coincidence. On the other hand, the *Litchfield Enquirer* in 1851 reported that the "Old Grimes" poem was indeed based upon William Grimes, who had become known to Greene during Greene's years studying law in Litchfield. This report seems inaccurate for the article confuses Albert Collins Greene (a Rhode Island senator who had studied law) with Albert Gordon Greene, the poet. Moreover, the years the *Litchfield*

Enquirer article cites don't precisely align with what we know about Grimes's life in Litch-field. Other Grimes references refer to the poem as based upon an entirely separate character, Ephraim Grimes of Hubbardstown, Massachusetts. But whatever the source, the fact that the real William Grimes appropriated a poem to signify his own heritage (in the form of his grandfather), to signify his own role in the community (such as when he used it to advertise his business), and later to cement his role in the historical and cultural imagination of the Yale community (by having the poem used in his own obituary) is telling. Grimes, as picaresque fugitive, was quite appropriately conflating his identity with a well-loved American trickster. See "'Old Grimes,' of Ancient Elegiac Fame; A Nonagenarian with an Inconvenient Memory Tells Some Sad Things About Him," *New York Times*, July 7, 1912; and "Old Grimes House Burned; A Landmark of Hubbardston, Mass. Is Destroyed," *New York Times*, February 4, 1907. See also "Old Grimes," *Litchfield Enquirer*, September 4, 1851.

CHAPTER 8. BOTTLES OF INK AND REAMS OF PAPER

The American Antiquarian Society supported research for this essay with a Jay and Deborah Last Fellowship in American Visual Culture. Many thanks are due to Brigitte Fielder and Elizabeth Maddock Dillon for making significant contributions during the writing and revision process. Thanks also to workshop and conference participants at Cornell University, Dartmouth College, and the McNeil Center for Early American Studies for providing feedback on early drafts.

1. Garrison to Elizabeth Pease, July 17, 1849, in William Edward Farrison, *William Wells Brown: Author and Reformer* (Chicago: University of Chicago Press, 1969), 143.

2. William L. Andrews, *To Tell a Free Story: The First Century of Afro-American Autobiography, 1760–1865* (Urbana: University of Illinois Press, 1986), xi, emphasis in original.

3. William Wells Brown, *Narrative of William W. Brown, a Fugitive Slave, Written by Himself* (Boston: Anti-Slavery Office, 1847), 29. Lovejoy's story was a national sensation in the late 1830s and in this passage Brown may be casting himself in Lovejoy's role in the well-known story. Brown is attacked while ferrying type and readers would remember Lovejoy's murder by an anti-abolitionist mob while defending his printing press.

4. Ibid., 27.

5. *Oxford English Dictionary*, 2nd ed., s.v. "stereotype" (n., def. 2, 3a, 3b).

6. William Wells Brown, *Narrative of William Wells Brown, an American Slave, Written By Himself* (London: Charles Gilpin, 1849), http://books.google.com/books?id=JWE6AAAAcAAJ.

7. Michael Omi and Howard Winant theorize racial formation as a "process of historically situated *projects* in which human bodies and social structures are represented and

organized." See *Racial Formation in the United States: From the 1960s to the 1990s,* 2nd ed. (New York: Routledge, 1994), 55–56. For other recent work on material textuality and early African American literature, see Marcy J. Dinius, "Look!! Look!!! at This!!!!": The Radical Typography of David Walker's *Appeal,*" *PMLA* 126 (January 2011): 55–72; and Beth A. McCoy, "Race and the (Para)Textual Condition," *PMLA* 121 (January 2006): 156–69.

8. This use of "common sense" owes to Jacques Rancière's concept of the distribution of the sensible (*le partage du sensible*), or the "implicit law governing the sensible order. . . . The distribution of the sensible . . . produces a system of self-evident facts of perception based on the set horizons and modalities of what is visible and audible as well as what can be said, thought, made, or done." See *The Politics of Aesthetics,* trans. Gabriel Rockhill (New York: Continuum, 2004), 85.

9. I refer to *Clotel,* or "the novel," across its title changes and revisions, as an ongoing project called *Clotel.* Samantha Marie Sommers develops the idea of *Clotel* as an unfolding project in "A Tangled Text: William Wells Brown's *Clotel* (1853, 1860, 1864, 1867)" (undergraduate thesis, Wesleyan University, 2009), http://wesscholar.wesleyan.edu/cgi/viewcontent.cgi?article=1264&context=etd_hon_theses. Except as noted, references to *Clotel* will be to Robert S. Levine's reprint of the 1853 edition, William Wells Brown, *Clotel; or, The President's Daughter: A Narrative of Slave Life in the United States* (1853), ed. Robert S. Levine (Boston: Bedford/St. Martin's, 2000).

10. For further discussion of this joke's history, and a reading of its racial significance in terms of print, publicity, and visual culture, see Marjorie Garber, *Shakespeare and Modern Culture* (New York: Pantheon Books, 2008), 154–77.

11. Michel Pastoureau, *Black: The History of a Color* (Princeton, N.J.: Princeton University Press, 2009), 114–18; Calvin quoted in ibid., 127, 114. For more on the meaning of black and white in the development of modern science of sight, mind, and thought, see the "White Science" chapter in Gary Taylor, *Buying Whiteness: Race, Culture, and Identity from Columbus to Hip Hop* (New York: Palgrave Macmillan, 2005), esp. 294–302.

12. *Oxford English Dictionary,* 2nd ed., s.vv. "black" (n., def. 2a; adj., def. 15b) and "white" (n., def. 7a).

13. George Lipsitz, *The Possessive Investment in Whiteness: How White People Profit from Identity Politics* (Philadelphia: Temple University Press, 2006), 1.

14. James Cutbush, *The American Artist's Manual; or, Dictionary of Practical Knowledge in the Application of Philosophy to the Arts and Manufactures,* vol. 2 (Philadelphia: Johnson and Warner, and R. Fisher, 1814), reprinted in *Early American Papermaking: Two Treatises on Manufacturing Techniques,* ed. John Bidwell (New Castle, Del.: Oak Knoll Books, 1990), 59. In his introduction to *Early American Papermaking* Bidwell notes that Cutbush cribbed entire passages from the *Encyclopedia Britannica,* including the one from which this quote was taken.

15. The "brownness" of brown paper takes on added racial significance in the twentieth century with "paper bag societies" and "paper bag parties," colorist African American associations that are said to have used brown paper bags to test the tones of a potential

member's skin. People with skin darker than the bag were ineligible for inclusion. See Audrey Elisa Kerr, *The Paper Bag Principle: Class, Colorism, and Rumor and the Case of Black Washington D.C.* (Knoxville: University of Tennessee Press, 2006).

16. D. Elliot to Tileston and Hollingsworth, March 9, 1833, in the Tileston and Hollingsworth Papers, American Antiquarian Society, Worcester, Mass.

17. The ideological value of whiteness that is constructed in relation to the paper trade appears in remarkably similar terms in relation to the slave trade, as Brown demonstrates in Clotel. The ragman's receipt documents whiteness as a valuable property in ways similar to the way whiteness functioned at the slave auction depicted in *Clotel*. The "still wet from the press" advertisement that includes notice of Clotel and Althesa's sale reads: "Notice: Thirty-eight negros will be offered for sale. . . . Also several mulatto girls of rare personal qualities: two of them very superior." This marketing of "superiority" comes just before Brown's description of Clotel as having "a complexion as white as those who were waiting with a wish to become her purchasers." Here, too, the possession of whiteness has quantifiable value. When Clotel is sold to Horatio Green, the narrator offers an itemized list of her worth. Her body is worth only five hundred dollars, but the virtues of white womanhood that she is said to possess are worth one thousand more: "This was a southern auction, at which the bones, muscles, sinews, blood, and nerves of a young lady of sixteen were sold for five hundred dollars; her moral character for two hundred; her improved intellect for one hundred; her Christianity for three hundred; and her chastity and virtue for four hundred dollars more." The itemization does not explicitly include her white skin, but shows Clotel's whiteness to be both physical and metaphysical, tying her physical whiteness to the trope of true white womanhood. The possession of whiteness, whether in the commodity of paper or in the body, is a promise of purity and refinement carrying with it quantifiably higher market value. Brown, *Clotel*, 84, 85, 88.

18. *Jack and the Beanstalk: A New Version* (Boston: T. H. Carter, 1837), 15, 30.

19. *Ink: Webster's Quotations, Facts, and Phrases* (San Diego: ICON Group International, 2008), 305

20. Cutbush, *American Artist's Manual*, 59.

21. Quoted in John Power, *A Handy-Book about Books, for Book-Lovers, Book-Buyers, and Book-Sellers* (London: John Wilson, 1870), 135.

22. For more on the racial significance of white goods in the antebellum United States, see Bridget T. Heneghan, *Whitewashing America: Material Culture and Race in the Antebellum Imagination* (Jackson: University Press of Mississippi, 2003).

23. Toni Morrison, "Unspeakable Things Unspoken: The Afro-American Presence in American Literature," *Michigan Quarterly Review* 28, no. 1 (Winter 1989): 16.

24. I am aware that the question of racial identification in the nineteenth century can be cut different ways depending on local contexts, laws, customs, and so on, and that these do not always result in categorization as either black or white. I remain interested here, however, in Brown's exploration of black and white as racial signifiers that are

flexible or ambiguous in certain registers like the visual, yet which are, in *Clotel*, in the end answerable to the legal constraints of hypodescent, or "one drop" logic.

25. Richard Dyer, *White* (New York: Routledge, 1997), 60, 57, 48.

26. See Cheryl Harris, "Whiteness as Property," *Harvard Law Review* 106, no. 8 (1993): 1707–91. While stating that legal whiteness is more defined than visual whiteness, I do not mean to suggest that it is homogeneous. Indeed, as Ian Haney-López has shown, local differences in population and power structures have mediated which populations are invited to participate in the property rights of whiteness. See *White by Law: The Legal Construction of Race* (New York: New York University Press, 2006).

27. Brown, *Clotel*, 87.

28. Ibid., 196.

29. Brown, *Clotelle; or, The Colored Heroine* (Boston: Lee and Shephard, 1867), 5.

30. Since the term "mulatto/a" is historically pejorative, I use it only to quote or paraphrase another text or when addressing the figure of the mulatta, which I take to be a cultural trope, not a descriptive term.

31. Announcement in the *New York Independent*, May 13, 1852, quoted in Trish Loughran, *The Republic in Print: Print Culture in the Age of U.S. Nation Building, 1770–1870* (New York: Columbia University Press, 2007), 364.

32. Brown, *Clotel*, 81.

33. Ann duCille writes of this passage that Brown's reference to ink and paper and his "use of quotation marks around the defining phrases he cites, indicate that he is himself is addressing the problem of representation" and how fiction "position[s] . . . black women as objects of the white male gaze." Ann duCille, *The Coupling Convention: Sex, Text, and Tradition in Black Women's Fiction* (New York: Oxford University Press, 1993), 22–23. In his annotations to the 1867 *Clotelle* in the Electronic Scholarly Edition, Christopher Mulvey notes, "The passage . . . is possibly taken from a printed source, but, if so, it has not been identified. [Brown] uses quotation marks for six of its phrases. These express stereotypes of exotic, particularly of mixed race, beauty. The quotation marks may indicate that they are quotations, or they may indicate that they are simply stock expressions." I would argue that Brown does not need a specific source for these lines because he is quoting print culture's habitual representation of mixed-race women. See Mulvey, ed., *Clotel: An Electronic Scholarly Edition* (Charlottesville: University of Virginia Press, 2006), http://rotunda.upress.virginia.edu:8080/clotel/.

34. Russ Castronovo, *Necro Citizenship: Death, Eroticism, and the Public Sphere in the Nineteenth-Century United States* (Durham, N.C.: Duke University Press, 2001), 41.

35. W. J. T. Mitchell, *Picture Theory: Essays on Verbal and Visual Culture* (Chicago: University of Chicago Press, 1994), 89.

36. Michael Gaudio, *Engraving the Savage: The New World and Techniques of Civilization* (Minneapolis: University of Minnesota Press, 2008), xii, 132.

37. See the title page of Harriet Beecher Stowe, *Uncle Tom's Cabin; or, The History of a Christian Slave, by Harriet Beecher Stowe; with an Introduction by Elihu Burritt; Illustrated by Sixteen Engravings by Johnston, from Original Designs by Anelay* (London: Partridge and Oakey: Saunders & Otley, 1852).

38. William Tait and Christian Isobel Johnstone, eds., review of *Uncle Tom's Cabin; or, The History of a Christian Slave*, by Harriet Beecher Stowe, *Tait's Edinburgh Magazine* 19 (December 1852): 761.

39. S[arah] E. Fuller, *A Manual of Instruction in the Art of Wood Engraving* (Boston: J. Watson, 1867), 46, 21.

40. For more on the nineteenth-century idea that race would always be manifest on the surface of the body, see Walter Johnson, "The Slave Trader, the White Slave, and the Politics of Racial Determination in the 1850s," *Journal of American History* 87 (June 2000): 27, 34. Johnson describes the case of *Morrison v. White*, in which the defendant successfully sued for her freedom using her white-looking body as evidence and arguing that "colored blood will stick out."

41. John Locke, *An Essay Concerning Human Understanding*, ed. Peter H. Nidditch (Oxford: Clarendon Press, 1975), 81.

42. Benjamin Franklin, "Paper: A Poem," in *The Works of Benjamin Franklin*, vol. 2, ed. Jared Sparks (Boston: Hilliard, Gray, and Company, 1836), 161–62. The editor of this volume registers his skepticism of Franklin's authorship. "This poem has been printed in nearly all the collections of Dr. Franklin's writings, and for that reason it is retained in the present edition; but I have seen no evidence which satisfies me that he is the author of it. In the *American Museum*, where it was printed in 1788, it was said to be '*ascribed* to Dr. Franklin'; and, on that authority, it was taken in Robinson's and then into Longman's edition, and then transferred, under Franklin's name, to various other publications in England the United States. It is not contained in W. T. Franklin's edition." Whether or not Franklin actually wrote the poem, it was widely reprinted in *The Columbian Orator*, a text most readily remembered, perhaps, as the one from which Frederick Douglass learned the master-slave dialectic.

43. Contemporary art is beyond the scope of this essay, but Glenn Ligon's 1990 *Untitled (I Feel Most Colored When I Am Thrown Against a Sharp White Background)* is worth mentioning because it compares the whiteness of writing surfaces to racial whiteness and the blackness of text to racial blackness. The phrase "I FEEL MOST COLORED WHEN I AM THROWN AGAINST A SHARP WHITE BACKGROUND" is stenciled in black and repeated down the length of a white door. The text is taken from Zora Neale Hurston's 1928 essay "How It Feels to Be Colored Me." As the border between white background and black text blurs, the repeated phrase becomes increasingly illegible toward the bottom of the panel. In this piece, racial legibility and print legibility depend on the distinction between black marks and white surfaces, and whiteness is constructed as the background against which all else becomes readable. For a reproduction of the painting, see Scott Rothkopf, ed., *Glenn Ligon: AMERICA* (New York: Whitney Museum of American Art, 2011), 98, published in conjunction with the exhibition of the same name, shown at the Whitney Museum of American Art in New York City.

44. Jean Genet also makes this connection between critical race theory and print legibility explicit: "In white America the Blacks are the characters in which history is written. They are the ink that gives the white page a meaning." See Genet, *Prisoner of Love* (New York: New York Review of Books, 2003), 245.

45. Julia Thomas, *Pictorial Victorians: The Inscription of Values in Word and Image* (Athens: Ohio University Press, 2004), 35–36.

46. Brown, *Clotel*, 101.

CHAPTER 9. NOTES FROM THE STATE OF SAINT DOMINGUE

1. Robert S. Levine's Bedford Cultural Edition of *Clotel* (2000, rev. 2011) offers the best available documentation of Brown's citations. However, forthcoming work by Dawn Coleman and Geoffrey Sanborn locates many other instances, and with the help of digital tools scholars may discover still more.

2. Robert F. Reid-Pharr, *Conjugal Union: The Body, the House, and the Black American* (Oxford: Oxford University Press, 1999), 38. Even J. Noel Heermance, one of the first twentieth-century scholars to make a case for Brown's importance as a writer and activist, laments, "What we finally have in *Clotel* . . . is not so much an artistic novel as a loosely structured skeleton of a plot on which the author can hang true and vivid anecdotes, stories, advertisements and Virginia legislature speeches." Heermance, *William Wells Brown and "Clotelle": A Portrait of the Artist in the First Negro Novel* ([Hamden, Conn.]: Archon Books, 1969), 164.

3. Ann duCille, *The Coupling Convention: Sex, Text, and Tradition in Black Women's Fiction* (New York: Oxford University Press, 1993), 451.

4. Robert B. Stepto, *From Behind the Veil: A Study of Afro-American Narrative* (Urbana: University of Illinois Press, 1979), 3–31.

5. Michel Foucault, "What Is an Author?" in *Language, Counter-Memory, Practice: Selected Essays and Interviews*, ed. Donald F. Bouchard and trans. Donald F. Bouchard and Sherry Simon (Ithaca, N.Y.: Cornell University Press, 1977), 138.

6. Harriet Beecher Stowe, *Uncle Tom's Cabin*, ed. Elizabeth Ammons (New York: Norton, 1994), 129. Subsequent citations in this chapter refer to this edition.

7. Foucault, "What Is an Author," 121.

8. William Edward Farrison, *William Wells Brown: Author and Reformer* (Chicago: University of Chicago Press, 1969), 414. John Ernest offers a more analytical take on some of Brown's self-citations in *Liberation Historiography: African American Writers and the Challenge of History, 1794–1861* (Chapel Hill: University of North Carolina Press, 2004), 336–40.

9. I thank Jordan Stein for some of the wording of this sentence—not to mention for contributing more to this essay than its own authorial attribution conveys.

10. See R. B. Lewis, *Light and Truth: Collected from the Bible and Ancient and Modern History*, rev. ed. (Boston: By a Committee of Colored Gentlemen, B. F. Roberts, printer, 1844); and David Walker, *Walker's Appeal, in Four Articles; Together with a Preamble, to the Coloured Citizens of the World*, 3rd ed. (Boston: David Walker, 1830). The same patchwork aesthetic governs a book with a title similar to Lewis's that appeared a few years later, from an author who identifies himself only as "Aaron"—*The Light and the Truth of Slavery: Aaron's History* (Worcester, Mass.: Printed for the author, ca. 1845), a work that

purports to be a slave narrative but proves to be something closer to a commonplace book assembled by the peripatetic author and his northern hosts.

11. Lauren Berlant, *The Female Complaint: The Unfinished Business of Sentimentality in American Culture* (Durham, N.C.: Duke University Press, 2008), 28.

12. Ibid., 45; Brown, *A Description of William Wells Brown's Original Panoramic Views of the Scenes in the Life of an American Slave* (London: Charles Gilpin, 1850), 33. Farrison notes that Brown himself probably based the scene on an incident that had been reported in the abolitionist press (*William Wells Brown*, 176).

13. See Meredith L. McGill, *American Literature and the Culture of Reprinting, 1834–1853* (Philadelphia: University of Pennsylvania Press, 2003).

14. John Ernest, *Resistance and Reformation in Nineteenth-Century African-American Literature: Brown, Wilson, Jacobs, Delany, Douglass, and Harper* (Jackson: University Press of Mississippi, 1995), 25.

15. William Wells Brown, *Clotel; or, The President's Daughter: A Narrative of Slave Life in the United States* (1853), ed. Robert S. Levine (Boston: Bedford/St. Martin's, 2000), 226. Subsequent citations of the 1853 *Clotel* are to this edition.

16. William Wells Brown, *Clotelle: A Tale of the Southern States* (Boston: James Redpath, 1864), 8.

17. Levine, introduction to Brown, *Clotel*, 6; see also "Sources and Revisions," 231–37.

18. Ezra Greenspan, introduction to *William Wells Brown: A Reader* (Athens: University of Georgia Press, 2008), xx, xi.

19. Ernest, *Liberation Historiography*, 86.

20. William Wells Brown, *The Black Man: His Antecedents, His Genius, and His Achievements*, Revised edition (New York: Thomas Hamilton, 1863), 59.

21. Trish Loughran, *The Republic in Print: Print Culture in the Age of U.S. Nation Building, 1770–1870* (New York: Columbia University Press, 2007), 416.

22. Brown, *Clotel*, 201.

23. Stowe, *Uncle Tom's Cabin*, 234.

24. John R. Beard, *The Life of Toussaint L'Ouverture, the Negro Patriot of Hayti* (1853; Westport, Conn.: Negro Universities Press, 1970), 19, 20–21, emphasis mine.

25. William Wells Brown, *St. Domingo: Its Revolutions and Its Patriots* (Boston: Bela Marsh, 1855), 12.

26. C. L. R. James, *The Black Jacobins: Toussaint L'Ouverture and the San Domingo Revolution*, 2nd ed., rev. (New York: Vintage, 1963), x.

27. Brown, *St. Domingo*, 32.

28. Brown, *The Black Man*, 75.

29. Brown, *Clotel*, 202.

30. Beard, *Life of Toussaint L'Ouverture*, 240.

31. Ibid.; Brown, 202.

32. Brown, *Clotel*, 195.

33. Beard, *Life of Toussaint L'Ouverture*, 219–20; the passage Brown copied word for word appears on 214–15.

34. Ibid., 83–84.

35. Ibid., 86 (original emphasis), 88.

36. Ibid., 94–95.

37. DuCille, *The Coupling Convention*, 25.

38. Ann duCille, "Where in the World Is William Wells Brown? Thomas Jefferson, Sally Hemings, and the DNA of African-American Literary History," *American Literary History* 12 (Autumn 2000): 453.

39. Jacques Rancière, *The Names of History: On the Poetics of Knowledge*, trans. Hassan Melehy (Minneapolis: University of Minnesota Press, 1994), 30.

40. Walter Benjamin, "Theses on the Philosophy of History," in *Illuminations*, ed. Hannah Arendt and trans. Harry Zohn (New York: Schocken, 1968), 256–57.

41. Brown, *Clotel*, 99.

42. Ibid., 208.

CHAPTER 10. THE CANON IN FRONT OF THEM

1. I thank Jason Camlot for alerting me to this episode.

2. For a detailed survey of *Frederick Douglass' Paper*'s literary content, see Patsy Brewington Perry, "The Literary Content of *Frederick Douglass's Paper* Through 1860," *CLA Journal* 17 (1973): 214–29. For further analysis, see Elizabeth McHenry, *Forgotten Readers: Recovering the Lost History of African American Literary Societies* (Durham, N.C.: Duke University Press, 2002), 115–29; Daniel Hack, "Close Reading at a Distance: The African Americanization of *Bleak House*," *Critical Inquiry* 34 (Summer 2008): 731–43. For a broader discussion of antebellum U.S. periodical reprinting practices, see Meredith L. McGill, *American Literature and the Culture of Reprinting, 1834–1853* (Philadelphia: University of Pennsylvania Press, 2003) and Meredith L. McGill, ed., *The Traffic in Poems: Nineteenth-Century Poetry and Transatlantic Exchange* (New Brunswick, N.J.: Rutgers University Press, 2008).

3. "Multiple News Items," *Frederick Douglass' Paper*, January 28, 1853.

4. "Fall of Sebastopol! The Allies Triumphant!!" *Frederick Douglass' Paper*, October 5, 1855.

5. Communipaw [James McCune Smith], "From Our New York Correspondent," *Frederick Douglass' Paper*, October 5, 1855.

6. One major exception is *Bleak House*, as I discuss in Hack, "Close Reading at a Distance," 729–53.

7. John Stauffer, introduction to *The Works of James McCune Smith, Black Intellectual and Abolitionist*, by James McCune Smith (New York: Oxford University Press, 2006), xiii. For further discussion of Smith, see David W. Blight, "In Search of Learning, Liberty, and Self-Definition: James McCune Smith and the Ordeal of the Antebellum Black Intellectual," *Afro-Americans in New York Life and History* 9, no. 2 (1985): 7–25; and John Stauffer, *The Black Hearts of Men: Radical Abolitionists and the Transformation of Race* (Cambridge, Mass.: Harvard University Press, 2001).

8. Communipaw [James McCune Smith], "From Our New York Correspondent," *Frederick Douglass' Paper*, January 12, 1855. This piece is reprinted in Smith, *The Works of James McCune Smith*, 108–13.

9. This article was reprinted in Gustave d'Alaux, *L'empereur Soulouque et son empire* (Paris: Michel Lévy Frères, 1856), 63–77. For a more recent discussion of the history and meaning of this chant, see David Geggus, "Haitian Voodoo in the Eighteenth Century: Language, Culture, Resistance," *Jahrbuch für Geschichte von Staat, Wirtschaft und Gesellschaft Lateinamerikas* 28 (1991): 21–51. Smith's version of the poem's genesis bears a striking resemblance to the version later related by Tennyson's son Hallam, who similarly claimed that "the origin of the metre of [the] poem" came from a passage in a periodical—specifically, from the phrase "some one had blundered" in the London *Times*. Before concluding, however, that Smith got the process right but the source wrong, we should recall that Hallam himself got the source wrong, as Christopher Ricks notes: this precise phrase did not appear in the *Times*. See Alfred Tennyson, *Tennyson: A Selected Edition*, ed. Christopher Ricks (Berkeley: University of California Press, 1989), 508.

10. Smith's investment in the authority that can accrue through charges of plagiarism is on further display later in the same column, where he goes on to accuse another of Douglass's contributors of plagiarizing both Charlotte Brontë's recent novel *Villette* and a speech by Frederick Douglass himself.

11. According to Ifeoma Kiddoe Nwankwo, "Whites' fear of the [Haitian] revolution and its presumably contagious nature forced people of African descent throughout the Americas, particularly those in the public and published eye, to name a relationship to the Haitian Revolution, in particular, and to a transnational idea of black community, in general." See Nwankwo, *Black Cosmopolitanism: Racial Consciousness and Transnational Identity in the Nineteenth-Century Americas* (Philadelphia: University of Pennsylvania Press, 2005), 7. Smith's column belongs in this tradition, or rather signifies on it, as Smith gleefully raises this topic but at the same time refuses to be pinned down to a particular position.

12. "Fylbel" himself, Philip A. Bell, reports on "The Light Brigade" being read at a fund-raiser for San Francisco's African Methodist Episcopal Zion Church. See [Philip A. Bell], "Lisle Lester," *Elevator*, July 28, 1865.

13. See Alice Dunbar-Nelson, "Negro Literature for Negro Pupils," *Southern Workman* 51, no. 2 (1922): 59.

14. Ibid., 60, 63.

15. Marcus Garvey, *Philosophy and Opinions of Marcus Garvey*, vol. 2 (Paterson, N.J.: Frank Cass, 1925), 201. The Black Star Line was founded in 1919.

16. "Letter from Alexandria, Va.," *Christian Recorder*, July 11, 1868.

17. "Mr. John H. Smith's Reading, in Sansom St. Hall," *Christian Recorder*, February 4, 1865.

18. George Henry Boker, "The Black Regiment," in *"Words for the Hour": A New Anthology of American Civil War Poetry*, ed. Faith Barrett and Cristanne Miller (Amherst: University of Massachusetts Press, 2005), 112–14.

19. Uriah Boston, letter to the editor, *Frederick Douglass' Paper*, April 20, 1855.

20. Tellingly, however, Dunbar-Nelson omits Boker's name, in contrast to her usual practice of identifying the (African American) authors of the works she recommends.

21. I omit here, for reasons of space, discussion of African American pastiches of "The Light Brigade," but see, for example, "Charge of the Border Ruffian Brigade," *Provincial Freeman*, July 19, 1856, which mocks the cowardice of a proslavery mob that sacked Lawrence, Kansas, in 1856.

22. James Madison Bell, *The Poetical Works of James Madison Bell* (Lansing, Mich.: Wynkoop, Hallenbeck, Crawford, 1901), 71. I am grateful to Cristanne Miller for alerting me to this poem.

23. Ibid., 65, 73.

24. Ibid., 73. The word "All" is italicized in all the anthologized versions of the poem I have seen, but the copies of the original 1864 pamphlet and the 1901 edition I have consulted (one of each) do not italicize it.

25. James Madison Bell and Philip A. Bell do not seem to have been related. Both were living in San Francisco in the 1860s, which helps account for their collaboration.

26. For another example, see James Thomas Franklin, "The Battle of Port Hudson," in *Jessamine Poems* (Memphis, Tenn.: [J. T. Franklin?], 1900), which returns to both the event George Henry Boker celebrates and the Tennysonian model he uses to do so:

> A regiment black as night
> Behold the cannon on their left
> And cannons on their right
> . . . .
> 'Tis but the gaping jaws of death
> The open gates of hell
> . . . .
> And thro' the storm of shot and shell
> Rushed into eternity.

27. Paul Laurence Dunbar, "The Colored Soldiers," *The Collected Poetry of Paul Laurence Dunbar*, ed. Joanne M. Braxton (Charlottesville: University Press of Virginia, 1993), 51.

28. Alfred Tennyson, *Tennyson: A Selected Edition*, ed. Christopher Ricks (Berkeley: University of California Press, 1989), 511.

29. Dunbar, "The Colored Soldiers," 51–52.

30. Jennifer Terry, "'When Dey 'Listed Colored Soldiers': Paul Laurence Dunbar's Poetic Engagement with the Civil War, Masculinity, and Violence," *African American Review* 41 (Summer 2007): 269.

31. H. T. Kealing, "Titular Twaddle," *Christian Recorder*, October 26, 1882.

32. Perhaps the first instance in which "The Light Brigade" is invoked to address this failure comes in Henry McNeal Turner's 1868 speech before the Georgia legislature.

Speaking on behalf of the newly elected African American representatives whom the legislature is refusing to seat, Turner states: "We are in a position somewhat similar to that of the famous 'Light Brigade,' of which Tennyson says, they had

'Cannon to right of them,
Cannon to left of them,
Cannon in front of them,
Volleyed and thundered.'"

"On the Eligibility of Colored Members to Seats in the Georgia Legislature" (1868), reprinted in *Respect Black: The Writings and Speeches of Henry McNeal Turner*, ed. Edwin S. Redkey (New York: Arno Press, 1971), 28.

33. W. E. B. Du Bois, *The Souls of Black Folk*, ed. Henry Louis Gates Jr. and Terri Hume Oliver (New York: Norton, 1999), 33.

34. Ibid., 30, emphasis added.

CHAPTER 11. ANOTHER LONG BRIDGE

1. A Member of Congress [Seth M. Gates], "Slavery in the District: The Escape," *New York Evangelist*, September 8, 1842.

2. Seth M. Gates, "The Long Bridge—The Escape," *Prisoner's Friend: A Monthly Magazine Devoted to Criminal Reform, Philosophy, Science, Literature, and Art*, September 10, 1845, 96.

3. Sarah J. Clarke, "The Escape," *Liberator*, September 20, 1844, 152; John Kemble Laskey, "The 'Long Bridge,'" *Liberator*, August 22, 1845, 136.

4. Frederick Douglass, "No Union with Slaveholders" (presented in Boston, May 28, 1844).

5. Jane Grey Swisshelm, *Half a Century* (Chicago: Jansen, McClurg, 1880), 129; Frances Harper, *Iola Leroy; or, Shadows Uplifted* (New York: Oxford University Press, 1988), 98; Norman B. Wood, *The White Side of a Black Subject: Enlarged and Brought Down to Date; A Vindication of the Afro-American Race: From the Landing of Slaves at St. Augustine, Florida, in 1565, to the Present Time* (Chicago: American Publishing House, 1897), 140.

6. William Wells Brown, *Clotel; or, The President's Daughter* (1853), ed. Robert S. Levine (Boston: Bedford/St. Martin, 2000); hereafter cited parenthetically.

7. In anticipation of the first installment of *Hagar's Daughter* two months later, the January 1901 *Colored American Magazine* establishes the relationship between these two authors in a number of ways, including Hopkins's biographical sketches of both Brown and herself. In her otherwise third-person sketch of Brown's life and work, Hopkins mentions in the first person that her father had introduced Brown in 1844 at an event in Aurora, New York. Her biography mentions Brown in connection with the essay "The Evils of Intemperance and Their Remedies," which she describes as her first

literary effort. Finally, portraits of Brown and Hopkins appear on facing pages, visually illustrating him as her predecessor, as he appears on the left page and she follows on the right.

8. Lois Brown demonstrates that *Hagar's Daughter* is "indebted to three works by and about William Wells Brown," especially an 1856 biography by Josephine Brown, his daughter, and Brown's own autobiographical account of his work for a slave trader named Walker. Lois Brown, *Pauline Elizabeth Hopkins: Black Daughter of the Revolution* (Chapel Hill: University of North Carolina Press, 2008), 346.

9. Pauline Hopkins, *Contending Forces: A Romance Illustrative of Negro Life North and South* (Boston: Colored Co-operative, 1900), 15.

10. Ibid.

11. Charles Chesnutt, *The Marrow of Tradition* (Boston: Houghton, Mifflin, 1901), 238.

12. Frederick L. Hoffman, *Race Traits and Tendencies of the American* Negro (New York: Macmillan, 1896), 176.

13. Ibid.

14. Paul Brandon Barringer, *The American Negro: His Past and Future* (Raleigh, N.C.: Edwards and Broughton, 1900), 13.

15. Ibid., 25. Interestingly, the Colored Co-Operative Publishing Company ran an advertisement in the April 1901 issue of *Colored American Magazine* (in which the second installment of *Hagar's Daughter* appeared) that publicized Hopkins's first novel *Contending Forces* alongside a forthcoming response to Barringer by Joseph E. Hayne titled *Progress or Reversion, Which?*

16. Chas. H. Williams, "The Race Problem," *Colored American Magazine*, September 1901, 355.

17. Ibid., 356.

18. Hanna Wallinger suggests that in *Hagar's Daughter*, slavery tears apart the white family in addition to the more traditional representation of black familial separations. Hanna Wallinger, *Pauline E. Hopkins: A Literary Biography* (Athens: University of Georgia Press, 2005), 174.

19. See Augusta Rohrbach, "To Be Continued: Double Identity, Multiplicity and Antigenealogy as Narrative Strategies in Pauline Hopkins' Magazine Fiction," *Callaloo* 22 (Spring 1999): 483; Rohrbach's excellent essay on Hopkins's magazine fiction has helpfully described this narrative mode as "antigenealogy," which disrupts the "monolithic (and hegemonic) conceptions of race promoted by generic conventions of the novel." Lois Brown also views intertexuality as this novel's primary tactic, examining at length not only allusions to the life and works of William Wells Brown but also Stowe's *Uncle Tom's Cabin*, Milton's *Paradise Lost*, and Tennyson's *Maud*. See chapter 12 of *Pauline Elizabeth Hopkins*.

20. Pauline Hopkins, *Hagar's Daughter* (1901–2), in *The Magazine Novels of Pauline Hopkins* (New York: Oxford University Press, 1990), 53; hereafter cited parenthetically.

21. William Benjamin Smith, *The Color Line: A Brief in Behalf of the Unborn* (New York: McClure, Phillips, 1905), 15.

22. Ibid., 10.

23. Wallinger, *Pauline E. Hopkins*, 175.

24. *Hagar's Daughter* broadcasts its engagement with atavism most explicitly through the character Cuthbert Sumner's remarks about narrowly escaping marriage to a mixed-race woman: "The mere thought of the grinning, toothless black hag that was her foreparent would forever rise between us" (271).

25. Dana Seitler, *Atavistic Tendencies: The Culture of Science in American Modernity* (Minneapolis: University of Minnesota Press, 2008), 2.

26. Ibid., 7.

27. Ibid., 20.

28. Lois Brown also observes that in *Hagar's Daughter*, Hopkins "focused deliberately on the lingering manifestations of slavery . . . that challenged notions of a reunited nation" (*Pauline Elizabeth Hopkins*, 319).

29. Lara Langer Cohen, "Notes from the State of Saint Domingue: The Practice of Citation in *Clotel*," Chapter 9, p. 164 in this volume.

30. See Charles Sumner, *A Bridge from Slavery to Freedom* (Washington: Polkinhorn and Sons, 1864), which presents the text of Sumner's speeches on the Freedmen's Bureau in the Senate on June 13 and 15, 1864.

31. S. C. Cross, "The Negro Problem and the Sunny South; or, Prejudice the Problem," *Colored American Magazine*, July 1902, 193.

32. Ibid., 197.

33. Rohrbach observes, "in a radical way, Hopkins' use of genre rebukes conventional notions of racial inheritance and identity by turning the argument away from the monolithic (and hegemonic) conceptions of race promoted by the generic conventions of the novel" ("To Be Continued," 483).

34. A character in Charles Chesnutt's *The Marrow of Tradition* describes the future of the African American race as "a tremendously interesting problem. It is a serial story which we are all reading, and which grows in vital interest with each successive installment" (51). This relationship between race progress and serial narrative progress further illuminates Hopkins's formal tactics in *Hagar's Daughter*.

35. Kristina Brooks "Mammies, Bucks, and Wenches: Minstrelsy, Racial Pornography, and Racial Politics in Pauline Hopkins's *Hagar's Daughter*," in *The Unruly Voice: Rediscovering Pauline Elizabeth Hopkins*, ed. John Cullen Gruesser (Champaign: University of Illinois Press, 1996), 133.

36. Ibid., 134. Also see Susan Hays Bussey, "Whose Will Be Done? Self-Determination in Pauline Hopkins's *Hagar's Daughter*," *African American Review* 39, no. 3 (2005): 299–313.

37. Claudia Tate notes that this "failed romantic consummation aborts the story of ideal family formation" (*Domestic Allegories of Political Desire: The Black Heroine's Text at the Turn of the Century* [New York: Oxford University Press, 1992], 200).

CHAPTER 12. "PHOTOGRAPHS TO ANSWER OUR PURPOSES"

1. Lugenbeel to Washington, December 2, 1854, ACS Papers, Library of Congress, Washington, D.C., reel 242, letter 131.

2. Irony and appropriation in abolitionists pictures is discussed by Phillip Lapsansky, "Graphic Discord: Abolitionist and Antiabolitionist Images," in *The Abolitionist Sisterhood: Women's Political Culture in Antebellum America*, ed. Jean Fagan Yellin and John C. Van Horne (Ithaca, N.Y.: Cornell University Press, 1994), 208–9; and detailed throughout Marcus Wood's *Blind Memory: Visual Representations of Slavery in England and America, 1780–1865* (New York: Routledge, 2000).

3. John Sekora, "Black Message/White Envelope: Genre, Authenticity, and Authority in the Antebellum Slave Narrative," *Callaloo* 32 (Summer 1987): 482–515.

4. The literature on the American Colonization Society is vast. A foundational text focused on the institutional identity of the ACS is P. J. Staudenraus, *The African Colonization Movement, 1816–1865* (New York: Columbia University Press, 1961). For scholarship that attends to both colonizationists and settlers in a more balanced fashion, see, for example, Claude Clegg, *The Price of Liberty: African Americans and the Making of Liberia* (Chapel Hill: University of North Carolina Press, 2004); and Eric Burin, *Slavery and the Peculiar Solution: A History of the American Colonization Society* (Gainesville: University Press of Florida, 2005).

5. This tension between sameness and difference in colonization rhetoric has already been observed by historians in a number of contexts. For a discussion of this in terms of nation and citizenship, see Nicholas Guyatt, "'The Outskirts of Our Happiness': Race and the Lure of Colonization in the Early Republic," *Journal of American History* 95, no. 4 (2009): 986–1011; Guyatt argues that before 1840, removal policies toward blacks and Native Americans were shaped by the logic that separation of the races would promote the uplift of nonwhite peoples. John Saillant and David Kazanjian locate the rhetoric of imitation and sameness of African Americans in Liberia to European Americans in the United States in Jefferson's Enlightenment values and emerging liberal thought. See John Saillant, "The American Enlightenment in Africa: Jefferson's Colonizationism and Black Virginians' Migration to Liberia, 1776–1840," *Eighteenth-Century Studies* 31 (Spring 1998): 273; and David Kazanjian, "Racial Governmentality: The African Colonization Movement," in *The Colonizing Trick: National Culture and Imperial Citizenship in Early America* (Minneapolis: University of Minnesota Press, 2003), 100. Analysis of colonization pictures demonstrates that this verbal rhetoric also has visual manifestations. See Dalila Scruggs, "'The Love of Liberty Has Brought Us Here': The American Colonization Society and the Imaging of African-American Settlers in Liberia" (Ph.D. diss., Harvard University, 2010).

6. "For the Colonization Herald [no title]," *Colonization Herald*, June 17, 1837, 214.

7. Ibid.

8. These issues receive greater treatment in Scruggs, "Love of Liberty," chap. 2. For settler life, see also Tom W. Shick, *Behold the Promised Land: A History of Afro-American Settler Society in Nineteenth-Century Liberia* (Baltimore: Johns Hopkins University Press, 1980).

9. Ann M. Shumard, *A Durable Memento: Portraits by Augustus Washington, African American Daguerreotypist* (Washington, D.C.: National Portrait Gallery, 1999), 2; Scruggs, "Love of Liberty," 17.

10. Examples of Washington's Hartford photographs are housed at the Connecticut Historical Society, the Smithsonian Institution's National Museum of American History, as well as in private collections.

11. Shumard, *A Durable Memento*, 5.

12. Ibid., 4.

13. Ibid., 11.

14. Peter B. Hales, *Silver Cities: The Photography of American Urbanization, 1839–1915* (Philadelphia: Temple University Press, 1984), 21.

15. For example, Grafton T. Brown was an artist, lithographer, and publisher who drew and published. See Samella Lewis, *African American Art and Artists* (Berkeley: University of California Press, 1990), 34–36.

16. "View of Monrovia," *African Repository* 27, no. 2 (February 1851): 51–52; also on the back cover of the *Eighteenth Annual Report of New-York Colonization Society* (1850).

17. James Fairhead et al., eds., *African-American Exploration in West Africa: Four Nineteenth-Century Diaries* (Bloomington: Indiana University Press, 2003), 13.

18. For a discussion of tropical medicine and reaction to malaria, see Philip D. Curtin, *The Image of Africa: British Ideas and Action, 1780–1850* (Madison: University of Wisconsin Press, 1964), esp. 71–80.

19. Ibid., 80–81.

20. Dolores A. Kilgo, *Likeness and Landscape: Thomas M. Easterly and the Art of the Daguerreotype* (Saint Louis: Missouri Historical Society Press, 1994), 157.

21. "View of Monrovia, Liberia," *New-York Colonization Journal*, January 1856.

22. Mary Louise Pratt, *Imperial Eyes: Travel Writing and Transculturation* (New York: Routledge, 1992), 201.

23. "View of Monrovia, Liberia."

24. Ibid.

25. "Monrovia and Messurado River, as Seen from the Lighthouse on the Summit of Cape Messurado," *New-York Colonization Journal*, June 1856.

26. John W. Reps, *Cities on Stone: Nineteenth-Century Lithograph Images of the Urban West* (Fort Worth, Tex.: Amon Carter Museum, 1976), 30.

27. Hales, *Silver Cities*, 29.

28. Beaumont Newhall, *The Daguerreotype in America* (New York: Duell, Sloan and Pearce, 1961), 84.

29. "Extracts from Liberia Correspondents," *New-York Colonization Journal*, August 1855.

30. Gerry Beegan, "The Mechanization of the Image: Facsimile, Photography, and Fragmentation in Nineteenth-century Wood Engraving" *Journal of Design History* 8, no. 4 (1995): 257–74.

31. In *Visual Communication and the Graphic Arts: Photographic Technologies in the Nineteenth Century* (London: R. R. Bowker Company, 1974), Estelle Jussim suggests that an image's artistic medium is a "syntax," or culturally defined mode of representation, constructed through the use of a material channel (the physical medium of communication

such as wood, metal, or paper) and a code (message units such as lines, dots, or half-tones). As a result, information is never completely extracted from, but instead is shaped by, its code, the limitations of which can distort or even obliterate a particular message (7–17). *Visual Communication* adds to the scholarship of William Ivins Jr., *Prints and Visual Communication* (Cambridge, Mass.: Harvard University Press, 1953).

32. Wilson Jeremiah Moses, ed., *Liberian Dreams: Back-to-Africa Narratives from the 1850s* (University Park: Pennsylvania State University Press, 1998), xxix.

33. See William Nesbit, *Four Months in Liberia; or, African Colonization Exposed* (1855), reprinted in Moses, *Liberian Dreams*, 79–125.

34. Ibid., 89.

35. Ibid., 94.

36. For changing symbolism of swamp, see David Miller's book *Dark Eden: The Swamp in Nineteenth-Century American Culture* (Cambridge: Cambridge University Press, 1989).

37. Martin Delany, introduction to *Four Months in Liberia*, reprinted in Moses, *Liberian Dreams*, 85.

38. Miller, *Dark Eden*, 1.

39. *New-York Colonization Journal*, September 1855, 2 (italics in original).

40. Thanks to Marie Tyler-McGraw for drawing my attention to this ongoing debate.

41. J. W. Lugenbeel, *Sketches of Liberia: Comprising a Brief Account of the Geography, Climate, Productions, and Diseases, of the Republic of Liberia* (Washington, D.C.: C. Alexander, Printer, 1850), 5 (his italics).

42. Allan Sekula, "Traffic in Photographs," *Art Journal* 41 (Spring 1981): 15–16.

43. Dan Schiller, "Realism, Photography and Journalistic Objectivity in Nineteenth-Century America," *Studies in the Anthropology of Visual Communication* 4, no. 2 (1977): 86–98, esp. 92–93.

44. Bell I. Wiley, ed., *Slaves No More: Letters from Liberia, 1833–1869* (Lexington: University Press of Kentucky, 1980), 7–8.

45. "View of Bassa Cove," *Colonization Herald*, June 17, 1837, 214.

46. This is part of R. J. M. Blackett's argument to demonstrate that African Americans are integral to the transatlantic success of the abolition movement in *Building an Antislavery Wall: Black Americans in the Atlantic Abolitionist Movement, 1830–1860* (Baton Rouge: Louisiana State University Press, 1983), 58–59.

47. Ibid.

48. For most of Washington's major published letters, see Moses, *Liberian Dreams*, 181–223.

49. The evolution of Washington's relationship with the Liberian landscape is more thoroughly examined in Scruggs, "Love of Liberty," chap. 2.

50. Moses, *Liberian Dreams*, 201.

51. Carol Johnson was the first to make the link between his landscapes and his written claims to objectivity. See "Faces of Freedom: Portraits from the American Colonization Society Collection," *Daguerreian Annual* (1996): 272. Washington's use of photographic

language as a rhetorical strategy for claiming accuracy and truth telling is the focus of
Marcy Dinius's scholarship on Washington in "My daguerreotype shall be a true one":
Daguerreotypy and the Liberian Colonization Movement," in Dinius, *The Camera and The
Pen: American Print Culture and Literature in the Daguerreian Age* (forthcoming).

52. Augustus Washington's "Liberia as It Is, 1854" appeared in *Frederic Douglass'
Paper* December 15, 1854, and *New York Tribune*, n.d.; full text in Moses, *Liberian
Dreams*, 205.

53. Lugenbeel to Dr. Henry J. Roberts, December 4, 1854, ACS Papers, Library of
Congress, reel 242, letter 132.

54. "Letter from Augustus Washington," *African Repository* 31, no. 10 (October
1855): 296.

55. For instances where Washington's "view of the anchorage" was reprinted, see "S.
A. Benson, President of Liberia," *National Magazine: Devoted to Literature, Art and Reli-
gion*, April 1856, 311; Rev. Morris Officer, *Western Africa, a Mission Field* (Pittsburgh: W.
S. Haven, 1856); and Thomas McCants Stewart, *Liberia: The Americo-African Republic*
(New York: Edward O. Jenkins' Sons, 1886). For examples of how the general composi-
tion was maintained in later representations of Monrovia, see "Monrovia," *Colonization
Herald*, September 1858; and "A Tour in Monrovia," *Frank Leslie's Illustrated Newspaper*,
July 24, 1858.

56. Charles G. Steffen, "Newspapers for Free: The Economies of Newspaper Circulation in the Early Republic," *Journal of the Early Republic* 23 (Autumn 2003): 409–10.

57. Meredith L. McGill, *American Literature and the Culture of Reprinting, 1834–1853*
(Philadelphia: University of Pennsylvania Press, 2003), 5.

58. Isabelle Lehuu, "The 'Lady's Book' and the Female Vernacular in Print Culture"
in *Carnival on the Page: Popular Print Media in Antebellum America* (Chapel Hill: University of North Carolina Press, 2000), 103.

59. "Editor's Table," *Ladies' Repository*, March 1859.

60. "Ashmun Street, Monrovia," *Colonization Herald* (October 1858), front page.

61. Alexander M. Cowan, *Liberia, as I Found It, in 1858* (Frankfurt, Ky.: A. G.
Hodges, 1858), quoted in "A Tour in Monrovia," *Frank Leslie's Illustrated Journal*, July 24,
1858, reprinted in the *Colonization Herald*, October 1858.

62. From the *Journal of the Alabama House of Representatives* (1840), 17, quoted in Ira
Berlin, *Slaves Without Masters: The Free Negro in the Antebellum South* (New York: Pantheon Books, 1975), 213.

63. For example, the acknowledgments on frontispiece of Morris Officer's *Western
Africa, a Mission Field* demonstrates that John B. Pinney, agent of the New-York Colonization Society and editor of its journal, provided plates for the reproduction of the harbor
view of Monrovia as well as a picture of President Joseph Jenkins Roberts's presidential
mansion. There is no indication that Pinney passed along the view of Monrovia from the
lighthouse. If he did, then Morris Officer did not use it.

64. "Negroland and the Negroes," *Harper's New Monthly Magazine*, July 1856, 161–
78. This article is an extract from a larger volume named *Western Africa: Its History, Present*

Condition, and Future Prospects, by Rev. J. Leighton Wilson (New York: Harper and Brothers, 1856).

65. "Negroland and the Negroes," 162.

66. Ibid.

67. Stewart, *Liberia*, 91.

68. Little other textual or visual analysis has been done on Stewart's *Liberia*. For an extremely brief mention, see Charles E. Wynes, "T. McCants Stewart: Peripatetic Black South Carolinian," *South Carolina Historical Magazine*, October 1979, 311–17.

69. In fact, most of the images in Stewart's book are appropriated from ACS literature published before 1866.

70. See Stewart, *Liberia,* 39.

71. Ibid., 89.

72. Augustus Washington, "Liberia As It Is" *New-York Colonization Journal* (November 1854).

73. This is to borrow John Sekora's phrase.

74. The "view from the anchorage" is reproduced in Clegg, *The Price of Liberty*; and in Max Belcher, Svend E. Holsoe, and Bernard L. Herman, *A Land and Life Remembered: Americo-Liberian Folk Architecture* (Athens: University of Georgia Press, 1988).

75. This observation follows Tanya Sheehan's critique of scholarship of the "image of the black" which often "run[s] the risk of oversimplifying the relationship between the (always mediated) image and the (always performing) body." Tanya Sheehan, review of *Portraits of a People: Picturing African Americans in the Nineteenth Century*, by Gwendolyn DuBois Shaw, *caa.reviews*, September 6, 2007, doi: 10.3202/caa.reviews.2007.76.

76. These conclusions rely heavily on Meredith McGill's investigation of reprinting as well as Marcus Wood's analysis of the function of woodcut illustrations in Henry Bibb's 1849 slave narrative. See McGill, *American Literature*, 39; and Wood, *Blind Memory*, 120.

CHAPTER 13. NETWORKING *UNCLE TOM'S CABIN*

1. See http://utc.iath.virginia.edu/. Railton has "directed" two other sites: an electronic archive, "Mark Twain in His Times"; and another for Faulkner, "Absalom, Absalom! Electronic, Interactive! Chronology."

2. "What we discover after all this time," said Professor Gates of Harvard, "is that it is the black American linguistic voice which forms the structuring principle of the great American novel, and that ain't bad." See Anthony DePalma, "A Scholar Finds Huck Finn's Voice in Twain's Writing About a Black Youth," *New York Times*, July 7, 1992. On Melville, see Sterling Stuckey, *African Culture and Melville's Art: The Creative Process in "Benito Cereno" and "Moby-Dick"* (London: Oxford University Press, 2008); on Poe ("no early American writer is more important to the concept of American Africanism than Poe"), see Toni Morrison, *Playing in the Dark: Whiteness and the Literary Imagination* (Cambridge, Mass.: Harvard University Press, 1992), 32.

NOTES TO PAGES 234–237

3. On the nineteenth-century origins of notions of the "web," before the advent of the Internet, see Laura Otis, *Networking: Communicating with Bodies and Machines in the Nineteenth Century* (Ann Arbor: University of Michigan Press, 2001); Tom Standage, *The Victorian Internet: The Remarkable Story of the Telegraph and the Nineteenth Century's Online Pioneers* (New York: Walker, 1998); Matt Cohen, *The Networked Wilderness: Communicating in Early New England* (Minneapolis: University of Minnesota Press, 2010); Mark C. Taylor, *The Moment of Complexity: Emerging Network Culture* (Chicago: University of Chicago Press, 2003); Christine L. Borgman, *Scholarship in the Digital Age: Information, Infrastructure, and the Internet* (Cambridge, Mass.: MIT Press, 2007).

4. For a critique of presumptions about new media and older literary forms, see Meredith L. McGill and Andrew Parker, "The Future of the Literary Past," *PMLA* 125, no. 4, Special Topic: Literary Criticism for the Twenty-First Century (October 2010): 959–67.

5. Thomas F. Gossett, *Uncle Tom's Cabin and American Culture* (Dallas: Southern Methodist University Press, 1985); Robert B. Stepto, "Sharing the Thunder: the Literary Exchanges of Harriet Beecher Stowe, Henry Bibb, and Frederick Douglass," in *A Home Elsewhere: Reading African American Classics in the Age of Obama* (Cambridge, Mass.: Harvard University Press, 2010), 100–120; Lauren Berlant, "Poor Eliza," in *The Female Complaint: The Unfinished Business of Sentimentality in American Culture* (Durham, N.C.: Duke University Press, 2008), 33–68; Robert S. Levine, *Martin Delany, Frederick Douglass, and the Politics of Representative Identity* (Chapel Hill: University of North Carolina Press, 1997); Denise Kohn, Sarah Meer, and Emily B. Todd, eds., *Transatlantic Stowe: Harriet Beecher Stowe and European Culture* (Iowa City: University of Iowa Press, 2006); Sarah Meer, *Uncle Tom Mania: Slavery, Minstrelsy and Transatlantic Culture in the 1850s* (Athens: University of Georgia Press, 2005); Claire Parfait, *The Publishing History of "Uncle Tom's Cabin," 1852–2002* (Burlington, Vt.: Ashgate, 2007); Jo-Ann Morgan, *"Uncle Tom's Cabin" as Visual Culture* (Columbia: University of Missouri Press, 2007).

6. Walter Mignolo, *Local Histories/Global Designs: Coloniality, Subaltern Knowledges, and Border Thinking* (Princeton, N.J.: Princeton University Press, 2000); see esp. chaps. 4 and 5 on the politics of language and culture and the politics of language and knowledge.

7. Toni Morrison, "Unspeakable Things Unspoken: The Afro-American Presence in American Literature," *Michigan Quarterly Review* 28, no. 1 (Winter 1989): 3.

8. Harriet Beecher Stowe, *Uncle Tom's Cabin; or, Life Among the Lowly*, ed. with introduction by Ann Douglas (New York: Penguin, 1987), 182. Parenthetical citations are to this edition.

9. Mary Boykin Chestnut, *Mary Chestnut's Civil War*, ed. C. Vann Woodward (New Haven, Conn.: Yale University Press, 1981), 168.

10. Barbara Jeanne Fields, "Ideology and Race in American History," in *Region, Race, and Reconstruction: Essays in Honor of C. Vann Woodward*, ed. J. Morgan Kousser and James M. McPherson (New York: Oxford University Press, 1982), 149. See also Fields, "Slavery, Race and Ideology in the United States of America," *New Left Review* 181 (May–June 1990): 95–118.

11. Morrison, "Unspeakable Things," 11.

12. Cindy Weinstein, ed., *The Cambridge Companion to Harriet Beecher Stowe* (New York: Cambridge University Press, 2004).

13. George Fredrickson, *The Black Image in the White Mind: The Debate on Afro-American Character and Destiny, 1817–1914* (Middletown, Conn.: Wesleyan University Press, 1987), 110.

14. Morrison, "Unspeakable Things," 3, 11.

15. Frederick Douglass, *Narrative of the Life of Frederick Douglass, An American Slave* (1845; rpt. New York: Cambridge University Press, 2011), 33.

16. Ada Ferrer, "Talk About Haiti: The Archive and the Atlantic's Haitian Revolution," in *Tree of Liberty: Cultural Legacies of the Haitian Revolution in the Atlantic World*, ed. Doris L. Garraway (Charlottesville: University of Virginia Press, 2008), 21–40.

17. Ibid., 35.

18. See Linda Williams, *Playing the Race Card: Melodramas of Black and White from Uncle Tom to O. J. Simpson* (Princeton, N.J.: Princeton University Press, 2002), 59–60.

19. Michel-Rolph Trouillot, *Silencing the Past: Power and the Production of History* (Boston: Beacon Press, 1995), 71.

20. Harriet Beecher Stowe, *The Key to Uncle Tom's Cabin: Presenting the Original Facts and Documents upon Which the Story Is Founded, Together with Corroborative Statements Verifying the Truth of the Work* (Boston: John P. Jewett, 1854), 5; *Uncle Tom's Cabin*, European ed. (Leipzig: Bernard Tauchnitz, 1852), v.

21. Thanks to David Kazanjian who noted, in his comment at the March 2010 conference "Early African American Print Culture in Theory and Practice," that we might add to this circuit the nineteenth-century Yucatán.

22. Julia Stern, "Spanish Masquerade and the Drama of Racial Identity in *Uncle Tom's Cabin*," in *Passing and the Fictions of Identity*, ed. Elaine K. Ginsberg (Durham, N.C.: Duke University Press, 1996), 103–30; on the historical unlikelihood of the George Harris Spanish masquerade, see 107–8, 110–11.

23. See Aníbal Quijano and Immanuel Wallerstein, "Americanity as a Concept, or the Americas in the Modern World System," *International Social Science Journal* 44 (November 1992): 549–57.

24. Susan Gillman and Kirsten Silva Gruesz, "Worlding America: The Hemispheric Text-Network," chap. 14 in *A Companion to American Literary Studies*, ed. Caroline F. Levander and Robert S. Levine (Oxford: Wiley-Blackwell, 2011), 232. See also Daniel L. Selden, "Text Networks," *Ancient Narrative* 8 (2009): 1–23.

25. See Helen Hunt Jackson's letters in which she made this (or similar comments), reprinted in *The Indian Reform Letters of Helen Hunt Jackson, 1879–1885*, ed. Valerie Sherer Mathes (Norman: University of Oklahoma Press, 1998), 258 (to Thomas Bailey Aldrich, May 4, 1883), 307 (to William Hayes Ward, January 1, 1884), and 319 (to Amelia Stone Quinton, April 2, 1884).

26. See Carolyn L. Karcher, "Stowe and the Literature of Social Change," in Weinstein, *Cambridge Companion to Harriet Beecher Stowe*, 210–11.

27. See Beth A. McCoy, "Race and the (Para)Textual Condition," *PMLA* 121 (January 2006): 156–69; on paratextuality and history, see Linda Hutcheon, *The Politics of Postmodernism* (New York: Routledge, 2002), 79–88.

28. See Elizabeth Gudrais, "Networked," *Harvard Magazine*, May–June 2010, http://harvardmagazine.com/2010/05/networked.

CHAPTER 14. THE LYRIC PUBLIC OF *LES CENELLES*

1. Henry Louis Gates Jr., "Canon-Formation, Literary History, and the Afro-American Tradition: From the Seen to the Told," in *Afro-American Literary Study in the 1990s*, ed. Houston A. Baker Jr. and Patricia Redmond (Chicago: University of Chicago Press, 1989), 14–38; Michel Fabre, "The New Orleans Press and French-Language Literature by Creoles of Color," in *Multilingual America: Transnationalism, Ethnicity, and the Language of American Literature*, ed. Werner Sollors (New York: New York University Press, 1998), 29–49.

2. Fabre, "New Orleans Press," 33.

3. See Shirley Elizabeth Thompson, *Exiles at Home: The Struggle to Become American in Creole New Orleans* (Cambridge, Mass.: Harvard University Press, 2009); Thomas F. Haddox, *Fears and Fascinations: Representing Catholicism in the American South* (New York: Fordham University Press, 2005); Caryn Cossè Bell, *Revolution, Romanticism, and the Afro-Creole Protest Tradition in Louisiana, 1718–1868* (Baton Rouge: Louisiana State University Press, 1997). For a critical history of the framing of New Orleans as a historical exception, see Barbara J. Eckstein, *Sustaining New Orleans: Literature, Local Memory, and the Fate of a City* (New York: Routledge, 2006).

4. Virginia Jackson, *Dickinson's Misery: A Theory of Lyric Reading* (Princeton, N.J.: Princeton University Press, 2005), 53.

5. Ibid., 156.

6. Ibid.

7. Michael Warner, *Publics and Counterpublics* (New York: Zone Books, 2002), 82.

8. Alexander G. Weheliye, "After Man," *American Literary History* 20 (Spring-Summer 2008): 321.

9. The relationship between the local and the global has in particular received a great deal of attention. See, for example, Rob Wilson and Wimal Dissanayake, eds., *Global/Local: Cultural Production and the Transnational Imaginary* (Durham, N.C.: Duke University Press, 1996).

10. Warner, *Publics and Counterpublics*, 68

11. Ibid., 66.

12. Meredith L. McGill, "Introduction: The Traffic in Poems," in *The Traffic in Poems: Nineteenth-Century Poetry and Transatlantic Exchange*, ed. Meredith L. McGill (New Brunswick, N.J.: Rutgers University Press, 2008), 1–2.

13. Gates, "Canon-Formation," 25.

14. Jerah Johnson, "*Les Cenelles*: What's in a Name?" *Louisiana History* 31 (Fall 1990): 407–10.

15. *The New Princeton Encyclopedia of Poetry and Poetics*, ed. Alex Preminger and T. V. F. Brogan et al. (Princeton, N.J.: Princeton University Press, 1993), s.v. "apostrophe."

16. Jonathan D. Culler, *The Pursuit of Signs: Semiotics, Literature, Deconstruction* (Ithaca, N.Y.: Cornell University Press, 1981), 61.

17. Ibid., 157.

18. Saidiya V. Hartman, *Scenes of Subjection: Terror, Slavery, and Self-Making in Nineteenth-Century America* (New York: Oxford University Press, 1997), 115–24; Hannah Arendt, *The Human Condition* (Chicago: University of Chicago Press, 1998).

19. *Creole Echoes: The Francophone Poetry of Nineteenth-Century Louisiana*, trans. Norman R. Shapiro, intro. and notes by M. Lynn Weiss (Urbana: University of Illinois Press, 2004), 216–17.

20. Jackson, *Dickinson's Misery*, 159.

21. J. Douglas Kneale, *Romantic Aversions: Aftermaths of Classicism in Wordsworth and Coleridge* (Montreal: McGill-Queen's University Press, 1999), 17.

22. Règine Latortue and Gleason R. W. Adams, trans., *Les Cenelles: A Collection of Poems of Creole Writers of the Early Nineteenth Century* (Boston: G. K. Hall, 1979), 4–5.

23. Ibid., 6–7.

24. Ibid., 16–17.

25. Ibid., 26–27.

26. Warner, *Publics and Counterpublics*, 75.

27. Georg Simmel, "The Stranger," in *The Sociology of Georg Simmel*, ed. and trans. Kurt H. Wolff (Glencoe, Ill.: Free Press, 1950), 402.

28. Warner, *Publics and Counterpublics*, 75–76.

29. See Erving Goffman, *Behavior in Public Places: Notes on the Social Organization of Gatherings* (New York: Free Press of Glencoe, 1963), 83–84:

> When persons are mutually present and not involved together in conversation or other focused interaction, it is possible for one person to stare openly and fixedly at others, gleaning what he can about them while frankly expressing on his face his response to what he sees—for example, the "hate stare" that a Southern white sometimes gratuitously gives to Negroes walking past him. It is also possible for one person to treat others as if they were not there at all, as objects not worthy of a glance, let alone close scrutiny. Moreover, it is possible for the individual, by his staring or his "not seeing," to alter his own appearance hardly at all in consequence of the presence of the others. Here we have "nonperson" treatment; it may be seen in our society in the way we sometimes treat children, servants, Negroes, and mental patients.

> Currently, in our society, this kind of treatment is to be contrasted with the kind generally felt to be more proper in most situations, which will here be called "civil inattention." What seems to be involved is that one gives to another

enough visual notice to demonstrate that one appreciates that the other is present (and that one admits openly to having seen him), while at the next moment
withdrawing one's attention from him so as to express that he does not constitute a target of special curiosity or design.

30. Latortue and Adams, *Les Cenelles*, 114–15.

31. Ibid., 48–49.

32. Ibid., 50–51.

33. Ibid.

34. Ibid., xxxvi–xxxvii.

35. Ibid.

CHAPTER 15. IMAGINING A STATE OF FELLOW CITIZENS

Part of the research for this essay was supported by grants from the Ford Foundation, the American Antiquarian Society, the Library Company of Philadelphia, the Social Science Research Council, and the Vanderbilt University College of Arts and Science. Many thanks to Dana Nelson, Teresa Goddu, and James Grady, as well as Lara Cohen, Jordan Alexander Stein, and the other contributors to this collection, without whom this essay would not have been possible.

1. By the end of the 1840s, only Maine, Massachusetts, Vermont, and Rhode Island
offered unrestricted suffrage to black voters. New York's 1821 constitution retained a $250
freehold estate requirement for black male suffrage while eliminating the same requirement
for white men; Pennsylvania's 1838 constitution restricted suffrage to "white men." In a reversal of the national trend, Rhode Island actually extended the franchise to black men in
1843, partially to gain crucial votes against the Dorr Convention. Anyone interested in the
black state conventions should begin with Philip S. Foner and George E. Walker, eds.,
Proceedings of the Black State Conventions, 1840–1865, 2 vols. (Philadelphia: Temple Univer-
sity Press, 1979–80). For more on the elective franchise in northern states, see Phyllis Field,
The Politics of Race in New York: The Struggle for Black Suffrage in the Civil War Era (Ithaca,
N.Y.: Cornell University Press, 1982); Leslie M. Harris, *In the Shadow of Slavery: African
Americans in New York City, 1626–1863* (Chicago: University of Chicago Press, 2003); Leon
A. Higginbotham Jr., *Shades of Freedom: Racial Politics and Presumptions of the American
Legal Process* (New York: Oxford University Press, 1996); Alex Kissar, *The Right to Vote: The
Contested History of Democracy in the United States* (New York: Basic, 2000); Leon F. Lit-
wack, *North of Slavery: The Negro in the Free States, 1790–1860* (Chicago: University of Chi-
cago Press, 1961); Christopher Malone, *Between Freedom and Bondage: Race, Party, and
Voting Rights in the Antebellum North* (New York: Routledge, 2008); Jane H. Pease and
William H. Pease, *They Who Would Be Free: Blacks' Search for Freedom, 1830–1861* (New
York: Athenaeum, 1974); Benjamin Quarles, *Black Abolitionists* (New York: Oxford University Press, 1977); Rogers Smith, *Civic Ideals: Conflicting Visions of Citizenship in U.S. History*

(New Haven, Conn.: Yale University Press, 1997); Xi Wang, "Make 'Every Slave Free, and Every Freeman a Voter': The African American Construction of Suffrage Discourse in the Age of Emancipation," in *Contested Democracy: Freedom, Race, and Power in American History*, ed. Manisha Sinha and Penny Von Eschen (New York: Columbia University Press, 2007); Mark S. Weiner, *Black Trials: Citizenship from the Beginnings of Slavery to the End of Caste* (Ann Arbor: University of Michigan Press, 2004); and Nicholas Wood, "'A Sacrifice on the Altar of Slavery': Doughface Politics and Black Disenfranchisement in Pennsylvania, 1837–1838," *Journal of the Early Republic* 31, no. 1 (2011): 75–106.

2. See Nancy Isenberg, *Sex and Citizenship in Antebellum America* (Chapel Hill: University of North Carolina Press, 1998), 15–41. Isenberg suggests that "such conventions had a constitutional precedent derived from the right of the people to assemble and petition the government" that offered a recognizable venue and structure for politics despite the participants' legal status (16).

3. As Wayne D. Moore argues of Frederick Douglass's constitutional politics, by exercising their right to sovereignty, the delegates become a part of the sovereign people; *Constitutional Rights and Powers of the People* (Princeton: Princeton University Press, 1996), 8–10. See also Nikhil Pal Singh, *Black Is a Country: Race and the Unfinished Struggle for Democracy* (Cambridge, Mass.: Harvard University Press, 2004), 18–19.

4. The black state conventions form the core of Jane and William Pease's 1974 analysis of the resurgence of political action in black activism of the 1840s (Pease and Pease, *They Who Would Be Free*); see also Jane H. Pease and William H. Pease, "Negro Conventions and the Problem of Black Leadership," *Journal of Black Studies* 2 (September 1971): 29–44. As Foner and Walker rightfully observe, "for keen analyses of the issues outlined and for breadth of research and argument, these addresses are among the outstanding political documents of the period," reflecting "a cross-section of this community" (*Proceedings*, 1: xv–xvi). More recently, Leslie Alexander presents New York's black state convention movement as central to black politics and identity formation during the 1840s; see *African or American? Black Identity and Political Activism in New York City, 1784–1861* (Chicago: University of Illinois Press, 2008), 102–19.

5. John Ernest, *Liberation Historiography: African American Writers and the Challenge of History, 1794–1861* (Chapel Hill: University of North Carolina Press, 2004), 252.

6. "New York State Convention," *Colored American*, August 29, 1840.

7. The Dorrite Conventions, or "Dorr War," of 1841–42 and their proposed "People's Constitution" provide a potent example of the revolutionary potential in these movements. Isenberg cites the Dorrite Convention as installing "the convention as a new kind of public and political forum and, perhaps for the first time, [sanctioning] revolution as a constitutional rather than a natural right" (*Sex and Citizenship*, 14). See also Ronald P. Formisano, *For the People: American Populist Movements from the Revolution to the 1850s* (Chapel Hill: University of North Carolina Press, 2008), 164–65; and Christian G. Fritz, *American Sovereigns: The People and America's Constitutional Tradition Before the Civil War* (New York: Cambridge University Press, 2008), 246–76.

8. See Litwack, *North of Slavery*, 82; and Dana D. Nelson, *National Manhood: Capitalist Citizenship and the Imagined Fraternity of White Men* (Durham, N.C.: Duke University Press, 1998), 6.

9. The loss of the franchise became foundational to further state-sanctioned stripping of African American civil rights. For instance, in the state of Connecticut's argument against black citizenship in *Crandall v. State of Connecticut* (1834) it was "evidence that that race were not embraced by the framers of the constitution, in the term citizen." See also Smith, *Civic Ideals*, 255–68.

10. The struggle for suffrage in Pennsylvania began even before the 1837–38 Pennsylvania state "Reform Convention" revised the suffrage qualification to read "every white freeman of the age of twenty-one years." See "Appeal of Forty Thousand Citizens, Threatened with Disfranchisement, to the People of Pennsylvania," in *Pamphlets of Protest: An Anthology of Early African American Protest Literature, 1790–1860*, ed. Richard Newman, Patrick Rael, and Phillip Lapsansky (New York: Routledge, 2001), 132–42.

11. Between 1840 and 1865, state conventions occurred in New York, Pennsylvania, Indiana, Michigan, Ohio, New Jersey, Connecticut, Maryland, Illinois, Massachusetts, California, Kansas, Missouri, Louisiana, Virginia, and South Carolina.

12. See, for instance, "A Call for a Convention of the Colored Inhabitants of the State of New York," *Colored American*, June 6, 1840.

13. Conventions usually convened in the state's capital city (Harrisburg, Pa.; Albany, N.Y.; Columbus, Ohio; and so on) in a public hall or church. The 1849 State Convention of the Colored Citizens of Ohio actually met in the Hall of the House of the Representatives in Ohio, spatially linking their activities to the official state government. See "Minutes and Address of the State Convention of the Colored Citizens of Ohio," in Foner and Walker, *Proceedings*, 1:218–40.

14. The usual periodicals included *Colored American, National Anti-Slavery Standard, Pennsylvania Freeman, Liberator*, and *North Star*. The conventions cite the periodical press as *the* medium through which its cause would be fought. As the delegates to the 1848 Pennsylvania convention argued, "we must draft on the benevolence and liberality of the *press*; for without its favourable influence, no cause, however pure, may hope to succeed, and with it truth and justice must prove invincible." Most conventions printed limited copies of their proceedings in pamphlet form, distributing them to states' assemblies and selling them to support the costs of the convention itself and the costs of carrying out its programs. See *Minutes of the State Convention of Coloured Citizens of Pennsylvania, Convened at Harrisburg, December 13th and 14th, 1848* (Philadelphia: Merrihew and Thompson, 1849), 125.

15. The 1840 New York convention, for instance, sold pamphlets for one dollar per dozen out of the office of the *Colored American* in New York City. Charles B. Ray delayed reprinting the proceedings in the *Colored American* until those pamphlets had nearly sold out.

16. See Jay Fliegelman, *Declaring Independence: Jefferson, Natural Language, and the Culture of Performance* (Stanford, Calif.: Stanford University Press, 1993), 144–51.

17. Smith eventually attended the 1841 convention as a delegate from New York City in accordance with his popular nomination. See "Reviving the Black Convention Movement," in *Black Abolitionist Papers,* vol. 3, *The United States, 1830–1846,* ed. Peter C. Ripley (Chapel Hill: University of North Carolina Press, 1991), 345–51; and James Mc-Cune Smith, "Position Defended," *Colored American,* August 15, 1840. Smith most likely penned this letter because the *Colored American* did not print his remarks in opposition to the convention in two previous meetings; see Ripley, *Black Abolitionist Papers,* 3:349 n. 1. For a detailed account of these tumultuous meetings and competing organizations like Thomas Van Rensellaer and David Ruggles's American Reform Board, see Alexander, *African or American,* 103–13.

18. *Colored American,* February 6, 1841. Sterling Stuckey has collected Whipper's letters with a series of responses by "Sidney" in appendix 2 of Sterling Stuckey, ed., *The Ideological Origins of Black Nationalism* (Boston: Beacon Press, 1972).

19. "Colored Convention," *National Anti-Slavery Standard,* June 18, 1840.

20. Ibid.

21. See for instance, "Fifteen Thousand Negro Balance-of-Power-Men Wanted, by the Whigs and Abolitionists!" reprinted in *National Anti-Slavery Standard,* October 9, 1845.

22. "William Whipper's Letters, No. 4," *Colored American,* February 13, 1841. See also Stuckey, *Ideological Origins,* 161. Stuckey frames Sidney's response to Whipper as one of the central texts in the "ideological origins" of black nationalism.

23. "Samuel Ringgold Ward to Nathaniel P. Rogers," in Ripley, *Black Abolitionist Papers,* 3:341.

24. Ibid., emphasis added.

25. For a discussion of "whiteness as property," see Cheryl Harris, "Whiteness as Property," *Harvard Law Review* 106, no. 8 (1993): 1707–91.

26. "Our Future Course," *Colored American,* May 23, 1840. See also Eric Gardner's essay, Chapter 4 in this volume, for another account of how black editors could leverage state conventions to bolster their paper's legitimacy.

27. "The Convention," *Colored American,* June 27, 1840; and "The *National Anti-Slavery Standard* vs. the Convention," *Colored American,* July 11, 1840. See also Pease and Pease, *They Who Would Be Free,* 80–85.

28. "*National Anti-Slavery Standard* vs. the Convention."

29. "The Convention."

30. Field, *Politics of Race in New York,* 45.

31. See Harris, *In the Shadow of Slavery,* 222. Initially led by Charles B. Ray and Philip Bell in 1837, the drive generated a standing corresponding committee of "colored young men" that expanded to the New York Association for the Political Elevation and Improvement of the People of Color by 1839, and ultimately resulted in the New York state convention movement.

32. Field reports that between 1837 and 1842, "the legislature received equal suffrage petitions from blacks in New York, Albany, Oneida, Dutchess, Erie, Onondaga, Sche-

nectady, Orange, Queens, and Rensselaer counties among others" (*Politics of Race*, 45). See *Report of the Debates and Proceedings of the Convention for the Revision of the Constitution of the State of New York: 1846* (Albany: Evening Atlas, 1846), 1029. Garnet was invited to speak before the state's judiciary committee on February 18, 1841. Garnet left the capital confident that the state assembly would repeal the franchise qualification, only to see the provision voted down (46–29) that April. See David E. Swift, *Black Prophets of Justice: Activist Clergy Before the Civil War* (Baton Rouge: Louisiana State University Press, 1989), 125–27; and *Colored American*, March 13, 1841.

33. Martin Delany would later describe the fugitive slave law and the legal restrictions placed on blacks as a "corruption of blood" (*The Condition, Elevation, Emigration, and Destiny of the Colored People of The United States* [1852; reprint, New York: Arno Press, 1968], 37), following the language of the 1793 fugitive slave provision.

34. In Foner and Walker, *Proceedings*, 1:16 (New York, 1840).

35. Ibid., 22.

36. See Smith, *Civic Ideals*, 167.

37. In Foner and Walker, *Proceedings*, 1:10 (New York, 1840). This petition was drafted by a committee led by Patrick H. Reason.

38. Ibid., 16.

39. Ibid.

40. Ibid.

41. Ibid., 18.

42. See Isenberg, *Sex and Citizenship*, xiv; and Smith, *Civic Ideals*, 167.

43. In Foner and Walker, *Proceedings*, 1:6 (New York, 1840). In some ways, the onlookers' approval mirrors the function of authenticating documents in narratives by former slaves.

44. Ibid., 6.

45. My use of "style" builds on Robert Hariman, *Political Style: The Artistry of Power* (Chicago: University of Chicago Press, 1995), 122–23. On the "theatrical" quality of conventions, see Isenberg, *Sex and Citizenship*, 213 n. 10.

46. For more on the distinction between deliberative and persuasive models of civil society, see John L. Brooke, "Consent, Civil Society, and the Public Sphere in the Age of Revolution and the Early American Republic," in *Beyond the Founders: New Approaches to the Political History of the Early American Republic*, ed. Jeffrey L. Pasley, Andrew W. Robertson, and David Waldstreicher (Chapel Hill: University of North Carolina Press, 2004), 207–50; and Jeannine Marie DeLombard, "Apprehending Early African American Literary History," Chapter 5 in this volume.

47. In Foner and Walker, *Proceedings*, 1:6 (New York, 1840).

48. Ibid.

49. Ibid., 12.

50. I borrow the concept of institutional heteroglossia from Mark Schoenfield's description of nineteenth-century British periodicals, "the language of which was often borrowed from prior texts, quoted from contemporary ones under review, and echoed

from one article to the next—was institutionally heteroglossic." See *British Periodicals and Romantic Identity: The "Literary Lower Empire"* (New York: Palgrave Macmillan, 2009), 37.

51. Mikhail Bakhtin, *The Dialogic Imagination: Four Essays*, ed. Michael Holquist, trans. Caryl Emerson and Michael Holquist (Austin: University of Texas Press, 2006), 314.

52. For a discussion of print counterpublics see Craig Calhoun, ed., *Habermas and the Public Sphere* (Cambridge, Mass.: MIT Press, 1992); Nancy Fraser, "Rethinking the Public Sphere: A Contribution to the Critique of Actually Existing Democracy," *Social Text* 25–26 (1990): 56–90; Paul Gilroy, *The Black Atlantic: Modernity and Double Consciousness* (Cambridge, Mass.: Harvard University Press, 1993); Michael Warner, *Publics and Counterpublics* (New York: Zone Books, 2002), 119–21; Catherine Squires, "The Black Press and the State: Attracting Unwanted (?) Attention," in *Counterpublics and the State*, ed. Robert Asen and Daniel C. Brouwer (Albany: State University of New York Press, 2001), 112; and especially Joanna Brooks, "The Early American Public Sphere and the Emergence of a Black Print Counterpublic," *William and Mary Quarterly* 62 (January 2005): 67–92. My argument also draws from the "black Founders" model offered by Richard S. Newman and Roy E. Finkenbine, "Forum: Black Founders in the New Republic: Introduction," *William and Mary Quarterly* 64 (January 2007): 83–94.

53. See Fraser, "Rethinking the Public Sphere," 67; Squires, "The Black Press and the State," 112; and Miranda Marie, *Homegirls in the Public Sphere* (Austin: University of Texas Press, 2003), 133.

54. Ironically, Whipper, who opposed the first New York convention of colored citizens because of its "complexional" nature, was a key member of the 1848 convention in Pennsylvania. For an excellent reading of the complexity of Whipper's evolving positions, see Samuel Otter, *Philadelphia Stories: America's Literature of Race and Freedom* (New York: Oxford University Press, 2010), 107–23, particularly his reading of the resemblances between the 1848 convention's "Appeal to the Colored Citizens" and "Our Elevation," Whipper's 1839 article in the *National Reformer*.

55. This contrasts to the 1840 New York conventions, which were separated by a month in the *Colored American* (November 21 and December 19, 1840). The Pennsylvania appeals appeared in the *Impartial Citizen*, December 5, 1849. The Library Company of Philadelphia and the Historical Society of Pennsylvania hold copies of the proceedings. See also "Suffrage Convention at Harrisburg," December 14, 1848, and "The Harrisburg Convention," December 21, 1848, in the *Pennsylvania Freeman*. The minutes also include a resolution that "the proceedings of this Convention be printed in the *North Star, Daily Republic*, and all other papers friendly" (in Foner and Walker, *Proceedings*, 1:112 (Pennsylvania, 1848).

56. In Foner and Walker, *Proceedings*, 1:123 (Pennsylvania, 1848).

57. Douglass famously proclaimed to his white listeners: "This Fourth of July is *yours*, not *mine*. *You* may rejoice, *I* must mourn" ("What to the Slave Is the Fourth of July?" in *Frederick Douglass Autobiographies*, ed. Henry Louis Gates Jr. [New York: Library of America, 1996], 431).

58. In Foner and Walker, *Proceedings*, 1:128 (Pennsylvania, 1848).

59. On the 1837–38 Pennsylvania constitutional convention, see Eric Ledell Smith, "The End of Black Voting Rights in Pennsylvania: African Americans and the Pennsylvania Constitutional Convention of 1837–1838," *Pennsylvania History* 65 (Summer 1998): 279–99; and Wood, "Sacrifice on the Altar of Slavery."

60. In Foner and Walker, *Proceedings*, 1:128 (Pennsylvania, 1848).

61. Rhode Island used a similar tactic, enfranchising its black citizens in exchange for their opposition to the Dorrites.

62. In Foner and Walker, *Proceedings*, 1:128 (Pennsylvania, 1848).

63. The Dorr Convention and the Continental Congress fall under this category of appeal.

64. In Foner and Walker, *Proceedings*, 1:124 (Pennsylvania, 1848).

65. Isenberg, *Sex and Citizenship*, 21.

66. "Appeal to the Voters," in Foner and Walker, *Proceedings*, 1:123 (Pennsylvania, 1848). See also Sacvan Bercovitch, *The Rites of Assent: Transformations in the Symbolic Construction of America* (New York: Routledge, 1992), 37–49.

67. In Foner and Walker, *Proceedings*, 1:124 (Pennsylvania, 1848).

68. "An Appeal to the Colored Citizens," PA 1848, in Foner and Walker, *Proceedings*, 1:127. See also "Minutes and Address of the State Convention of the Colored Citizens of Ohio" in which delegates ask their audience to read Garnet's "Address" and Walker's *Appeal* (Foner and Walker, *Proceedings*, 1:229).

69. Foner and Walker, *Proceedings*, 1:125 (Pennsylvania, 1848).

70. "Appeal of Forty Thousand Citizens, Threatened with Disfranchisement, to the People of Pennsylvania," in Newman, Rael, and Lapsansky, *Pamphlets of Protest*, 142.

71. The "Appeal of Forty Thousand Citizens," for instance, was read during Pennsylvania's Reform Convention in 1837, sparking a prolonged debate among delegates (almost twenty pages), first over printing and distributing the petition to the convention, and then over a wide range of questions including the petitioners' status as citizens, and the implications of accepting the petition for Pennsylvania's relation to other states. The convention eventually decided to at least print and distribute the petition. See Foner and Walker, *Proceedings*, 1:683–701.

CHAPTER 16. "KEEP IT BEFORE THE PEOPLE"

1. See *Second Annual Report of the American Anti-Slavery Society of America* (New York: Dorr and Butterfield, 1835), n.p.; and *Third Annual Report of the American Anti-Slavery Society* (New York: William S. Dorr, 1836), 32.

2. Jean Fagan Yellin, *Women and Sisters: The Antislavery Feminists in American Culture* (New Haven, Conn.: Yale University Press, 1989), 5.

3. Joseph Horace Kimball, "Pictorials," *Herald of Freedom*, January 23, 1836, 95; and John R. McKivigan and Mitchell Snay, "Religion and the Problem of Slavery in Antebel-

lum America," in *Religion and the Antebellum Debate over Slavery*, ed. John R. McKivigan and Mitchell Snay (Athens: University of Georgia Press, 1998), 6.

4. Notable exceptions here include the work of Jean Fagan Yellin, Karen Halttunen, Elizabeth Clark, Saidiya V. Hartman, and Daniel Wickberg.

5. Karen Halttunen, "Humanitarianism and the Pornography of Pain in Anglo-American Culture," *American Historical Review* 100 (1995): 305.

6. Ibid., 307.

7. Ibid., 304.

8. Ibid.

9. Ibid., 303.

10. Elizabeth B. Clark, "The Sacred Rights of the Weak: Pain, Sympathy, and the Culture of Individual Rights in Antebellum America," *Journal of American History* 82 (September 1995): 478.

11. Adam Smith, *The Theory of Moral Sentiments*, ed. D. D. Raphael and A. L. Macfie (Indianapolis, Ind.: Liberty Fund, 1976), 9, 25.

12. Ibid., 206–7.

13. Ibid., 9.

14. Ibid.

15. See W. J. T. Mitchell, *Iconology: Image, Text, Ideology* (Chicago: University of Chicago Press, 1986), 7–46.

16. *Liberty Almanac* (New York: William Harned, 1848), title page, and Kimball, "Pictorials," 95.

17. Elizur Wright Jr., "Address of the Executive Committee of the American Anti-Slavery Society," in *Third Annual Report of the American Anti-Slavery Society* (New York: William S. Dorr, 1836), n.p.

18. Anonymous verse, quoted in Debbie Lee, *Slavery and the Romantic Imagination* (Philadelphia: University of Pennsylvania Press, 2002), 212.

19. For more on the British origins of American evangelical abolitionism, see Phillip Lapsansky's "Graphic Discord: Abolitionist and Antiabolitionist Images," in *The Abolitionist Sisterhood: Women's Political Culture in Antebellum America*, ed. Jean Fagan Yellin and John C. Van Horne (Ithaca, N.Y.: Cornell University Press, 1994), 201–30.

20. *Third Annual Report of the Board of Managers of the New England Anti-Slavery Society* (Boston: William Lloyd Garrison, 1835), 12–13.

21. David Paul Nord, "The Evangelical Origins of Mass Media in America, 1815–1835," *Journalism Monographs* 88 (May 1994): 24.

22. Harriet Martineau, "Persevere," in *The Liberty Bell*, by Friends of Freedom (Boston: Massachusetts Anti-Slavery Fair, printed by Oliver Johnson, 1843), 33.

23. N. Southard, ed., *The Anti-Slavery Almanac for 1838* (Boston: D. K. Hitchcock, 1837), 5.

24. Ibid.

25. G. B. Armenini, *De' veri precetti della pittura*, quoted in David Freedberg, *The Power of Images* (Chicago: University of Chicago Press, 1989), 2.

26. This and all subsequent biblical citations are quoted from Michael Coogan et al., eds., *The New Oxford Annotated Bible* (New York: Oxford University Press, 2001).

27. Jon Cruz, *Culture on the Margins: The Black Spiritual and the Rise of American Cultural Interpretation* (Princeton, N.J.: University of Princeton Press, 1999), 89.

28. *First Annual Report of the American Anti-Slavery Society* (New York: Dorr and Butterfield, 1834), n.p.

29. See *Anti-Slavery Record*, January 1835, 8; May 1835, 59; and May 1836, 3.

30. S. E. Sewall, "Mr. Prejudice," *Slave's Friend* 2, no. 8 (1836): 3.

31. "The Colored American," *Slave's Friend* 2, no. 11 (1836): 2–3.

32. Letter from Sarah Douglass to William L. Garrison, *Liberator*, June 21, 1839, 98.

33. William Ellery Channing, *The Complete Works of William E. Channing*, reprint ed. (Boston: American Unitarian Association, 1903), 705.

34. Wilson Armistead, *Tribute to the Negro: Being a Vindication of the Moral, Intellectual, and Religious Capabilities of the Colored Portion of Mankind; with Particular Reference to the African Race* (London: Charles Gilpin, 1848), 100–102.

35. Jessica Riskin, *Science in the Age of Sensibility: The Sentimental Empiricists of the French Enlightenment* (Chicago: University of Chicago Press, 2002), 61.

36. Armistead, *Tribute to the Negro*, 100.

37. Charles Ball, *Slavery in the United States: A Narrative of the Life and Adventures of Charles Ball, a Black Man, Who Lived Forty Years in Maryland, South Carolina and Georgia, as a Slave Under Various Masters, and Was One Year in the Navy with Commodore Barney, During the Late War* (New York: John S. Taylor, 1837), xi.

38. See Michael A. Chaney, *Fugitive Vision: Slave Image and Black Identity in Antebellum Narrative* (Bloomington: Indiana University Press, 2008), 1–13.

39. *Second Annual Report*, 48.

40. See Leonard L. Richards, *Gentlemen of Property and Standing: Anti-Abolition Mobs in Jacksonian America* (New York: Oxford University Press, 1971), 52.

41. See *Second Annual Report*, 15–16; and "Colorphobia," *Anti-Slavery Record*, May 1835, 60.

42. Armistead, *Tribute to the Negro*, 102.

43. Ibid., 101.

44. See *Second Annual Report*, 65; and *Third Annual Report*, 33.

45. "The Generous Planter," *Anti-Slavery Record*. August 1835, 91. All subsequent citations will be given parenthetically in the text.

46. Smith, *Theory of Moral Sentiments*, 130.

47. Harriet Martineau, "The Martyr Age of the United States," in *Writings on Slavery and the American Civil War*, ed. Deborah Anna Logan (Dekalb: Northern Illinois University Press, 2002), 55.

48. Richard Terdiman, *Present Past: Modernity and the Memory Crisis* (Ithaca, N.Y.: Cornell University Press, 1993), 7.

49. Ibid., 8–9.

50. Susan Sontag, *Regarding the Pain of Others* (New York: Picador, 2003), 89; Terdiman, *Present Past*, 8.

51. Terdiman, *Present Past*, 8.

52. John F. Kasson, *Rudeness and Civility: Manners in Nineteenth-Century Urban America* (New York: Hill and Wang, 1990), 174–75.

53. *Second Annual Report*, n.p.

54. Elise Virginia Lemire, *Miscegenation: Making Race in America* (Philadelphia: University of Pennsylvania Press, 2002), 99.

55. See Richards, *Gentlemen of Property and Standing.*

56. Harriet Beecher Stowe, quoted in Jim O'Loughlin, "Articulating *Uncle Tom's Cabin*," *New Literary History* 31 (Summer 2000): 592.

57. Maria Weston Chapman, ed., *Harriet Martineau's Autobiography*, vol. 1 (Boston: James R. Osgood, 1877), 407.

58. Morgan, *Protestants and Pictures*, 6.

CHAPTER 17. JOHN MARRANT BLOWS THE FRENCH HORN

1. John Marrant, *A Narrative of the Lord's Wonderful Dealings with John Marrant, a Black*, 4th ed. (1785), reprinted in *"Face Zion Forward": First Writers of the Black Atlantic, 1785–1789*, ed. Joanna Brooks and John Saillant (Boston: Northeastern University Press, 2002), 53.

2. The French horn was not a valved instrument in the late eighteenth century, thus it was not identical to the contemporary French horn. For a history of the development of the instrument, see R. Morley-Pegge, *The French Horn: Some Notes on the Evolution of the Instrument and of Its Technique*, 2nd ed. (New York: W. W. Norton, 1973).

3. *Monthly Review; or, Literary Journal*, November 1785, 399.

4. For the classic account of the public sphere, see Jürgen Habermas, *The Structural Transformation of the Public Sphere: An Inquiry into a Category of Bourgeois Society*, trans. Thomas Burger with Frederick Lawrence (Cambridge, Mass.: MIT Press, 1991); note that Habermas's public sphere is not limited to print alone, although much work in the wake of Habermas has turned in this direction. For discussion of disembodiment in relation to the print public sphere in early America, see Michael Warner, *The Letters of the Republic: Publication and the Public Sphere in Eighteenth-Century America* (Cambridge, Mass.: Harvard University Press, 1990).

5. Marrant, *Narrative*, 51–52.

6. Jacques Rancière, *The Politics of Aesthetics*, trans. Gabriel Rockhill (New York: Continuum, 2004), 12.

7. Ibid., 13.

8. Paul Gilroy, *The Black Atlantic: Modernity and Double Consciousness* (Cambridge, Mass.: Harvard University Press, 1993), 57.

9. This view is eloquently expressed by Frederick Douglass in his famous speech, "What to the Slave Is the Fourth of July?" in *Narrative of the Life of Frederick Douglass,*

ed. William L. Andrews and William S. McFeely (New York: Norton, 1997), 116–27. Douglass points out that the illogic and immorality of slavery are so manifest that rational debate is not a legitimate expressive response to its injustice: "What, am I to argue that it is wrong to make men brutes, to rob them of their liberty, to work them without wages, to keep them ignorant of their relations to their fellow men, to beat them with sticks, to flay their flesh with the lash, to load their limbs with irons, to hunt them with dogs, to sell them at auction, to sunder their families, to knock out their teeth, to burn their flesh, to starve them into obedience and submission to their masters? Must I argue that a system thus marked with blood, and stained with pollution, is *wrong*? No! I will not. . . . At a time like this, scorching irony, not convincing argument, is needed" (126).

10. Thoughtful challenges to, and extenuations of, Gilroy's influential arguments can be found in the work of Ronald Radano, *Lying Up a Nation: Race and Black Music* (Chicago: University of Chicago Press, 2003), 39–42; and Sibylle Fischer, *Modernity Disavowed: Haiti and the Cultures of Slavery in the Age of Revolution* (Durham, N.C.: Duke University Press, 2004), 35–38.

11. Édouard Glissant, *Caribbean Discourse: Selected Essays by Édouard Glissant*, trans. J. Michael Dash (Charlottesville: University Press of Virginia, 1999), 127–28.

12. Jacques Rancière, "Who Is the Subject of the Rights of Man?" *South Atlantic Quarterly* 103, nos. 2–3 (2004): 304.

13. Fred Moten, *In the Break: The Aesthetics of the Black Radical Tradition* (Minneapolis: University of Minnesota Press, 2003), 14.

14. Ibid., 6.

15. Warner, *Letters of the Republic*, 11–13.

16. For a powerful analysis of the significance of networks to early African American print culture, see Joanna Brooks's account of Phillis Wheatley's writing and publishing strategies, "Our Phillis, Ourselves," *American Literature* 82 (March 2010): 1–28.

17. See Bruno Latour, *Reassembling the Social: An Introduction to Actor-Network Theory* (New York: Oxford University Press, 2005), for an analysis of "assemblage" in relation to the social world. Latour's account of a network of "actors" that are indiscriminately either subjects or objects (people or commodities or musical instruments, for instance) has proven particularly suggestive with respect to the ideas under discussion in this essay.

18. Josiah Quincy, "Journal of Josiah Quincy, Junior, 1773," ed. Mark DeWolfe Howe, *Massachusetts Historical Society Proceedings* 49 (1916): 451.

19. For the history of the St. Cecilia Society, see Nicholas Michael Butler, *The St. Cecilia Society and the Patronage of Concert Music in Charleston, South Carolina, 1766–1820* (Columbia: University of South Carolina Press, 2007).

20. Marrant, *Narrative*, 49.

21. Ibid., 50, emphasis added.

22. As Philip Gould points out, Marrant's language is similar in this passage to that of Olaudah Equiano who writes of becoming "master" of a few pounds through trading; amassing this money subsequently enables Equiano to purchase his freedom from slavery. See Philip Gould, "Free Carpenter, Venture Capitalist: Reading the Lives of the Early Black Atlantic," *American Literary History* 12 (Winter 2000): 668.

23. David J. McCord, ed., *The Statutes at Large of South Carolina*, vol. 7 (Columbia, S.C.: A. S. Johnston, 1840), 399–400.

24. Ibid., 410. See also John Belton O'Neall, *The Negro Law of South Carolina* (Columbia, S.C.: J. G. Bowman, 1848).

25. Reprinted in Mark M. Smith, ed., *Stono: Documenting and Interpreting a Southern Slave Revolt* (Columbia: University of South Carolina Press, 2005), 14–15.

26. In *How Early American Sounded* (Ithaca, N.Y.: Cornell University Press, 2003), Richard Cullen Rath reports the passage of laws prohibiting drums and horns in Jamaica (1688 and 1717), Barbados (1699), and Saint Kitts (1711 and 1722). Rath explains, "Planters passed laws against drums and drumming several times, and in various forms, indicating that their control was less than absolute. European[s] . . . feared drums as loud signals that could lead men on a battlefield. Thus, they banned loud instruments, ignoring quieter ones in their laws. They understood only the soundways of military and state drumming that they shared with Africans: planters failed to comprehend how African Americans could represent themselves and their agendas in their music rather than just signal with it" (79). Note that Radano argues that drumming was not the subject of a particular fear among whites in the United States; however, Radano's argument seems largely aimed at countering the notion that slave drumming can be seen as evidence of the "'naturally rhythmic' character of blacks" (Radano, *Lying Up a Nation*, 102). I am in agreement with Radano's argument in this latter respect and concur with his emphasis on the polysemic possibilities of African American music. Indeed, the 1740 Negro Act indicates precisely the concern of whites to exert control over such polysemic possibilities.

27. Saidiya V. Hartman, *Scenes of Subjection: Terror, Slavery, and Self-Making in Nineteenth-Century America* (New York: Oxford University Press, 1997), 43–44.

28. Richard Cullen Rath, "Drums and Power: Ways of Creolizing Music in Coastal South Carolina and Georgia, 1730–90," in *Creolization in the Americas*, ed. David Buisseret and Steven G. Reinhardt (College Station: Texas A&M Press, 2000), 113, 118.

29. Hartman, *Scenes of Subjection*, 70.

30. *South Carolina Gazette*, September 17, 1772, cited by Peter Wood, *Black Majority: Negroes in South Carolina from 1670 to the Stono Rebellion* (New York: Alfred Knopf, 1974), 342–43.

31. *The Concise Oxford English Dictionary*, 12th ed. (Oxford: Oxford University Press, 2008), s.v. "rout¹ n."

32. The dance described above was not an isolated event. Historian Bernard Powers reports that dances were common in the black community of Charleston in the late eighteenth and early nineteenth centuries. In *Black Charlestonians: A Social History, 1822–1885* (Fayetteville: University of Arkansas Press, 1994), Bernard Powers relates that in 1804, for instance, an observer reported seeing forty slave men and women arrive early in the morning in Charleston by boat from the neighboring Sullivan's Island; the slaves said they had been "dancing and carousing all night" (23). Although the period Powers focuses on in this study is slightly later than the one under consideration here, Powers provides ample evidence that the legal statutes governing public gatherings of slaves and

free blacks were routinely ignored in Charleston: thus, for example, "Although slaves were not permitted to be on the streets without a pass after the evening curfew, between September 1836 and September 1837, 573 were convicted of this offense or for being at large in some illegal place" (22).

33. Marrant, *Narrative*, 51.

34. Marrant was not enslaved but apprenticed, thus some provisions of the Negro Act do not explicitly apply to him: however, the language of the Negro Act often specifies that both slaves *and* free blacks are subject to its regulation, particularly with regard to the prohibition of assemblies. Accordingly, Marrant would have been subject to the terms that prohibited assembly.

35. *South Carolina Gazette*, March 4–6, 1784.

36. I have found additional references to black French horn players in the Atlantic world in the same period: in a print titled *A View of Cheapside, as It Appeared on Lord Mayor's Day Last*, published in 1761, London engraver John June depicts a street scene that includes a black French horn player. (My thanks to Catherine Molineux for bringing this image to my attention.) Further, a runaway slave advertisement from a newspaper in Jamaica describes a "Negro Man Slave Named RICHARD . . . belonging to his Excellency Gen. DALLING, and lately the property of Mr. Thomas Dolbeare, of Kingston, merchant. He is remarkably tall, well-made, likely fellow, speaks good English, is very plausible, and plays well on the French horn, he is well known in Kingston and Spanish Town, having for a considerable time past attended his Excellency, together with a Sambo fellow belonging to Dr. Duncan M'Glasham, named BILLY HARE, who has also absconded, and, as it is apprehended, in company with the said Richard" (*Gazette of Saint Jago de la Vega*, February 8–15, 1781). At the same time, an advertisement for Richard's compatriot, Billy Hare, appeared in another Jamaican paper: "RUN AWAY, from the Subscriber, a Sambo man, called, BILLY, ALIAS WILLIAM HARE, He has been for several months past in the Governor's service, and absconded when ordered home. He blows the French Horn plays on the Violin, Pipe and Tabor, writes and reads, and is well known all over the Island, pretends to be free, and has a design of getting off the Island in some of the ships going with the next Country for England" (*Royal Gazette*, February 3–10, 1784). The evocative terms of these advertisements point, to my mind, to how free and enslaved blacks, like Marrant, navigated a complex imperial/Atlantic world in ways that we have not fully understood, and in ways that are usefully viewed in relation to the concept of assemblage.

37. Marrant, *Narrative*, 60.

38. Ibid., 61.

39. Cedric May, "John Marrant and the Narrative Construction of an Early Black Methodist Evangelical," *African American Review* 38 (Winter 2004): 553–70.

40. Samuel Whitchurch, *The Negro Convert, a Poem: Being the Substance of the Experience of Mr. John Marrant, a Negro, as Related by Himself, Previous to His Ordination at the Countess of Huntingdon's Chapel, in Bath, on Sunday the 15th of May, 1785; Together with a Concise Account of the Most Remarkable Events in His Very Singular Life* (Bath: S. Hazard, 1785).

41. For discussion of the evidence of Marrant's editorial hand in the fourth edition and the distinction between this edition and others, see Brooks and Saillant, *Face Zion Forward*, 38–39.

42. Marrant, *Narrative*, 49.

43. John Sekora, "Black Message/White Envelope: Genre, Authenticity, and Authority in Antebellum Slave Narratives," *Callaloo* 10 (1987): 482–515.

44. Daphne Brooks, *Bodies in Dissent: Spectacular Performances of Race and Freedom, 1850–1910* (Durham, N.C.: Duke University Press, 2006), 65.

45. For a superb collection of essays on the history of the book in the Atlantic world, see, in particular, Hugh Amory and David D. Hall, eds., *A History of the Book in America*, vol. 1, *The Colonial Book in the Atlantic World* (New York: Cambridge University Press, 2000).

CONTRIBUTORS

SUSANNA ASHTON is an associate professor of English at Clemson University. She is the editor of *I Belong to South Carolina: South Carolina Slave Narratives* (Columbia: University of South Carolina Press, 2010) and *The South Carolina Roots of African American Thought: A Reader*, co-edited with Rhondda Thomas (Columbia: University of South Carolina Press, 2012).

JOANNA BROOKS is an associate professor in the Department of English at San Diego State University. Her book, *American Lazarus: Religion and the Rise of African-American and Native American Literatures* (Oxford: Oxford University Press, 2003), won the MLA's William Sanders Scarborough Award for outstanding book in African American literature.

COREY CAPERS is an assistant professor of history and African American studies at the University of Illinois at Chicago. His book, *Public Blackness, Printed Bodies*, is forthcoming from the University of Pennsylvania Press.

LARA LANGER COHEN is an assistant professor of English at Wayne State University. She is the author of *The Fabrication of American Literature: Fraudulence and Antebellum Print Culture* (Philadelphia: University of Pennsylvania Press, 2012).

RADICLANI CLYTUS is an assistant professor of English at Tufts University. He is finishing a book entitled *Envisioning Slavery: American Abolitionism and the Primacy of the Visual*.

JEANNINE MARIE DELOMBARD is an associate professor of English at the University of Toronto, where she is also affiliated with the Collaborative Program in Book History and Print Culture. Her most recent book is *In the Shadow of the Gallows: Race, Crime, and American Civic Identity* (Philadelphia: University of Pennsylvania Press, 2012).

ELIZABETH MADDOCK DILLON is an associate professor in the Department of English at Northeastern University. Her book *The Gender of Freedom: Fictions of Liberalism and the Literary Public Sphere* (Stanford, Calif.: Stanford University Press, 2004) won the Heyman Prize for Outstanding Publication in the humanities at Yale University.

ERIC GARDNER is a professor of English at Saginaw Valley State University and the author most recently of *Unexpected Places: Relocating Nineteenth-Century African American Literature* (Jackson: University Press of Mississippi, 2009), which won the inaugural EBSCOhost / Research Society for American Periodicals Book Prize in 2010.

SUSAN GILLMAN is a professor of literature at the University of California Santa Cruz. Her book *Blood Talk: American Race Melodrama and the Culture of the Occult* (Chicago, 2003) received honorable mention for the MLA's William Sanders Scarborough Award.

DANIEL HACK is an associate professor at the University of Michigan and the author of *The Material Interests of the Victorian Novel* (Charlottesville: University of Virginia Press, 2005). His 2008 essay "Close Reading at a Distance: The African Americanization of *Bleak House*" received honorable mention for the Donald Gray Prize from the North American Victorian Studies Association.

HOLLY JACKSON is an assistant professor at Skidmore College. Her essays have appeared in *PMLA*, *ESQ*, and the *New England Quarterly*.

MEREDITH L. MCGILL is an associate professor of English and director of the Center of Cultural Analysis at Rutgers University. Her publications include *American Literature and the Culture of Reprinting, 1834–1853* (Philadelphia: University of Pennsylvania Press, 2003).

LLOYD PRATT is a university lecturer in American literature at Linacre College, Oxford. His publications include *Archives of American Time: Literature and Modernity in the Nineteenth Century* (Philadelphia: University of Pennsylvania Press, 2010).

JOSEPH REZEK is an assistant professor at Boston University. His essay "The Orations on the Abolition of the Slave Trade and the Uses of Print in the Early Black Atlantic" won the Richard Beale Davis Prize for best essay in *Early American Literature*, 2009–10.

DALILA SCRUGGS is the Mellon Curatorial Fellow at the Williams College Museum of Art. She completed a Ph.D. in the History of Art and Architecture Department at Harvard University. Her dissertation studies representations of African Americans in the context of Liberian colonization.

JONATHAN SENCHYNE is an assistant professor at the University of Wisconsin-Madison. His contribution to the present volume was awarded Cornell University's Moses Coit Tyler Prize for the best graduate student essay in American literature, history, and folklore in 2011.

DERRICK R. SPIRES is a doctoral candidate in the Department of English at Vanderbilt University. His dissertation is titled "Black Theories of Citizenship in the Early U.S., 1793–1860."

JORDAN ALEXANDER STEIN is an assistant professor of English at the University of Colorado at Boulder. He is completing a study of print and the novel, tentatively titled *The People Are Clarissa*.

INDEX

abolitionist iconography, 291, 292, 294–97, 301–17

abolitionist lecture circuit, 50, 56, 57, 62–64, 66–68, 70, 74, 140, 148, 317

abolitionist publishing, 51, 64, 66, 132, 135, 138, 166, 206, 305. *See also* newspapers

Adams, John Quincy, 83, 316

adaptation, 15, 231–48

address: modes of, 12, 36, 54, 62–64, 66, 67, 70, 73–74, 257, 263–69; second-person, 317; songs as, 336. *See also* first-person narrative voice

advertisements, 20, 22, 24, 144, 297, 333–34

aesthetics, 4, 34, 183, 214, 292; in African American culture, 325; experience, 23; judgment, 22, 25, 33, 36, 38, 282; and politics, 93, 97, 126, 322–23, 326; of slave narratives, 97

affiliation: voluntary forms of, 12, 259, 268–69, 287. *See also* kinship

African American literature, 1, 2, 3, 14, 16, 96, 99; Anglophone bias of, 268; and the author function, 162; institutionalization of, 4–5, 93; links between literacy and freedom, 140–41, 162; neglect of Western writing, 76; penal origins of, 94–99

African Methodist Episcopal Church, 1, 49, 50, 56, 63, 77, 84, 87, 98, 190, 222

African Repository, 209, 211–13

Afrocentrism, 259

Aldridge, William, 43, 46, 337

allegory, 116, 236, 352–53n26

Allen, Richard, 24, 49, 50, 98, 112, 366n6

alphabet, 141, 290

amalgamation, 314–16

The American Anti-Slavery Society, 13, 140, 291, 292, 296, 297, 300–302, 305–8, 311–12, 316, 317; 1835 pamphlet campaign of, 291, 305–6, 316

American Colonization Society, 203, 206–9, 211, 214, 217–19, 221–22, 226, 228, 230

American West. *See* geography

Anderson, Benedict, 14

Anderson, Peter, 79–81

Andrews, William L., 94, 97, 128, 140, 162, 163

Anelay, Henry, 152–56

anthologies, 12, 62, 89, 253, 263

Anti-Slavery Almanac, 206

Anti-Slavery Record, 301, 306, 307, 309, 310

Appeal to the Colored Citizens of the World (Walker), 164, 277, 287

Armistead, Wilson, 303–6

assemblages, 166, 327, 329, 331, 333, 334, 335, 336, 338

atavism, 198, 381n24

Attucks, Crispus, 70–71, 168

authorship, 1, 14–16, 24, 25, 32, 38, 56–57, 101, 136, 162, 186; corporate, 283; entrepreneurial, 50, 51; versus editing, 163, 166–67, 337; women's, 82

autobiography, 127. *See also* slave narratives

B., Valcour, 267, 270

Ball, Charles, 304

Banneker, Benjamin, 24, 86

Baraka, Amiri, 179

Barringer, Paul Brandon, 194

Beard, John Relly, 161, 164–65, 169–74, 176

Bell, James Madison, 186–89

Bell, Philip A., 76, 81, 82–89, 181, 183, 187

Benjamin, Walter, 176

Béranger, Pierre-Jean de, 272

Bible, 41, 43, 106, 137, 144, 297, 301, 305, 312, 336, 337

bibliographic scholarship, 3, 16, 55, 349n9. *See also* book history

ACKNOWLEDGMENTS

Our ideas for this volume were galvanized by the conference "Early African American Print Culture in Theory and Practice," held in Philadelphia in 2010. We are incredibly grateful to John Van Horne of the Library Company of Philadelphia, Daniel Richter of the McNeil Center for Early American Studies, and Diane Turner of the Temple University Libraries for signing on early and generously as sponsors. For additional sponsorship, we're indebted to the Africana Studies Program at the University of Pennsylvania. For on-the-ground support, we extend a warm thanks to Amy Baxter-Bellamy and Barbara Natello at the McNeil Center. Lauren Propst performed similar work at the Library Company, where Nicole Scalessa also designed a beautiful program and website. Aslaku Berhanu curated a fantastic tour of Temple's Charles Blockson Afro-Americana collection, materializing the matter of print. Carrie Hyde and Megan Walsh assisted at the conference in both tangible and intangible ways. Tara Bynum, Thadious Davis, Marcy Dinius, Teresa Goddu, Ezra Greenspan, Miles Grier, Leon Jackson, David Kazanjian, Janet Neary, Joshua Ratner, Gus Stadler, David Waldstreicher, and Edlie Wong were crucial to that weekend's conversation—as was Frances Smith Foster, whose brilliant work and lively presence continue to provoke and inspire. Every scholar of early African America is indebted to the career-long contributions of Phil Lapsansky, and we remain humbled to be working on his turf in every sense.

At the University of Pennsylvania Press, Jerry Singerman's perfect combination of warmth and skepticism helped us to make the volume stronger and more coherent. Two anonymous readers for the Press offered welcome support and incisive suggestions. Also at Penn Press, Erica Ginsburg and Caroline Winschel shepherded the book through production with grace and care, and Jennifer Shenk proved that copyediting is an art. Ben Beck provided valuable research assistance with the final manuscript. Ashley Cataldo of the American Antiquarian Society found the book's cover image in a remarkable feat of detective work. John Van Horne supported this project again at the publication stage, and we are excited to be publishing in conjunction with both Penn Press and the Library Company of Philadelphia.

All of this volume's contributors have been collaborators in the ongoing project of establishing and refining our sense of what early African American print culture is and could be. Joe Rezek organized a panel at the 2008 American Studies Association meeting that initiated this project, and Meredith McGill suggested it take shape as a conference. In addition, we would like to thank Adam Bradley, Robert Chang, Jim Green, Leon Jackson, William Kuskin, John Pat Leary, Trish Loughran, and Peter Stallybrass. Without their conversation, sage advice, and (in a few cases) polite cautions, this volume would not be assembled today.